WHEN WE RULED

WHEN WE RULED

The Rise and Fall of Twelve African Queens and Warriors

Paula Akpan

First published in Great Britain in 2025 by Trapeze,
an imprint of The Orion Publishing Group Ltd
Carmelite House, 50 Victoria Embankment
London EC4Y 0DZ

An Hachette UK Company

The authorised representative in the EEA is Hachette Ireland,
8 Castlecourt Centre, Dublin 15, D15 XTP3, Ireland
(email: info@hbgi.ie)

1 3 5 7 9 10 8 6 4 2

A CIP catalogue record for this book is
available from the British Library.

ISBN (Hardback) 978 1 3987 1989 7
ISBN (Export Trade Paperback) 978 1 3987 1990 3
ISBN (Ebook) 978 1 3987 1992 7
ISBN (Audio) 978 1 3987 1993 4

Typeset at The Spartan Press Ltd,
Lymington, Hants

Printed and bound in Great Britain by Clays Ltd,
Elcograf S.p.A.

www.orionbooks.co.uk

For Elianne Andam, for Shakia Ama Bonsu Asamoah and for the numberless Black women and girls taken from us too soon

Nnipa nyinaa ye Onyame mma; obi nye asase ba
All [wo]men are the children of Onyame [the supreme being];
none is a child of the earth

– AKAN PROVERB

The land knows you, even when you are lost

– ROBIN WALL KIMMERER

CONTENTS

INTRODUCTION

Softness and vulnerability aren't extended to us, an interviewee told me. It's a sentiment this Black woman and many others are intimately acquainted with. Instead, the logic of antiblackness frames us as figures who must endure, suffer and flirt with pain.

But my interviewee wasn't talking about Black women collectively. She wasn't referring to African women in general. Instead, this young woman from Bénin was describing the lot of her fellow countrywomen.

As we broke bread together in the country's largest city, Cotonou, she had run through some of the stereotypes. Togolese women are good cooks and know how to please a man. The Congolese are known for their beauty. The Beninese, however, are strong, they're fighters. Within her country, this gets parsed out even further. The women from the north of this West African nation are better wives because they know the place of men. Their sisters down south, however, are framed as difficult women. They have too much pride. They do not submit easily. Why? Because these women – especially from around Abomey – are still today measured against the history of the land and the women who once stalked it. Abomey, the capital of the historic royal kingdom of Dahomey, was once defended by an all-women regiment known as the *agooɖojĭè*. And this squad of fighters, according to local historians, was created by the kingdom's only woman ruler: Tassi Hangbé.[1]

Hangbé is one of many African queens and warriors whose history is considered 'untold', even though the weight of her legacy is borne by some of her people today. Others, especially (but not limited to) scholars and historians outside Bénin, question whether she even existed. Despite the adamance of many Abomey historians and storytellers who assert that she was real and that she ruled, colonial accounts and internal disputes have ushered in an element of enduring doubt.

History is written by the victors, a white man said. It continues to be taught by the victors. From formative school years through university, history has always been presented as concrete, whole, lacking any veneer. We learnt about the Irish Potato Famine (albeit with British colonialism pushed to the margins), the Cold War (US = good, Soviet Union = very bad) and US civil rights (Martin Luther King Jr the paragon of respectable, nonviolent protest, unlike the hard-talking, implicitly villainous Malcolm X) as if they were each one inarguable, past reality. When it comes to race, the determinedly outward-facing focus of the UK national curriculum wouldn't become clear and obvious until I was beyond its grasp.

The gentle romance of history as gathered fragments, offering glimpses of a bygone society gave way to a more steely process, one guided by curation and self-awareness. Nowhere was this clearer than when I encountered Stephanie E. Smallwood's work on the eighteenth-century *Cape Coast* vessel incident during my master's degree.

The historian recounted how thirteen men and four boys – all African, captured and intended for a lifetime of enslavement – escaped when the British ship ran aground off the coast of present-day Ghana on 6 September 1721.[2] In correspondence between the English Royal African Company and its employees, officials noted that the seventeen men and boys were unchained before they escaped, otherwise the enslaved Africans rising up against seven white men would make for a 'very unaccountable history.'[3] This was a revealing admission: that the colonial state wished to present a history that would make sense to its intended readership, that there were certain histories – counter-histories – that would derail their narrative.

Over time, I've learnt that history is also written by the hungry, those keenly aware of the lack, the voids. Those in search of the counter-histories. After all, world-ending and world-building events on the African continent weren't just imparted with ink onto paper.

Societal shifts announced themselves in migrating communities and expanding circles of kin. Experiences of loss and gain, wealth and frugality, becoming the conqueror and the subjugated, wrote themselves into familial bloodlines. Supple Black flesh bore horrors we can never wholly conceptualise. The land, its people and their descendants carry the scores of time – how can such lack emerge when the consequences have been so abundant?

The digital age has provided newer tools for redressing and challenging this lack. A quick search for any facet of African history will spurn a wave of dedicated blogs and sites. Blog posts on afrolegends.com span histories of African fabrics and textiles, collect an array of proverbs and jokes from around the continent, and examine scientific contributions on African soil. Blackpast. org, a US-based resource, lists primary documents central to the shaping of Africa and its far-flung diaspora, like *The Book of Negroes* from 1783 or the South African Students Organisation (SASO)'s 1969 manifesto. The history section of WeAfrique, a site primarily dedicated to famous and historical figures of African descent, is packed with articles like '80 Quick Lies Told About Africa', '100 Famous African Kings that Have Ruled in Ancient Times' and '5 Greatest African Empires and How They Fell'.

Among these resources, you'll find plenty on African independence. The 'Year of Africa' was 1960. Seventeen new countries were created across the continent that year, eighteen the next, with a further thirteen countries realising the possibilities of independence by 1970.[4] As the likes of Ghana and the Democratic Republic of the Congo came into being, the period ushered in huge excitement in excavating the African past, imbued with nationalist, often Pan-Africanist fervour. This included locating long-overlooked African queens and warriors, emblems of an illustrious past and symbols for future freedom.[5]

There's a heady allure to these figures. For those of us who have grown up with British presentations of royalty, it connotes numerous, sprawling palaces and castles, plush fabric and finery, and stolen jewels winking from solid gold adornments. These are all incompatible with the images of a barren, starving Africa that we've been fed by these former colonial empires. As we acquaint ourselves with these African women rulers – as well as the figures who were not men and did not understand themselves as 'queens' – we're confronted with the glorious possibilities of royalty headed up by actors that are often relegated to the footnotes: Black, African women and people whose identities pre-date terms like 'trans' and 'queer'.

So many of us of African descent seize upon these stories.

The story where an elderly chief took on the might of a colonial power in defence of her kingdom. The story where a sovereign used cunning means to save her people. The story where rule and rainmaking secrets have been exclusively passed from mother to daughter, aunt to niece, for 200 years. African nation-making endeavours have imbued bravery, courage and determination into their every action, elevating them from fallible individuals to legendary characters worthy of national pride. They embody correctives to painful legacies – welcome platforms for moving away from difficult histories. These nationalist agendas often buff out the rough edges, like the way the elderly chief's kingdom built much of its wealth on trading enslaved Africans for guns or that, in the kingdom of the rainmaking queens, there is a precedent of families handing over their daughters as debt payments. In an attempt to counteract the grim stories of African history that the West tries to teach us, we enshrine stories of African royalty. It's a deeply understandable impulse but one that robs us of complexity.

Then there are the other legacies. The ones where rulers flouted social conventions and broke with entrenched traditions. The ones who ruled through violence and devastation, like the queen who had been disowned by her people for falling pregnant while unmarried. The ruler whose self-interest saw them leverage their own people against a colonial power as a means to an end, and the sovereign whose struggle against encroaching Europeans saw her poison, torture and kill large swathes of her population.

To examine their histories we must establish what these rulers were at the most fundamental level: members of the elite upper echelon and (sometimes joint) occupants of the highest seat in the land. A place gained through birthright, internal challenge and suppression.

What they were *not* was representative of the everyday African woman, or the millions of women on the continent who continue to struggle against modern Western imperialism.[6] Their stations padded by established lineage, the elites' structural positions and participations in government and public life cannot and should not be understood as 'a general index to female political activity.'[7] Monarchical rule requires the often violent oppression and manipulation of all other classes, whether the monarch is African or otherwise.

At its core, this is a book about power. Together, we'll explore the elite might wielded by these rulers, often against their own people. This, too, forms part of our African histories. Examining these uncomfortable truths allows us to engage these rulers with greater nuance and move beyond their figurehead status. Alongside an in-depth look at these African royals, we can glimpse at the lands they reigned over, the people they presided over and, critically, how these legacies are understood within countries today built on ancient kingdoms.

I travelled through nearly a dozen African countries – Côte d'Ivoire, Bénin, Ghana, Nigeria, Angola, South Africa, Madagascar, eSwatini, Rwanda and Burundi – across almost two months. For reasons I'll explain later, I couldn't travel to Ethiopia. No amount of time would have ever been enough; however, for a host of reasons, a longer research trip was not possible. The idea of attempting to entirely engage with these histories from my London home without ever deigning to set foot in these lands would have mirrored a number of colonial historians who published tomes on African kingdoms without ever entering the realms themselves. Such actions reek of the belief that African histories, specifically those south of the Sahara Desert, don't require the same care and veracity as other disciplines nor the interventions of the people of those lands. The very least I could do was commit myself to this undertaking and seek out the stewards of these histories, so I set out on the trip that took me from Africa's west coast, down to its southern tip and back up towards the continent's centre. I spent time at heritage and cultural sites of preservation, speaking to people – taxi drivers and museum curators, tour guides and plane seat companions. There would be no book without their insights because no one could know the stories of a land better than them. I am entirely indebted to every person who entrusted me with their knowledge. Some of their names have been changed to protect identities, relationships and livelihoods.

This work became a project of untangling: decentring the fixed assumptions that have been left behind by white colonial historians, comparing and contrasting the 'unaccountable' with indigenous history, tugging at the uncomfortable in anticipation of what it can reveal. Influenced by Smallwood's methods, I've written this book with and against the archive. I've written with the knowledge that colonial 'accountable' histories can never entirely disappear the counter-history it seeks to supplant.[8]

It's not easy to tease apart what you've always known – what you've been *told* – to be true. I was instructed from a young age that history follows a set series of events that only happened in one way. We're not privy to the edits or augmentations. We don't consider the way our imaginations have been curtailed, nor what is lost when we systematically and uncritically apply Western models to indigenous histories.

For myself, and others, this unpicking will be a lifelong endeavour. But when you get a glimpse of how the societies we live in have been formed and at the hands of whom, when you trouble myths of white superiority, when you lean closer to hear the voices that have been stifled or dismissed, things begin to click. I started making better sense of my present once I turned my head and hand to the past.

It's my aim to facilitate the same unpicking for others, particularly Africans – continental and of the diaspora. These particular histories are not easy to access, both by design and the erosion of time. So I hope that in gathering just a few, these African histories – *our* histories – feel closer. That things continue to click for you too. That colonial storytelling of lands they plundered and denigrated – of people they feared, reviled and demeaned – may, instead, present themselves to you as a 'very unaccountable history'.

You hold in your hands the histories of twelve queens and warriors who led, conquered and annihilated during the last one thousand years. They garnered fear, loyalty and revulsion. The messy, knotted threads of these sovereigns' lives run through Africa's vast tapestry. Their rules present different fragments of, not only African rule, but the kinship, gender, sexuality, love, loss, conquests, submissions, divinities and imperialism that have contoured the continent.

There will always remain unknowable loose ends, such is the nature of working with the past. But if we attend to these legacies carefully, painstakingly, we can trace the lines – faded as they may be – from bygone eras through today. Let's seek out the counter-histories, the intertwined vulnerability and violence, together.

CHAPTER 1

Mọrèmi Àjàṣorò

The Spy Queen

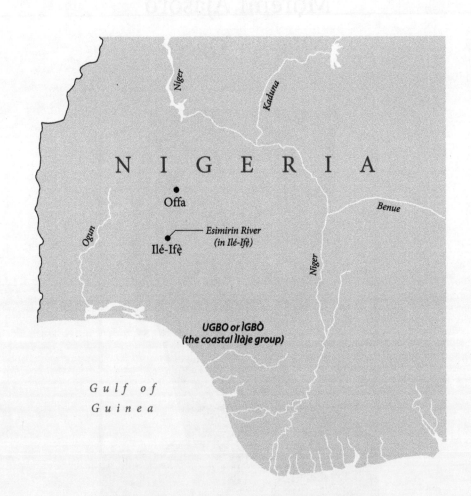

Niger

Kaduna

N I G E R I A

Offa

Ogun

Esimirin River
(in Ilé-Ifè)

Ilé-Ifè

Benue

Niger

UGBO or ÌGBÒ
(the coastal Ìlàje group)

Gulf of
Guinea

The beginning belonged to Olódùmarè. A being vaster than the skies, a force that planets and galaxies fold themselves into, the keeper of knowledge, the owner of the secrets that turn the universe.

In one of the many versions of the Yorùbá creation story, it is said that Olódùmarè, the Supreme Being, gathered all their wealth into one place before sending a messenger to call upon the 401 Irúnmọlè, their intermediaries between realms. The messenger had a task for this supernatural fleet: to carry Olódùmarè's treasures from Ìkọ̀lé Ọrun to Ilé Ayé, from the otherworldly realm to Earth.

But first, the Irúnmọlè were each ordered to entertain and prepare food for their guest, the messenger: a potful of steaming soup, kola nuts swaddled by their reddish-brown husks, a lump of pounded yam inviting searching fingers to tear into its dough. They were also told to provide goats and poultry offerings, and thousands of cowries.

However, none of the Irúnmọlè followed the instructions. None but Ọrúnmìlà, the only among them to greet Olódùmarè's guest with a hearty welcome. Belly full, the guest disclosed to Ọrúnmìlà that the most important treasure would be underneath Olódùmarè's seat.

Later, when the Irúnmọlè assembled before the Supreme Being, vying for the most valuable contents to carry, Ọrúnmìlà was patient. As the other Irúnmọlè departed for Ilé Ayé with money, food and other vestiges of wealth, Ọrúnmìlà looked on. When they had finally all left, Ọrúnmìlà looked under Olódùmarè's seat and found a snail shell.

Ọrúnmìlà followed the other Irúnmọlè and found them gathered at the end of the path that led from Ìkọ̀lé Ọrun to Ilé Ayé. Their descent had been thwarted by the water that covered the Earth's surface, leaving no place to step foot. It was from within the snail shell that Ọrúnmìlà found the tools necessary for an earthly landing: a net to cast upon the water, soil to place upon the net and a rooster to spread the soil on both the net and water.

The ground spread, slowly at first and then with haste once Ọrúnmìlà descended, following the being's order to expand itself

with speed. Ọrúnmìlà became the first being to stand on Earth and
the ground under Ọrúnmìlà's feet came to be known as Ifẹ̀ Wàrà
in Ilé-Ifẹ̀. The other hundreds of *Irúnmọlẹ̀* descended shortly after,
256 in total. And, once they had carried out their work of making
Ilé Ayé habitable for human life, soon came the *òrìṣà* – humans
who spent their lives as apprentices of each *Irúnmọlẹ̀*, and passed
their learnt skills onto their own descendants. With these practices
preserved through to the present day, a person becomes an *òrìṣà*
during their lifetime, accruing fitting powers for their position.
The *òrìṣà* are numbered as '400+1', as a shorthand for 'as many as
your mind can comprehend, and then add one'. This innumerable
enclave is the link between Olódùmarè and the humans who would
populate the earth.[1]

Olódùmarè's knowledge and wisdom were to be mediated
through Ọrúnmìlà, the witness to not only earthly creation but
human destinies. *Ifá*, the divination and pedagogical system that
has shaped the lives of Yorùbá communities on the continent and
across the African diaspora, is also credited to the wise figure.

By 2000 BCE (Before Common Era), the land Ọrúnmìlà had
stepped upon, Ilé-Ifẹ̀, had flourished. It was during 'The Bronze
Age' (2000 BCE to 500 BCE) that the indigenous Nok peoples,
specifically those who had made a sacred home of Ilé-Ifẹ̀, were
visited by a Yorùbá contingent led by Odùduwà.[2]

Some say Odùduwà descended from the skies to Earth on a
chain, others that they were a migrant from neighbouring lands
or even as far as Mecca.[3] They appear as woman, man and *òrìṣà*. It
is generally agreed, however, that this figure claimed the Ilé-Ifẹ̀ seat
as their own, the seat that most, if not all, Yorùbá settlements and
kingdoms trace their origins to. Of course, some of these claims
of descent may have been fabricated to underscore a future ruler's
legitimacy as validation lay with Odùduwà's legacy in the sacred
city.[4] After all, while Odùduwà was an *òrìṣà*, they had a descendant
of the same name who became the first *ọ̀ọ̀ni* of Ilé-Ifẹ̀ – the title
given to the highest priest and paramount steward of knowledge
in old Yorùbáland. (Yorùbá people often bear the names of their
progenitors, as surnames came with schooling systems.[5])

As documented in *Ifá*, during Odùduwà's lifetime and shortly after their death, their children and grandchildren dispersed from Ilé-Ifẹ̀. Although scattered, they were bound to one another by a primary mission: to settle, occupy and found their own empires.[6] With their exploits likely funded by the Odùduwà line, the descendants paid taxes back to the dynastic house once their empires, cities and territories were established.[7] Ọ̀yọ́, Ketu and Bénin sat among these original dominions which dominated the territory to the right of the kingdom of Dahomey and the left of the Nupe territories.[8] As the fourteenth century rushed forth, the focus of the Odùduwà-linked lands shifted from agriculture to conquest, laying the foundations for the Yorùbá domination that was to come.[9]

'Yorùbá' and 'Yorùbáland' as loosely affixed terms are misleading. Though these subgroups would go on to occupy an expansive territory and share a common tongue and culture, the use of 'Yorùbá' as a catch-all is a recent development that emerged after the nineteenth century.[10] In fact, 'Yorùbá' originally only referred to one kingdom, the Ọ̀yọ́, with historians finding that the various Yorùbá-speaking groups didn't seem to refer to themselves by any common name.[11] Their differing beliefs, social structures and dialects set them apart.[12] Ilé-Ifẹ̀ was the common factor that drew the different subgroups into its orbit, the spiritual and cultural capital of the region.

However, as the 1400s approached, the star of the Ìfẹ Empire was fading. As the regional picture shifted, with power transferred from one empire to the next, new towns were still being established.

One such town, Offa – which sits around 100km north-east of present-day Ilé-Ifẹ̀ – was founded between 1000 and 1395 by a crown prince from the growing Ọ̀yọ́ dynasty.[13] It's said that Offa is the hometown claimed by Mọrèmi Àjàṣorò.

As fat and juices dripped from the cooking meat, the aroma would've hazily drifted through the gathered celebrants, provoking moisture in mouths that would soon acquaint themselves with the source of temptation. The smell itself signalled the mood of the occasion.

When an animal is offered, a trained holy figure, often a *babalawo*, a priest of *Ifá*, skins and cooks it. The meat is laden with *àṣẹ* bequeathed by Olódùmarè – the ability to activate and utilise innate energy and power believed to reside in all beings, animals, natural phenomena and divine entities.[14] The *àṣẹ* is passed from the meat onto all who partake, whether there to mark events like the birth of a child, or, in this case, a spousal union.[15] Waste has no place in *òrìṣà* practices, as they centre on community, economy and protecting the most vulnerable. To eat well is to give the body the ultimate offering – *ẹnu l'ẹbọ*.[16]

Was Mọrèmi overwhelmed by the rites and rituals that accompanied her union, like the premarital use of *Ifá* divination to test the compatibility of the couple, helping them avoid unforeseen tragedy within their relationship?[17] Did she have any worries about whether her *ori* – inner head – would be aligned with that of her betrothed or if they would be advised by *Ifá* to 'think deeply' about the potential ramifications?[18]

Was the Offawoman swept away in the preparation? If Ìfẹ marriage traditions ran parallel to those documented in Ọyọ-Yorùbá, was she subsumed by the betrothal period? There was the celebration of her *òrìṣà*, receiving the food, money and cherished objects gifted to Mọrèmi's family by the family she was 'marrying'.[19] Was she burdened by expectation, lost to the rituals she needed to observe? Or, if she was indeed already a princess of Offa as has been suggested by some researchers, was such lavished attention simply par for the course?[20]

The threshold over which Mọrèmi was carried was in Ilé-Ifẹ and its compound belonged to the kingdom's *ọọni*.[21] The question of which *ọọni* she married, however, has pulled historians down differing paths. The popular answers to these questions shed light on uneasy grips on power in the region.

The popular choice is Ọrànmíyàn, positioned both as a son and grandson of Odùduwà; the man who founded Ọyọ-Ilé, the seed that would grow into the Ọyọ Empire.[22] Overseeing this budding kingdom, Ọ̀rànmíyàn is said to have become its first *aláàfin* in the 1300s – a term which roughly translates as 'the custodian of the palace'.[23] *Aláàfin* and *ọ̀ọ̀ni* are often incorrectly used interchangeably to describe Ọ̀rànmíyàn and the rulers who follow him as the highest positions in two different Yorùbá power structures. *Aláàfin* is exclusively used for Ọ̀yọ́ title holders, while *ọ̀ọ̀ni* is strictly for Ìfẹ̀.[24] There is still further confusion over who ruled where and when, with Ọ̀rànmíyàn returning to reign in Ilé-Ifẹ̀ and described as anywhere between the city-state's fourth and sixth *ọ̀ọ̀ni*.[25] Even his status as *aláàfin* is contested, with suggestions that he actually installed his son as the title's first holder.[26] Crucially, like Odùduwà, there was more than one Ọ̀rànmíyàn as, for identification purposes, people were named after their grandparents and the guilds (membership-based profession schemes, i.e. weavers, farmers, blacksmiths and traders) they belonged to.[27]

The figure of Ọbalùfọ̀n Aláyémọrẹ, or Ọbalùfọ̀n II, also complicates the picture. Referred to as the third *ọ̀ọ̀ni* of Ìfẹ̀, Ọbalùfọ̀n was likely forced out of power by Ọ̀rànmíyàn and only reclaimed the throne following his adversary's death.[28] As a result, Mọrèmi's spouse changed alongside the flow of power – a wife to Ọ̀rànmíyàn and then to Ọbalùfọ̀n II when he seized authority once more.[29] This might not have been her first time celebrating a union.

Like the heady scent of a cooking sacrifice dispersing through the air and refusing to be tethered, the timeline of Mọrèmi dances around the thirteenth and fourteenth centuries but, as of yet, cannot be known for sure. However, her legacy has been sealed as *Olorì* Mọrèmi – a princess consort to the *ọ̀ọ̀ni*.

'Western storytelling is fixed on dates and location but Yorùbá storytelling is more hinged on the ability of each story to be archived,' says ayọ̀délé olọ́fintúádé from across our table in the Kokodome in Ìbàdàn, the populous city you have to pass through to get from Lagos to Ilé-Ifẹ̀.

Our raised perch is a prime spot for people-watching as we observe a lazy Sunday afternoon crowd milling through the restaurant doors. The humidity blanketing us is welcome and makes

my luminescent glass-encased Fanta Orange (no ice, of course)
all the sweeter. After a difficult few days in Lagos which gave me
a glimpse of the vocal sexual objectification, cat-calling and intimidation that Nigerian feminists regularly highlight, in ayòdélé's
company, the tight band of anxiety around my chest eases.

As with almost every person I'll interview on my travels, this
is our first meeting and it was orchestrated on social media. After
sending a DM riding the wings of hope and a few further exchanges
with the acclaimed author of *Lákíríboto Chronicles: A Brief History
of Badly Behaved Women* and *Eno's Story*, we're finally together. As
I sip my glowing drink, ayòdélé's candour and no-nonsense affabil-
ity warm me. Donning an airy, striped jumpsuit and strings of
multicoloured beads around her neck, she mulls over my question
of the place of folklore in Yorùbá storytelling with a smoking slim
cigarette hanging from her fingers.

To her mind, Yorùbá traditions such as the ones I outline here
cannot be archived in books or videos. Those don't last, she tells me.
Those are temporal. The preservation of *Odu Ifá* and *Ese Ifá* – sacred
scriptures and verses – has never been rooted in these mediums.

'Our verses have been around for hundreds of thousands of
years,' the writer explains. 'They keep adding to them and they
keep expanding, but there's still a core. There's a way a story is told
and when someone refers to it, you remember it. If not maybe the
title, then the story itself because [you recognise] the pattern in the
way stories are told.'

For the Yorùbá, it's the power of the tongue that steers precious
fragments from then to now. According to one Yorùbá saying, 'Bi
omo o ba itan, a ba àròbá, àròbá, baba itan' or, 'If a child doesn't
witness history, the child will hear tales; tales, father of history.'[30]
These traditions, particularly *rara* – praise poems – skew towards
the elite classes including rulers, the wealthy and those deemed
exceptionally brave.[31] As such, a fantastical and mythical register
runs through these retellings. Ìbàdàn-based linguistics and communications scholar Abiola Odejide calls the result 'faction' – a
mix of fact and fiction – which 'allows licence in recreating actual

events and the use of motifs and symbols from oral tradition even though the recent past is its temporal setting.'[32]

These modes of storytelling demand the suspension, at least temporarily, of Western-formed registers, ayọ̀délé explains. '[For example] praise poems require you to have a shift in mindset and if you're going into that space with a very Westernised understanding, hinged on dates and locations, you lose so much of the legend and folklore.'

Odejide emphatically agrees: 'For the unsophisticated reader who applies only the rigid conventions of the realistic story, it is a disorienting world.'[33]

Yet, it's not just oral modes of Yorùbá collective memory that bend, challenge and disrupt the lenses of those of us with entrenched Eurocentric concepts.

There's the language, for example, that is not only gender-free (i.e. there are no gender-specific words that denote son, daughter, brother, sister, ruler[34]) but alive with music. When describing translating the musical quality of Yorùbá into English, Ulli Beier notes that 'poetry is what is left out.'[35] In a note on Yorùbá orthography – the conventional spelling system of the Yorùbá language – in her seminal book *The Invention of Women: Making an African Sense of Western Gender Discourses*, Oyèrónkẹ́ Oyěwùmí demonstrates the three underlying pitch levels. 'The low tone is marked with a grave accent (e.g. à, ì, ò), the midtone is unmarked and the high tone is indicated with an acute accent (e.g. é, ó, ú)' alongside subscript marks where 'the ẹ is approximately equivalent to the *e* in the English word "yet"; the ọ is close to the *o* sound in "dog"; and the ṣ is close to the English *sh* sound.'[36] However, with so many names and words unmarked, particularly in scholarly works, Oyěwùmí flags that there is a tendency to discount the diacritics in African languages (although, in English language publications, this can be extended to nearly all languages except French). And yet, 'without the diacritics, those words do not make sense.'[37]

There are the relationships between the peoples, the land and lineage. 'Having children is one of the few ways of ensuring your stewardship of land is maintained,' ayɔ̀délé had told me. '[It is] one of the reasons why there was a lot of adoption going on in Yorùbá city-states back then. Adoption rights [were] done in such a way that you can trace your ancestors.' In fact, growing up, ayɔ̀délé herself didn't know who had birthed her, given that she was raised by a number of women. There was no centralised 'mother' figure in her household, reflective of how groups of women tend to operate within Yorùbá societies. My companion referred to how incumbent *obas* (rulers) are often surrounded by clouds of women who aid with decision-making.

There's also the manner in which wealth is understood and accrued, linked to offspring and land. For Ìbàdàn women, ayɔ̀délé had specified, 'if they'd have a child with you, they'd make sure you have land and come from a wealthy place. They'd have that child with you then look for another person who has wealth and have a child with that person.' Perhaps having three or four children for as many households, the bearer of them ultimately gets shares further down the line when issues of inheritance arise. It's a practice that has lasted through to the present, although today, no one talks about it or other behaviours that can be linked back to sex.[38] This is even more pronounced when navigated in the English language. If poetry is what is lost in translation, it's ignominy that fills the void. 'Nobody's shy about these things but once you start talking about these things and sex in English, you start blushing,' ayɔ̀délé had told me. 'The language of sex in the English language is very closely tied to shame.' As such, far-stretching practices are ubiquitously cloaked in imported stigma.

Then, there's the marketplace.

When appraising the *ọjà* (market), Mọrèmi would've watched the sun's fingers lazily trailing over the buzzing mass of bodies, channelling warmth into the ground beneath brown feet, sandalled soles and the hooves of bleating livestock. The searching hands appraising over hairy *iṣu* (yams), kola nuts and cassava, seeking out imperfections only known to the finger pad, under the watchful eyes of the women *olónjes* – food sellers. An errant child pulled out of one of the *ọjà*'s main earthen paths, narrowly avoiding passing women with their balanced woven baskets filled with pots, calabashes, firewood and bundles of leaves for protecting food. Wrapped babies mewling into the backs of guardians locked in conversation. The smell of bananas, spices and palm oil puncturing the air, rising above the enticements of canny vendors – *olojà* – and the haggling of consumers reluctant to relinquish too many cowries.[39] Little takes place that misses the eye of the *Ìyáloja* (or the *babalojà*). Every *ọjà* has one. If the market itself is considered a state, an empire, a kingdom of its own, then its highest position belongs to them as the chief marketer.

Yorùbá *ọjà* held financial significance as a vital link in the marketing process, with most agricultural products entering the exchange economy through local markets, alongside access to certain crafts like weaving, smithing, dyeing and calabash-carving.[40] These economic hubs – normally found in the centre of a town – were primarily run by women who traded and set the prices.[41]

Mọrèmi, better than most, would've known the alluring pull of the *ọjà*, how it beckons people from different towns and national-ities, as well as different 'beings' altogether.[42] For her, the presence of spirits and *òrìṣà* roaming the marketplace would've been a given, making the *ọjà* a divine site – especially at night. When the night markets closed, after midnight, the *ọjà* historically had to be vacated by humans and 'turned over to the spirits'.[43]

The marketplace is frequented by Ọya who, aligned with sudden change, winds and storms, is also the *òrìṣà* of the marketplace where money changes hands and fortunes can be shifted through profit and loss; offerings to Ọya are often made at an *ọjà*.[44] Appearances are made by Èṣù, the possessor of *àṣẹ*, a maker of mischief and the representation of choice and crossroads – both of which are plentiful in and around Yorùbá markets.[45] There's also Ajé, an *òrìṣà* representing wealth, trade and money but is also tied to fertility and reproduction, a being who is invoked in the day-to-day of the *ọjà*. 'Ajé óò wa,' customers respond to the *olojà* whose wares they won't be purchasing that day. *Ajé will come. Profit and wealth will come to you, even though I have refused you.*[46]

These *òrìṣà*, and others, stalk the marketplace, a domain shared with humans. And if the *ojà* is generally a location of spiritual gravitas, then the marketplace in the sacred city of Ilé-Ifẹ̀ drips with divine primacy. However, as Mọrèmi would learn, what is sacred to one, may be a target to another.

Some historians believe that it was the coastal Ìgbò who would regularly descend upon the Ilé-Ifẹ̀ *ojà* to steal and abduct. Each time, the raiders made off with the vendors' produce, animals and Ifẹ̀ peoples – the latter intended for enslavement. And each time, they left a furious and terrified Ifẹ̀ community in their wake who felt helpless in the face of what they understood as a spiritual attack.[47]

It's worth noting that the name of this people (who are part of the Ìlàje linguistic group) has since become a bone of contention for Nigerians today. 'Ìgbò', a Yorùbá word, translates as 'bush' or 'forest' – as does 'Ugbo'; both are used interchangeably. Similarly, both 'ule' and 'ilé' refer to a house.

The issue arises when Ìgbò/Ugbo is used to describe a different population that stem from the historic Igboland. Inhabiting southeastern Nigeria, the Igbo people are one of the largest ethnic groups in Africa. The feudal divisions between the three dominant ethnic groups in Nigeria – Hausa-Fulani, Yorùbá and Igbo – erupted after Nigeria became independent in 1960. The predominantly Igbo Republic of Biafra declared its independence from Nigeria in 1967 and an almost three-year long war killed between 1,000,000 and 3,000,000 civilians largely through starvation. Almost as many were left malnourished and displaced.[48] Against this loaded, traumatic history, it feels vital to clarify that, in this chapter, 'Ìgbò' refers only to the coastal Ìlàje group.

Although they dwell in the Delta regions presently, the Ìgbò once claimed Ilé-Ifẹ̀ as their home, considering themselves to be the 'original' inhabitants of the city. Changes in power, political manipulation and familial disputes had driven them out.[49] Each time they swarmed the Ifẹ̀ market, this surely sharpened their desire to plunder Mọrèmi's lands.

Covered from head to toe in *iko* – clothing made from the dried leaf fronds of raffia palms – the marauders would've cut intimidating figures. Not only are the leaves, fibres and bark useful for making mats, brooms, furniture and other day-to-day objects ('The Yorùbá believe that there's no part of the palm tree that goes to waste,' ayọ̀délé explained) but the raffia tree is spiritually significant. Its leaves, for example, are often used to barricade shrines and sacred forestland belonging to the *òrìṣà*.[50]

Whenever the attackers burst through the city, they unleashed fear and chaos on the *ọjà*. When they were busy sending produce flying one way and unsettled livestock the other, was Mọrèmi sometimes present? Did her eyes take in the abject panic that seized her people? Did she call out warnings, direct them on where to hide or use that same voice to plead with the *iko*-clad looters? Did she watch a terrified Ifẹ̀ people scatter in all directions, grabbing what they could while pulling their children towards them in earnest? Did Mọrèmi clutch her own child – Olúorogbo or Oluogbo – closer, all too aware of how capture often heralded a lifetime of separation from kinfolk and kingdom?

Though convinced that spiritual forces were cowing the Ifẹ̀ people into submission, it didn't stop it being an affront. It was bad enough for the *ọjà* in Ilé-Ifẹ̀ – the 'mother of all markets in Yorùbáland' – to be commercially disrupted given its key position within trade routes which beckoned craftsmen, artists, traders, warriors and more. It was worse still for raids to take place in a sacred kingdom and result in the capture of Mọrèmi's people, descendants of the imperious Odùduwà.[51]

For Ifẹ̀ was more than just a busy community centre. It buzzed with sanctified intensity, with divine vibrancy. According to traditions, it was the centre of creation for the world; it was a living altar.[52] And it was to be protected at all costs.

*

According to the *Ifá* belief system, there are only two predetermined events in our lives: the day we are born and the day we will die. During the time in between, the Yorùbá people are guardians of the land – not its owners. Connection to the earth, as well as the *òrìsà*, means that there is a constant loop to both, with the latter particularly nurtured through honour and emulation. After all, according to *Ifá* traditions, it was the *òrìsà* who came together to design each human body.

Sipping our drinks by the Kokodome pool, ayòdélé paints a picture of divine mechanics. The work of Ògún, *òrìsà* of technology and engineering, on the human frame, with Obatalá moulding them from clay and carving the orifices of the face; Oya, with their sudden winds and gusts, represents the respiratory system and the air that enters our lungs; Sàngó, *òrìsà* of virility, wrath and oratory skill, occupies our tongues and genitalia while Osanyìn, whose domain is healing, herbal medicine and nature, connects humans to the food and medicine that nourish us.[53] Once the being has been formed, it is the breath of Olódùmarè that brings life and activation.

And so, to stem the flow of raids, Morèmi determined that the aid she required was not of this world. The deliverance of the defenceless Ilé-Ifè could be sought at one of her realm's *ojúbo* – sacred places.

There are as many *ojúbo* as there are *òrìsà* or *Irúnmolè*. In fact, there can be two, three or more *ojúbo* dedicated to the same entity in a single village or town.[54] These are living spaces as well as a space where the *òrìsà* or *Irúnmolè* is cared for, honoured and sanctified. In many cases, the *òrìsà* of each family live in the same space.[55] *Ojúbo* can be found in *ojà* and at road junctions, erected at the main entrances to towns and villages, by trees, on hills, at the banks of rivers, lakes and lagoons. 'No *ojúbo* is a permanent or singular abode for a deity', writes J. Omosade Awolalu, a scholar of African traditional faiths. 'They can be invoked at any *ojúbo*.'[56]

When Morèmi stood on the banks of the Esimirin River, that, too, was an *ojúbo*. Historians like David Abiodun explain that, after communing with *Ifá*, the *Olorì* was told to appease the river, that it would give her the tactics needed to stop the raids, that she would be forever indebted to the river spirit.[57] Help often comes at a cost.

She consulted the waters and began to plan.

Moremi premiered in 2018 at the ọ̀ọ̀ni's palace in the modern-day Osun State (which encompasses Ilé-Ifẹ̀), with the *Olorì* played by Abiodun Dúró-Ládiípọ̀ who also directed the film. We watch as she is presented before the effusive Ìgbò leader and his court as he delights in what his raffia-trussed warriors have delivered from their latest raid on the sacred city.[58]

Gone are the colourful necklaces that adorned Mọrèmi's neck, the intricate beadwork that graced the crown of her head and the smalls of her wrists, the evidence that signalled her status in Ilé-Ifẹ̀. Receiving plaudits from their chief, the warriors have removed the heads of their costumes, their very ordinary, sweaty human faces revealed. It's not long before Mọrèmi's beauty catches the eye of the Ìgbò men and soon, their chief too.

A forlorn-looking Mọrèmi – her initial woes presented, in part, because of jealous mistreatment at the hands of the Ìgbò leader's wives – eventually earns the trust of the most senior wife. It is she who reveals that the masquerades used by her people are only grass, while informing the new palace inhabitant that it is forbidden to take fire near where the unwieldy *iko* costumes are stored, an act punishable by death. 'O ma ṣe o,' Mọrèmi says with a shake of the head as she turns briefly to stare down the camera, splintering the fourth wall. *What a pity.*

Scholars have built upon this narrative: that, having allowed herself to be captured during the latest Ìgbò raid, Mọrèmi studied their ways with the goal of understanding the masquerades and where their weaknesses lay; that she used 'her beauty and seductive powers' to wed the enemy ruler; that she quietly held onto her gathered information while telling the Ìgbò leader – widely believed to have installed her as his wife – that she would have to return to her people and observe the proper customs before sexual appetites could be whetted; that, actually, instead of seeking permission, she escaped instead.[59]

All of their interpretations arrive at the same point: the woman who had made a home of Ifẹ̀ managed to return to it, with the knowledge that the ọjà was set to be raided again – and soon.

Outside my Ilé-Ifẹ̀ hotel, my soon-to-be driver and I share a laugh beside his car. I know he's hustling me and he knows I know I'm being hustled. He gestures towards his vehicle, its sleek, expensive-looking body a justification for the price. The security guard whose post is normally at the compound's entrance looks on with amusement. Since he insisted on fetching cigarettes for me the night before, I've acquired a new escort. Ultimately, all three of us know how this will go. In most, if not all, of my transactions across the trip, there is an unspoken, bilaterally agreed dynamic: the stated price is inclusive of an English accent tax which means that I can afford it.

Once all settled against the red leather interior, we head into the sacred city. Under a grey sky and against corrugated metal-topped buildings lining the road, Ilé-Ifẹ̀ quickly flashes past with sparks of colour breaking up the brown roadside tableau. Stacked fizzy drink bottles on red crates, a tempting sight for thirsty throats. Orange wheelbarrows and blue, red and grey loops of pipe arranged outside a trade tools shopfront, next to rows of parked bikes. People walking along the road in sliders as red-bodied motorcycles zoom in the opposite direction.

The next four or five hours are no less of a whirlwind. We pass by the grove and shrine which holds the commemorative monument of former ruler Ọ̀rànmíyàn's ọ̀pa (staff) which is described as the essence of the city. I'm taken to another ojúbọ, this time honouring Ajé and prayers made here hinge on wealth and prosperity. Barefoot, we follow the white-clad Ìyálórìṣà – caretaker of the òrìṣà – up steps embedded with cowries and place naira notes at the base of the mounds of crystallised salt. After, we're led around Ifẹ̀'s National Museum by three of its custodians, all hugged in colours of sky blue and azure.

Walking through the museum, it feels like both my driver and escort are experiencing the history held in its rooms for the first time. They take pictures and record, the flash from their phones running over every artefact we pass: the eroded ṣìgìdì – human-made terra-cotta effigies whose name translates into English as 'robot' – that bear human features and were used to divinely inflict pain on enemies during wars; an ìbòjú ọbàlùfọn, a face mask made of bronze that is used during the installation and funeral rites of an ọọni; a gourd sur-rounded by a net of beads called sèkèrè which is shaken and twisted only when there is jubilation and merriment, never in mourning.

And, of course, we visit the Mọrèmi Àjàṣọrò statue.

Towering over the city at forty-two feet – making it the tallest statue in Nigeria – time has stolen flecks of gold from all over the ruler's likeness.[60] Erected in 2016 by Ilé-Ifẹ's current ọọni, Adeyeye Enitan Ogunwusi, Mọrèmi raises a blazing torch high with her right arm, earning her the colloquial title of 'Queen Mọrèmi Statue of Liberty'. A monument for a woman who followed divine instruction, gave herself to the raiders and then gave again to the waters. The second offering, however, was not herself. Instead, it was her son.

'Although Mọrèmi is not one of the primordial deities (òrìṣà afẹ̀wọ̀nrọ̀) featured in the creation of the city,' writes Jacob K. Olúpọ̀nà, a scholar of indigenous African divinity traditions, 'she has a stronger presence in Ifẹ̀ myths, rituals and symbol[s] because her story is indispensable to Ìfẹ̀ salvation history'.[61] The statue, the institutional buildings named in her honour, the *Edi* festival which commemorates the defeat of the Ìgbò, and her *oríkì* – a form of praise that straddles music and poetry while claiming neither – cement Mọrèmi's place in its past, as well as the sacrifice itself.

One of her popular *oríkì* includes the phrase *Mọrèmi a f'òbò ṣ'ẹ̀tẹ̀*: Mọrèmi uses her vagina to destroy enemies' intrigues, or evil schemes.[62] 'When *òbò* – vagina – is used in this context, it is meant as using her creative force and genius to conquer,' ayọ̀délé later tells me. '*Òbò* is often used to describe reproduction rather than sex in *òrìṣà* practices.'[63] One interpretation could be that the debt she paid the river had emerged from her own body with her offspring, Olúorogbo, cast into the waters.[64]

There are clear cultural, divine and social meanings laced up in Mọrèmi's narrative: a heroic sacrifice in the face of repeated incursions against her people; her deployed sexuality demonstrating the sacred, innate power believed to be held in a woman's sexual organs; a selfless mother who would relinquish even her child for the good of the people; the assertion of Ilé-Ifẹ̀ as a central, venerated hub that requires protection.[65]

She is another of the quasi-mythical African figures particularly celebrated after independence set the continent ablaze, often found in the biography books of children.[66] Mọrèmi has emerged as a cultural hero – a standard bearer for Yorùbá women everywhere.

The sacrifice of Olúorogbo – and the wider traditions around Mọrèmi – also sat suspect for ayọ̀délé when we discussed it in the Kokodome but for slightly different reasons.

'Giving up her *only child*? A Yorùbá woman?' The cackle surged out of her chest. Even more incredulous to her was the idea of a singular figure liberating their people. 'There is no superhero anywhere in Yorùbá [traditions]. Even the òrìṣà don't work alone, they work in groups. There's always this circular division of labour and profit that is missing from Mọrèmi's story.'

That's not all. Aside from her potential husbands, there's little that binds Mọrèmi to a particular time in history, which is unusual for Yorùbá record-keeping. 'People mark time by rooting it to a war [or] another particular event to tie it down,' ayọ̀délé had explained. Another important marker is the presence of multiple witnesses. For example, in *Ifá*, when a story is being told, the researchers involved will often be mentioned to historically anchor retellings of the events. Any event that doesn't have three witnesses or researchers establishing that story, and that doesn't repeat – if not in the exact same way but at least with the same core tenets – that story likely isn't from *Ifá*. These are, of course, critical for community historians and storytellers.[67]

According to the Ìbàdàn author, with all stories from prehistoric times, even up to the sixteenth century – which saw imperialism,

enslavement and the destruction of education patterns across
the lands that are now the sum of Nigeria – there are women
in the village of Bodé who specialise in record-keeping. They
painstakingly oversee the community's history, tracing it alongside wars, conflicts, accessions, deaths and more. 'If any of your
ancestors have been to this part of the world before the West had
done anything in these parts, they can trace your roots back to
wherever you come from,' she had said. 'They know what your
great-grandparents look like and the things they did.'

ayọ̀délé's own research into Mọrèmi yielded more questions
than answers, especially given that there are multiple figures in
the records by the same name. However sparse the details may be
and no matter how tightly the Offawoman's story aligns with a
pedagogical, superhero register, the possibility of her existence
cannot – or should not – be dismissed. 'Like everything else, I'm
sure there's a true story behind the legend.' That possibility has
been further supported by the recovery of figures, cast in copper
alloy, recovered from the *Ita Yemoo* site, a temple complex not
far from where the annual *Edi* festival ends. At least two of them
have been identified with Mọrèmi, including one where her figure
is interlocked with another, believed to be her potential husband,
Ọbalùfọ̀n II.[68] However, as ayọ̀délé notes, two interlocked figures
means a 'twinning' – either the figure is a twin or is non-binary
with two distinct genders. 'This links back to Yorùbá beliefs about
people having the ability to mutate and change. This includes
gender, profession and other aspects of being human. They do not
believe in one rigid structure maintained throughout one's life.'[69]

When it comes to Mọrèmi, there's one thing that my new friend
was resolute about, however, and it hinges on the detail in her *oríkì*.
She pointed to examples that feature the *òrìṣà*, painting vivid pictures with words. The sensual figure of Ọ̀ṣun whose *oríkì* describes
them as 'wiping their hands on the breasts of nubile, beautiful girls'.
One of mischief-maker Èṣù's depictions suggests that they're short
with a huge, disproportionate penis. Descriptions you'd never
forget, ayọ̀délé had chuckled. If someone is tall, the height will be
described exactly. If someone is dark-skinned or light-skinned, that

will be mentioned too. The size of a vulva, the girth of a shaft, no detail is spared because you must be able to picture the anatomy of the *oríkì*'s subject. They seek to exactly capture the person who will become a legend.[70]

'They're visceral and descriptive because they're archival,' ayọ̀délé had added. 'You can't fake *oríkì*.'

A different day sees me trailing ayọ̀délé as she strides towards the Ìbàdàn marketplace, dodging oncoming motos and *kekes* – sunshine-yellow commercial three-wheeled vehicles.

She knows what she wants as she approaches the women perched behind wooden stalls groaning under the weight of fresh produce, wrinkled naira notes in hand. Against the noise of bartering, ayọ̀délé briefly chatters with the different vendors who she knows on sight. They do business under sunbeaten parasols, their prolonged exposure having bled the colours from vibrant to pastel. Only a couple of weeks into my trip, I'm grateful to be directed, carried under someone else's steam, referring to another's plan rather than my extensive spreadsheet-based itinerary.

With turkey and yam in ayọ̀délé's hands and a few frozen (but swiftly melting) drinks in mine, we return to the *keke* that brought us to this side of Ìbàdàn. As we begin trundling towards her home, my companion begins to tell me about the market women of Ìbàdàn.

Through her own research – including trawling articles on JSTOR – ayọ̀délé gained a better understanding of the prominence of women scattered across pre-colonial Yorùbá territories: the way that all able women engaged in trade, crafts or household production, if not a combination of all three; the manner in which young girls began their tutelage as future traders from an early age as they picked up skills including weaving, pottery, soap-making, beer-brewing and more; how women traders travelled up and down old Yorùbáland and beyond in large caravans, hawking their produce, kola nuts, palm oil, cloth, arms and ammunition.[71]

Ìbàdàn women, in particular, are remembered as travelling in caravans to towns like Ikire and Apomu for corn and other foodstuffs, ultimately supplying their hometown with food 'while men were engaged in slave hunting'.[72] These women not only controlled their own economic activities and the profits made from them, but also employed workers and took advantage of the labour of enslaved people, controlled the prices in the market, oversaw the movement of goods and headed up their own trade associations.[73]

'The colonials came and discovered that, actually, the so-called men, or the people that colonials *decided* were men, were not the people who [held] economic power,' ayọ̀délé explains while our *keke* dredges up plumes of sun-kissed sand behind us. 'So the first thing they decided to do was destroy the market system but it was stronger than them.'

Following British occupation in the late eighteenth century, the *ọjà* suffered. The rise of Christian missionary-led education – and the access to more lucrative occupations that it provided – saw some traders move away from the market space. Rulers installed by the colonialists imposed themselves on market dealings. Pottery, basketry and other trade skills declined and those who sustained these crafts found themselves competing with imported European commodities (and later locally manufactured goods). These were all factors in the downsizing of the market industry. Still, through to the present day, the women of the market continue to serve a considerable consumer base.[74]

'Market women have been fighting back for the past two centuries now for their right to be independent of government interference,' ayọ̀délé adds. The writer refers back to the 1940s when Madam Alimotu Pelewura, the leader of the Lagos Women's Market Association, campaigned against price control measures the British imposed to help finance their endeavours in the Second World War. She gained the support of two key women's organisations for the educated and wealthy – the Lagos Women's League (founded 1901) and the Women's Party (founded 1944).[75]

Meanwhile, sixty miles north of Lagos lay the city-state of Abeokuta, ruled over by *Alake* Ademola II. The paramount ruler of the Egba clan, the *alake* had become a key part of British colonial occupation through indirect rule. Here, the market women had joined forces with the Abeokuta Women's Union, founded in 1946 by Funmilayo Aníkúlápó-Kuti, as they demonstrated against an enforced special tax on the market women: in addition to paying income and water rate taxes, market women were required to pay the salaries of the market supervisors.[76] By November 1947, the women had organised mass demonstrations that saw tens of thousands attend, while Aníkúlápó-Kuti held training sessions in her home. She trained women on mass resistance and dealing with tear gas – including picking up the canisters and throwing them back at the police.[77] In early 1949, the sustained uprising forced the temporary abdication of Ademola II.[78]

The women of Yorùbá markets shoulder weighty histories of resistance, consciousness-raising and solidarity with the public. ayòdélé reflects on the process of price-setting, for example. Every day, before anything is brought to the market, farmers and market vendors meet to decide on the prices, appraise the value of the goods that will wink at consumers that day.

'It's always market women who are on the side of the citizens,' my companion tells me. 'They try as much as possible to not put their money in banks where the government will keep taking from it so instead they have co-ops – you put your money in the co-op, they give it to someone who needs it and will refund it [at a given time].' Of course, these informal savings systems aren't unique to the Yorùbá or even the African continent, with *pardna* schemes established in Jamaica and the wider Caribbean, as well as the rest of the world.[79] The money spins round and round, spurning institutional meddling.

Even so, it's not enough. The price of transportation, fuel, food and more continue to upwardly spiral in Ìbàdàn and wider Nigeria. ayòdélé adds: 'You can still see those women fighting to keep the price of goods down so that people can afford to eat. They'll leave the prices up for a while and then push it, push it, push it until it can accommodate everybody.' The way these vendors – scattered from south-west Yorùbá territories to the Hausa lands of northern Nigeria – organise together through underground channels, for ayòdélé, defines radical praxis and community care. Resistance has long been stamped into *ọjà* floors. Mọrèmi is one of many women who have drawn battle lines through the sand of the marketplace.

Our *keke* pulls up outside the low brown brick wall surrounding her home. The sky is still heavy with clouds but the air around us remains warm as we unload our bags and see our driver off. ayọdélé leads the way and my suitcase trundles behind me.

'When people talk about feminist women in Nigeria, I laugh. The people that we see on TV, that are writing tomes, are not the feminist women,' she concludes with mirth. 'It's the market women fighting the government.'

Did jubilation add extra swing to her arms as she stalked forward? Did pride swell up her chest and leave a twinkle in her eyes as Mọrèmi spied the familiar banks of the Esimirin? Was there self-satisfaction sat at the corners of her mouth that only victory could have lodged there?

Were her senses still heightened from the clamour of recent events? The sound of her heartbeat in her ears as she made her way back to Ilé-Ifè's embrace, through escape or otherwise. The pitch of her voice as she explained to her husband Ọ̀ọ̀ni and his court what she had learnt during her time in Ìgbò captivity and what they needed to do next. The tenor of the warning cries that alerted Mọrèmi's people to the Ìgbò party's approach. The taste of sweat that has trickled its way to unsuspecting lips. The raw stench of fear and anticipation. The crackle of flames licking the end of the *ògùsọ̀s* (torches) which had been dried, dipped in palm oil and sparked into action.[80] The shadows dancing across the faces of their bearers. The smell of grass meeting amber heat, curling into a disintegrating, blackened husk. The screams of the burnt and the moans of the captured meeting the relieved cries of the market people. The flavour of triumph.

Even if her skin was still warmed with the excitement of driving off the marauders with flames, the time had come for Mọrèmi to pay her debt. And though she might have been brimming with thanks for the river, threatening to overrun, no words would be satisfactory recompense. The shimmering depths awaited her approach, ready to demand the greatest wealth a Yorùbá mother could give.

While my driver navigates Ilé-Ifẹ̀'s potholes, my attention is caught by the numerous posters that line almost every roadside we pass. HELL IS REAL, one proclaims. *Also know that RELIGION DECEIVES and THE gods ARE DEAD. Don't say you were not told.*

The local praise chapel's advertisement crystallises the way that *Ifá* jostles for space with Islam and Christianity in a locality understood as its altar. The latter arrived in Yorùbá territories with the zeal of European missionaries, as their colonial governments expanded their choking grip on West Africa from the 1700s onwards; the smatterings of settlements and forts were yet to develop into a full-scale chattel slavery and plantation-toiling matrix. Where missionaries met indigenous belief systems, the goal was to supplant and eradicate them – often creating dire conditions through violence, the introduction of charges of 'witchcraft' (which is still on the Nigerian constitution today) and indirect interference, where the local population felt that they had no choice. 'Some [Africans] denounced the traditional gods; others did not even credit their existence,' writes Trinidadian and Tobagonian scholar Maureen Warner-Lewis. 'On the other hand, a large number maintained traditional beliefs and practices alongside Christianity, using one spiritual resource to supplement and complement the other.'[81]

Baba Ifa Karade, who has written extensively about *Ifá* culture, points to the way Yorùbá communities maintained their traditions through syncretism – the (attempted) merging of different religions, cultures or schools of thought. 'The ability to keep [the òrìṣà] alive in the world-reality of the Yoruba led to the conscious masking of them behind Catholic saints and related social-ritual performances.'[82] He points to 'African' influences on the enforced Christianity: the field hollers sung by enslaved labourers across America's cotton fields, railway construction sites and turpentine camps, the 'negro spirituals' that succeeded them, receiving the holy ghost, speaking in tongues, praise dancing and more.[83]

The amalgamation of faiths explains why, as my driver explains, you'll still see Ifẹ̀'s regular churchgoers heading to *ojúbọ* and making offerings. However, as we pass from one sacred space to the next, contempt, cynicism and fear of *Ifá* follows us in the form of the eye-catching flyers and signs plastered along the road. They make some fractures around religion and divinity in these lands visible, others are not.

Just north-west of Ifẹ̀, in the community of Ẹdẹ, devotion to Ṣàngó – the first *aláàfin* of Ọ̀yọ́ who became a powerful *òrìṣà* of thunder, bravery, destruction and virility – is prominent. Like with a marriage union, devotees are joined to the *òrìṣà* through initiation, regardless of gender. Highly positioned practitioners are always regarded as *Ìyàwó òrìṣà* – wife of the *òrìṣà*. When they are 'mounted' by Ṣàngó, the *òrìṣà*'s will subjects their own. It includes the heat of a sexual act where, again, the genders of the participants hold no meaning.[84] Elsewhere, what we understand as 'sapphistry' or 'lesbianism' exists in *Ifá* traditions, for example, when Òfurufú-ko-ṣe-feyinti and Láárúfín, both with female anatomy, slept together and Láárúfín gave birth to Ọrúnmìlà.[85] Among the Hausa, the pre-colonial term of *Yan Daudu* was used to describe 'effeminate men and male wives.'[86]

There's a great deal of evidence that underscores, not only queer existence but pre-colonial social norms, behaviours and language that would have negated the need for such a classifier. However, the dawn of Western imperialism, vociferous missionary work and Nigeria's legal system on sexuality and gender deriving from English law are just a few of the factors that have aided the revising of history. They were, for example, foundational to the passing of the Same Sex Marriage (Prohibition) Act in 2013, which was 'the outcome of legislative lobby by a powerful Christian elite in Nigeria.'[87]

There's a wilful tangling of what is or isn't 'African' with *Ifá* observance and satanic connotations. It leads to visible queer individuals like ayọ̀délé often at risk of being accused of witchcraft, knowing that it is tied to her sexuality and gender and – in her case – not leaving the house for weeks on end out of fear.[88] Many of these thoughts, unwieldy mental loads, sit in my mind as I'm driven back down to Ìbàdàn where I'll reunite with the author before our detour to the market.

But that evening, after ayòdélé has grabbed me a towel, pushed me towards her shower and told me to wash off the day, after the warming turkey and yam cooked by her housemate K which leaves me rotund, after we've danced around their living room to Aṣa, Spyro and Burna Boy, after the three of us have discussed familial estrangement, contemporary Black women's feminist movements in Nigeria and the UK and how lesbians were maligned in both, after we've pored over how the artist Tems manages to sustain her hooded-eye mystique, after ayòdélé gives and (at my request) signs for me a copy of *Lákíríboto Chronicles* which I'll later discover has a main character named Moremi, after the pair organise my taxi for the long drive to the Lagos airport and run to fetch me four boxes of slim cigarettes, after they wave me off until they're small figures from the car's rear window, after I sit and meditate on how Black queer people continue to nourish one another, keep each other safe and create new modes of care even as we walk with targets on our backs, the thoughts finally subside to background noise.

According to Yorùbá ontology, after Olódùmarè's breath animates Obatalá's clay bodies, the sculpture remains alive as long as that vital breath remains within it. When it is lost, the buried *ara* – the physical body – decomposes into clay. However, this death does not mark the end of life, but rather a transformation from one realm to the next.[89]

For the majority of 'culture-heroes', their deaths come about through walking into a cave connected to a different realm or being turned into stone sculptures.[90] With Mọrèmi, as of yet, we simply do not know how or when she died.

What we do know is that she is credited with survival of the sacred city and its people. It's in the hubbub of the Ilé-Ifè *ọjà* with its bustling bodies that you'll find her legacy – both alive and intangible.

Mọrèmi Àjàṣorò, a sculpture of clay, a body of flesh and a statue of gold.

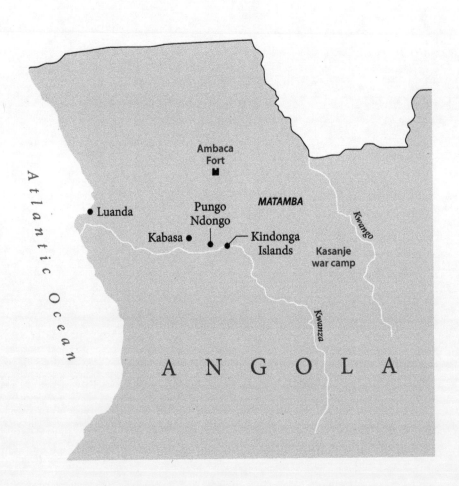

Atlantic Ocean

● Luanda

Ambaca
Fort ◼

MATAMBA

Pungo
Ndongo

Kabasa ●   ● ← Kindonga
                  Islands

Kasanje
war camp

Kwango

Kwanza

A N G O L A

CHAPTER 2

Njinga a Mbande

The Gender-Blurring Ruler

Kengela ka Nkombe had been here before. Groaning, writhing, willing the occupant of her womb a safe but swift exit. As she pushed, surrounded by *ngangas* (Kimbundu for priest or ritual practitioner), her attendants noticed something alarming as they guided the slick bundle out of Kengela.

An upturned face and the umbilical cord wrapped around a tiny neck is what we'd call a 'nuchal cord', occurring in 10–29 per cent of foetuses.[1] Over 400 years ago, it presented an omen for Mbundu peoples: any baby born in this 'so-called unnatural manner' would not live a normal life, for they believed that the conditions of a person's birth shaped their character.[2]

As she rode waves of oxytocin and adrenaline, her sweat-dappled body surely exhausted from the effort, perhaps Kengela appraised the way Mbande a Ngola interacted with the newborn. Her lover, already a father of other children and now this latest addition, her husband in all ways bar the title. Maybe she could read weariness imprinted on his face, the clamour of fighting and the anxiety of unending raids against their people leaving visible marks on the man she had been chosen for. He was already married when she was sent to him as a gift and Kengela had been made his principal concubine, holding a status that sat just below that of his chief wife. He hadn't been reserved in the way he lavished more favour on her than his other partners and now their union had borne more life.[3]

As the father appraised the squirming mass, a child who

tradition dictated would not be able to follow him as a direct heir, the birth still signalled a future that none in that room could predict. That day which fell around 1582, under a Kabasa sky, the heir to the Ndongo throne named his baby 'Njinga'. Coming from the Kimbundu root *kujinga*, it means 'to twist, to turn, to wrap'.[4]

The royal family that Njinga had been born into had not been around for very long. While the *ngola* (ruler) line had reigned over the kingdom of Ndongo since its inception in 1515, it had held tributary status to the more powerful Kingdom of Kongo. Raids had been carried out against Ndongo's agricultural population to bring it under Kongo submission.[5] However, by the reign of Njinga's ancestor, *Ngola* Kiluanje kia Ndambi (1561–75), Ndongo had been firmly established as an independent state. When Njinga's father, Mbande a Ngola, ascended the throne in 1592, he was only the kingdom's fifth sovereign.

Grand baobab trees sprouted from the land, providing water, food, shelter and medicinal resources for the Mbundu peoples who inhabited the land. The crashing waters of the Kwanza River offered up imposing waterfalls with swamps laden with crocodiles and hippopotami, and further upstream, ripe grounds for fishing – enough, in some cases, to support whole villages.[6] It was the highlands where you would find the capital of Kabasa, however. The young Njinga knew the city as a home, a birthplace, and the base of power. It was from here that Ndongo's *ngolas* ruled over their dominion.

By the time Mbande a Ngola had taken up the position of ruler, Kengela's child had traded animated gabbling for critical thought. So advanced were Njinga's intellectual and physical capabilities from childhood into early adulthood, a gap emerged between them and the other young people at court, including their older brother.[7] The warmth that the *ngola* held towards his favourite concubine had been passed onto their child who showed interest in law, military strategy and understanding the inner workings of the Ndongo political system.[8]

This was unique access for the child of any ruler, let alone a dynast with multiple paramours and extended family who could take such favouritism as a slight. If that wasn't enough, some historians suggest that Njinga had also inherited royal status through their mother Kengela, a member of another Mbundu royal lineage.[9] If this is, indeed, true, it could go some way to explaining why Njinga was granted special permissions. It was a childhood marked by their attendance at a host of judicial and military councils, among others, that were presided over by their father – much to the gall of his officials.[10] And so, at the feet of their father, Njinga's education began.

The reception to Njinga is important to note because as the second-largest political structure after Kongo, Ndongo's internal organisation was built on networks of kinship. These connections, shaped by lineage, dictated its hierarchy.[11]

Under the *ngola* were the *sobas*, a form of local authority with officials who carried out the day-to-day running of the villages. Njinga's father made the most important decisions alongside the *makotas*, powerful advisors and territorially based nobles. Each *soba* offered the reigning *Ngola a Kiluanje* – the ruler's full title, named for the kingdom's founder Ngola Kiluanje kia Samba – an annual tribute called *luanda*. It symbolised public acknowledgement of their power as the 'ultimate title holder in the Ndongo'.[12]

Alongside great political power, the *ngola* also owned some state lands and controlled the lives of the people who lived on them. Free peasants made up the bulk of the population while *kijikos* (serfs) worked the *ngola*'s land. The *kijikos* could not be forced off the land nor sold, due to the land being held by royal lineage. *Mukibas*, on the other hand, could be sold or removed at will. These enslaved people were owned outright by the sovereign. This was done to them through a number of means: capture as spoils of war from neighbouring kingdoms, abduction through the excursions of Ndongo's military forces, condemnation by judges for spiritual transgressions or civil infractions like treason and adultery – especially if the latter involved one of the *ngola*'s many wives.[13]

Perhaps the most pivotal lesson Njinga learnt was the spiritual

centrality their father possessed once he became *ngola*. To the
Mbundu peoples he ruled over, his body was imbued with divine
power. The rain and the fertility of the soil, both of which sustained
his people, lay in Mbande a Ngola's control.[14] Njinga absorbed that,
as the conduit between the otherworldly and their Ndongo population, an *ngola* held both life and death in their hands.

When the Portuguese arrived at the *ngola's banza* – village or city
of main importance, in this case, Kabasa – around 1560, it came
after the Ndongo rulers had first made contact.[15] Since 1518, decades
before Njinga's birth, *ngolas* had been sending their own emissaries
to Portugal to request missionaries and lay down the foundations
for a trading relationship.[16]

They had seen the benefits that had been afforded to their
Kongolese neighbours since they first received the Europeans
around 1483, and the Ndongo elite sought them too.[17] There were
the Portuguese cloths, beverages, wines and *geribita*, a sugar cane
spirit from their Brazilian colony. Access to Portugal's developed
marine technology, firearms, weaponry and building technology
– the things Kongo had most craved from Europe – had only
further boosted the already powerful kingdom.[18] By 1491, the
entire Kongo ruling class, including the monarch, had converted
to Catholicism.[19] Crucially, as the sixteenth century ticked on, the
Kingdom of Kongo could call upon Portuguese military might
to help quell threats from beyond its reach. The relationship also
allowed Kongo and Portugal to secure areas producing goods that
couldn't be found in the kingdom, like cloth or iron.[20]

As much as the Ndongo elite sought a rapport with the Portuguese, much about the 1560 visit gave them pause. The tenets
of the Christian faith that the missionaries wanted them to adopt
would trouble the *ngola's* spiritual and legal authority. The political relationship that the head of the military party, Paulo Dias
de Novais, spoke of sounded a lot like the Portuguese monarch
would dilute the *ngola's* power over provincial leaders and in rela-
tion to the rulers of surrounding states. The Europeans brought
with them different cultural values on justice, social and inherited

statuses, freedom and enslavement, hospitality and more, all of which threatened the Ndongo way of life.[21]

The Ndongo made it clear that meddling or any form of submission to the Portuguese would not be welcomed. And they held them at bay, especially after a new *ngola* in the form of Njinga's great-grandfather, Kiluanje kia Ndambi, expelled the Portuguese delegation he deemed suspicious. Instead, he spent the next few years expanding the kingdom's borders.[22] And then, in 1575, the Portuguese struck.

The Portuguese were looking for a way through to the interior of Africa, driven by hopes of seizing all-important salt mines for trade, as well as the reputed silver mines of Cambambe that they'd never find.[23] Crucially, the Portuguese Empire was looking to supply labour for its newly claimed colony of Brazil in the form of enslaved Africans.[24]

By 1574, the Kongo sovereign had given the Portuguese permission to build a settlement on the island of Luanda, an area that the Kongo Kingdom laid claim to. It was from there that the Europeans set about their new mission. At the head of an armada, Dias de Novais returned to Luanda with new credentials: he had been elevated to first governor and *capitão-mor da conquista do reino de Angola* – captain-general of the conquered kingdom of Angola. The instructions he had received from his sovereign were simple: to 'subjugate and conquer the kingdom of Angola.'[25]

They set about seizing over 200 miles of Ndongo territory while they simultaneously turned the port city of Luanda into a bustling hub that beckoned Portuguese missionaries, farmers and merchants. In 1582, the year that a baby Njinga entered the world wrapped in their own lifeline, the Portuguese had completed their first interior fort and were levying their first attacks. Having gleaned that the *ngola*'s sovereignty, in part, rested on the collection of tribute, the colonists targeted the hierarchical structure. *Luanda* from the *sobas* and other local chiefs was now to be paid to the settlers, not the Ndongo sovereign.[26]

Hopes or pretences of partnership evaporated as the Portuguese sought to destabilise and rebuild the Mbundu state. The *sobas* and other local authorities saw their land invaded and looted by the Europeans, their people rounded up, bound and transported. Brazilian plantations were determined as their final destination. Njinga was taking wobbly first steps as these raids were carried out, had learnt about the political system as an inquisitive pre-teen while, not far away, the Portuguese were taking strides towards demolishing it. The Portuguese had some success. A number of Ndongo provincial lords eventually accepted their status as 'vassals' – subjects, subordinates, feudal tenants – of Portugal's king.[27]

An upbringing scored with their father's resistance and the violence of Portuguese occupation, Njinga would've been around twenty years old when the Portuguese established the Cambambe Fort in 1603 on the banks of the Kwanza River. The edifice, left in ruins today though reconstructed multiple times, would be used to hold captured Mbundu people the Portuguese planned to transport using the river. As the colonial mission moved further inland, they raised prisons and fortresses from the ground.[28] The stone structures they built as they went communicated intent: the Portuguese were here and they planned to stay.

Luanda's administrative centre or 'old town' flashes past my taxi window in pinks and greens. Beneath the low-hanging clouds suppressing the sun, dusky flamingo-coloured walls line the pavements, an effort to curb the sprawl of abundant bushy growth. The Governo da Província de Luanda building sports the same rosy hue, as do the headquarters for the Banco Nacional de Angola. I step out of the cab unable to go further down the one-way system, get lost and then directed to the building I'm after, finding that so, too, does the Museu Nacional de Antropologia, its many windows and doors replete with thick white trimming. The visually stunning structures are relics from a Portuguese colonial architectural approach that fused together simplicity, modernity and basic requirements like ventilation.[29]

Once home to an eighteenth-century noble family of Portuguese settlers, the mansion housed the headquarters of the Companhia de

Diamantes de Angola, a Western-backed company that exploited Angolan diamond mines for much of the twentieth century.[30] Today, it hosts thousands of artefacts in its collection, primarily preserved remnants of pre-colonial life. 'This space is important for future generations,' my assigned museum staff member tells me, pushing heavy locs over his shoulder. 'They can know where they have come from and [have] a good view of where we're going.'

He walks me past an interior courtyard, its perimeter lined with potted trees and shrubs. We slowly pass through one room after another, each filled with time-worn objects. There's an *ngundja*, a large wooden chair with an animal skin seat. Used as the seat of the sovereign by Cokwe and Lunda ethnic groups, the rungs between the legs of the chair and its back are lined with intricately carved figurines. There are *tsysakulu* from the Ngangela, wooden combs with long prongs, one topped with an antelope carving and the other with a rooster. There's a *kinda*, a tightly woven basket made of straw and vegetable fibres used to serve and conserve fruits among the Mbundu ethnic group – or Ambundu, as the museum plaque notes. Njinga's people.

I'm shown a *mutopa*, a hookah pipe fashioned out of a young gourd used to smoke tobacco, then we head through a different corridor lined with the tools of hunters and warriors. As we walk, he tells me that Angola should be called Ngola, after the Ndongo sovereign, but that colonists struggled with the spelling.

Poison-tipped spears, protective amulets and uniquely shaped arrowheads (the different heads indicated which hunter had made the kill) give way to more modern instruments of war and hunting. Together, we appraise the dark metal guns, varied in length, size and design. They've rested in many hands, colonial and indigenous, before ending up encased in glass. When trade with Europeans was established, the local African populations could get their hands on these weapons in return for land.

'It was a poor deal for them,' my companion observes. He's not wrong: guns need bullets and bullets are finite. 'And every time you needed more [ammunition], you had to give more land.'

*

Despite steadily losing authority, tribute-paying lands and supporters, the sudden death of Mbande a Ngola in 1617 shook the
kingdom. Ambushed and murdered by his own disgruntled men,
he died with just a fraction of the kingdom his father had passed
down to him intact.[31]

The royal court erupted into the necessary chaos of choosing
a successor: officials tasked with electing the next *ngola* hurried
around Kabasa, the children and relatives of the deceased ruler's
wives and concubines jostled with one another as they pushed
forward their candidates, challengers from eligible lineages mobil-
ised support in the hopes of seizing the capital and its royal seat.[32]

As the fervour built around a now 35-year-old Njinga, perhaps
they were lost in mourning for the father who had heaped attention on them, who had made this child so decidedly his favourite.
As is the way of grief, maybe Njinga's mind ruminated on words
left unsaid, as old memories crystallised, now weighty with new,
sombre meaning. Or, with Njinga's belly having swelled with new
life, was their own mortality – and that of their shortly arriving
baby – foregrounded in the wake of this loss?

Njinga's sex life was an active one with multiple lovers across
their life. As the royal got older, they indulged in the same sensual
pleasures afforded to male counterparts, seeking out sweaty, greedy
delight that would've sparked frowns and gossip around court.
Alongside their host of enslaved women and attendants, Njinga
had a large number of male concubines.[33] Like father, like child,
the Ndongo royal had a favourite among them, Kia Ituxi, the lover
whose offspring ripened in their womb.[34]

But while favour nourishes and builds, elsewhere, its lack starves
and withers. Ngola a Mbande (who I'll call Mbande the Younger)
had spent a childhood in the shadow of his younger sibling. Despite
being the old *ngola*'s eldest, he surely heard the whispers of how
Njinga was treated as the son of the ruler, one who was more intel-
lectually and physically formidable than him. Njinga would later
boast of their skill with likely the *cimbuiya*, a decorative small axe
used in dances and the royal symbol of the Ndongo. They outshone
their brother in all the ways that mattered.[35]

For once, however, Mbande the Younger emerged on top. Having swiftly called upon the support of his partisans, he argued that his father's presumptive heir – Mbande the Older's son with his principal wife and therefore, Mbande the Younger's unnamed older half-brother – was ineligible as his mother had been convicted of adultery. In the same year of his father's death, Mbande the Younger proclaimed himself *ngola*, before many Ndongo electors had even convened in Kabasa to cast their votes.[36]

The seizure of power was underscored quickly and brutally. The freshly self-appointed monarch dispensed of his potential rivals in speedy succession. The half-brother, the half-brother's mother and all her siblings were murdered. Prominent members of court were slaughtered alongside their families. And Njinga's mewling male newborn, only a few days old but old enough to pose a threat, was not spared.[37]

As he eliminated his rivals, Mbande the Younger was shoring up his future, a reign that he wanted uninterrupted by challenges for his seat. So he went further. According to Njinga's partisans in reports collected years later, he had Njinga and their two younger sisters, Nkambu and Nfungi, forcibly sterilised. Though there are no eyewitness accounts of the act, neither Njinga nor their sisters are known to have given birth to any children after 1617.[38]

Perhaps riding waves of anguish – for their father, their child, the family members they had grown up with, the way in which their own body had been weaponised against them – Njinga left Kabasa. They retreated to the neighbouring kingdom of Matamba, just east of Ndongo; somewhere the aggrieved royal could withdraw to and make sense of the hand they had been drawn.[39]

If Mbande the Younger believed that he could triumph where his father had fallen short, the optimism was short-lived. The *sobas*, whose changed allegiance had foreshadowed the old ruler's demise, were still not fully loyal to the new *ngola*. Meanwhile, the Portuguese continued their campaign of military expansion.[40]

The manner in which these Europeans demolished kingdoms with exacting violence was not new to Ndongo. Neighbouring regions that were subordinate to the *ngola*'s authority had borne brutality and destruction at Portuguese hands. In 1581, near the salt-rich province of Kisama, 150 Portuguese swarmed the lands of a local lord in vengeance after the deaths of their comrades. They enslaved around one hundred people before razing the villages to the ground. Elsewhere, a provincial lord negotiated with the colonists for his life, offering one hundred enslaved people as ransom. After accepting the enslaved people, the Portuguese publicly decapitated the lord anyway.[41]

More of the same was in store for Ndongo. Enslavement, famine and the pilfering of natural resources and goods ravaged their lands. In 1618, the Portuguese built another structure, the Ambaca Fort, in the centre of Ndongo territory.[42] The destruction reached fever-pitch when the Portuguese enlisted the help of the Imbangala, also referred to as the Jaga. These nomadic armed communities – who had crossed the Cuango River in 1568 and sacked Kongo's capital – lived by the logic of pillaging, making them handy allies.[43]

As the cries of '*Ita! Ita!*' (War! War!) filled the air, the *ngongo* (a double clapperless war bell) emphasised the message as it sounded through the settlements.[44] Ndongo's most vulnerable – the elderly, some women, and most children – were instructed to scramble for the hills or other hiding places until the fighting was ended, while the Portuguese–Imbangala alliance hacked its way through the kingdom's defences, enslaving and imprisoning as they went. They'd even reach the undefended Kabasa royal palace and manage to drive out Mbande the Younger. He left behind his mother and wives who, with other captives, were carried away.[45]

The colonial onslaught was a calculated effort that superseded physical destruction. Portuguese Jesuit missionaries set about attempting to weaken the peoples' faith in their *ngangas*. These senior practitioners presided over major religious ceremonies, like those before entering into battle, while village *ngangas* officiated local births, naming rituals, illnesses and deaths. The European Catholics burnt everything: the shrines and ancestral homes they built, the huts they stored their divination tools in or where rituals were carried out and the physical representations of their deities.

Crosses were erected in their place. *Ngangas*, alongside villagers, were involuntarily converted – some were arrested first before being forced to learn 'the things of God'.[46]

Meanwhile, since 1605, the dominance of slave-trading settlers in Luanda had become increasingly clear: the 'so-called captains of the [Kwanza]' married into the families of the *sobas*, taking their daughters for wives and earning the descriptor of 'white *sobas*' from some historians.[47] In line with the demands of settler colonialism, the Portuguese were making good on a mission of demolishing, usurping and extracting.

Yet, the Ndongo managed to remain independent and not pay tribute to the European power laying siege to their lands. Alongside having a huge military force, it still had an extensive tribute base from a significant population, making the kingdom difficult to subjugate in its entirety.[48] From his refuge in the Kindonga Islands, located upstream in the Kwanza River, the embattled *ngola* pursued a peace treaty with the Portuguese, while his guerillas continued to attack their fortresses.[49] Mbande the Younger even managed to make an alliance with Jaga leaders who had become disillusioned with the Europeans. It still wouldn't be enough.

The kidnapping, enslavement and displacement of Mbundu peoples had devastated the kingdom. Across just four years, more than 55,000 of their people had been enslaved and transported to the Americas. Hundreds of thousands of *kijikos* had been bequeathed to settlers to use as their personal property on budding plantations near Luanda and around Portuguese fortresses.[50] By 1621, Mbande the Younger was at a loss and saw only one viable method of ending the violent campaigns against Ndongo and regaining seized lands: diplomacy. To his mind, there was no one better to turn to than Njinga, the sibling he'd had sterilised.

Njinga had held their own in Matamba, perhaps channelling grief into organising troops against the Portuguese campaigns taking place in the kingdom they had sought refuge in, as well as eastern Ndongo. In 1620, Njinga even joined forces with Imbangala leaders after their allegiance switch.[51] The Portuguese would lament not being able to share news with those based in Luanda because

'Ginga' had blocked their routes and prevented all communication.[52] However, when Mbande the Younger discovered that João Correia de Souza had been installed as the new governor in 1621 and would be arriving in Luanda imminently, he nominated his estranged sibling Njinga to head up a peace-seeking delegation, correctly gambling on their political ambitions taking priority over any lingering resentment.

Months later, joined by a sizeable military escort, musicians, enslaved people destined as greeting gifts for the governor, pages, waiting women and more, official envoy Njinga and their delegation wound through Kabasa and into the port city claimed by the Europeans. There, in Luanda, they were received with the aplomb of military salutes and music before the work of negotiating began.[53]

With large multicoloured feathers threaded through the kinks of their hair, priceless jewels dangling from their arms and legs, gemstones covering everywhere the swathes of rich clothes did not, and flanked by their ensemble, Njinga entered the palace saloon.[54]

As they placed one foot after the other, the rustle of fabric and tinkle of finery marking a rhythm, Njinga moved towards what they had already known would be waiting. Some historians describe it as a simple floor mat, others as 'velvet covers on a carpet on the floor'.[55] Unlike the velvet-covered chair embroidered with gold belonging to the Portuguese governor, Correia de Souza, Mbundu dignitaries visiting Luanda were expected to sit on the floor, permeating any negotiation attempts with an unspoken power dynamic.[56]

Maybe with a haughty, lazy signal, or with the quick utterance of a few words, one of the Ndongo royal's entourage – most likely an enslaved person – dropped to the ground on all fours and Njinga sat on their back, bringing them to eye-level with the governor.[57] They were now ready to conduct the business required of them. Armed with proficiency in Portuguese said to be taught by visiting missionaries, Njinga was the bearer of the *ngola*'s word.[58]

As Njinga sat on the back of another person, their presence as unremarkable and unimportant as the chair they were imitating, the royal outlined Mbande the Younger's position. The *ngola* would live in peace with the Portuguese, cease military attacks and return the Portuguese-claimed enslaved people who had since fled to join the Ndongo ruler. Ndongo land concessions as well as acceptance of Christianity and the presence of Catholic missionaries were also rolled into the deal. The Portuguese pledged to withdraw from the Ambaca Fort. With these conditions met, Njinga wagered, together both powers could take on common enemies as allies.[59]

There was one notable demand, however, to which Njinga refused to acquiesce. When the issue of an annual tribute of enslaved Ndongo peoples to the Portuguese sovereign was raised, Njinga reportedly reminded the governor that their brother was seeking friendship, not servitude.[60]

When Njinga exited that saloon, leaving behind the hunched individual because 'it was not proper for the ambassador of a great king to use the same chair twice', the assurances of a treaty between Ndongo and the Portuguese settlers were carried back to Kabasa.[61] It wasn't without surrendering more on Njinga's part.

One of the demanded concessions was Njinga's conversion to Christianity. They had grown up with an understanding that their father's authority was inextricable from the divine. The throne was advised and counselled by the *ngangas* and below them, the *xingulas*. The latter occupied a similar role but were spiritual figures who acted as a conduit to the ancestral world. Through them, the wishes of the bygone could be transmitted to the ruler to aid their deliberations.[62] They guided the *ngolas* with the words of the ancestors, underscored the ruler's divine powers and connected them to the Mbundu people. Njinga's decision to convert was no small thing.

When any ruler entered into serious negotiations with devout seventeenth-century Iberian monarchs, their acceptance of Christian baptism was a prerequisite.[63] Mbande had already given his sibling permission to undertake a public baptism should it offer Ndongo leverage, so Njinga simply extended their stay in Luanda. They threw themselves into preparing for conversion. Around 1623, before nobles, government figures and church officials, Njinga was anointed with holy waters in a Jesuit-built church in Luanda.

They emerged with the baptismal name of 'Ana de Souza' and the governor as their godfather.[64]

Like a number of Ndongo *sobas* and provincial lords, Njinga understood conversion, and religion more largely, as central to Portuguese politics. Not only could a public embrace of Christianity earn the respect of the Europeans, but it could also garner the support of the many converted Mbundu who were enslaved in the city, toiling over plantations, or were refugees in their flight from the fighting.[65]

With their Christian baptism, Njinga entered the realms of colonial high society. The Ndongo royal presented themselves as 'a potential bearer of Portuguese evangelical hopes for the conversion of the Ngola kingdom to Christianity.'[66]

Compared to their brother, Njinga presented a flexible, willing option to the colonial power. But, in doing so, the already strained ties between the royal lineage and the unconverted Mbundu peoples – those who continued to turn to their spiritual leaders as danger closed around them – grew even tauter. Whatever Njinga was willing to gain with the Portuguese came at the cost of loyalty, both from and towards the people of Ndongo.

It is no surprise that when Mbande the Younger died in 1624, rumours, gossip and excavations for truth flew thick and fast. It's said that after vehemently refusing to be baptised, 'melancholy' or depression gathered up the besieged ruler of dwindling lands. That, by his own hand, he ingested poison – a common practice among their ancestors. Elsewhere, Portuguese chroniclers fanned flames by intimating that Njinga had played a part in his demise.[67] The truth is lost to us but what we do know is that the dance of succession began again.

Any political designs Njinga had on the *ngola* seat, however, were blighted with obstacles. One living, breathing problem was Mbande the Younger's son and legitimate male heir – a minor who had been entrusted to the care and guidance of a leader of the Jaga, to train the young child as a soldier. In the wake of their brother's death, Njinga became a regent for the young boy, believed to be around eight years old, as they eased themselves closer to true power.[68]

Another issue was the different lineages left by past *ngolas*, their kin all with varying claims to the office. Living in the capital or in communities close by, they offered fierce competition for any challenger.

However, it was the subjects of Ndongo themselves who posed one of the greatest problems for Njinga's potential succession. The European application of the term 'sister' to Njinga didn't align with Mbundu lineage. Instead, it blurred their codes – especially as not all believed (or believe, in the case of contemporary historians) that Mbande the Younger and Njinga shared the same mother. These distinctions mattered to the Mbundu and informed their rites of succession. If it was indeed the case that Njinga was a half-sibling of Mbande, this difference possessed the power to split the hopeful ruler's aspirations wide open. As historian Joseph Miller writes, 'a half-"sister" through a co-wife of the father was no kin at all'.[69]

These reasons for disqualification slid off Njinga's back like water. And where problems couldn't be ignored, they were dealt with robustly.

The nephew they acted as a regent for was under the wing of a Chief Jaga, named as Kasanje da Matamba or simply Kasa. Kasa's *kilombo* (war camp) was located in the Kina region in Kasanje, near Njinga's base.[70] Njinga biographer Linda Heywood paints a tableau of single-minded seduction. In it sits a ruthless Njinga, one who may have made their principal concubine, Kia Ituxi, their 'king' before tossing them aside in favour of Kasa. Wiles, wealth, public declarations of love and affection cloud the frame. At first, Kasa appears to have resisted the romantic favours of someone much older than him who he was sure was attempting to manipulate him for the boy. Any founded suspicions didn't stop him from acquiescing to the union – one that the Portuguese literally understood as a 'marriage' – and ultimately giving up the boy. Some accounts state that the ceremony had not yet come to a close before Njinga had their nephew murdered, his body thrown into the depths of the Kwanza River and 'declared that [they] had revenged [their] son'.[71] Like the enslaved person expected to fold themselves into furniture, it was yet another bleak exercise of Njinga's power.

All ritual objects and symbols – essential markers of authority – found their way into the sole possession of Njinga. Their staunch belief in their 'right to rule' Ndongo trumped disgruntled chatter from the *sobas*, *makotas* and the classes below. This was maybe even bolstered by Mbande the Younger, who had come to increasingly rely on his young sibling's counsel, allegedly indicating that Njinga should rule after him.[72] As far as Njinga may have been concerned, the masses – those nameless, faceless, anonymous masses only fit for subjecthood or sale – could believe whatever they wanted.

In 1624, Mbande the Younger's successor seized power and their name was Njinga a Mbande.

A scratching stylus leaked Njinga's reminders of unfulfilled Portuguese promises onto parchment.[73]

The symbols arranged themselves into words that implored the newly appointed Portuguese governor, Fernão de Souza, to respect the promises of his predecessors: to remove the Ambaca Fort, as agreed two years prior, and return the since-taken *kijikos* and *sobas* (serfs and local officials) to Ndongo. The letters carried in sweaty palms of emissaries outlined Njinga's predicament for the Portuguese. Only once these conditions were released could the ruler safely leave the Kindonga Islands where they held court and return to the traditional base of power in Kabasa. These were the agreed terms, wrote Njinga in August 1624, terms that meant that markets could then be re-opened, allowing goods and enslaved people to be sold, and then the agricultural industry could churn into action once more. Ndongo was willing to meet demands in opening trade routes, they emphasised.[74]

The colonial onslaught against Ndongo had destroyed the trade in enslaved lives and the Portuguese were looking to get it up and running. To that end, they sent Njinga a proposal from Luanda. *Sobas*, enslaved people, and *kimbares* – Mbundu soldiers serving under Portuguese officers – had fled the Europeans' control and into Njinga's camp. The Portuguese wanted them back. They also wanted an acceptance of Christianity, its missionaries and tribute paid to the Portuguese sovereign. As far as the Europeans were concerned, their conditions hadn't changed. These demands, the governor responded, had to be met before the Portuguese would return the people that *they* had taken.[75]

The much-deliberated fort still stood deep in Ndongo territory. Relations with Luanda were, once again, dipping into crisis. Yet, maybe bolstered by their ranks swelling with hired Imbangala bands as mercenaries and displaced Mbundu people offering support in return for protection, Njinga turned the proposal down.[76] They cited the illegality of the demand: Mbundu laws did not permit the return of runaway war captives to enslavement because escape to their homeland immediately granted amnesty.[77] Instead, with newly fortified numbers, Njinga took to the battlefield – a location called Pungo Ndongo, an area belonging to an opposing lineage.[78]

The alliance between the Portuguese and Pungo Ndongo's *soba*, the Hari a Kiluanje, was one that took advantage of a historic rivalry: the *soba* was a descendant of the kingdom's founder but his lineage had lost out on the throne when Njinga's grandfather, Kilombo kia Kasenda, ascended to the office of *ngola* in 1575.[79]

The ousted lineage had grown close to the Portuguese across Mbande the Younger's reign. From 1624 onwards, the colonists had pumped military resources into the Hari *soba*'s dominion and their joint efforts to track down Njinga.[80] By 1625, amid their fruitless pursuit, Governor de Souza began to consider Hari a Kiluanje as the legitimate heir to the throne, helped by the fact that the Hari lands had become a vassalage of the Portuguese sovereign. Before the year was out, despite widespread Mbundu uproar and uprising over his ineligibility to rule, the *soba* was named King of Ndongo by the Portuguese.[81]

Incensed – because Hari a Kiluanje was a puppet king betraying his people and their traditions, because he was a child of the third wife and 'therefore of housekeeper status', because the Portuguese clandestinely supported then elevated their rival, because the *soba*-turned-*ngola* was willing to give up what they had refused – Njinga attacked Hari lands in December 1625.[82] The governor responded by sending Portuguese and African soldiers and archers to defend them. Njinga's side endured a number of casualties and captures, while managing to kill three Portuguese – including the captain – and seize six captives of their own.[83]

Njinga fled into hiding in the Kindonga Islands which, since they came to power, had become their new capital of Ndongo.[84] The escaped ruler continued to attack Hari a Kiluanje until he succumbed to the grip of smallpox in late 1626.[85] The void he left was filled by his half-brother, Ngola Hari – also referred to as Filipe (or Philipe) Hari I. Here was another member of the competing lineage, another figure with a questionable matrilineal claim to the throne, another Portuguese-supported candidate pushed forward to underscore Njinga's disqualification for rule on the basis of gender.

Under intense pressure from de Souza, the *sobas*, *makotas* and other electors in the kingdom took the only option put before them. They elected Ngola Hari on 12 October 1626 at the fort in Ambaca. The newly minted ruler took the oath of vassalage to the Portuguese king and agreed to hand over one hundred 'prime' enslaved people every year, among other obligations.[86] It signalled the end of the Ndongo Kingdom's autonomy while the Portuguese settlers heralded the establishment of 'The New Kingdom of Dongo'.[87]

Despite the governor sending Ngola Hari military reinforcements to destroy their headquarters in 1627, Njinga remained beyond reach, launching attacks from their fortified island base.[88] Their sisters, however, did not.

By 1629, Nkambu and Nfungi had both been imprisoned, baptised and given Christian names. Upon their capture, the pair, their aunt and eleven *sobas* and *makotas* were paraded naked on their way through Ndongo before arriving in Luanda. It reeked of petty desperation from de Souza. There were still rebellious *sobas* refusing to pay tribute, fleeing with enslaved people to join Njinga's armies and the departing swathes were severely jeopardising the flow of business out of Luanda's port. Njinga had once again turned to their alliances with Imbangala groups, meanwhile converting the kingdom was proving difficult with the *ngangas* still occupying central divine roles.[89] The Portuguese crusade was faltering.

The governor couldn't get his hands on the sibling he wanted but remained haunted by their presence.

Over the years, it became apparent that Njinga's symbolic ceremony with Kasa didn't necessarily make the alliance a secure one and security was exactly what Njinga needed as they launched attacks against the joint Hari-Portuguese campaigns. After two Imbangala armies changed sides in the middle of a battle in 1628, Njinga had taken matters into their own hands.[90] Having already introduced their followers to the military techniques, rituals and ways of living of Kasa's people, Njinga decided to become an Imbangala (or Jaga) themselves – reportedly assuming the role of *tembanza*, a major title reserved for women which heralded authority over both war and politics.[91]

Approaching 1630, the Portuguese couldn't reach Njinga without broaching Imbangala lands. It offered the sovereign a strategic advantage as they led considerably inflated Mbundu-Imbangala military armies. This wasn't to last. Kasa and other Imbangala defected to the Portuguese, effectively exiling an almost 50-year-old Njinga for lacking authentic Imbangala ancestry.[92]

With no allies and still being hunted by a Portuguese army, the former *tembanza* fled east to the lands they had called home when their brother had laid siege to both their family and body. Njinga was in need of a political base and the familiar Matamba had historically been a tributary of the Ndongo *ngola*.[93] Thanks to years of incessant raids by Imbangala and Portuguese forces, the kingdom of Matamba – which had a precedent for female rulers – had since been left in political disarray.[94]

Njinga moved with purpose. Still flanked by the numerous Mbundu people, they made their way to the kingdom's capital of Mkaria ka Matamba where its queen, Muongo, held court. After fierce fighting, the war-hardened chief emerged triumphant with the queen and her daughter as captives. Muongo's swift deposition – and later, banishment from the capital – saw the flight of her closest allies and, by 1635, Njinga occupied the kingdom and had established themselves as Matamba's ruler.[95]

The African authorities in Ndongo, Kasanje and beyond had come to understand that whoever controlled the movement of enslaved people controlled wealth and power. The more Africans – bound to one another by metal and rope, wearing only the scraps of cloth they were permitted, their bodies worn with the licks of whips and merciless sun – trailed through Njinga-controlled domains, the more resources the ruler gained for army-building. Having diverted much of the trading routes from surrounding regions into Matamba, Njinga rebuilt the once-faltering kingdom until it was the largest state in the region during the 1640s.[96]

For all their success at their relocated base, as far as Njinga was concerned, they were sovereign of Matamba *and* Ndongo. Even if they'd had to rule from a capital far from the walls of Kabasa. Even if they'd had to yield much of Ndongo's original territory. Even if there was another *ngola* who, by 1640, had been ruling for almost a decade and a half with the help of the Europeans.

The Portuguese manufactured Njinga as a deeply unsuitable monarch.

Belligerent, determined and garnering support, the Ndongo royal and their goal of sovereignty were a threat to a colonial project approaching seventy years in the making. Njinga's gender, then, made for a convenient vehicle for disqualification. 'A woman had never governed this kingdom,' penned Governor Fernão de Souza to the Portuguese king.[97]

Njinga embodied transgression, especially of European norms. They commanded their own troops into battle; they wore what was understood by the Portuguese as masculine garb; they used a male-coded name, especially in military settings, and would answer to no other.[98] Njinga had also declared themselves 'Lady [of Ndongo]' before their people and had sent letters to Governor de Souza from 1624 onwards as '*Dona* Anna, the *senhora de Angola*'.[99] They presented a walking contradiction. What kind of *dona* or queen was this?

The deployment of these terms in African contexts already stretched Western imaginations to breaking point. Preconceptions around the continent and its inhabitants collided. Missionaries and colonial settlers transmitted messages on the morality, decency and modesty of women. These merged with notions of the morally decayed 'savage' in need of salvation.[100] And it seemed Njinga needed salvation more than most.

Here was a figure that the Portuguese called 'woman', sexually exploiting the bodies of the unfree, draping their own body in male attire and engaging in the brutality of war – all decidedly masculine behaviours that weren't permissible for the Ndongo ruler.[101] To them, this African flouting their civilised values of feminine morality was inherently deviant. A 'volatile, unstable, and abject ruler who was to be distrusted and ultimately removed from power.'[102] Njinga was thoroughly incompatible for the role of queen.

But Njinga did not understand themselves as a queen – they did not have the language for it. The language of the Mbundu people, Kimbundu, did not have gendered pronouns, let alone distinct terms assigned on the basis of gender alone. Although the Ndongo held a precedent of male rulers, the title of *ngola* – which emerges from the root of *'ngolo'* meaning 'strength' – is not inherently gendered. *'Ngola'* cannot be accurately translated as 'king' or 'queen'.[103] It's an issue that continues to throw contemporary historians: in a footnote, Belgian historian Jan Vansina noted that 'the [historical] tradition does not mention *Queen* Nzinga, but *King* Nzinga, even when speaking of Queen Dona Anna Nzinga.'[104] He questions whether the 'Nzinga' reference could be describing Njinga or perhaps even their deceased brother.

Trans history scholar Kit Heyam suggests it's likely that Njinga requested to be addressed as 'king' in gendered languages, a desire to wear the same title as the Portuguese sovereign they viewed as an equal.[105] But perhaps their bargaining position against a more powerful occupier meant that the new *ngola* sometimes accepted the use of gendered titles, like 'queen' and *'dona'*, that carried notes of respect and sovereignty.

Could it be possible that, given that Njinga had to learn gendered language to specifically deal with the Europeans, they didn't struggle with entrenched attachments to the terms? Perhaps it even allowed for a certain playful deliberateness in when and how they expressed all parts of themselves. Here was a coy-looking feminine figure, as romanticised by Portuguese artists, couched in rich furs, golden regalia and feather plumes but also a military-minded general barking out brash directives in male-coded cloth.

It's unclear how many others there were in the kingdom who, like Njinga, were assigned female at birth but expressed themselves fluidly or lived as men. We know, however, that Njinga's dominion teemed with other gender-variant people, including *kimbandas* (or *chibados*): people assigned male at birth who lived as women.

They embodied another form of divine connection between the people of Ndongo and unearthly realms. Of the fifty *kimbandas* Njinga was said to have at court, each one – clad in feminine attire – could be called upon as 'spiritual arbiters' in political and military decisions, as well as to perform the rituals required to usher the deceased's onward journeys.[106] The belief that they could not only cure diseases but also force secrets out into the open, unveiling criminal identities and activities, rested a special status on their heads.[107] *Kimbandas* married men, with their unions 'honoured and even prized' among the Mbundu and the Imbangala.[108] One elderly *kimbanda* would lead the caste, the contours of time carved into her aged body, responding to the call of 'grandmother'.[109] So entrenched were the ritual traditions of Kimbanda throughout the kingdom, overseen by individuals who predate the term 'trans', it travelled across the Atlantic alongside enslaved people ferried through Njinga's lands to Brazil and beyond. With its key tenets surviving over 400 years, it forms the foundation for the Afro-Brazilian denomination of Quimbanda observed today.[110]

The lives of Njinga, the *kimbandas* and, no doubt, unnamed others within the Ndongo kingdom repudiate a number of assertions. These include the belief that there is something 'traditional' about understanding gender as essentialised, or that it can be understood as a recent development, a novel trend, a fanciful fabrication.[111]

The confines of European tongues could not, and still cannot, capture Njinga. It's why, as you'll have noticed, I've used 'they/ them' pronouns to describe the ruler. It's an imperfect approach: I've made a choice – linguistic and political – that Njinga didn't make. I do not suggest that Njinga would have used these pronouns to describe themselves. Instead, like Heyam, I want to avoid presumptions of gender *and* honour the plurality with which Njinga explored theirs. Until there are better linguistic tools for exploring gender neutrality in the English language, until there is greater acknowledgement of how our languages impose pronouns on people who did not have them in their own language, I hope that for now, 'they/them' can suffice.[112]

It's also important to note that there are certain colonial chroniclers that appear in the footnotes again and again. Much of what we know about Njinga is, in some way, filtered through their accounts. There's Gaeta, an Italian missionary who resided in Njinga's court in the late 1650s.[113] Cadornega, a Portuguese military officer who turned his hand to slave trading and historical documentation after participating in the 1626–7 campaigns against Ndongo.[114] Cavazzi, Gaeta's fellow Capuchin priest, presented as Njinga's missionary confidante, advisor and biographer.[115]

Many of the texts were pumped out of Luanda, their contents heavy with accounts created to support settler interests, decisions and strategy. The records are selective, often focusing on what the Portuguese did or how the Ndongo reacted to the former's presence. There was a tendency to emphasise Portuguese victories, while some sources, like Cadornega, almost entirely omitted their defeats.[116] Historians Heintze and Rieck assert that Gaeta and Cavazzi came to Angola together, most likely stayed in contact via letters and periodically met in person across the years. They add that if both missionaries were recording traditions in Matamba, they theoretically had the chance – as a number of primary eyewitnesses have done – to compare, contrast and supplement their versions.[117]

For example, it's through these men that we're introduced to cannibalistic rituals among the Imbangala, naturally implicating Njinga too. Mercenaries who devoured brown flesh on a daily basis, mouths contorted around human gristle and bone, became a subject that would be repeated through works created across the following centuries.[118] There are also other claims like Njinga '[instituting] mutilation of the genitals as punishment for infidelity among [their] male consorts'.[119] With a stated Christian mission of saving the African continent from itself, European imaginations danced with imagery that only fortified white supremacy. 'If European society represented the heights of civilised society,' writes scholar Rachel Briard, Njinga and the Imbangala demonstrated the 'barbarity and crassness' of undelivered African societies.[120]

As we've seen, Njinga's use of brutal power is evident across their reign. However, we must ask, how has their capacity for cruelty been distorted by disparate dynamics of power, gender and race?

I reckon that it was a Lagosian goat peppersoup that felled me in Luanda. My Nigerian heritage meant it wasn't my first. Being raised in a household where a Trinidadian mother's liberal use of scotch bonnet had also fortified my capacity for spice – or so I thought. My stomach didn't start churning until long after I had taken to the skies from Lagos's heaving metropolis on a three-hour flight to Angola's capital. However, after a day spent at the Museu Nacional de Antropologia, back in my hotel on downtown Luanda's busy strip of Rua da Missão, it came for me.

In between falling in and out of restless sweaty stupor, bemusedly watching out of my room's window the karaoke-indulging revellers at the café-turned-bar across the street belting out impassioned renditions of George Michael's 'Careless Whisper' into the night air, and clutching the cool body of the toilet for the umpteenth time thanks to an inability to hold down food or water, I had messaged Líria asking to reschedule our meeting. Falling ill had more than halved my time in Luanda. But whether it was the peppersoup, fatigue from constantly moving, an overall inconsistent diet on my travels, a stomach virus or none of the above, meeting the people behind Arquivo de Identidade Angolano (AIA) was a priority.

Stood in humid air, I carry the signature, and frankly embarrassing, apologism that coats the behaviours of most raised in the UK. Not only had AIA generously fitted me into a busy Saturday of activities, not only had crawling city traffic made me late, but I'd also managed to slip into knee-deep dirty – likely sewage-laden – water as I rushed out of my taxi to try to find the centre's discreet front door. I was saved from finding out how much further I could sink by instinctively clutching onto a passer-by, obviously earning their rebukes in quick Portuguese. It's with murky viscous liquid drenching the bottom half of my culottes, bare legs and trainers, under the gaze of curious drivers locked in a jam that hadn't moved in at least ten minutes, that Líria and Fally open the door to me.

They gently but firmly dispense of my flustered explanations. In the centre's pastel yellow front room, the pair quickly organise others to help me slough off the waste on my legs with a bucket wash as well as washing and drying my trainers. Moments later, I'm directed to a sofa next to a wall with bright artwork and assorted AIA flyers for past and upcoming events. I'm soon joined by Fally, whose silver nose and septum piercings flash against their black beard and dark skin. Líria, and her open smiling face, sits in a chair across from me. I open my small notepad and start the recording.

AIA was established in 2017 as an LGBTQ+ Angolan feminist collective, Líria – one of the co-founders – tells me, largely translated through Fally who dips in and out of rapid Portuguese and English with an American accent. Their activities rest on core pillars like advocacy with government institutions, cross-organisation work with other LGBTQ+ initiatives and creating educational content for young people, educators, politicians and media and health professionals.[121] Another is to create a safe refuge for their queer communities.

The building we're sat in is not just an events space but also a physical shelter for people fleeing violence – physical, mental, emotional, financial and more – and experiencing homelessness.

Angola only decriminalised 'same-sex sexual activity' and brought in anti-discrimination protections in 2021.[122] Queer couples looking to have their relationship recognised by the state still have no recourse, there are no provisions for lesbians to access IVF and there is no right to legally change gender.[123]

Entrenched social attitudes cannot be quickly undone – if undone at all – with legislative reform. Líria's collective was forced to move to the location we're sat in after enduring violence and attacks from the previous neighbourhood and a nearby church. Here, AIA's offerings are plentiful: vocational training; an on-hand psychologist; cultural activities like dance and theatre; shared meals; a space to chill and refuel; escapism. All these prongs combined, Líria's mission is simple: 'We're attempting to decolonise the idea of homosexuality, diverse marginalised sexuality or gender expression as "Eurocentric". It's African. There are lots of examples of diverse sexualities in African histories.'

That said, their initial introductions to Njinga were threadbare. Líria has only managed to access scraps of information on the ruler and didn't learn about them at school, home or elsewhere. Meanwhile, Fally remembers reading about Njinga in a third-year classbook and it presented a warrior queen with no allusions to sex, sexuality or gender. 'As an adult, I discovered this diverse sexuality of Njinga and the different people they had intimacies with,' they share with a note of incredulity. 'Where was this story when we were growing up? That's what we question every day. People just want this shallow version of Njinga and African history.' It's in line with a matrix of Angolan institutional structures that Líria identifies as patriarchal, religious and deeply conservative. Within this, the story of Njinga is constructed in a way that reinforces extolled moral values. 'Our system can't bear anything less.'

Across our conversation, the pair pause occasionally to greet the centre's users who trickle through the door, some solitary, some excitedly greeting friends, some clutching the hands of partners. A few rush in through the door, escaping Luanda's now-turned weather as rain batters the roof. Under its thunderous cacophony, I ask Fally about the gendering in Portuguese language and how they navigate it as a trans non-binary person. In short, it's tricky with the linguistic structure often used as a vehicle for misgendering, including within queer communities. 'It doesn't matter if it's a gendered language,' they explain. 'If someone identifies in a gender-diverse way, a way beyond the binary, we are supposed to adapt and not question why.' Fally's first language was English, a far cry from the way that 'a' signals a Portuguese word is feminine and 'o' masculine.

'What does adaptation look like in practice?' I ask. 'Could the "a" and "o" be used interchangeably?'

Fally plays with their thick glasses frames. They reference their own experiences – they try not to use either, employing phrases with no gender assigned.

'For example, a *fulana* – meaning a 'so-and-so' whose name is not known – indicates a female subject, *fulano* is male,' they explain. 'I prefer to use *fulane*. Not male, not female, not in-between, maybe above.'

Since at least 1598, the Dutch had been tied up in Portuguese affairs, as the former sought to upend the latter's dominance over the global trade network. They stated their intention through launching attacks against Portuguese naval power and assaulting their occupied territories, like the series of invasions of Brazil that began in 1624.[124] Decades later, the Dutch loomed closer still. Having seized the Brazilian sugar-producing lands, they were now looking to secure a reliable stream of enslaved people to work them.[125] So, accordingly, the Dutch invaded Luanda in 1641, forcing the Portuguese to take refuge further inland. They had 'invaded the invaders'.[126]

For Njinga, Dutch arrival offered a new alliance and reignited hopes of a Portuguese expulsion. By 1642, their power had stretched to such an extent that Njinga was powerful in traditionally rebellious regions while the Portuguese settlers were penned into four inland forts. The *ngola's* benefits as an ally to the Dutch – maintaining trade routes and supplying goods and enslaved people – were undeniable.[127] An uneasy coalition formed between the Dutch,

Njinga, the Kongo, the Dembos and other rulers and *sobas* who had never accepted Portuguese rule or contended their vassal status.[128]

While consumed by their mission to flush out Portugal's colonial presence, the now 60-year-old Njinga never forgot about their sisters still captive in enemy hands nor their sisters, them. In fact, from wherever they were held in Luanda, Nfungi managed to send their sibling letters that detailed all the Portuguese manoeuvres, aiding Njinga's decision-making elsewhere in the region. When the penned scraps of precious intel were found during the invasion of Njinga's *kilombo* in 1646, the Portuguese discovery cost Nfungi her life. She was murdered by drowning in Luanda.[129]

Nfungi's murder was just one element of a bleak picture sharpening into focus for the beleaguered *ngola*. Not only did Njinga's established military might and growing strategic control frighten the Portuguese, but it also made their tenuous allies, like the Dutch and Kongo, wary and suspicious.[130]

Despite combining with Njinga and local African rulers in defeating the Portuguese army at the Battle of Kombi in 1647, and maybe unsure of when they might be on the receiving end of a coordinated African attack themselves, the Dutch struck up a deal with their fellow Europeans before exiting the region in 1648. They sailed away, leaving broken agreements of allyship trailing in the split waters.[131]

With the Dutch gone, other alliances fragmented, the destruction of their base, resumed Portuguese attacks, the loss of Nfungi and its ramifications for the still captive Nkambu's safety, Njinga's hand had been forced.

Dependent on the support of outsiders all throughout their military career, even at their most successful, driving out the Portuguese colonists was no longer a realistic prospect. As the ageing chief entered their seventies, in a similar fashion to their brother in his final years, they switched tack. It was time to return to statecraft.

After re-converting to Catholicism, letters spooled from Njinga's hand to the Vatican. Through them, they deferentially and successfully sought the Pope's diplomatic recognition of their sovereignty and requested missionaries to be sent to their kingdoms.[132] Once lost, a 1651 letter claimed, Njinga – who was erecting churches in the kingdom – had now wandered back to the Catholic God: 'I confess that I am very grateful to your Lordships for this favour; because now we have knowledge of the true God who once we did not help, so we were deceived in our idolatry, in the power of the devil...'[133]

Messages also sent to Portuguese officials hinted at steadily rising desperation. In 1655, Njinga wrote a complaint to the latest governor, Luís Mendes de Souza Chichorro, about how they had delivered 'infinite' enslaved people to the colonial power and still did not have their sister. Pointedly noting in the letter that Chichorro was a relative of João Correia de Souza, 'my Godfather', they added: 'Past governors... always they will promise to hand over my Sister, for whom I have given countless pieces... and they have never handed her over, but rather they will immediately start wars, which will make me uneasy.'[134]

Njinga wasn't just uneasy – they were out of options. In October 1656, against the will of principal advisors in Matamba, Njinga signed a formal peace treaty with the Portuguese.[135]

Nkambu was released that same year but the price of her freedom – and the end of attacks against parts of Ndongo and Matamba – was not cheap. Njinga relinquished claims to strategic lands their armies had fought over ten years to control, opened Matamba to Portuguese enslavers, welcomed missionaries into their court, committed to sending an annual tribute of enslaved peoples and providing military support to the Portuguese when required, and publicly repudiated the ways of the Imbangala.[136]

Having largely repeated the fundamental concessions they had made in the palace saloon back in 1622, Njinga still stood to make some personal gains. They solidified their own position with a monopoly on the exports of enslaved people by directing trade through a *feira* (fair) at their capital, saw some benefit to the presence of Portuguese allies, traders and officials in helping keep internal control and, most importantly, carefully demanded that the Portuguese recognise Njinga's only living sibling – known to them by the Christian name of Bárbara – as their heir to fend off any ambitious nobles.[137] With the Portuguese happy to support Njinga's claim to the throne, Ngola Hari, after three decades of rule, was effectively deposed.[138]

Despite the agreement, despite being forced into a position of subjugation, Njinga firmly asserted that they would never recognise Portuguese sovereignty over their domains: 'As to paying the tribute, then, which you want, this has no reason whatsoever, because since I was born to rule my kingdom, I do not have to obey nor recognize another sovereign.'[139]

Finally, after almost four decades, Njinga took their place as the recognised *ngola* of Ndongo and Matamba.

Njinga defied thirteen Portuguese governors who were installed over the kingdom from 1622 to 1663.[140] Their single-mindedness as well as military and diplomatic prowess meant that, in the 1960s and 1970s, Njinga rose to symbol status.[141] They became, for example, an emblem of the People's Movement for the Liberation of Angola during a 27-year-long civil war which had a base among the Kimbundu people.[142] To be a proto-nationalist, however, is to champion the interests of one's own people against outsiders, at least in theory.[143] With Njinga, it seems that throughout their reign, they had understood that all those who did not stand with them were against them.

At the age of seventy-five, they entered into a Catholic marriage with a young courtier named Sebastião. They adopted Catholic practices across their kingdoms. Njinga told their biographer Gaeta that they had always been a Christian and that it was extreme circumstances that had driven them to join the Imbangala.[144]

Up until their death after only seven years of recognised rule, Njinga contributed to the conflicting portraits of themselves: the resistance leader, the Mbundu politician, the devout Christian and the Portuguese ally.[145] Over the years, scholars have taken more critical approaches to Njinga's legacy where depictions of heroism yield space for grappling with the Ndongo leader's pragmatism, self-interest and dogged chase of legitimacy and recognition.

A lung infection claimed a fragile Njinga a Mbande in September

1663. Despite a number of Christian overtures, the ruler was laid to rest in the ways of their Mbundu and Matamba peoples.[146] In accordance with their wishes, Nkambu ruled after them. The *ngola* position was no longer a role read as exclusively male – it became gender-neutral. In fact, for at least 80 of the 104 years following Njinga's death, the monarch of Ndongo and Matamba was a woman.[147]

Njinga's relationship with Catholicism, its religious principles flirted with when advantageous, could be read as a means to an end. Twisting, turning, manoeuvring like their birth and name had forewarned. So, too, can their regard for the people they ruled over, specifically the unfree. Not only did Njinga accept the trade and transportation of enslaved people through their lands, but transports increased significantly under their watch – a departure from *ngolas* who ruled before them.[148]

These enslaved individuals, their autonomy, their livelihoods, their relationships, their community ties changed in an instant as they were shifted like pawns across a gameboard.

They appear, unnamed spectres, across Njinga's legacy as bargaining chips, furniture, tributary gifts and sexual playthings. They are lost to us forever and, yet, resist complete erasure. They sit resolutely as hollows in Njinga's heroism.

CHAPTER 3

Tassi Hangbé

The Dahomey Leader

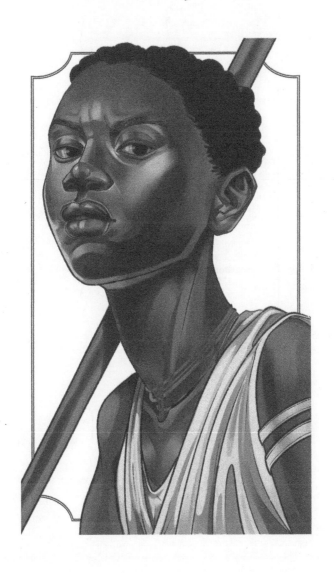

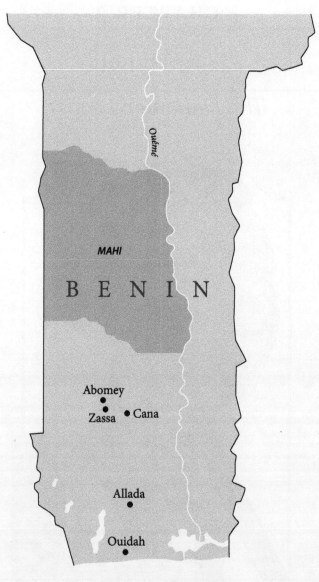

Ouémé

MAHI

B E N I N

Abomey
●
Zassa ● Cana
●

Allada
●

Ouidah
●

Bight of Benin

In the car, I pass the grey concrete roads and buildings of Cotonou, the largest city in Bénin. Within its white and pastel painted shop-fronts and never-ending stream of weaving motos, my driver, Sosthène, winds us away from Bénin's coast and up to the city of Abomey. Almost three hours later, shops are still adorned in pastels but now there's a greater presence of those with rusted, corrugated metal awnings as well as wooden roadside stalls sheltered under weather-beaten parasols. The procession of motos has slowed to a trickle.

Like the majority of the cities and towns I pass through on this trip, the drive has been punctuated by vendors dotted along the road with bags of fruits and nuts dangling from their wrists, tempting motorists with mid-drive snacks. Further north, for long stretches, all you can see are emerald fronds and rust-coloured ground, before the occasional interruption of metal-topped shacks.

'We consult the oracle, Mawu-Lisa, on the future and important decisions,' explains my tour guide an hour later, as we walk on the burnt orange dust floor of what was the Kingdom of Dahomey's capital of Abomey. 'The [diviner's] tablet, shells, nuts are all used to call upon the ancestors and get advice on the unknown.'

We are here to explore one of the many still-standing palaces in this land, once home to Dahomey's royals, and he leads me over to a squat statue depicting the supreme god he speaks of. With a breast one side, and a flat chest on the other, Mawu-Lisa's gender – or lack of – is etched into stone. The entity's gift to us of day and night is depicted by the moon and sun that rest in their hands. Though there's no sun in the museum statue's grip, having broken off long ago, there are still shells around the neck. Once currency, the cowrie shells demonstrate the riches bequeathed to the world by the divine.[1]

Just like my tour guide, advice seekers have consulted this divine entity for guidance and wisdom on their troubles, from the physical to the spiritual, for centuries. In Dahomey, the people revered the powerful potential of complementary forces. Two sides of the same coin, two crescents of the same cowrie shell, the male and the female and neither all at once. The Dahomey belief systems mirror the Yorùbá *Ifá* in this way. And so, just as they understood the divine, the Fon people of Dahomey (or simply Dahomeans), believed duality was central to every part of their lives.

The offices of ministers of state, the heads of families, the commanders of army wings, the primary stewards of the houses of the gods – all of these positions were to be held jointly along a male-female binary. Sex wasn't the only basis for doubled appointments. A certain dualism could be found in the way that women employed in service outside the palace walls corresponded with women on the inside doing the same. Or the way that living lineages were mirrored in *kutome* – 'the land of the dead' in Fongbe – in which the spread of a living family network is believed to be exactly aligned with that of their ancestors.[2]

The orange-red sand I will walk on during my tour, is the same earthen material used to build the palace that Tassi Hangbé and Akaba had played and grown up in. Not only were they siblings, they were also twins. In keeping with Dahomean ideology, any twins born within Fon society were to be treated with 'perfect even-handedness'; whatever one received, their twin was entitled to the same.[3] I learn that, with twins where both female, if one enters a marriage, her spouse must offer the same honours and gifts to her sister.[4]

Hangbé and Akaba's status as twins marked not only them, but also members of their family. A former Dahomey court chronicler named Agbidinoukoun would explain in the early twentieth century that the twins had a younger brother. His name of Dosu was, as the scribe relayed, the name given by the Fon to the first son born after twins.[5]

The three siblings' mother, Adonon, was not only the wife of the kingdom's foundational ruler Wegbaja (reigned 1645–c.1680–85), but she was also a descendant of Aligbonu – the kingdom's 'ancestral mother' who straddles the cross-section of being a critical historical actor and a cultural myth. Adonon and Aligbonu are often conflated, with Agbidinoukoun and other chroniclers presenting them as the same. However, the romantic and sexual disputes that troubled Wegbaja, the man largely recorded as Dahomey's first *ahosu* (king) are credited solely to Adonon.[6]

Dakodonu (c.1620–c.1645), identified in historical accounts as Wegbaja's father, was said to be Adonon's original betrothed. However, before she joined her husband-to-be, she fell pregnant by Wegbaja who was also serving as his father's emissary. In the middle of establishing the first settlements that would spawn Dahomey's basic structure, a furious Dakodonu had Wegbaja expelled.

Wegbaja promptly went into the service of one of his father's enemies, Adenyin. It was only when Wegbaja killed Adenyin over a dispute that things changed. 'The day he killed Adenyin, it is that day Dakodonu took him [back] as a child,' claimed court minister Humase Adjaho, a man descended from generations of political managers and judges within the Dahomey kingdom. Although not members of the royal family, as custodians, the Adjaho family were privy to the inner machinations of dynastic rule, including court gossip, internal fighting, *coups d'état* and largely hidden personal agendas.[7]

Some oral traditions and historians posit that it's likely Adonon remained as Dakodonu's wife. As a result, although Hangbé, Akaba and Dosu are understood as the children of their mother and Wegbaja in Bénin today, they can also be considered Dakodonu's offspring.[8] The disputed nature of their parentage adds another layer of intrigue to the royal twins and their brother, children destined to rule.

Power passed from Dakodonu to Wegbaja and by the 1680s – the final years of the latter's reign – Dahomey developed a reputation as an ideal coastal market for the purchase of enslaved people.[9] It fit into a West African coast that would come to be known as 'Slave Coast', already teeming with Portuguese settlers who had been driving regular trade for centuries.

The bottomless-seeming voids of Portuguese plantation-powered colonies, in both São Tomé and Brazil, demanded more and more African bodies to fall into them. Decades prior, in 1620, it was reported that only one or two Portuguese ships called upon Allada (a sovereign kingdom that was later absorbed as part of Dahomey) annually with the Europeans having established trade with the kingdom at the beginning of the century. This quickly intensified.[10] (Although the Dutch, English and French empires had already begun colonising the Americas, they were yet to truly enter the fray in search of their own supply of enslaved people for Caribbean colonies.)

As the frequency and volume with which enslaved Africans were led onto boats starkly increased, so too did the import of European firearms. By the 1680s, alongside a robust reputation for slave-trading, Dahomeans began to replace traditional missile weaponry, like javelins and bows, with smoking muskets and pistols.[11] The increased militarisation of Dahomey society was directly linked to the overseas demand, and ultimate profitability, of trading in enslaved lives.

The political, economic and social head of this society, the *ahosu*, a station imbued with divine credence, depended on the goodwill of their subjects, particularly their court officials. Their approval was usually required before any major decision or act of reform – political, military, economic or otherwise – could be made. In fact, for some historians, it's apparent that the *ahosu* couldn't do anything without the consent of his council – they could depose him or even force him to die by suicide if his advisors felt that he had strayed beyond his granted powers.[12]

Among the *ahosu*'s trusted counsel sat women in the Dahomey royal family, occupying positions of ministers of state, commanders and governors of provinces.[13] However, when Wegbaja passed rule onto his son and successor, Akaba (1680–85), Hangbé was entitled to more than a council seat. Cyrelene Amoah-Boampong and Christabel Agyeiwaa, scholars of women in pre-colonial Africa, note that she ruled as co-sovereign.[14]

We know little about Akaba's – or the twins' – late seventeenth century ascent to power. Historians have yet to establish when the siblings were born, let alone what either sole or joint rule might have looked like in their hands. With a reign that fell short of the defining legacy of their father, indigenous traditions relay little about Akaba, save for the fact that 'he came to power at a relatively old age.'[15] With the *ahosu*'s death generally dated to 1708 but occasionally as late as 1716, what we do know is that conjecture, assumptions and confusion sweep through this period in Dahomean history.[16]

Material on Hangbé is limited, perhaps in part due to her reign taking place before sustained contact with written-record-keeping British and French colonisers, as well as the secrecy that shrouds Dahomean historical traditions.

In Fongbe, 'history' translates as *hwenoho*, or literally 'old-time story' while 'story', in terms of creative tales, is *hoho*. It creates clear linguistic distinctions between what is a collectively established narrative and what is not. However, historical traditions, more or less, belonged to their corresponding *ako* – lineages or clans – rather than to an imagined Dahomean community at large.[17]

The identity of each *ako* was indivisibly tied to shared descent from their *tohwiyo* – a *vodun*-founding ancestor. The origins of the different Dahomey *akos* are plump with world-bending detail. Aligbonu, for example, is *tohwiyo* for the royal lineage. Once a princess, Aligbonu is said to have mated with a leopard, resulting in the birth of Agasu, a creature with leopard-like features who would go on to found the ruling dynasty and join his mother in *tohwiyo* status.[18]

The achievements of their *tohwiyo*, alongside wider historical traditions, were guarded by the elders of the *ako*, jointly headed up by the eldest male and female family members.[19] They preserved and then shared the narratives when deemed appropriate. This was true even for the ruling class: the Agasu origin narrative was only shared by the reigning *ahosu* with their heir apparent when the latter was 'formally designated'. Cocooned in secrecy, not only were important *ako* traditions barely divulged publicly or in the clan, but they were also withheld from members within the circle of *ako* elders.[20] The measures taken to aid preservation cannot be overstated, nor the impact on contemporary historians attempting to build an accurate picture.

As a result, the contradictions are monumental. Agbidinoukoun

asserts that rather than leaving behind a co-*ahosu* with the ability
to rule in her own stead, Akaba specifically chose another close
family member as his heir to evade any future conflict between
his and Hangbé's children.[21] Anatole Coissy, a Dahomean school
director working on the kingdom's history who 'considerably aug-
mented' Agbidinoukoun's insights, suggests that, rather, Hangbé
was appointed regent because the late *ahosu*'s designated successor,
his son Agbo-Sasso, was too young to rule.[22] Still another historian
contends that a surely just as 'old' Hangbé supported Agbo-Sasso
in a bloody, violent title challenge that would prove unsuccessful.[23]

According to official records, amid the fray of infighting and
instability, a victor emerged to claim the *zinkpo* – the Dahomey
throne. His name following the ascension was Agaja, formerly
Dosu.

Sosthène brings me to the Palais des rois d'Abomey – the Royal
Palaces of Abomey – today a UNESCO World Heritage Site that
houses ten palaces across forty-seven hectares.[24] While Sosthène
seizes a moment for a nap, reclining his seat and settling in behind
the wheel, I step out of the vehicle to be swallowed up by the red-
toned former royal capital. My hardy leather sandals, purchased
from an Asante artisan in Ghana's Kumasi, raise dust as I head
towards what I'm sure is the entrance of the Musée historique
d'Abomey – the Historical Museum of Abomey – which is housed
in the palaces of *Ahosu* Ghézo (1818–58) and his son and successor,
Glélé (1858–89).

I pass a sign titled LE PALAIS DU ROI AGONGLO and underneath, the virtues of this *ahosu* (1789–97) are extolled, including
the social reforms he brought in like a new tax system and supporting the arts. A ramp leads into the building, one central opening
of the five that exist, separated by chipped and faded pillars that
boast coloured engravings and restored bas-relief work of divine
symbols, animals and vegetation. I'd later learn that these architectural designs told a story and held the emblems for each ruler
of Dahomey, as each new ruler built their own palace. But there

are twelve rulers who once resided on this protected site and only ten palatial homes.

I walk further. LE PALAIS DU ROI GLÉLÉ reads the next sign in front of the museum's reception building.

Inside, the cool walls are a welcome respite from Abomey's sticky humidity, the floor is littered with pairs of shoes and sandals. It's here that I meet Adaze, my guide, a slight young man who barely reaches my shoulder. He tells me that I need to remove my sandals. The current *ahosu*, Georges Collinet Béhanzin, is here doing a ritual. Adaze is quick to correct my unfounded assumption that the ruler would be in the area for a few days. It's early April 2023 and the man who had assumed the ceremonial position just the year prior has been on site for at least ten months.

'In the past, only the king can wear shoes, a hat and an umbrella,' Adaze explains haltingly. 'His presence means that we have to leave our shoes.' Plus, he adds, no shoes are allowed in the interior court anyway. I slip out of my sandals and we step forward. The hot ground kisses my soles and tiny grains find home between my toes.

Photos are only allowed to be taken in the exterior court of Glélé's palace and I start snapping: at the stalls piled high with colourful handmade bags, aprons, appliqué artworks, brass and silver bangles and key chains laid out for the next swarm of tourists, at the two giant trees sprouting from the centre of the court's barren ground and sheltering a dozen motorcycles from the sun, at the sand wall and buildings that line the perimeter of this Abomey palace, and have done for centuries.

From the central hub of Abomey, the *ahosu* ruled over three different social classes, each represented by information laden plinths in one of the museum's buildings. The first was made up of descendants of the royal family, the guide explains, and you recognised them by the way they dressed and styled their robes: their *pagnes* – brightly decorated fabric – were arranged around the torso rather than on the shoulder. Below them sat the artisans, the weavers, blacksmiths, painters and sculptors, much like those sat behind us in the interior court market. 'The last social class were the slaves,' Adaze finishes. He doesn't have much to add about them and, unlike the other two classes, there is no picture on the plinth depicting them.

Within the interior court, Adaze leads us over the *djexo*, a small spiritual building erected after the death of an *ahosu*. The responsibility for its construction falls to the new ruler – the *djexo* must be erected so that the spirit of their predecessor can rest within. My guide reels off the elements required for the building's structure: the blood of forty-one enslaved people, animal blood, shells, sea water, cannon powder and palm oil, all mixed together with sand. Animal bones lie heaped around Glélé's *djexo* because, the Beninese man explains, today only animals – specifically cows – are sacrificed following the end of the Dahomean human sacrifice practice in the late nineteenth century.[25]

The buildings conjured from sand are sites of veneration, divine power and a conduit to ancestral realms. For these Fon people, to build was to honour the past while steering a new course for the future. When a new *ahosu* took the *zinkpo*, they would normally stay in the palace of their predecessor – usually their father – while building their own nearby palace which they'd move into upon completion.

I ask Adaze if he knows why each *ahosu* wanted a new palace rather than using what was already built. For him, it's a foregone conclusion: they wanted to grow the kingdom. What better manifestation of sovereign strength than a city filled with the sprawling palaces of rulers past and present? 'Each king, each palace,' I'm told with frank finality. Before I have the chance to open my mouth with yet another question, Adaze has already pre-empted it.

'If twelve *ahosu* stayed here, why did two of them not build a palace?' he asks with the air of a guide who has already heard, on multiple occasions, the question you had hoped was original. 'We have Hangbé who stayed in the palace of her twin Akaba, and King Adandozan who stayed in the palace of his father Agonglo.' As of yet, it's not clear why Hangbé did not have her own palace erected.

Some historians say Hangbé ruled for as long as a few years, others for as little as three months. Where her reign has been

referenced, it is one characterised as 'bacchanalian' with the surviving twin's claimed hedonistic lifestyle scandalising factions of
her court. Rumours leaked: she entertained lovers from the rival
Yorùbá kingdom; while they chased bliss between her thighs,
she was sharing state secrets; members of the council were ready
to depose her. Agbidinoukoun states that those officials made
themselves brutally clear: they assassinated her only son. The
grief-stricken Hangbé resigned.[26]

There's an air of doubt and shakiness around Hangbé's history.
Every step towards rediscovering her is a tentative one, in the fear
that the ground might be ripped away at any second. Historians
contradict and clash over her legacy, if she is acknowledged at all.
One claim is immediately rebutted by another, again and again
until it feels like there is just negative space left. However, any
ambiguity about her seems louder from those outside of Bénin.

When I ask Adaze about Hangbé, there's no hesitation in his
voice, just quiet assuredness. 'For three years, 1708 to 1711,' he says
in the flow of a custodian delivering his time-worn patter, 'Tassi
Hangbé was our queen.' It's telling that where historians have hesi-
tated, for local storytellers and guides, there is only surety.

The recognised ruler that followed Akaba, however, was Agaja,
the third of these siblings to claim the highest seat. Unlike his sister,
Agaja built himself a palace. His foundations remain yet there's
a cloud of confusion that still obfuscates his image – was he a
usurper as some said? Did he have anything to do with his nephew
Agbo-Sassa's alleged migration away from Dahomey, leaving the
right to rule to his uncle? Or, rather, did he refuse to hand over
power to his brother's son?[27] The dissent he weathered, including
other rival claimants to the throne in 1718, didn't detract from the
mark the newly installed *ahosu* would leave on the kingdom.[28]

Dahomey had existed since the early seventeenth century but
it was under Agaja's reign that it realised its imperial potential.
On his orders, his forces invaded and subjugated their southern
neighbours of Allada (1724) and Ouidah (1727).[29] Not only did it
cement the Fon kingdom as a regional power but also put it in

direct contact with the European enslavers occupying the coast. This was despite, however, Dahomeans having to pay tribute to the Yorùbá Empire of Ọ̀yọ́. From 1726 to 1748, Ọ̀yọ́, with its greater military advantage, invaded Agaja's kingdom at least seven times. The treaty that ended the fighting outlined Dahomey's subordinate status and the annual tribute it owed. Thankfully for the *ahosu*, the agreement did not restrict the kingdom's freedom in areas considered beyond Ọ̀yọ́'s 'sphere of interest'.[30]

Of course, Agaja's quest for complete domination didn't apply just to those beyond the borders of his kingdom. The search for control shaped the lives and roles within the walls of his palace, specifically women. Women of different classes traversed the earthen grounds. There was the *kpojito*, the woman the ruler named as a reign-mate from among the wives of their predecessor. Like her co-wives, she was a mother to the new *ahosu* and therefore a queen mother. The richest and most powerful woman in the kingdom, the *kpojito* – a symbol of continuity – held her office in perpetuity and passed on both her name and estate to a female heir. By the end of the nineteenth century, visitors of the Abomey court noted the appearances of, not only the incumbent *kpojito*, but also the preceding holders of her office.[31]

The *kpojito* title-holders belonged to a massive network of women and eunuchs who embodied – and were referred to – as the 'palace'. It's estimated that between 3,000 to 8,000 women served both as 'a state bureaucracy and the [*ahosu*'s] personal household'.[32] Women captured as spoils of war mingled with those of Dahomey's upper classes, sisters and daughters of the sitting *ahosu* crossed paths with the freeborn women of the lower classes, while enslaved women drifted around and beyond them. A number of the men who ruled over Dahomey exercised their constitutional right to select their wives from among the free-born and enslaved women and girls alike, the latter often brought back from military campaigns in other dominions. These wives would go on to become *kposi*, a title denoting their outlander status with no Fon royal blood in them.[33]

'No man sleeps within the walls of [my palace] after sun-sett but myselfe,' Agaja explained in 1726, with other chroniclers reporting that men couldn't enter the interior of the palace.[34] As such, it was women – and also the relatively few eunuchs who were exempt from restrictions applying to 'males' – who guarded the doors of his palace; it was they who, when Agaja held court, stood behind his *zinkpo* with muskets in hand.[35]

Despite women being trusted to shoulder the weight of weaponry, Agaja would still specifically note in the late 1720s that though his people were 'bred to war... the women stay at home to plant and manure the earth.'[36] However, historians point to evidence of gender roles being assigned differently in Fon society than they were in Europe – women worked the land alongside domestic responsibilities, trade and handicraft production, even though this agricultural labour was considered a difficult task and primarily the remit of men.[37]

Amoah-Boampong and Agyeiwaa argue that in Dahomey, like other West African societies as well as those around the globe, gender was – and is – a social construct. Gender was engaged differently in traditional West African societies, for example, there was an absence of gendered pronouns in their languages nor were there codes of personal dress and adornment for ritual and ceremonial roles.[38] Gender – a social identity where society shapes our understanding of biological sex categories and cultural meanings are attached to the roles of men and women – was not the most important stratifying category, the pair argue; seniority dictated the flow of power, rather than gender.[39]

However, in Dahomey, gender still had a foundational part to play. It was a kingdom that had established itself as a strong link in a chain that ran from West Africa to the plantations of the Americas, one where enslaved women deemed 'pretty and well built' were not sold to foreign traders but kept in the palace for the pleasure of the *ahosu* and the *ahovi* (princes), where enslaved girls and women were distributed as gifts to chiefs, ministers, officers, princes, soldiers, patriotic citizens and European traders and visitors. Historians point to the fact that a number of women in Dahomey – if not most – were unfree individuals.[40] While there may have been a de-emphasis in certain spheres, gender directed certain and specific violences towards women, including the denial of their bodily autonomy.

Primarily enslaved women joined soldiers on their military excursions, preparing their food and carrying it to the fighters in their war camps. They were even used as spies to aid reconnaissance in enemy territory. Meanwhile, enslaved people who were deemed to have special skills were not sold into the Atlantic slaving complex but kept in Dahomey. Those skilled roles included *adjinonto*, women who were skilled in the delivery of babies and were kept to aid childbirth across the kingdom. Sex workers in the kingdom were often punished with enslavement and sold out of the kingdom, while adultery was also an offence that could lead to a lifetime of servitude.[41] In Dahomey markets, where the price of an enslaved person rose or fell on the basis of their ethnic origin, the indigenous population had 'a notoriety for being troublesome slaves', while some Fon women steered their own futures, electing to die by suicide rather than live in slavery.[42]

Though women of different classes, statuses, lineages, origins and more all passed through the palace, walking the same ground that I traversed while in Abomey, unseen chasms split them apart. A world existed between the likes of Hangbé and other royal women – who were known to trade enslaved people for jewellery and other goods – and the women who served them, who were ushered through and beyond the boundaries of Dahomey on the whims of others.[43]

Twitter (now X) was – before it became what it is today – an excellent medium for locating African feminists, both on the continent and far flung within the diaspora. Among the different branches and strands of African-based feminism, including those working in the NGO and policy work sectors, I was looking for people with personal and intimate connections to the historical figure in question in whatever form that might come. It's how I ended up in touch with Beninese feminists Chanceline and Carine who are both part of the country's feminist organising spheres. In separate conversations, they generously offered their time and availability but signalled that they don't consider themselves the best people to discuss Hangbé's legacy. Instead, they both suggested someone else: Mafoya.

'I actually wrote an article about Hangbé a few years ago,' Mafoya says once we're seated at the largely empty restaurant of L'Institut français de Cotonou, as she unfolds a printout she's brought to our interview. Thin black locs escaped a hair tie to frame Mafoya's round face, fine silver frames with round lenses perch on her nose. It's noon but the *brasserie* is yet to fill up with the lunchtime crowd. The arms of overhead fans sweep through the warm air.

It's her patrilineal link to the royal bloodline that underpins her interest in Hangbé, as she tells me of her father who grew up in his village with his love of history nursed and developed by his parents and elders. Mafoya has since inherited that same itch and only recently turned to her father to fill the gaps still remaining after her school education: 'I learnt [at school] that a woman had reigned over Dahomey for three years but no more information because the focus, until recently, didn't really talk about her.'

It was through her father, for example, that she learnt that 'Hangbé' means 'the voice of the song.' 'They say she had a beautiful voice, like a nightingale, and she tended to sing to her brothers when they were little.' Mafoya's words conjure images of three small siblings, lost in the headiness of childish glee, singing, dancing, playing drums. As they shed their baby years, the children – at least Hangbé and Akaba – continued to grow and develop together. 'When her brothers were learning the art of war and how to fight, she also learnt how to fight. She was a twin,' Mafoya adds matter-of-factly.

The bloodlines that have emerged from the lineages of Dahomey rulers and their many spouses are sprawling. Mafoya's own grand-father, for example, had twenty-two children. As a result, Mafoya – who doesn't descend directly from Hangbé's bloodline – doesn't know any descendants from the woman ruler. Particularly given the nature of patrilineal descent where the name of the father is inherited, the young Beninese woman doesn't know if the name of Hangbé is even used as a family name today.

Much memory and retention lies in an inherited family name. But, of course, the woman sat across from me would know. As we take a break to attend to our food orders, my head is swimming. I could not have imagined that hopeful Twitter DMs would lead me to a woman bearing the name of Mafoya Glélé Kakaï, descended from *Ahosu* Glélé who is, in turn, an indirect descendant of Hangbé. Just a few years ago, Mafoya set up the *Agoodojiè* feminist blog and adjoining collective. Both are named for the famed women warriors of Dahomey whose histories have long been tied to Hangbé's.

The warrior women of Dahomey are a legacy of the Fon people that have taken on a life of their own. This West African all-female military regiment has sparked imaginations and even inspired a Hollywood blockbuster film.

In the few images taken of them, the fighters stare down the camera, beaded and feathered adornments resting on their heads and around their necks. Gold and ivory pendants, silver crowns and coronets signal those of high rank. Rings and beads sitting in copper, iron and tin decorate their limbs.[44] Taut and tensed muscles peek out under the *chokoto* (uniform), which is often depicted as a blue-and-white striped, sleeveless tunic with long shorts and a cap, other times with knee-length skirts and short trousers underneath.[45] Arranged in rows, ranging from toddlers to adults, machete-like weapons sit upright in the hands of most, while others clutch thin sticks[46] – these hinted at the strength of the warriors, skilled in hand-to-hand combat and proficient with muskets which they fired from the shoulder, likely for better aim, unlike male soldiers who shot from the hip.[47] Hardened by the intense training required of new recruits – said to include scaling thorny hedges, wrestling one another and surviving in forests for up to nine days on minimum rations – French settlers would claim that a Dahomean male soldier would take fifty seconds to reload and fire a weapon; an *agoodojiè* could do it in less than thirty.[48] It makes their name all the more fitting: *agoodojiè* translates as 'the last defence before the king'.

By the 1860s, a hundred and fifty years after Hangbé and just a few decades before the kingdom would take up arms to resist French imperialism, the contingent of Dahomey's women soldiers had featured in a number of conflicts, according to European chroniclers. They subjugated the Mahi region in 1845, with *agoodojǐè* fighters reportedly seen carrying scalps as trophies.[49] When Dahomey attacked the city of Abeokuta in the Yorùbá-founded Owu Kingdom in 1851, it's believed that an army of 6,000 *agoodojǐè* took on 10,000 men. Where they had once fought with slingshots, clubs, cutlasses and axes, over time, flintlock muskets, howitzers and cannons had increasingly become weapons of choice for an onslaught such as this.[50] Storytellers in Abeokuta would later tell of a crushing defeat for the Dahomeans, sparked by their gender: when their opponents sought to castrate a fallen *agoodojǐè* and discovered their sex, the shame of defeat was said to spur on their efforts.[51] One account claims that as many as 2,000 of Dahomey's women soldiers were killed in the campaign.[52]

This army was also integral in the Dahomean trade in enslaved people. Following successful military campaigns, the *agoodojǐè* returned to their kingdom with captives in tow. Immediately earning enslaved status, the peoples of rival lands – including large numbers of women – became property of the *ahosu*. They were the ruler's to distribute among the *ahovi*, ministers and officers if they elected to do so, including the commanders of the *agoodojǐè*.[53] Enslaved women not only served in their military camps, but would also enter into their ranks, especially since the numerous wars waged by the sovereigns of Dahomey reduced military numbers as well as the wider population.[54] They joined other *agoodojǐè* who were recruited through conscription, voluntarily and by lottery – the latter through cowrie divination where families were gathered and a set of cowries thrown with selection resting on whose cowrie fell into a basket.

Chastity was expected of the *agoodojǐè*, especially considering that they were all legally married to the reigning *ahosu*. It was illegal to have sex with the *ahosi* (wives) and adultery with an *agoodojǐè* was punishable by death for both the soldier and their lover. Dahomeans liked to joke that more soldiers lost their lives attempting to scale the walls into the *agoodojiè* quarters than they did in battle.[55] Though few women fighters reportedly had sex with the *ahosu*, those who were favoured in this way would be effectively stood down from active military service.[56] They were known as the Leopard Wives.[57]

Buried away in a footnote of his account, British consul and anthropologist Richard Francis Burton notes that 'as a rule, these fighting célibataires prefer the *morosa voluptas* (translates roughly as "sexual deviance" or "delights") of the schoolmen, and the peculiarities of the Tenth Muse.'[58] Referring to the poet Sappho of the Isle of Lesbos, Burton uses hooded terms to allude to romantic and sexual relationships between the *agoodojiè* and other women – potentially even between the fighters too. Elsewhere, he notes that while sex workers were licensed to serve the male population, there was another corresponding group that served the inside of the woman-dominated palace.[59] Other historians have since downplayed its significance, seeing it as the Dahomean principle of duality 'carried to its logical extreme' rather than being actually intended for – or used by – the occupants of the palace.[60]

But then there's another obfuscation: heteronormativity. The idea that the services of sex workers might be engaged by people who were not men sits erringly close to 'illogical' in the minds of these scholars. This comes despite evidence of intimacies in pre-colonial African societies that we would call 'lesbian' or 'sapphic' today: the *sangomas* – traditional healers – of the Zulu people who could marry any gender; daughters within the royal palaces of Northern Sudan who were given enslaved girls for purposes of sex; long-standing erotic relationships between Basotho women in present-day Lesotho who chose women lovers exclusively.[61] 'Outsiders have a long history of interpreting African sexuality and relationships through their own lenses to long-lasting, dangerous ends,' writes scholar Jesse Brimmer.[62]

As famed and popularised as Dahomey's women warriors have become, what we know about their origins remains scant. Contested dates for the formation of the *mino* soldiers largely congregate around the first half of the eighteenth century, with accounts on them more widely available from the 1760s onwards. Others question whether the soldiers might've existed as far back as the reign of Wegbaja in the mid-seventeenth century.[63] The hypotheses around the unit's original purpose are plentiful and muddled. They were policewomen who became soldiers. They were palace guards who became royal guards. They were simply extra bodies to pad out Agaja's army to mask depleted numbers.[64]

While traditions around the connection between Hangbé and the *agoodojìè* are just as scarce, they exist. In their oral traditions, the Ouéménou people speak of having to face women soldiers donned in raffia cloth in Akaba and Hangbé's time, while an *agoodojìè* song details defeating their ruler, Yahazé, with swords under the orders of Akaba. Another song refers to the fighting unit camping around the shallows of Ouémé River, east of Abomey. Historians believe that the Ouéménou were so impressed by the *ahosu*'s fighters, they attempted to start their own unit of women with little success.[65]

Another fragment is sourced from a French writer, Victore-Louis Maire, who published a book on Abomey in 1905 based on information he had gathered in the kingdom's capital in 1894. He listed the names of fifty-nine 'companies' of the Dahomean army created from Wegbaja all the way through to Dahomey's last truly independent *ahosu*, Béhanzin (1889–94), which he states are all male. The eighth unit he refers to is 'Zokhénou', which Maire says was created under Akaba and also known as the 'Company of Queen Angbé, daughter of Teckbessou.'[66] Historians note that it is chronologically impossible for a unit founded during Akaba's time to bear the name of a daughter of the ruler Tegbesu (1740–74) who came after him. They question the mistaking of Tegbesu for Wegbaja: plausible error or deliberately laid misinformation?[67]

There are no such question marks for my guide, Adaze. 'The *agoodojìè* were created during the reign of Tassi Hangbé,' he proclaims before briefly explaining that the fighters were chosen between the ages of twelve and fifteen, trained and then became warriors. Agaja used the army, he says, but only after the kingdom's first and only queen had established it, with her brother expanding their role and status. 'Under Hangbé, they only fought in wars. She was not creative,' the guide adds frankly.

For a man who spends his days leading predominantly foreign visitors around the royal city of his ancestors, the omittance of Hangbé within the emergence of the *agooḍojìè* is undeniable erasure. It brings him back to the only viable conclusion he repeats across the tour.

'They couldn't accept a woman as king.'

Where the all-woman Dora Milaje soldiers of Marvel's *Black Panther* teased, with its nod to the *agooḍojìè*, director Gina Prince-Bythewood's *The Woman King* makes explicit.

Set in Dahomey in 1823, we meet the fighters led by battle-hardened General Nanisca, played by Viola Davis – defenders of the kingdom ruled by John Boyega's Ghézo. They stand as defenders against the ever-encroaching Ọyọ́ empire which has been attacking villages, like those of the Mahi, under Dahomey's control. We're ushered past the walls of a bustling Abomey palace, rich with the artisans and vendors Adaze had described, and into the inner sanctum of the *agooḍojìè*. It's here that we watch them train, including new young recruits like Nawi, played by Thuso Mbedu, and ready themselves for battle against the constraints of Ọyọ́ dominion. The reception to the film, however, cracked open the wrought tensions just below the surface, displaying both its achievements and limitations. What made it possible for some critics to call for its boycott as a movie that obfuscates colonial harm while others heralded it for condemning enslavement and its specific impact on African women?

Visually, it stuns. 'The women soldiers, their bodies oiled to a high gleam, emerge like hallucinations that Prince-Bythewood makes palpably real,' writes Manohla Dargis for the *New York Times*. 'She puts you right on the ground so that you can watch these women fly. They do just that, not with superhero capes and fairy-tale enchantments, but with swords, javelins, twirling ropes and an occasional gun...'[68] The rarity of seeing a host of dark-skinned Black women central to a plot based on real African

fighters, let alone in a thrilling historical action epic with its familial and romantic subplots, is compelling – particularly in a climate
where words like 'visibility' and 'representation' form part of our
common parlance.

But similar to how representation politics – where an individual's
identity is of itself greater testimony than their moral or political
views and actions – leaves us largely unsatisfied, so too does *The
Woman King*, particularly with its handling of enslavement. The
Ọ̀yọ́ soldiers appear as our villains, alongside a Portuguese slave
trader, which is drawn in contrast with Nanisca who, across the
film, states her argument to the *ahosu* for a Dahomey free of
enslaving and selling its people.

It's a narrative that elides the accounts and traditions that say
otherwise. Film critic Antol Bitel summarises it well:

> Even as the film concedes from the outset the uncomfortable
> truth that the real Dahomey under Ghezo was no less actively
> involved in slave-trading than its enemy the Ọ̀yọ́ Empire, it also
> implies that by the film's end, such practices, at Nanisca's urging,
> would soon be replaced with palm oil production – whereas in
> reality, Ghezo was still selling into slavery both captives from
> raids (often conducted by the Agojie) and even Dahomey's own
> citizens till the end of his reign three decades later.[69]

The end to Dahomey's participation in the Atlantic slaving system
would come about in 1852 when Ghézo came under pressure from
Britain who had *officially** closed its doors on enslavement.[70]

---

* The British Government passed the 1833 Act of Abolition of Slavery, which
was in effect in 1834 with the caveats of compensation to slave-owners and an
apprenticeship period. This period oversaw a 'transition' from enslavement to
waged labour and enslaved people were made to work for the slave-owners
for another half a decade. This is why historians consider the real beginning
of emancipation to have begun in 1838 when apprenticeship was abolished.
Although, even with it gone, many newly-free individuals had little choice but
to continue working for former masters for minimal pay. It's worth noting that
Britain continued to rely on enslavement in Cuba, Brazil and the US South.[71]

Perhaps this is where the issue lies. *The Woman King* is stretch-
ing for something it never quite reaches. A desire to tell a truer,
more accountable history is there – it seeks to hold a steely gaze
and take in the ways in which Africans were complicit in establishing a colonial world order. Except it flinches. It takes a shortcut
and establishes a binary and, although the parameters are blurred,
it's necessary for us to understand that the *agoodojiè* are Good™.
Feminism, empowerment, uplifting Black women dictate that they
must be. To explore their own integral role in Dahomean slave-
trading is too much; it muddies the waters we wish to drink from.

Complications arise for Mafoya too as we discuss the film over
our freshly arrived lunch orders in the Cotonou *brasserie* – for her,
a sandwich and for me, the fermented corn dough of *akassa* next
to smoked fish lathered in spicy *monyo*, a sauce rich with fresh
tomatoes, onions and peppers. For someone who doesn't like fish
and made an accidental order, it slaps. My hands move from mouth
to bowl and back again while Mafoya speaks.

When I ask her about her feelings on Dahomey's prominent role
in enslavement, she shifts in her seat. 'This is a part of the story
of my family that I'm really not proud of. It was really difficult
as I grew up and learnt about the triangular slave trade.' A subtle
wince on her face. She's descended from *Ahosu* Glélé, son of Ghézo,
after all.

Mafoya's words evidence the internal struggle, the delicate yet
unwieldy work of troubling African complicity.

'It's a hard pill to swallow.' She pauses. 'I don't want to excuse
them because it's not a good thing but I think that the way enslavement was done in West Africa – perhaps they didn't think much
about what they were doing?'

While picking at her sandwich, Mafoya continues through a
carousel of explanations and excuses, in search of an answer that
will sit satisfactorily, perhaps more for her than for me. 'The geography of Dahomey was often at war. The kingdom wasn't that big
compared to Asante, for example, so when there is war, there are
war prisoners.'

'As seen in *The Woman King*, you can see how [enslaved people] were assimilated into the culture, like how orphans could join the *agooḍojìè*. [Dahomey society tended] to assimilate the culture of the enslaved peoples to create a homogenous population. It's why so much of the mythical ideology is the same – for example, the Yorùbá have *Ifá* and we have *Fa*.'

'The violence of enslavement in America wasn't as violent here. Yes, there were blood sacrifices and I don't know how those selections were made but there were Dahomeans and enslaved people [sacrificed].'

The thoughts put forward by Mafoya are not too dissimilar to those of historians attempting to untangle the threads underpinning the slaving complex that ravaged Africa. Historians like Dr Boniface Obichere point to the 'positives' or more 'benevolent' details of enslavement in Dahomey. That enslaved people labouring in domestic environments 'were sometimes treated with kindness and entrusted with responsibilities of great importance' and even might be 'considered as part of the family', that the practice of 'slave breeding' ultimately 'replenished' a war-stricken, depleted Dahomey.[72]

These are incomplete tableaus of the kingdom, and so too are the arguments that paint a peaceful Dahomey corrupted under the heavy influence of Europeans and their slave-trading agendas. Abolitionists of the period would describe the way the kingdom became 'despotic and militarized' only *after* contact with the trade, ultimately offering a sanitised appraisal of the pre-colonial society.[73] Some abolitionists, historians and Fon people apportion the blame for the unsavoury features found within Dahomey externally, mitigating the task of appraising the society in depth.

'You are a man,' former *agooḍojìè* soldier Tata Ajachè was told after she had killed and disembowelled her first enemy combatant. Taken captive from her village and brought to Abomey, the experiences shared by Ajachè in the 1920s demonstrated entrenched associations between courage and masculinity, and femininity and cowardice.[74] Following a victory over Atakpame in 1850, the *agooḍojìè* were recording singing 'we marched against the Atahpahms as against men, we came and found them women.'[75]

For Hangbé, masculinity may have also acted as a shield. There are Fon traditions which run counter to established narratives: these counter-histories sit at odds with the belief that she was quickly unseated by Agaja or that her reign consisted only of minding the throne for her nephew.

They, instead, point to Hangbé impersonating her twin during a war against the Ouéménou, after Akaba was killed by smallpox. Masked by their shared features, she sought to conceal the passing of the *ahosu* in order to lead Dahomey forces to victory.[76] Adaze adds that, while her officials and soldiers believed that she was Akaba, it was Agaja who recognised her, precipitating the deposition of Hangbé. Next came the expunging.

Question marks float around a ruler who stalks the margins. You find her tangled in confusion in the footnotes where her inconclusive status is probed at. You find her peeking out from fragments carried over from her era, like the Fon *récade* – a hatchet-like baton of authority with an iron head featuring two bells – once held at the Musée de l'Homme in Paris. According to some historians, the bells symbolise Hangbé and Akaba with its design reminiscent of *asen* – ceremonial iron sculptures placed in front of altars that honour twins.[77] You find her in Agaja's birth name – Dosu – signalling the twins before him. Another scholar asserts that Dahomeans have always been aware that Akaba had a twin and 'since no one has ever mentioned a male twin, they may also have been aware it was a female.'[78] Even so, Hangbé's existence has been called into question.

The aim was to disappear her, Adaze would later explain adamantly. 'They cleaned her name in the history and said that the *agoodojïè* were created by Ghézo, when actually,' my guide stressed, 'they were created by Hangbé and *improved* by Ghézo.' It's only now, he says, that Bénin's government is making efforts to restore her omitted histories.

The cleanse of Hangbé has been so thoroughly conducted that her existence is considered by some as 'a late invention, perhaps devised as a sort of mythical charter for the Amazons' (the name Europeans gave the *agooɖojiè*).[79] In fact, her indirect descendant Ghézo would receive credit again from some historians, this time for promoting the concept of Hangbé and Akaba in the nineteenth century in order to 'present his institutional innovations as a revival of tradition'. Those proponents argue that the *ahosu* introduced dualism into Dahomey as a means of creating a 'balance of power' against possible disloyalty among his chiefs.[80] This might be more persuasive if Hangbé wasn't the only Dahomey sovereign put through the 'cleaning'.

Adandozan, Ghézo's older brother, came to power in 1797 – nearly ninety years after Hangbé's reign – following the assassination of their father. He's remembered as 'the cruellest king in Dahomean history' by some, and a creative monarch who 'tried to lead his people away from slave trading' and back towards agricultural labour by others.[81] After Ghézo deposed Adandozan in an 1818 military coup, the latter's name was banned from the official history of Dahomey, no doubt aided by the secretive clan traditions.

Like Hangbé, Adandozan did not have a palace built. Like her, his name was not included the list of *ahosu*. It makes it difficult to ascertain which parts of Adandozan's fragmented history approach truth and which are the fruits of Ghézo's blacklisting.[82] As noted by another historian, to this day, appliqué wall hangings made in Abomey that boast the symbols of twelve *ahosu* of Dahomey omit Adandozan, leaving a gap of twenty-one years within the dynasty.[83] The deposed *ahosu*, however, couldn't be erased from European records, for example, given that those powers were already in contact with Abomey. Hangbé, with a reign that predated direct engagement with Europe, could.[84] Both, however, have been preserved in the oral traditions that were forced underground. Both have survived the purges of memory.

When Dahomey was claimed by French settlers following wars that spanned 1890 to 1894, and then ceased to exist as a political entity in 1900, the *agooɖojiè* also disappeared. They fought their last battle on 4 November 1892 at the gates of Cana against men under the orders of the French president. They had finally fallen.

With the arrival of the European occupying power, the women within the kingdom likely experienced the same gendered colonial violence introduced into other West African societies. Despite contributing significantly to the economic development of their kingdoms, the status, power and agency of women were systemically eroded. Taxation systems were imposed by colonialists on male household heads, pushing the work of women – like food crop production – to the margins as it didn't create enough income for tax. Meanwhile, the designation of land titles by colonial governments saw farmlands controlled by women bequeathed to new male owners. The contributions of women in Dahomey have been unremembered, Hangbé among them.

Before Mafoya and I departed the *brasserie* to head our separate ways, she had shared a last lingering thought.

'It's a little bittersweet to know that we only had a queen because she was a twin, it reinforced the patriarchy they lived in.' She had paused. 'Her twin status overthrew her woman status.'

My heart is skipping in my chest. I should've asked if I'm allowed to look at her. The air in this small house is warm, still and heavy. Stately elders stare down at me from burnished frames on the wall. In one of the pictures, there are three figures – two standing and one crouched. All resplendent in the vibrant, clashing fabrics characteristic of Abomey. Behind them stands an attendant holding an umbrella and, together, its panels read '*Reine* Hangbe' in appliqué design. Queen Hangbé. Her name sits under symbols of animals and weaponry used in battle by the *agoodojiè*. Unlike other *ahosus*, Hangbé doesn't have her own official insignia.[85]

I'm invited to sit in a chair across from the bed she's perched on. A single string of coloured beads hang from her neck with a blue and yellow *pagne* wrapped around her, baring her shoulders. Her feet rest on green plastic flip-flops. As I set up the recording, someone else pours water for me. You must always greet a stranger in your home with water Adaze explains from his seat beside me.

Sat against the far wall are two men. One of them had joined Adaze and I in the car, spirited across the short distance by a roused Sosthène. The other had greeted us at the sand-coloured entrance, sheltered under corrugated metal. Large letters above its four pillars spelling out the compound's *raison d'être*: PALAIS ROYAL TASSI HANGBE.

The second man's easy smile and demeanour had given no hints as to his position but now, as he converses with her, I'm unsure. He's her interpreter, Adaze answers my whispered question in kind. If she cannot herself answer a question or chooses not to, this is the man who helps her. When he speaks, it is she speaking through him. She is *DaDa* and, as her representative, he is *Da*.

Carried on the vibrations of *Da*'s deep voice, mediated through the hushed tones of my guide, she tells me about Hangbé. How, after telling no one of Akaba's passing, only she – bearing his face – could steward the kingdom towards stability. That the wars she waged ultimately brought peace to the kingdom and only then would she reveal her identity. The way she would experience the acute pain of familial betrayal as Agaja sought to remove her. How the *agoodojìè* as a unit was born in the village of Zassa, a few kilometres south-west of Abomey; there they trained under Hangbé's orders.

She sits silently on the bed, observing the exchange, as the voices of men bear her words.

Following Hangbé's deposal, there was no rain, no water, environmental disasters, children in the kingdom born with unprecedented features. They thought it was because of the overthrowing of the queen, she says, so they went to Zassa to beg her to bring stability once again. She accepted that, allowing for peace, and left the *zinkpo* to Agaja. Though her legacy would be scrubbed, Dahomeans would later consult the oracle *Fa* who spoke of a queen whose ignored achievements required acknowledgement; to secure the future of the kingdom, rituals in her honour were demanded. 'Now they give importance to her,' Adaze translates.

Her laughter greets my question of whether she knows the location or year of Hangbé's birth. 'She's born in the kingdom of

Dahomey,' Adaze offers with a smile. 'They don't know exactly the birthday of this queen, only the date of her reign.' Those familiar dates, heard across my time in Bénin, are repeated like a comfort: 1708 to 1711. Like most, they don't know what became of the ruler.

Da explains how the woman sat before us was selected among the descendants. When the last occupant died, they consulted *Fa*, for *Fa* always chooses who will be the next. After she's chosen and the adjoining ritual is complete, power has been transferred. She's a bastion in the community – women come to her with their problems, they leave with advice and solutions. She works with the current *ahosu*, a descendant of Dahomey's last independent ruler Béhanzin, solving issues among the royal lineages of the kingdom. If the sitting sovereign, Georges Collinet Béhanzin, wants to carry out ceremonies and rituals, he must seek her permission first, always bearing gifts.

I ask Adaze whether I should hand the colourful franc bank-notes to her directly or not. Before getting into the car, I had been advised that a minimum of 10,000 XOF was required as a tribute.

As signalled, I approach the wooden bed, notes in hand. Once accepted, my guide whispers at me to kneel.

'She'll pray for you,' says *Da*, breaking from Fongbe to English.

She is handed the cup of water that I was greeted with. She speaks.

'Peace for you,' Adaze translates rapidly behind me.

'Husband, children, money.' A small stream of water escapes its tipped vessel, pooling at the woman's feet. I initially believe she's pouring it for me to wash my hands. She is not.

'Say amen,' hisses my guide.

Three separate pours of the water are followed by a stream of brown liquor from a nearby bottle.

'Prosperity, peace, no danger, always peace.'

'Amen, amen, amen, amen.'

All gifts given, all blessings received, it's time to take our leave. But first, the men in the room suggest we take a picture together. My phone is enthusiastically seized as I'm directed to get closer to her. She rests a small hand on my shoulder. When I'll appraise the pictures later, all I'll be able to see is how my nervous and surprised smile, with hands clutched in lap, juxtaposes her stoic, unsmiling face with an upturned chin.

She invites me to take pictures of the various frames decorating the room. As I diligently begin capturing the photographed figures who are likely her ancestors, through Adaze, she explains that she's ill and normally wouldn't agree to see anyone. She only saw us because a fellow descendant of her line works at the Abomey museum and managed to get us a special meeting.

The current Queen Tassi Hangbé, descended from the eponymous forebearer she represents today – a bloodline that even other Fon people aren't sure has survived – speaks with a small smile.

'She said that the next time you visit, she'll wear nice clothes.'

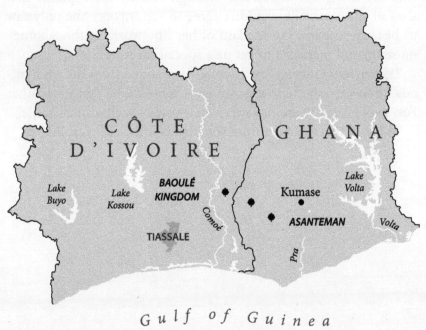

Lake
Buyo

CÔTE
D'IVOIRE

Lake
Kossou

**BAOULÉ
KINGDOM**

Comoé

GHANA

Kumase

Lake
Volta

ASANTEMAN

Pra

Volta

TIASSALE

Gulf of Guinea

CHAPTER 4

Abla Pokou

The Ruler Who Ran

Listen more often to things than to beings.
Hear the fire's voice,
Hear the voice of water,
Hear, in the wind, the sobbing of the trees,
It is the breath of the ancestors.

The dead are not gone forever.
They are in the paling shadows,
They are in the darkening shadows,
The dead are not beneath the ground.
They are in the rustling tree,
In the murmuring wood
The flowing water,
The still water,
In the lonely place, in the crowd.
The dead are never dead.

– BIRAGO DIOP, 'BREATHS'

Amid the discordant thoughts, Abla (also referred to as Abena and Abra) Pokou would've had to find order. As the woman selected which objects to take with her, was her head filled with cacophonous noise? Did she ask herself questions like, *what happens now? What does this mean for me? What does this mean for us? Who will come to my aid? Will anyone?*

It seems she wasn't prepared to stake survival on help that might never come. Perhaps she sifted through belongings like beads, cowrie shells, swathes of fabric, feline-headed manes, mentally separating them.[1] She may have weighed up what might be useful for trade, if necessary, along the journey before her. Maybe she packed a small memento of the kingdom she was fleeing.

Or perhaps there was little sentimentality as she gathered her things. Leaving would ensure the safety of her baby, her only child, whose life was in just as much danger. It would not be an easy journey, but every precaution had to be taken to protect her family.

Packed with a bouncing infant in tow, her feet would've followed earthen pathways from the palace and into the nearby forest. Her imprints in the ground were joined by others. Others whose hands and backs bore the weight of possessions that could not be relinquished.

Before bending tree boughs coaxed herself and her followers into the forest's depths, perhaps Pokou looked back a final time, surveying the home and life she had built in Kumase, now disintegrating before her very eyes. Maybe there was no need if the fleeing woman held the belief that she and her child would be returning imminently. Or perhaps there was no room or time for such romanticism. There was only survival. One foot placed before the other, eyes firmly fixed on what lay ahead.

History toys with us. It allows us glimpses into names, locations and events and challenges us to piece them together through mediums like oral traditions and the written word. While the date of Pokou's exodus remains largely unsettled, historians place it between 1730 and 1750. The kingdom she had left behind was just a handful of decades old.[2]

The seventeenth century had seen Akan peoples drift northwards, away from the states that were being birthed within the basin formed by the Pra and Ofin rivers in the land that is known today as Ghana.[3] The states they left behind heaved with overpopulation. Plus, monarchical rule was springing up across the region: an unwelcome concept to small communities bound by kinship, clan ties and trade. The arbitration of deities and their divine representatives, and temporary military leadership in times of peril had previously been enough.[4] Among the Akan groups moved to migrate north of the Pra-Ofin cradle were the ancestors to the Asante, and the ancestors of Abla Pokou.

They inhabited the abundant hills of Kwaaman – which means 'forest state' in Twi. It was land that was already home to clan communities like the Dormaa, Kaase and Wonoo.[5] The settlers ushered in insecurity, usurpation and internal conflict. Clans struggled over rivers rich with gold and evergreen trees laden with kola nuts. It was emblematic of the intense trade industry that had enveloped the coast – a trade where a lifetime spent in bondage had been weighed against the grains of gold dust proffered to Akan traders since at least the 1400s.[6]

During the latter half of the fraught 1600s, the military prowess inscribed into the history of the Oyoko tribe ensured that this community floated to the top of the hierarchy. Kwaaman developed as an Oyoko state.[7] Under the Oyoko leader Osei Kofi Tutu I, who was comfortably ruling the state by 1695, Kwaaman became Kumase and power became more centralised – in part, as a response to the Denkyira, an Akan state that had grown plump with power because of its inland supply of gold and enslaved people to Europeans.[8]

Having emerged as a powerful kingdom of southern Akan people in the mid-seventeenth century, Denkyira forced states within a twenty-mile radius of Kumase into the subservient role of tributaries. It became the dominant power among Twi-speaking Akan people of the region.[9] Among those tributary states were four of Oyoko origin – Kokofu, Nsuta, Bekwai and Dwaben. It would be these states that Kwaaman would merge with, alongside the Bretuo state of Mampon, to defeat the unwanted overlordship of the Denkyira.[10] With a decisive victory over them at the Battle of Feyiase in 1701, the Osei Tutu-led, cross-clan military union became a permanent one: Asanteman, the Asante state.

Asanteman rose to become the paramount Akan kingdom. In truth, it was a confederacy of chieftaincies led by the largest,

Kumase, which supplied the Asante ruler – the *asantehene*.[11] The first to wear the title, Osei Kofi Tutu I ushered in waves of change: centralising authority so that, for example, only he could carry out capital punishment; establishing a constitution for the Asante nation which underpinned an expansionist foreign policy; requiring the paramount chiefs to pledge an oath of faithful service and loyalty to the *asantehene*.[12] Regardless of previous resistance to being ruled, the Asante were a people who now had a sovereign, a monarchy that has survived over three centuries. Osei Tutu's lineage would form the royal line, with each successive Asante ruler descended from the Oyoko dynasty. Among those bequeathed with royal stature was his niece, Pokou, a princess of the kingdom.

When Osei Kofi Tutu I crossed the River Pra around 1717 to wage war against the south-eastern Akyem people, they ambushed him, bringing about the demise of Pokou's uncle.[13] He left behind an Asanteman that sought access to trades being conducted with Europeans from their forts and castles along the coast. A state that was constantly at war with its northern and southern neighbours.[14] The death of its first *asantehene* led to a succession war in efforts to name the next.

The figure of Dakon, believed to be the brother of Pokou, refuses historians' attempts to pin him down. He appears after the death of Osei Tutu around 1720 as one of the late ruler's nephews battling for the throne with his cousin, and eventual victor, Opoku Ware. Killed in the ensuing struggle, Dakon leaves his followers with no leader other than his sister whose sights were set on what lay beyond Kumase.[15] In a different set of traditions, Dakon is understood to have made his unsuccessful bid for the highest Asante position around 1749, following Opoku Ware's death.[16] Meanwhile, Pokou's unnamed husband is said to have died in an ambush, leaving her widowed with a young child.[17]

Whether or not Pokou's departure was as a result of her brother's demise, Asante civil war after her uncle's passing would have rocked the stability of her position. And so, she fled, flanked by the Warɛbo, the Faafwɛ, the Nzipri, and the Sa – all of noble rank and attached to groups conquered by the Asante.[18] Together, they headed westwards.

Unruly forest floor cracking and rustling under tired feet. Impatient hands brushing away the dangling arms of tropical growth. Hungry mouths suckling on the available offerings from branch and bush. Paw marks on the ground and shaking branches above the travellers' heads would've hinted at the life surrounding them.

The animals encountered by Pokou's migrating band all fell within the Asante classification system. Monkeys and their tree-swinging relatives were *asorommoa* – animals primarily living above ground, on and in trees. *Ntummoa* consisted of cawing birds and bats who swooped through the air, while *ntɛtemmoa* prowled the earth by hoof or paw.[19] Within Asante divinity, all of these beings, whether covered by feathers, scales, tough thick skin or fur, are animated by a force – as are the rocks and twigs Pokou's people would've stepped over and the minerals and vegetables they'd have ingested.

'In this Africa, the living and the dead are joined in a powerful reality named "existence",' writes French-Senegalese painter and scholar, Iba Ndiaye Diadji.[20] Each being, alive or not, flows with a force. That force is placed within a hierarchy, from grains of sand to gods and deities, all possessing a distinct spiritual essence. Citing Diadji in her work, Ivorian writer Véronique Tadjo points to the existence of a hidden Africa that penetrates our living one – often defined as 'animism'.[21] Contemporary historians, like Zeinab Badawi, make the point that African belief systems, like 'animism', were often framed by European anthropologists as 'religions', influenced by their own Abrahamic traditions. It obfuscates how fundamental and core African beliefs were: that a transcendent force was present in all aspect of nature.[22]

Together, Tadjo and Diadji assert that the visible world of the living is inextricably tied to the invisible world of the dead. This understanding is what ripples through Diop's poem as he describes the essence of departed ancestors ruffling trees and ever-present in the ebb and flow of water. This is foundational in many African divinity systems, where gods channel their will through agricultural elements, communicating their wishes through rain, wind, water, animal and plant.[23] These beliefs were common among Akan peoples whose territory eventually spanned from present-day Côte d'Ivoire to Togo.

For scholars like Tadjo, whose practice is rooted in indigenous tradition, there's an onus on the part of the living: 'Those who live in the "visible" world have the duty to keep the communication open and to nurture the "invisible" world in the same way as the "body" is animated by an invisible "breath" coming out of its mouth.'[24]

Acknowledgement of these invisible vital forces is demanded. We must accept our responsibility to keep those channels open, we're told, from ancient times through to today. Pokou and her people who followed her through those forests would have understood this. As they picked their way through verdant depths, they believed that a force hummed through everything that surrounded them. A force that could help or hinder.

When Pokou and her people finally emerged from the belly of the forest, they were met with a gushing Comoé River at its flood stage. It lapped at the banks on which they stood, demonstrating its might against rocks and boulders.[25] Perhaps eyes fervently searched the surroundings for means of crossing, while others simply stared into the river's depths, lost to its display of beautiful violence. There was no way across, and going back wasn't an option. According to some scholars, an Asante army was hot on their tracks, possibly under the authority of Opoku Ware.[26]

Like the waters that branch off from the Comoé – plotting new, searching courses through the terrain – the oral traditions that have sustained the narrative of Pokou's voyage split and diverge here. Accounts of the eighteenth-century Asante princess take on new life with each narration. Tadjo, who grew up with Pokou's story in Côte d'Ivoire, describes it as simultaneously a 'myth of foundation and a historical fact'.[27] Pokou existed and can be traced back to the Asante kingdom, offering the fact. However, after her departure, myth is ushered in.

We access Pokou through an intricate web of truth and legend, shaped by divinity and oral retellings. They each uniquely mark her tale while, at the same time, pushing against what the West routinely prescribes as 'proper' history work. Rather than inflexibly denoting something as 'truth' or 'myth', the oral traditions on Pokou and her people – and the new life ushered in with each fresh recounting – challenge us to trouble the murky waters in between.

The plane has filled up, all of us about to embark on the five-hour journey from Algiers to Côte d'Ivoire's economic centre of Abidjan. Luck, divine forces and/or Air Algérie have smiled down kindly on my three-person row, where an empty middle seat separates me from a fellow passenger after everyone has finally boarded. Immaculately, modestly dressed, the muted colours of her outfit are accented by small red patent heels.

She looks sublime and I lean over to tell her so, earning a bashful smile with thanks. Later, as our flight imperceptibly makes its way over Algeria's expanse, lights dimmed to induce stupor, she offers me her unopened snacks from the earlier roaming food trolley. In a matter of minutes, I'm chatting to her, a woman I learn is a Liberian business owner named Hawa.

We share titbits of our lives and our reasons for flying, with Hawa on her way to visit her husband. She's particularly intrigued by my research project and Abla Pokou sparks her interest, a shadowy figure she remembers learning about in school. We hover over a continent shrouded in darkness, save for a few scattered dots of light. Spirituality, water and animal life were formative to Hawa's upbringing. She explains how her family don't eat silure – a large species of catfish – because the fish had saved their people during difficult times. It's a narrative that appears repeatedly, including within Pokou's people.

'These animals did plenty for them,' she says with a small smile under the cabin's muted lights. 'But they also asked for sacrifices.' Hawa goes on to tell me that, when Pokou and her followers were confronted by the churn of the Comoé, 'animals came out of the water and formed a bridge.'

The day after next, while steering through Abidjan traffic, my taxi driver recalls that crocodiles emerged to aid Pokou's people with their gnarly armour providing stepping stones. Our short journey to the Musée des Civilisations de Côte d'Ivoire is punctuated by our enthusiastic teaching – and correcting – of one another's first languages. In halting French, I ask how he first learnt about Pokou. 'At school,' he replies, his trepidation at practising English quickly giving way to the pride of being understood, 'everyone knows about Pokou.'

The story shifts depending on the person you speak to, but the heart remains the same. Even scholarly accounts provide an array of differing elements: helpful hippopotami breaching the surface, the river's waters parting to allow the group safe passage, a large tree falling to create a bridge between both sides.[28] Many suggest that salvation for Pokou and her stranded followers had been delivered through the final Asante animal classification of *nsuommoa* – animals who primarily or partially live in water.[29]

We don't know through which means this fatigued band of followers came to stand on the other side of the bank, eluding any Asante fighters tasked with their capture. The echoes of Moses's harried voyage through the Red Sea in Abrahamic religions are poignant.

As Hawa flagged, however, little is free. And, as the oral traditions suggest, passing the Comoé River came at a cost.

While her fellow travellers relinquished trinkets of ivory and bracelets of gold into a pile at the feet of a diviner or priest, did Pokou look on? Was she, too, deflated when the divine representative asserted that the jewels could never quell the river's roar?[30]

Did she look down at her little infant, distracted by their coos or alert to any burbles of discomfort, before raising her eyes to meet the silent stares of her people? Did an awareness of what truly constituted 'value' quietly sweep through their numbers with a murmur? Or was this conclusion reached with forceful aplomb?

When the price of crossing sharpened into focus, was the

princess suddenly aware of the dryness of her throat? Once the ask had been put forth, did her grip on her only child tighten?

We can only imagine what Pokou felt during the seconds, minutes, hours or days it took to deliberate. Was she reliving moments of delirious joy, like when she had carried her little one through Kumase on her back, as was custom, while gifts, money and well wishes rained down on them? Did the prayers and invocations for wisdom, intelligence and a long life for her baby still ring in her ears?[31]

But Pokou was no longer in Kumase, long gone were the red-dust walls of the kingdom that had once kept her safe. None of it mattered, not anymore.

The water demanded a sacrifice and nothing less than her cooing baby would do.

Purity and purification, healing, knowledge, cleansing, energy, wisdom, transformation, nourishment, protection, awakening, life. Water has a wide symbolic reach within spiritual, divine and religious spaces and its importance ripples through many African traditions.

Some Bantu peoples, spread across central and southern Africa, believe that the story of creation began in a great whirlpool of water or a reed bed. Among the Bamiléké, who have long inhabited the Western High Plateau of present-day Cameroon, a father blesses his daughter on her wedding day with water in which *fefe* leaves have been soaking – a plant that, not only represents harmony, but is also believed to treat fertility problems. For the Diola people, today largely located in the Gambia and Senegal, in the beginning, there were only two gods: Amontong, the god of drought, and Montogari, the god of rain.[32] Whole dynasties, like South Africa's Modjadji rulers, are centred on the ability to make rain.

Resplendent with a scaly, shimmering tail in Vodún waters, or standing tall on shapely legs, with long flowing black locs or a tightly coiled afro, the image of Mami Wata has taken on many forms as word of the water deity drifted around the world from the fifteenth century onwards. Sometimes Mami Wata appears in a masculine form, though they are understood to more likely make themselves known as a feminine person.[33] The water spirit is, however, rarely depicted without snakes looped around their neck or threaded through their hair. The figure of Mami Wata is often linked to the arrival of foreigners but much like their image, their personality and powers shift depending on cultural context.[34] Believed to be a notoriously jealous deity who demands sexual abstinence in return for riches, Mami Wata is deemed to bring monetary wealth that is acquired outside the kinship system, rather than inherited. From her seat of dominion – the crest of waves, the unknowable depths of open water – this divine being promised riches but also delivered death and disease whenever one of her many prohibitions was transgressed.[35]

Harnessing the power of water was not just the domain of the gods. Back on an aircraft heading to Côte d'Ivoire, Hawa's mind has returned to her maternal grandmother's compound. With whispered words, my companion conjures an image of an elderly woman who, when she didn't want rain, would conduct a ritual to stop it. As a younger, curious and less-polished Hawa watched on, her grandmother would take a stick, set it in the ground, dash salt around it and utter some words. The rain would stop. 'She would do the same when she missed her children and wanted to see them,' she softly chuckles. 'After the ritual, they would come.'

Water beckons and repels, gifts and punishes. Its plurality is highlighted through the construction of 'life-water' and 'death-water'. It becomes life-water when it purifies, and death-water when it soils. The scholar Diadji purposefully points out that is not 'dead water' – water can be a sign of life or of death, but it is always full of existence.[36] Therefore, he probes, how can it be dead when water is never spent? How can we, as mortal beings, attempt to frame such an omnipotent force with our incomplete terms of 'dead' and 'alive'?

'Water,' Diadji continues, '[has] the capacity to rejuvenate, to heal and especially to draw life forth from death and to bring death upon life.'[37]

*

The group continued on westwards, leaving the Comoé River behind them. They then headed south towards the Tiassalé region, where Pokou and her people would displace local populations, leaving some followers there to settle. From there, Pokou led her fellow wanderers northwards. Some of them had been with her since Kumase, others had been absorbed along the way, voluntarily or forcefully through displacement. They travelled until they reached the region just south-west of the present-day city of Bouaké, a city initially named Gbèkèkro after Gossan Kwa Gbeke, a man who would lead her people in the 1800s.[38]

As they walked, leaving their imprints on sand, soil and forest floor, did the hoarse riverside cries of Pokou still rattle in their ears? After bearing witness to the delivery of the royal's baby to churning waters, were her people haunted by guttural moans ripped from her throat? No matter how traditions diverge, they all come to the same point: Pokou secured her people's safe voyage by releasing her child into the Comoé's rushing waters. As the group travelled onwards, swelling and accruing, were their gains still underscored by their leader's unspeakable loss, the same kind known to Ilé-Ifè's Morèmi?

The sacrifice followed them to the new lands they inhabited and Pokou's offering would indelibly mark them. Her people would be henceforth known as the Baoulé. Baoulé means 'the child is dead.'[39]

This formation of the Baoulé kingdom – anywhere between 1730 and 1760 – ushered in a new chapter of the former Asantewoman's life: Queen Pokou.

Beyond the ability to navigate trepidatious travels, she already had the reputation of a formidable leader. Some historians believe that, when she had established a village for her people, nearby indigenous communities began to come to her as an arbiter over grievances. This rankled the leader of the existing occupants, Agpatou Mhenif, to whom Pokou had come to seek land from for her people, and it wasn't long before he declared war on the royal.[40] Despite their respectively small numbers, guns and munitions gained Pokou's partisans the upper hand. Whether the weaponry was brought all the way from the Asante capital of Kumase or was acquired along the way remains unclear. Pokou's victory over Agpatou, however, is not in question. He began paying tribute to the new queen, stamping her authority over the entire area.[41]

Rule over the Baoulé continued in a similar vein to how it began. Widely recognised as a conciliator for local disputes, Pokou's attributes as a judicial figure sustained her reign and influence. She would reportedly only deploy military tactics in self-defence.[42] Under her rule developed a society where there were barely village chiefs, let alone tribal leaders. Instead, as the Baoulé built themselves villages of mortar-based homes with thatched or wooden roofs on red dust, heads of extended families were the crucial link between the people and the emerging royal class.[43] A centralised political system, like those of the Akan states east of the Baoulé, wouldn't emerge until after the end of the nineteenth century – well beyond Pokou's lifetime.

The former princess would reign until her death around 1760, passing on the throne she'd forged to her niece, Akwa Boni. However, Pokou lives on – through the people and kingdom named for her lost child.

'If you listen to the stories that have been told for generations, elements of fantasy, s/f [science fiction] have always existed within them... I am just a new generation of storyteller, using cinema as my tool,' explains Kenyan film director Wanuri Kahiu. For her, myth, orality and indigenous belief systems have always been integral to African modes of speculative storytelling.[44]

These are enduring practices which offer different 'conceptual blueprints' within fields dominated by the loud cries of Western science, objectivity and realism.[45] To grapple with African story-telling – and, by extension, African modes of record-keeping – requires us (especially those of us in the West) to relinquish the practices drilled into our minds on how history *should* or *must* be done. We have to reckon with the ways our social conditioning shapes the history we consume and produce – for example, the way that oral histories, steadily gaining recognition in the West as a 'legitimate' historical method, are often regarded as less authoritative than the written document. Yet, it's primarily the oral medium that has allowed us access to the likes of Hangbé and Morèmi.

Similarly, as many historians have argued over the last century and a half, we must suspend the belief that Western historical frameworks can be uniformly applied to every historical context.[46] When a society understands, for instance, its dead as being reborn in every fragment of life – in the dust, in gentle waters, in the laughter of children, in every seed buried beneath the soil – which thereby impacts the historical events within that society and how they've been recorded, how do you diligently capture that within the stringent confines of 'objective' Western history? And when we have cases like the *Cape Coast* ship mentioned in the introduction, what makes Western history any less speculative?

When speaking to the oral tradition of Pokou's legacy, Kofi Anyidoho – who penned the introduction to Tadjo's novel, *Queen Pokou: Concerto for a Sacrifice* – calls attention to how historically rooted storytelling can take on the air of legend: 'In the mouth of each creative raconteur, the legend comes to life again and again as it is re-enacted in its proper historical context but with long shadows over the present.'[47]

It's why the novel presents us with a number of different Pokous, capturing the complexity and ambiguity of the figure herself, but also the disseminated variations of the narrative. One Pokou offers up the sacrifice of her infant with little hesitance, the picture of selflessness. Another Pokou, overcome with grief and regret, throws herself into the water in a search for her child, before the weight of anguish morphs her into a vengeful deity. Tadjo also presents us with a version of the Asante princess who refuses to sacrifice her son, defying the will of the gods.[48]

Alongside teasing out the many possible faces of Pokou – the ideal woman, the merciless ruler, the rational leader, the murderous avenger – Tadjo's fictive work underscores real, historical responsibilities. Great care must be taken in retelling stories of origin to avoid overly facile interpretations that can be used to serve social or political agendas.[49] For example, Pokou has often been folded into superhero narratives in African popular media which emerged towards the end of the 1970s.[50] In a continent-wide pressure cooker of independence movements, Pan-Africanism and Black consciousness, Pokou was – and continues to be – presented in stories for children with 'overtly didactic objectives'; a paragon of morality and unselfishness in the name of community-building.[51]

If anything, the varied interpretations of Pokou and her life only highlight how unlikely it is that we will ever conjure up an image true to the founder of the Baoulé people, presenting her as she was.

As our first and last in-person conversation draws to a close, Hawa describes the mixed education she received in school where European and African history were taught in parallel. She remembers learning about Pokou at the same time that she was introduced to Christopher Columbus. 'This was a real story,' she recalls with relish. 'This was a story about us.' As she grew up and, later, absorbed a Baoulé sister-in-law into her family, it's a narrative that has, no doubt, only felt more present to the Yacouba woman.

My companion was one of many learning about Pokou's legacy, whether in the classroom or at the feet of elders. Today, Pokou, her journey and sacrifice are called upon as the official version of Baoulé origins, with her now remembered by all the Akan groups in today's Côte d'Ivoire, from the Agni to the Ébrié.[52]

Her cultural significance, however, obscures a dearth of written materials or texts on Pokou. Despite journeying around Abidjan with *Tante* Lucie, the kind and generous aunt of a friend, to find scraps of the sovereign in the city's universities and libraries, we repeatedly came up empty-handed. While sat across from scholars in their offices, they admitted that it's difficult to find primary source material or texts on Pokou. Going into a library, you'd be hard-pressed to find anything on her outside of children's books.[53]

It's the spoken word, delivered from mouth to ear, that has largely carried Pokou and her unnamed infant far and wide. Dripping with the mythical, the fantastical and the unknowable, it is the oral tradition that sustains her place in history.

I cannot rise for air. Many must think
me dead as I do too with some scaly
darkness coming over, over me. A great
fish has swallowed me whole, giving breath
and rounded eyes to see hippopotamuses
lined in a row and on their backs my people
crossing into safety. Their thankful
praying quiets the surf and last I hear
is the voice of my mother, drumming pain:
'Baoulé, he is gone. Baoulé, he is dead.'

'No, no,' I try to say. 'No, I'm still alive!'
But the Great Fish swims the opposite way.
'Do not be afraid,' the Great Fish tells me.
'Do not be afraid. You have given them a name.'

Coming to the water they
Found a way over
Coming to the water they
Found a new home.

– MELVIN DIXON, 'BOBO BAOULÉ'

CHAPTER 5

Məntəwwab

The Ambitious Empress

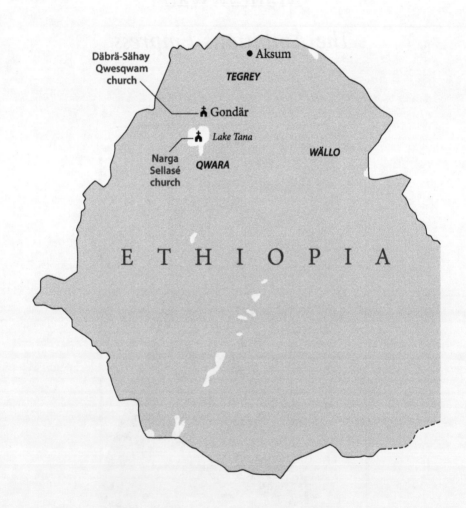

Däbrä-Sähay
Qwesqwam
church

● Aksum

TEGREY

♁ Gondär

♁ *Lake Tana*

Narga
Sellasé
church

QWARA

WÄLLO

E T H I O P I A

On a day warmed up by Ethiopian sun, in the early eighteenth century, a wealthy old man living atop a hill opened his doors to a fever-stricken stranger.

Däjazmach Mänbär, whose title suggests time spent command-ing Ethiopian army formations in the field, ushered the man into his home in Qwara. Perhaps with the help of his wife, *Wäyzäro* Enkoyä, Mänbär tended to his distressed guest.[1] It's not clear how much time passed as they worked to loosen the fever's grip, but we're told by local and colonial accounts that the couple's daugh-ter who wore the baptismal name of Wälättä Giyorgis left the deepest impression on the stranger. She was beautiful and gentle, affable and prudent. She was the darling of her family, of all her neighbourhood.[2] She was a paragon of the Ethiopian nobility she belonged to.

Naturally, the stranger she aided back to good health was none other than the *atse* (ruler) of Ethiopia – known as 'Ïtyoṗyā in the Ge'ez language. It was reportedly the custom of the empire's sovereigns to 'disappear for a time, without any warning', often assuming the appearance of their impoverished subjects as they visited parts of their realm.[3] *Atse* Bäkafa, who had ascended the seat of power in 1719, had followed in his predecessors' footsteps and they had led him to Wälättä's door. Even after he had bid his hosts farewell and hurried back to his Gondär palace, we're told that the Qemant girl from Qwara played on his mind.[4] Soon her father would open the door, not to a feverish fellow, but to a messenger with guards and attendants.[5]

By 1723, Wälättä had been hurried away from her home and pre-sented before the *atse*.[6] Some believe that the girl's appearance at court – and subsequent rise – was down to the engineering of her maternal grandmother, Yolyana. That it was she who sent the young woman – noted as 'still a virgin' – to court at Bäkafa's insist-ence and then acted as her sponsor and patron.[7]

We're all familiar with narratives of aiding the befallen stranger and girls being plucked from obscurity. They have been drummed into many heads from young, with folklore, fairy tales and other traditions passed from one generation to the next. Are they seeded as proverbs to remind us to be kind and generous to all, including strangers, for you never know who you might cross paths with? Moral advice for women and girls, that a gentle, diligent disposition will increase your value and desirability? Or a convenient reminder that the ruling classes may deign to walk among the people, even succumbing to misfortune and ill health just like the rest of us?

In this case, it's a mixture of all. It laid the foundations for Wälättä to enter the royal class. She'd become Bäkafa's *itege* and would eventually take the throne name of Berhan Mogasa. However, she's better known as Məntəwwab, Empress of 'Ītyoṗyā.

Before Bäkafa, there was a carousel of 'four feeble kings'. Their reigns, all together, only spanned fifteen years.[8] The first of them, Täklä-Häymanot I (r. 1706–08), sparked the nearly two decades of political instability when he ordered the assassination of his predecessor: his father, Iyasu I the Great.

Gondär had been established as the empire's permanent capital for decades by the time Iyasu I became *atse* in 1682, and the realm was in the wake of an 'Ethiopian Renaissance'. Alongside his military invasions and occupations of nearby territories, the *atse* undertook extensive architectural projects, including building Gondär's political and aesthetic pull. His assassination, therefore, destabilised not only the empire at large, but the capital city's influence.[9] The four rulers that followed each fell in quick succession, all assassinated, deposed or dying under mysterious circumstances. 'The kingdom was set on a disastrous course,' writes history scholar Habtamu Mengistie Tegegne. 'Only the ascent of King Bäkafa (r. 1721–30) reversed the downward slide... [he] managed to restore order and peace which lasted until 1769.'[10]

According to his royal chronicler and other sources, Məntəwwab's new paramour was a 'forceful and decisive personality.' He quickly and severely punished rebels, nonconformists and pretenders.[11] For example, when a claimant to the throne named Hezqeyas made himself known, Bäkafa ordered his upper limbs cut off.[12]

Under Bäkafa's authoritarian rule, some semblance of stability returned. The empire continued to enjoy its relations with Indian, Arab and Mediterranean realms, trading links that were established in the early fourteenth century. In return for enslaved people, ivory, musk, wax, and later, coffee, the ruling classes of 'Ityoṗyā were well-supplied with swords, helmets, silk, cushions, carpets and more.[13] The kingdom's nobility sat at the apex of a society where the peasant class was organised into fiefs, the lower classes trapped into dependence on their patrons.[14]

In medieval 'Ityoṗyā, Amharic had developed into the *lesanä negus* – the 'language of the king.' Although a multi-linguistic land, it was the tongue of the Amhara people that was used at court and, likely, for most government affairs.[15] It paved the way for Amharic to become the administration's official language and a widely used lingua franca. As Ethiopian researchers Mulugeta Gebrehiwot Berhe and Feseha Habtetsion Gebresilassie outline, ethnic Amharas and their cultures were dominant in the empire. 'Even the Oromo and Gurage soldiers in the emperor's army spoke Amharic and professed Orthodox Christianity, the key cultural labels of being an Amhara,' they explain. 'Regardless of their origins, therefore, these traits made them "Amhara" in the eyes of the local population.'[16]

Like all empires, 'Ityoṗyā was built on the conquest and hardships of subjugated groups whose stolen lands fell within its boundaries. Unable to identify with the state nor the language, culture or customs they were expected to embody as their own, the foundations of the realm were shaky.[17] And as the years ticked on, the grievances that hinged on identity, ethnicity and the concentration of power only widened fractures into chasms. Gaping rifts that, today, are still swallowing up the children of 'Ityoṗyā whole.

As the restaurant's playlist of Ethio-jazz tinkles around us, I beam across the table at my dinner companion. Our paths have criss-crossed around London for years but this is the first time we're actually sitting down to talk.

As a mild summer day blended into a milder evening, I'd entered the proudly family-owned and family-run Addis restaurant and admired the detailed wood panelling, much of it adorned with Amharic, with mounted landscape photography and artwork of Ethiopia and its people. Here I break injera with Magdalene Abraha.

The writer and publisher has made a name of herself in London, particularly with the book series she spearheaded (A Quick Ting On) at Black-owned publishing firm Jacaranda Books. But, rather than books and writing, we're here to talk about her other great love: her home country. After we've ordered an 'Addis Special' for two and our drinks have arrived, we settle in.

'There are so many!' Mags exclaims, taking a sip of her mango juice before returning to my question on the ethnic groups in present-day Ethiopia. 'I'm not sure if anyone knows exactly how many there are. People just know that there are over seventy, some say over eighty, but there are loads. They are vast and so different.'

What do we mean when we talk about 'ethnicity'? Anthropologist and historian Jon Abbink offers a useful definition that refutes essentialism: 'a cultural interpretation of descent and historical tradition by a group of people, as opposed to others, and expressed in a certain behavioural or cultural style... a kind of "expanded, fictive kinship".'[18]

For example, the Harari people, a Semitic-speaking group, largely live within the walled city of Harar in eastern Ethiopia, a city they were forced to leave when they were ethnically cleansed under Haile Selassie's regime. Known for their basketry craft, replete with stunning geometric designs, the Harari crystallise as part of an 'ethnic group' due to their shared historical memory, cultural identity and their past (and present) movements to secure collective interest.[19] There's the agricultural Irob people who predominantly reside in the highlands of Ethiopia and Eritrea today, renowned for their honey and *tej* (honey wine) and their poetry-like oral tradition of *Adar*. The nomadic Nyangatom – or Donyiro – people who inhabit the border of south-western Ethiopia and south-eastern South Sudan are characterised by their heavy necklaces made of dry seeds (more often glass beads today), customs of ornamental scarification of their faces and torsos, and their historic reputation as great warriors.[20] Like the rest of the Solomonic rulers (although debated with certain rulers), Bäkafa and his new *itege* were the latest faces of a dynasty once referred to as the 'kings of Amhara'.

Despite the abundance of peoples and lands claimed under the Ethiopian empire, as Mags notes, 'historically, politically, there has been a dominant three: Amhara, Tigray and Oromo.' Alongside the Somali people, they make up the bulk of the country's population. Historically, the Amhara have been the politically – and economically – dominant group. However, the Ethiopian state traces its roots back to the ancient Aksumite Empire – founded in the first century – which was centralised in the Tigray – or Tegrey – region.[21] As Mags explains, it became a province synonymous with Coptic Christianity: 'Christianity in Ethiopia was founded in Tigray. The oldest mosque in Ethiopia was founded in Tigray. It's the bearer of a lot of the history that Ethiopia prides itself on.' Although the Tigray would emerge as a politically dominant group right at the tail end of the twentieth century, their province has a long history of marginalisation within an empire-state where Amharas were overrepresented.[22] Meanwhile, the Oromo, a Cushistic ethnic group, were subordinated, economically and politically.[23]

The politicisation of ethnicity shaped the fate of this land and the many peoples that made up this empire, reverberating from ancient times through to the ongoing Ethiopian armed conflict. It laid the foundations of the recent devastation that has carved the country open: the Tigrayan genocide. We'll attend to this later.

Some say that Mǝntǝwwab and Bäkafa never formally married and she simply became his consort.[24] Others say that, not only did they marry, but she was also not the *atse*'s first wife. One historian writes that Bäkafa's first wife 'mysteriously died just hours after [Mǝntǝwwab's] coronation.'[25] Not in dispute, however, is her status as *itege* of 'Ītyoṗyä and that the child – a son – she would shortly bear would follow in his father's footsteps. Little and less is documented about the couple's daughter, Wälättä Täklä-Häymanot.

When the new royal entered Bäkafa's court, the Qwaräñña swept in with her – a faction named for her home province and her immediate family. As Məntəwwab rose, so too did her kinship network. From relative obscurity, they attained prominence, wealth and influence. A number of her family members received court appointments by the late 1720s – including Məntəwwab's great-uncle, Niqolawas, and her uncle, Arkälädis.[26]

Being surrounded by family at court certainly helped when, in 1730, Bäkafa died. Niqolawas is said to be the 'sole possessor of the emperor's dying words concerning the succession' and he immediately shared them with his sister Yolyana and Məntəwwab.[27] The itege's family moved quickly. They declared Bäkafa's son – the seven-year-old Iyasu II – as the next atse. Naturally, the Qwaräñña decided, Məntəwwab was best suited to reign during the young ruler's minority. It seems that rather than just taking the title of 'regent', she had herself crowned in the same year as her son, presenting herself as a co-ruler instead.[28] Encircled by her relatives, so began Məntəwwab's grip on real power.

In the empire she ruled over, the social groups can be summed up as the ruling classes and a largely unrecognised class of peasants. Proof of the latter's existence appears in land charters, administrative manuals for religious institutions and other sources in passing.[29] The Amharic term for the class, zégoch, can be translated quite simply: serfs. The landed property that they were associated with is called rim. It was this system of serfdom that the political and social power of the Ethiopian ruling classes was rooted in from the 1700s onwards.[30]

To be a zéga – or exist in a state of zéganät – was to live in 'abject poverty, in servitude or socioeconomic dependency'; to define people as zégoch was to say that they lacked status, with their lives defined by humiliation and subjection.[31] Rim property was confiscated land still used and lived upon by the peasant class. The system gave them the land back – but as tenants who had to accept their status as zégoch to landlords.[32]

Portrayals of this subjugated class remain in flux. Some sources distinguish the zégoch as landless, subordinate individuals who worked the lands of lords but were still able to leave of their own free will. Elsewhere, they're understood as closer to enslaved peoples, the property of their overlords who would pass on their rights in *rim* land to their descendants.[33] In fact, it was possible to, not only dispose of the labourers, but to also trade them for agricultural fields deemed more valuable. It was something that Mǝntǝwwab did herself when she traded 'Wärädé's cotton [fields] in exchange for *zéga*' in the Qäräfu locality.[34] The impoverished labourers had to pay tribute, tax and rent alongside carrying out specific tasks like erecting and repairing buildings, while the ruling classes shuffled them around at will. Mere possessions in the eyes of Ethiopia's nobles, they drew up wills in which they passed the peasants tied to their stolen land onto their heirs.[35] The *zégoch* were completely and utterly beholden to their *rim* owners in all senses, including judiciary – their lords held extensive private power over them.[36]

The granting of *rim* in Gondär reached its climax under Mǝnt- ǝwwab and the Qwaräñña were key beneficiaries.[37] 'All in all, Mentewwab, along with her well known relatives and their families, held around 97 *gasha* of land accounting for nearly 10 percent of the total lands distributed," writes Tegegne.[38] One *gasha* is about eighty to one hundred acres.[39] Meanwhile, the *itege*'s grants saw the lands of peasants broken up into smaller plots and redistributed among the clergy.[40]

The ruling class seized control of land in the name of churches, with widespread dispossession making way for the erection of beautiful religious buildings.[41] Power at the top of the hierarchy swelled as their dependents sunk deeper into subjection.

We cannot feign to know the experiences of 'Ītyoṗyä's enslaved people. With their experiences scarcely documented and their presence mediated through their oppressors, no historian can – or should – attempt to act as their mouthpiece. However, given the distribution of power and wealth and the source material available, a few extrapolations can be made – particularly about the figure of the peasant woman in 'Ītyoṗyä compared to their noble counterparts. It was one of subservience, writes historian Salome Gebre Egziabher. 'She was always treated as inferior and expected to act as subordinate. Whereas the woman from the nobility was treated as an equal to the males of her class [sic].'[42]

The idea that women of nobility were treated as equal is not a wholly founded assertion. While the likes of Məntəwwab could partake in various land transfer processes – a noble woman could buy, sell or act as a guarantor, underscoring some degree of parity – the Ethiopian society was patriarchally organised, and wealth and land still remained secondary to gender.[43] Despite the land rights held by noble women, they were not exercised equally. 'Men dominated and controlled land and where women had it, men tended to get it.'[44]

Once a consort, and now a ruler in her own stead who could grant *rim*, Məntəwwab occupied a unique position, and this extended to her romantic life. Following the death of her *atse*, she entered into a 'variety of attachments' with men, each short in duration.[45] One that stuck, however, is the relationship with one of Bäkafa's younger family members, Melmal Iyasu. A grandson of Iyasu I (and a potential successor to the throne), historians point to Məntəwwab's lover being a *Grazmach* – a military commander of the left flank of 'Ītyop̄yä's armed forces.[46] Younger than the ruler, Melmal Iyasu earned the sarcastic – perhaps even snide – moniker of 'Iyasu the Kept' by court officials. They had three daughters together: Aletash, Astér and Wälätä-Isra'el.[47]

As the *itege* continued to pad her station into the 1730s, and that of the Qwaräñña, the other *mäkwanent* – senior nobles – began to resent them. They begrudged the monopoly of power her family held and made their feelings known through rebellion. The nobles laid siege to the Gondär royal residence itself in 1732.[48] Seeking to reassure her war council of her right to lead them, a confident Məntəwwab is quoted by historians as announcing: 'If I am a woman by the manner of my creation, my gifts, which I have received from God, from below [on earth] and from above [heaven], are those of a man amongst men.'[49]

When she quashed the rebellion and several others, Məntəwwab's decisive actions likely validated her belief that she was not like other women – or perhaps even superseded them. Even the believed death of her grandmother Yolyana that same year, months before the rebellion, didn't impact the influence of her family at court.[50] If anything, her grip tightened and the power of the Qwaräñña was established. Significantly, Məntəwwab's brother Wäldä-Le'ul was elevated to the office of *behtwäddäd* – guardian of the *atse* – in 1733.[51]

Early on, Məntəwwab oversaw the devolution of power that would characterise her rule, entrenching her power and that of highly placed *mäkwanent* close to her. It also created fertile ground for the emergence of other ruling lines in their own territories, their claims to reign staked on kinship ties, land and ethnicity.[52]

As we scoop up lamb *tibs* (sautéed lamb) and *doro wot* (chicken stew) with spongy injera, Mags mulls on her identity between bites.

Her mother is Amhara. Her father is from Tigray, although his mother is from Gondär. Mags was named after the Tigrayan church where her paternal grandfather, who passed before she was born, was baptised. A child of mixed ethnicity referring to herself as an Ethiopian used to be straightforward and accurate. That all changed recently, although it was decades in the making.

Romanticised as a god to the Rastafari people, a benevolent ruler and the famous resister of Italian colonialism, the legacy of Ethiopia's last emperor – Haile Selassie I – is often wiped clean of his crimes and those of his associates. 'The autocrat is remembered in Tigray for inviting the British Royal Air Force to bomb the region in 1943 to quell what came to be known as the first Woyane Rebellion... he was also harsh towards those Ethiopian patriots who fought against the Italians while he fled to Britain. For example, Belay Zeleke, a national war hero (who led the resistance movement in Gojjam from 1936 to 1941) was hung on his orders,' writes Dr Yohannes Woldemariam.[53]

Selassie was deposed in 1974 and, the following year, the monarchy was abolished by the Derg. A Marxist-Leninist regime that would held power across the next two decades, the military junta sought to make ethnic identities 'irrelevant' through 'scientific socialism'.[54] They themselves would be toppled in 1991 by the

Ethiopian People's Revolutionary Democratic Front (EPRDF) which established a government where power was disseminated among ethnic regional governments.

The four regional parties were the Tigray People's Liberation Front (TPLF), the Amhara Democratic Party, the Oromo Democratic Party and the Southern Ethiopian Peoples's Democratic Movement. Out of all of them, the TPLF dominated the coalition (despite representing a small percentage of the population), controlling most of the important political and military posts in the EPRDF.[55]

After nearly three decades of this ruling system, Abiy Ahmed, an Oromo politician, was appointed as prime minister in 2018. He immediately set about making changes. Ahmed merged the EPRDF coalition into a single party, the Prosperity Party, which he became the leader of with a view to centralise Ethiopian governance and break up the TPLF's influence.[56] Within a year, Ahmed received the 2019 Nobel Peace Prize for, in particular, 'his decisive initiative to resolve the border conflict with neighbouring Eritrea.'[57] Meanwhile, the TPLF refused to join Ahmed's revamped party, resenting not only the contested deal with Eritrea, but also their loss of power in the new government.[58]

Things came to a head in 2020 with the onset of the COVID-19 pandemic. When Ahmed received parliamentary approval to postpone the elections – meaning he would remain in power unopposed until new elections could be held – the TPLF accused him of making authoritarian moves. The party held their own autonomous regional elections in Tigray. Proclaiming the Tigrayan election illegal, the prime minister cut funds to the region's government. That was evidently insufficient, however, as escalation soon followed on 4 November 2020. Ahmed announced a military offensive in Tigray led by Ethiopian armed forces and aided by Amhara regional militias and Eritrean troops.[59]

'When [on 4 Nov] the Ethiopian Prime Minister, Abiy Ahmed, a Nobel peace prize winner, announced a military offensive in Tigray, it was hard to predict the scale of the human suffering that would ensue,' Mags wrote for the *Guardian* in 2021. 'But almost instantly Tigray, a region in the far north of a country home to more than 7 million people, was cut off from the world: phone lines were shut down, the internet was cut off, banks were closed and journalists were barred from the region.[60]

In the piece, she touched on the many horrors that had unfolded over just a year: Ethiopian soldiers shut the border with Sudan to reduce the number of Tigrayan refugees who could flee; concentration camps controlled by Ethiopian forces housed ethnic Tigrayans including infants as young as two; abduction and gang-rape of women and girls at the hands of Ethiopian troops, Eritrean soldiers and armed militia; Tigray's healthcare system collapsed as soldiers looted 79 per cent of facilities; a man-made famine drove mass starvation.[61]

In December 2022, Mags's follow-up article was sobering, coming one month after the conflict 'formally came to an end'.[62] Against the backdrop of Russia invading Ukraine, which received – and continues to receive – widespread coverage from Western mainstream media, the loss of an estimated 600,000 lives in Ethiopia was largely ignored.

'This year we have seen what is possible when the world decides a conflict and the lives destroyed by it are worth caring about,' she penned. 'It's a tragedy that Tigray has become a forgotten catastrophe. As I write this, much of Tigray is still inaccessible or uncontactable, civilians are unable to access their money, they are starving, the health crisis is immense and they are still being terrorised by militia soldiers.'[63]

With the voices of the victims effectively silenced, Mags – and other Tigrayans in the diaspora – were compelled to amplify the violence their people were enduring, pushing against a very strong, top-down state narrative. These articles, alongside other pieces and radio interviews, saw Mags's name placed on a list that meant she couldn't enter Ethiopia. 'I didn't want to,' she tells me. 'I was writing the opposite of what the government was saying. I was getting messages accusing me of being paid by the Tigrayan government. I was on the receiving end of threats for writing or speaking about what was happening to the people of Tigray. So

I was like, damn, if I'm getting this here, what on earth are the people back home getting?'

Two years on, while it's now possible to travel to Tigray, fighting has spread to the Amhara region, making her family home in Gondär, where she'd spent whole summers, unsafe to visit. It's why we're talking at a restaurant in north London.

The genocide has since shattered ideals that Mags was once so sure of.

'I felt pain, anger, sadness, betrayal, heartbreak. I've never honestly been the same. After, everything I thought I knew was called into question. From a family perspective, it meant that people were on different...' she pauses, a questioning inflection adding an upward lilt, 'sides? For me there's only one side, the right side which is the victims.'

The emotional toll weighed on her, including witnessing the psychological impacts of war. 'Seeing my dad's experience is probably the most painful for me because that was very visceral and I was spending a lot of time with him.' Sorrow lines her words, her shoulders slightly dip. 'He was hoping to retire [in Tigray] so he was robbed of a lot of dreams, as was his generation because, that region, I don't think Tigray will ever really recover again after what it went through.'

There was also the abject denial of what was happening in Tigray, what was being done to Tigrayans. While she was trying to be 'as logical as possible' in order to advocate, she was trying to reconcile the fact that 'there were people who looked like me, [that I was] raised with, spent time with, who didn't see my pain.' She corrects herself, 'Actually, didn't *believe* my pain.'

She leans back in her seat, our food – a *bäyaynätu* spread – forgotten.

'I remember there was one conversation that I had and it was one of the more painful ones. I spoke to my cousin before the blackout and he shared a story of him basically witnessing somebody, an old woman, get murdered by soldiers. I told my friend and her response was, "Are you sure? Doesn't really sound believable". How do I respond to that?'

While the Tigrayan genocide looms large in its brutality and recency, Mags notes that it is not entirely unique to the country. 'Every ethnic group you ask will have a painful story to tell, where their hardships came from, maybe because of Ethiopia [in general] or against the ruling group at the time. Somehow, because identity is always linked to this, it always results in another ethnic group feeling attacked. And if the people in power are from your ethnicity, then by default, you are implicated.'

'It showed me how we can all, in some ways – I don't want to give too much grace – almost be tricked into supporting something so harmful because of how people behave when they feel their identity is threatened. I learnt a lot.'

Məntəwwab was also learning, namely how to strengthen her position and better stem the uprisings that would pepper the 1730s. To ensure this, she relied on one of the best tools at her disposal. Strategic marriage alliances.

Offering her daughters with Melmal Iyasu to the lords of northern 'Ityoṗyā presented a bloodless way of binding them to the *itege*. Keeping things in the family, Astér was married to *Däjazmach* YäMaryam Barya who was a prominent Qwaräñña himself. Her sisters, however, were married further afield. For Wälätä-Isra'el, Məntəwwab selected *Däjazmach* Yosédéq whose descendants would go on to rule Gojjam – a province that neighboured Qwara – into the twentieth century. The immediate view of the alliances was that they were a success, with political networks skilfully interlinked.[64]

Crucially, Məntəwwab brokered a marriage alliance with the Oromo of Wällo. The negotiations highlighted a shift in the status held by the Oromo. By the close of the sixteenth century, the Oromo had migrated from the southern border of the realm towards its centre. But, in truth, they occupied most of 'Ityoṗyā's territories, ultimately forming economic and military obstacles for the *itege*.[65] Not only would the alliance be an inter-religious and inter-ethnic union, but it would be of great political and economic expediency. Plus, there was a level of safeguarding, given that an

Oromo family could have no claim to the Solomonic throne that originated from ancient Amhara.[66]

With that, her son, *Atse* Iyasu II was married to Wäbi – or Wobit – a Muslim Oromo princess or daughter of a lord. However, the union was contingent on her baptism.[67]

Not far from where Məntəwwab had ruled – and three centuries later – a team of archaeologists working in northern Ethiopia published their findings in 2019: they had uncovered the oldest known Christian church in the region.

Just thirty miles north-east of Aksum, the capital of the Aksumite Empire, radiocarbon dating placed the establishment of the uncovered structure within the fourth century – fourteen centuries before the *itege* came to power. It means that the new religion had travelled quickly, nearly 3,000 miles from Rome, potentially through the long-distance trading networks that linked Africa, South Asia and the Mediterranean via the Red Sea. The Aksumite Empire began to decline in the eighth and ninth centuries. But, even as the teachings of Islam began to spread across the region and Ottoman-backed armies attempted to conquer the realm, Christianity in 'Ītyop̈yä was there to stay.[68]

The 1530s had been dominated by the invasion of the Adal Sultanate, a Sunni Muslim Empire backed by the more powerful Ottoman Empire, into Christian 'Ītyop̈yä. And although the east African realm, with the backing of Portuguese allies, avoided being wholly subsumed, it was greatly weakened. It lost much of the territory that would eventually become present-day Eritrea. From the 1550s, Jesuit missionaries had been determined to establish the Roman Catholic Church in 'Ītyop̈yä, despite Ottoman military activity in the Red Sea that ensured they were isolated from support. So great was Pope Gregory XIII's fear of 'losing the Christian country to the Muslim world', he had not allowed members of the Society of Jesus to withdraw from 'Ītyop̈yä.[69]

By the sixteenth century, 'Christological controversies' were pulling the empire in different directions, inspired by the arrival of Jesuit Catholic missionaries. Through their influence over *Atse* Susenyos I (r. 1607–32), the teachings of the traditional Orthodox

Church were banned and Catholicism was proclaimed the official state religion in 1622. This led to revolts and uprisings that continued until 1632. After choosing to restore the ancient Orthodox Church over more bloodshed, the ruler abdicated his power to his son and successor, Fasilädäs (r. 1632–67).[70]

Although the Jesuits were eventually expelled, the sectarian divisions that they had sparked – and doctrinal questions raised – remained long after their departure. Halfway through the seventeenth century, disparate sects emerged, including the *Qebat* – who emphasised the role of the Holy Spirit – and the *Säga* – who placed greater emphasis on Jesus as the Son of God.[71] Their conflicting interpretations and rituals on different calendars became the bed of much antagonism.

By the 1700s, both sects – now rival followers – vied for control at court, with the *Qebat* edging out their adversaries. The *Säga* were exiled, with some of their clergy massacred in 1721. The four weak rulers who preceded Bäkafa had bent to the will of the *Qebat* practitioners. In fact, it reached a point where deferring to the *Qebat* partisans become a condition of preserving one's political standing.[72]

Like much of the Qwaränña, Mǝntǝwwab was a *Qebat* partisan and therefore, it should be little surprise that the *Qebat* gained prominence at her Gondär court. But that wasn't enough. The *itege* wanted to leave a visible, lasting mark of her commitment to the Church and, specifically, her religious sect. Not only did she patronise churches around the region – in Bägémeder, Tegray, Gojjam and Saraye (the latter found in present-day Eritrea) – but Mǝntǝwwab set about building her own. Among her best-known constructions are Däbrä-Sähay Qwesqwam in Gondär and Narga Sellasé in Lake Tana, both intended to serve as centres of *Qebat* teaching to counter rival churches.[73]

Since the introduction of Christianity, the Ethiopian Orthodox Church has sat at the centre of art production – particularly paintings. The ruler's own churches and commissions were no different.[74] Especially devoted to the Virgin Mary, for one commission, Mǝntǝwwab instructed a painter to use precious gold, silver and

blue silk material – a rarely applied method given the expense –
for Mary's mantle instead of paint, and to make the dress of the
Child out of brocade.[75]

Given the increased power of the clergy at the royal court, it
then became politically symbolic for nobles to become a patron
of the arts. Donating paintings to, or commissioning works for, a
church meant that patrons could garner religious support from
those institutions.[76] When nobles fought for power, they often used
art to enhance their personal power and prestige. It was perfectly
advantageous for the Church, used as a tugging rope between
vying patrons. To even attempt to lay a claim on the throne,
noble donations to important churches and monasteries became
essential.[77]

During this period, ego also entered the frame. It has since
become evident that some patrons wanted to be recognisable in
church paintings. Məntəwwab, for example, is always depicted
with her hair pulled back from her face, giving the impression
of a crown, with the fine frontal braids and loose falling curls
resembling the hugely popularised *shuruba* hairstyle worn by
Habesha peoples today. It makes her 'immediately identifiable in
her portraits.'[78]

These were displays of power and also personal memorials.
After all, Məntəwwab had already thought ahead with one of her
structures. Whenever her end came, the ruler intended for the
Qwesqwam church, alongside a space for teaching and worship,
to also be her mausoleum and final resting place.[79]

But the next death that came was not hers. According to the
annals of his reign, Iyasu II died on 21 Säne 7247, or 27 June 1755.
Rumours shroud his passing but there's little obfuscation around
what happened next. Within a few days, the late *atse*'s son and
Məntəwwab's grandson, Iyo'as I, was titled as the empire's new
sovereign.[80]

With another newly named *atse* who was but a child, Məntəwwab and the Qwaräñña had been here before. It was decided
that, once more, the aged *itege* would rule in his stead, just as she
had held true power for her deceased son. After holding a council

with her *mäkwanent*, Məntəwwab decided that another marriage alliance was required to ensure smooth governance and seal the co-operation of a powerful figure in the realm.[81]

However, unbeknownst to her, this dynastic union would bring about her unravelling.

Huge swathes of what we know about Məntəwwab and the dynasty she married into are filtered through James Bruce, a Scottish wine merchant who fashioned himself as an 'explorer' and 'adventurer'. After he succeeded his father as the Laird of Kinnaird in 1758 and coal was discovered on his land, the new-found wealth allowed him to undertake extensive expeditions around the African continent and the Middle East. This included 'his paramount desire... to travel even further afield and ultimately, to discover the source of the Blue Nile, what is now called Lake Tana.'[82]

He's remembered favourably – and whimsically – by some. The National Galleries of Scotland take note of his 'impressive figure', standing at six foot four inches.[83] The Devon & Exeter Institution remarks on his ambition and aptitude for languages when the Stirlingshire landowner was made 'Consul-General' at Algiers in 1763. On its website, it describes his best-known work, *Travels to Discover the Source of the Nile* – which is a source for this chapter – as 'intended... to equal, if not outdo' the works of Captain James Cook. The Exeter-based historic library opines that Bruce's *Travels* were a 'tale of courage and scholarly endeavour combined with excessive self-belief and self-promotion' – despite 'accusations of inaccuracy'.[84] Historic UK makes the bold claim that his 'most impressive achievement and ironically perhaps his least known, is not what virgin territory he discovered on his travels, which was arguably not very much, but what he brought back with him.'[85]

The ludicrous assertion that he – and other British 'explorers' of the time – discovered 'virgin territory' that had been inhabited by indigenous communities for centuries is one repeatedly invoked by colonial and present-day historians. It speaks to the imperial desire to claim and extract, while presenting the agenda as one that benefits all, including the people from whom they steal.

This is surely what drove Bruce to return from his travels with three copies of the Book of Enoch, written in original Ge'ez and a religious text of the Ethiopian Orthodox Church. Bruce gave one copy to the French king, Louis XV, another to the Bodleian Library at Oxford and held onto the third – which eventually passed to the Oxford library anyway. The author of the Historic UK article does not delve into the ethical implications or challenge whether these places have any right to hold these stolen materials (they do not). They only remark that 'amazingly, Bruce brings back not just one copy, nor two, but three! Three copies of this text, which was previously thought to have been lost to the West forever.'[86]

Given that Bruce spent time in 'Ītyop̄yā and at the royal court, there is still some credence to his accounts, but it must be tempered. His unreliability as a source has since been noted, with other historians challenging his capacity to fabricate and his evident pride in his medical knowledge which is marked in his writing.[87] Plus, given that his contacts lay with the Qwarāññā, it's argued that he romanticises the Amhara noble classes while displaying contempt for other ethnic groups, particularly the Oromo people.[88]

It's through Bruce that we learn of the huge wealth of *Däjazmach* Mika'el Sehul, a powerful warlord in Tegray whose ancestors claimed descent from the ruling dynasty. Mika'el was already known to Məntəwwab's court after aiding Iyasu II in maintaining his authority in the final years of his reign.[89] The Tegrey noble was so 'lavish in his money' that 'all Gondär were his friends', making it 'plain' to 'everybody that nothing could stop' his 'growing fortune'.[90] Although we must take Bruce's penchant for exaggeration into account, it seems to be accurate, given Məntəwwab's determination to keep Mika'el onside. Bruce is yet another reminder of the dilemmas posed by using colonial sources: the use they can offer in locating historical figures, while existing as a testimony to coloniality. If we do not unravel their colonial context, we're at risk of repeating their untruths.

Shortly after observing the funeral commemoration for Iyasu II, the ruler's youngest daughter, Aletash, was married into the ruling house of Tegrey through her union with Wäldä Häwaryat, the son of *Däjazmach* Mika'el, on 2 September 1755.[91] Before the nuptials, Mika'el pledged lands to his son alongside many guns, carpets, swords, cows, oxen and enslaved people. It was all sealed in a brief marriage contract, numbering just over 200 words.[92]

As pomp and fanfare swallowed the royal capital, what was also clinched was Mika'el Sehul's all-powerful position.[93] The figure, believed to be around seventy, ended up as the most powerful lord in the empire.[94] Mika'el's newly claimed station even survived the death of his son – and the *itege*'s son-in-law – in 1760.[95] As far as Məntəwwab was concerned, the loyalty of a critical ally had been bought.

What she likely didn't account for was the threat posed by the mother of Iyo'as, the new *atse*.

There was a shift of political power towards Wäbi and her Wällo people.[96] Brought into the fold of national politics by Məntəwwab through the marriage to her late son Iyasu II, the Wällo grew in influence after Iyo'as's ascension – in particular, Wäbi's brothers, Birälé and Lubo.[97] Multiple sources describe an Iyo'as who, when he came of age, was determined to shake the influence of his grandmother and her close confidantes. Increasingly reliant on his maternal relatives, Iyo'as was surrounded by his Wällo kin who supported his attempts to free himself from the *itege*'s dominance.[98]

With historians describing Wäbi as '[taking] the government into her hands, supported by her [Oromo] relatives and tribes-men', it's also possible that Iyo'as's mother was ready to step into authority on her own terms.[99] The elderly Məntəwwab had enjoyed her time as the strategist behind the throne, but, despite her best efforts, the sun was setting on her reign. It was time for *Atse* Iyo'as to take his place, supported or led by a new rising faction, perhaps headed up by a new *itege*.

'Ītyop̣yä's ruling dynasty was split by uncertainty and rivalling kins. So when Məntəwwab's brother Wäldä-Le'ul, the guardian of the empire's sovereign and most powerful figure at court, died in early 1767, the looming crisis saw fit to explode.[100]

For Wäldä-Le'ul's passing epitomised the waning power of the Qwarañña. By the late 1760s, many members of Məntəwwab's kinship network had died or were dying. And with them – particularly Wäldä-Le'ul as *behtwäddäd* – faded their influence over the fractious noble class. Even the loyalty of chieftains of northern 'Ityoṗyā, meant to be bonded to the royal court through marriage, evaporated.[101]

Mәntәwwab leant even more on her powerful allies and extended family. Months after the loss of her brother, Mika'el Sehul was promoted to the title of *ras*, 'a civil military title below the king' and her uncle Géta became the new *behtwäddäd*.[102] It was them she turned to as 1767 came to a close, when it became increasingly clear that the clamour from Wäbi's supporters was not subsiding. In haste, she summoned the newly named *ras* from Tegrey to Gondär.[103] It was Mәntәwwab's great miscalculation.

Mika'el arrived in the royal capital around January 1768 but shortly after, headed to the residence of Géta. He kicked out Mәntәwwab's barely settled uncle and seized the *behtwäddäd* title for himself. Coups, conspiracies and assassinations marked the following few years. Chief among them was the assassination of Iyo'as in 1769 in the Gondär palace, killed for 'treachery towards Mika'el.'[104] It's also suggested by some sources that around this time, the *ras* married Mәntәwwab's widowed daughter, Astér – although others have placed their union earlier, perhaps even happening at the same time as Aletash and Wäldä Häwaryat's ceremony.[105]

Also in 1769, Mika'el placed his own puppet *atse* on the throne, by the name of Yohännes II, the son of Iyasu I the Great and brother of Bäkafa. The murder of Iyo'as spelt the dawn of a new political era in 'Ityoṗyā. It was the end of the Gondärine period and the rise of the *Zämänä-Mäsafent* – the Era of the Princes.[106]

Mәntәwwab had been outmanoeuvred, once and for all.

There are fault lines that run through today's Ethiopia that can be followed back to these foundational dynasties and the hierarchies, systems and values that they established. Crucial events in Ethiopia's history, including the impact of Mussolini's 1930s invasion and the ethnic-based violence spearheaded by Selassie, fed upon pre-existing strains.

We're called upon to interrogate linkages and probe with difficult questions. For example, what does it mean that Məntəwwab's beauty is widely mentioned by historians and chroniclers (her name even translating as 'how beautiful'[107]), perhaps sporting the same features – often mid-tone brown skin, slim noses, large foreheads, lengthy 3A to 3C hair – prized among Amhara and Tigrayans today?[108] How do we appraise the way that colourism, texturism and featurism have established a specific and dominant framing of Ethiopian beauty that has endured centuries?[109]

What about the country's legacy of *rim*, trading and owning enslaved Ethiopians? 'They are hiding the story because they feel ashamed,' Zerfe Argaw, outside her farmstead near the southern town of Dalbo, told the *Guardian* in 2023. 'It is seen as a closed subject; people don't want to talk about it.'[110] You won't find plaques, monuments, inscriptions or museum exhibits that explore domestic enslavement but its marks are everywhere. After Haile Selassie decreed the abolition of enslavement in 1942, it lingered until the rise of the Derg in the mid-seventies. And, even after enslaved people became part of the families of their former masters, their descendants are still positioned as 'impure', with some barred from participating in ceremonies, like funerals, or marrying into other clans and ethnic groups. It's why marrying someone descended from enslaved Ethiopians is seen as 'like a curse'; it's why it's still 'common to hear light-skinned highlanders refer to darker-skinned people from southern Ethiopia as "bariya"'. It means slave.[111] Then, of course, there's the government-led Tigrayan genocide and ensuing conflict.

These are just a few reasons why an 'Ethiopian state' feels like a fallacy to some, and wishful thinking to others.

With stomachs so heavy we fight over who must take the leftovers we can't fathom eating, Mags and I prepare to step out of the restaurant and back into the rush of London streets. First, however, she queries aloud what will be next for the country she once claimed with gusto.

'I know so many people who are no longer going to raise their children as Ethiopian but, rather, their ethnic groups. What does that mean? I used to once feel very safe when I would see [the Ethiopian flag] but now there's an unease because that flag was thrown about in support of the death of Tigrayan people.

'What is "Ethiopianness" going to mean for people?' Her question hangs in the air.

It surely didn't take long for the news to reach her.

Was the loss – the tireless, raging grief – one that she could share with the other woman who had loved Iyo'as? Was Məntəwwab's anguish magnified by the realisation that the power she had worked so hard to establish had been finally wrestled from her? Or did the numbing effect of denial delay such clarity? Did she attempt to gather herself for one last ploy or final alliance?

Perhaps she watched on from the personal villa she had built next to her Qwesqwam church as her usurper, *Ras* Mika'el, swapped in *atse* after *atse* – Yohännes II, Täklä-Häymanot II, Susenyos II – deposing (or killing) each to replace them with the next. Was there any satisfaction when Mika'el and his tyranny were finally defeated in 1771?[112]

When Məntəwwab died, believed to be in 1773, her wish was honoured.[113] She was laid to rest at the church that had once been a symbol of the dizzying heights she had been propelled to and had desperately sought to maintain – for herself, for the Qwaräñña, for the nobility.

The Qemant girl who became an *itege*, then co-ruler, is a pivotal figure in Ethiopia's history. But Məntəwwab, the wife of an *atse* and the 'regent' of two more, learnt a timeless lesson.

All empires and their sovereigns eventually fall; they – and their regimes – always return to the soil.

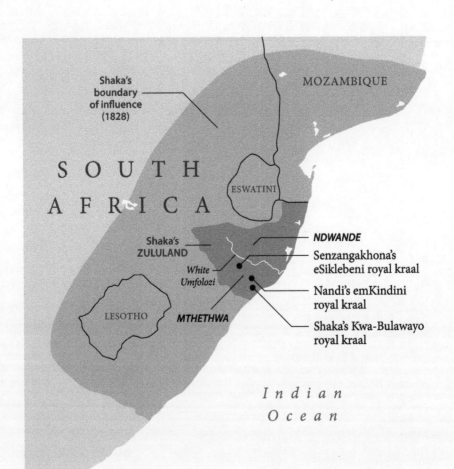

Shaka's
boundary
of influence
(1828)

MOZAMBIQUE

S O U T H
A F R I C A

ESWATINI

NDWANDE

Shaka's
ZULULAND

Senzangakhona's
eSiklebeni royal kraal

White
Umfolozi

Nandi's emKindini
royal kraal

LESOTHO

MTHETHWA

Shaka's Kwa-Bulawayo
royal kraal

Indian
Ocean

CHAPTER 6

Nandi kaBhebhe

The Scorned She-Elephant

The village of Babanango is listed as an ideal stopover for any tourists following the Battlefields route through present-day South Africa's KwaZulu-Natal. The province is home to at least eighty-two battlefields, museums, old fortifications and places of remembrance.[1] Babanango – noted as the highest village in Zululand – is seen in fleeting glimpses as holidaymakers and scholars explore the land that has swallowed the blood of the Zulu, British and Boers for centuries.

A cursory online search lists a variety of results on the Babanango Game Reserve before there are any references to the village or the upper White Umfolozi River Valley in which it sits. Blogs beckon visitors to the reserve which spans over 20,000 hectares with promises of unmatched topography, an eclectic mix of birds, plants, insects, reptiles and mammals, and specialised safari experiences with guides.[2]

But before there were the game lodges with chefs and viewing decks and swimming pools, before the safari vacations and visitors in their 'safari chic', before the game drives and bush walks and stargazing sessions and conservation helicopter flights, there were hills. A rolling expanse of sea-green hilltops reaching for the clouds, each couched in dense, thick foliage. Winding streams breaking up the landscape's uniform colour palette, further punctured by mangrove swamps and the dry browned bristle of the bush.

Soaking in one of the valley's natural baths over 200 years ago,

allowing its waters to clean and caress her, was a woman who had
an encounter that would alter the course of Zulu history forever.

Now, whether King Senzangakhona came across Nandi bathing,
or they crossed paths deep in the bowels of bushland, or while
Senzangakhona and his cohort of young men were out herding
cattle, the story goes that her lauded beauty distracted and intrigued
him and something was set in motion.[3] Interest sparked and lust
roared. However, status was supposed to constrain them. For while
attraction pulled at the pair, neither was a stranger to the rules of
love and sex that bound them – she, the daughter of the chief of the
eLangeni people, and he, the ruler of the Zulu peoples, including
hers.[4]

There was another king above Senzangakhona. Jobe kaKayi of
the Mthethwa sat at the peak of the hierarchy from the close of the
eighteenth century into the dawn of the next, having conquered and
absorbed nearby chiefdoms to strengthen his power. 'Mthethwa'
appropriately translates as 'the one who rules'. The Zulu were one
of a number of communities overseen by the Mthethwa dynasty.
Zulu peoples were part of the wider Nguni ethnic group, tying
them closely – ethnically, linguistically, culturally – to other Nguni
people like the Xhosa and the Swazi. Among those interlocking,
overlapping customs were those of love play.

To sexually fulfil his partner was the greatest satisfaction for a
Nguni man. He revelled in – gloried in – what he was able to give,
rather than receive. It was a prize to lead his lover to the edge of
delicious, unbearable frenzy. He ideally left a trail of sated, bliss-
filled lovers in his wake. The ultimate marker of his success was
to keep multiple wives content as they made a life together, their
homestead consisting of circular, thatched and intricately woven
indu – traditional Zulu home – with each wife's *indu* ordered
hierarchically.[5]

Maybe Nandi invited Senzangakhona to sample the waters with
her or the ruler left the company of his men to speak to the young
woman in her twenties. The details of that first encounter are lost
to time. What is not is that they soon sought out *ama hlay endlela*
in one another's arms – 'the fun of the roads' in IsiZulu.[6] The love

play they embarked on had its own codes of conduct. Penetrative premarital sex was forbidden in traditional Zulu society – the non-penetrative kind, however, was not. As long as it didn't take place between members of the same family group, they were free to whet their appetites.[7]

This external sexual intercourse, where the intimacy of being between another's thighs was enough, had two names: *ukuhlobonga* and *ukusoma*. Virtually synonymous, it was only marital status that set them apart. The latter was to have this form of sex with your own wife, while *ukuhlobonga* was sex between unmarried people – or another's wife. It often took place in secret under the cover of night, its practice deemed 'disgraceful' though traditionally sanctioned.[8] Like lovers locked in rising passion, these traditional codes rub against one another, tangling with one another in a complex web. Though condoned, stigma was never far off.

Women swapped their lovers with regularity, having frequent *ukuhlobonga* with the partner of their choice for a short time, before 'throwing' them for another.[9] Simultaneously, a 'typically well-bred [Zulu] girl' wouldn't 'initiate emotions of love for a man' and before she even considered entertaining his first advances, played the 'hard to get' game in line with cultural expectations.[10]

However, even this type of love play had firm limits – namely, do not lose your head.[11] Even if the casual and unattached nature of *ukuhlobonga* carried a shame-laden taint, it did not contravene Zulu social behaviours. Getting pregnant outside of wedlock did.

When Nandi's stomach began to swell with promises of new life, her network of kin shrank back with pronounced disgust and horror. The young expectant mother, born somewhere around 1760, was quickly learning the repercussions of falling foul of traditional custom. As she moved through one trimester to the next, shame and repudiation marked the pregnancy.

When unmarried Zulu women fell pregnant, they were understood as having been 'damaged' and the prospective father was expected to pay compensation for having committed the offence. The crime was taking what was not his to take, the perceived virginal value of this now tarnished woman, rather than the pregnancy

WHEN WE RULED

itself. Payment in the form of a goat or a cow, for example, would settle the transgression.[12]

When such a case was put forward on Nandi's behalf, it was met with denial. Impossible, she and her family were emphatically told by the clan's elders, the girl is simply harbouring *iShaka*. Pregnancy as the reason for her rounded belly was spurned in favour of an intestinal beetle.[13] Perhaps, they may have thought, this was punishment for Nandi's further transgression, for she had crossed forbidden degrees of kinship. Her mother, Mfunda, was of the Qwabe clan, close relatives of the Zulu; intermarriage between them was taboo.[14] To the minds of those around her, Nandi was reaping the incestual seed she had sowed.

And so when the time came for her to grunt and push, her baby traded her warmth for a society that had little interest in receiving him. Not only would he be named Shaka, a reminder of the beetle that never was, but spelt as 'Chaka', it also meant a poor fellow, a servant, a subordinate.[15]

The product of a sordid union, Shaka entered the world in 1787, his name signifying both his and his mother's prescribed place among their people.

Having let me through its imposing gates, a security guard points out the museum's entrance. Lush ficuses line the all-white exterior of the building, tree trunks and shrub stems alike reach for the favour of the sun as it dazzles over the city of Durban.

During my time here, the building before me is referred to as the Killie Campbell Museum. It is also, more formally, known as the Campbell Collections. 'This home belonged to the descendants of William Campbell and John Blamey, both Byrne settlers who sailed in 1849 and 1850 for the shores of Natal and it was given to the city of Durban by their grandson, William in 1855,' announces a bronze plaque next to the door.

Referring to the building as 'Muckleneuk', a name shared with a Pretoria neighbourhood, the plaque states that it was given in memory of '[William's] parents Sir Marshall and Lady Campbell and of those British settlers who, in great numbers emigrated and made their home in South Africa, in comradeship and unity of purpose with pioneers from other countries.' Outlining that the Campbell dynasty traded their lives in wars against a common enemy, endured severe hardships and devoted their skill and wealth to developing South Africa, the final words etched in the metal plate read: 'They helped to build a nation.'

The sun's rays barely reach across the threshold, and once my eyes adjust to the darkness, staircases and hallways appear, leading to dark rooms I'll later discover are filled with antiques and artefacts, each object heavy with the weight of its own history. It's quiet and empty and as far as I can tell, I'm the sole visitor in the building. The only light comes in the form of my tour guide, a local expert and museologist, a woman with a giggle that dances around the cold corners of the building. I follow her and her laugh through different rooms. She explains the ways in which Zulu women have historically communicated through intricate beadwork, muses over demonisation of traditional healers ('The term "witch doctor" doesn't even make sense, which is it?' she scoffs) and we connect over our common experiences with – and departures from – Christianity.

Over the next couple of days, I drift between the main museum house, the adjoining Africana Library and the bountiful grounds where insects zoom between the outstretched calathea leaves and the vibrant orange points of birds-of-paradise. Birds beckon one another from their palm perches, vocal above me each time I take a break from poring over the library's offerings and steal away for a quick vape.

On my last full day in Durban, I walk through the city in search of my affable museologist, finding her in her office. When I had first explained my research and asked her about Nandi's ill-fated relationship with Senzangakhona, the custodian had told me that when Nandi became pregnant, she had stood up for herself. 'She marched to the royal court and demanded to be married,' the museologist had said. 'Nandi said, "I know who I am and I know that, according to the culture you guys preach, I should be married."' Keenly aware that my time in the city is dwindling, I have many more questions for her.

Our conversation, which spans hours, is paused at times for the museologist to pick up her daughter from school and occasionally to make sure she is, in actual fact, doing her homework. A divorced single mother, she resonates with Nandi's experiences – all at once painful and indicative of the patriarchal structure of Zulu, Xhosa and other Bantu societies to which they both belong. 'The rule in [many African cultures] is that no child should grow from a single parent,' she explains from across her wooden desk. 'When a wife passes on, within two months – maybe even two weeks – the husband must take another wife to tend to these children.'

She uses herself as an example. 'If my husband passes on, I'm not allowed to go home. My husband's brother is supposed to take me as his wife. Why? For the children.' Her face is lined with frustration. 'Can you see why this upsets me?'

Nguni women marry the clan as much as the individual, strengthening intercommunal ties. In a societal system made up of countless clans, access hinges on lineage. If people do not know your clan, they do not know your ancestors, where you are from, nor how you might be associated with them and their clan. Patrilineal inheritance rules the social order of Nguni groups and therefore, a single mother is presented as an abomination.[16]

The museologist describes a culture where there is no uncle and rather, your father's brother is your father; where a woman remains married to a family even in the absence of her husband to sustain his bloodline; where to envelop and absorb kin is a way of life.

So why is it, she asks, that when a woman like Nandi becomes pregnant, it is so easy to let go of her? To disown her, as her father eventually would? Why was it so simple to allow her to slip through integral bonds of kinship?

There would be no wedding feast for Nandi. There was an absence of the usual ceremonial fanfare that would accompany a Zulu bride leaving the home she had always known and joining the family home of her groom. None of the raucous revelry, the heady, snaking scent of *impepho* – incense – nor the sight of mingling families, lips and hips loosened by beer, would follow this bride, already with child, into her marriage with Senzangakhona.[17] After the ruler's denials of paternity had been exhausted and disparaged, Nandi became the ruler's third wife.[18]

As an *umlobokazi* – young or newly wed wife – Nandi was entrusted into the care of Mkabi, Senzangakhona's 'Great Wife'. Not only was it largely Mkabi's role to oversee the younger wives as they adjusted to life at the eSiklebeni royal kraal, but she was also closely related to Nandi's mother.[19] But even the interventions of this motherly figure could do little about the shifting sands on which Nandi and her now-husband's relationship was built. Though they'd reconcile enough to have a second child, this time a daughter named Nomcoba, it was a union too strained for any form of intimacy or love play to remedy. Historians have bandied around theories for what would lead to Nandi and Shaka's departure from the kraal – from hypotheses on Nandi's disagreeability and temper to beliefs that a six-year-old Shaka allowed a dog to kill one of his father's favourite animals during his herding duties.[20]

Whether they fled or were expelled remains a point of historical dispute, but it marked the beginning of a mother's hunt for a welcome, some sort of embrace, for her and her children. However, there was little relief from the insults and mockery that met them wherever they tried to settle, whether among the Qwabe people of Nandi's mother or the Mhlongo kin of her father.[21] Not only was she a dishonourable bride, but in the eyes of her peers, Nandi's shame was compounded by failing in her duties as a wife. She had violated the notion of *kuyobekezelwa emendweni* – a woman should always persevere in her marriage.[22]

It was from within the belly of hostility that Nandi raised Shaka. She observed him turn from a child to a teenager, bore witness to his breaking voice and spurting growth from the margins of communities that wanted nothing to do with them. When he was fifteen, Shaka was taken to his father's kraal for puberty ceremonies but the youth's refusal to fully participate only fanned hungry belligerent flames.[23] Nandi and Shaka were made to leave once more, returning to the enduring search for somewhere to call home.

*

Whenever her gaze fell upon Ngwadi, gabbling and gurgling as young children are prone to do, perhaps the sight of her son sometimes reminded Nandi of the intimacy and companionship she had found again, after Senzangakhona. Of course, the fateful meeting with the Zulu ruler and all its enduring consequences were surely never far from her mind, but she had made a life of sorts for herself and her children. During her time among the Qwabe, she had found the embrace of a man named Ngendeyana, at least for a time. Though the animosity among the people of Nandi's mother would prove too much to bear, the fruits of that union had given her Ngwadi, her third child, just as the 1800s drew closer.[24] Then, she relocated her family again.

In the quiet moments between caring for her younger children and maintaining their home – cooking, fetching water, tending to livestock – maybe Nandi paused to consider just how much it had taken to get her family to the refuge of the Mthethwa people. Under the ruling hand of Jobe, the Mthethwa controlled the coastal area while the other dominant force of the Ndwandwe led by their ruler Zwide controlled the north. With the Mthethwa still the overseers of tributaries like the Zulu, under this blanket of power, Nandi and her children were more or less untouchable.[25] That wouldn't change even when power swapped hands, from Jobe to his son Dingiswayo after the latter conspired, with his brother Tana, against their father. Tana was eventually put to death for his role while Dingiswayo escaped execution by fleeing, returning only around 1806 to seize the reins of power when Jobe died.[26]

Perhaps Nandi also thought about what she had wanted for her firstborn, versus the reality that faced them. What Shaka's childhood might have looked like if it hadn't been pockmarked with contempt and ridicule. Much of the bullying was at the hands of older herd boys, their grievances with Shaka had likely trickled down to them from elders, sprouting from hushed, critical admonitions of his mother.[27] Their people had demonstrated that their scorn wasn't reserved just for Nandi, they had plenty in reserve for her offspring too.

It is unlikely the eLangeni woman could have imagined what

the future would look like for Shaka, then a growing 16-year-old on the cusp of manhood. That within six years, before her very eyes, her son would ascend the ranks of Dingiswayo's army and establish himself as a distinguished commander.[28] That he would become renowned for his actions that included spurning the taking of prisoners and killing all wounded enemies as well as his own incapacitated soldiers.[29]

Shaka's ascent carries the markers of an epic hero narrative. Padded out with fictionalisations around his birth and later military prowess, we're presented with an illegitimate heir, cast out by his kin, who excels as a warrior.[30] Our imaginations are captured by the prince who, against the adverse and scandalous conditions of his birth, paved a path to the Zulu throne. The typology of the epic hero – an archetype in which greatness rests on admired characteristics like warring ability, undertaking perilous travels, bravery and humility – demands that little can stand in the way of said impervious hero, not even an official heir.[31]

After the death of Senzangakhona around 1816, the successor of the Zulu kingship was named – his son, Sigujana.[32] With the blessing and military backing of his mentor, Dingiswayo, Shaka made the journey back to Zululand, the land from which he had been ousted. He relieved his half-brother of the throne he had barely warmed.[33] Shaka, with the help of Dingiswayo, had Sigujana assassinated. Bolstered by the support of his allies, Shaka kaSenzangakhona seized the title that he had never been considered fit to wear: ruler of the Zulu people.[34]

What was once a clan grew into an empire under Shaka. The innumerable Nguni-speaking groups in the KwaZulu-Natal area were swept up within the orbit of his power.[35] Building upon his warring experience after almost a decade spent among the Mthethwa fighters, the new ruler created disciplined regiments, grouped into military kraals.[36] With innovative weaponry and fighting techniques, in 1816, Shaka laid the foundations for his rule which would last over a decade. Guided by his hand, the Zulu grew from 2,000 people to a state deploying an army of 40,000 into warfare at a time.[37]

The term *Zulu* itself morphed following Shaka's ascendancy. It had once referred only to a clan that recognised Zulu I kaMalandela as its founding ancestor. It came to encompass the hundreds of clans under the remit of the Zulu monarchy.[38] Though these clans would still retain their individual chiefs, they were now one people answering to one man. When Dingiswayo succumbed to the battlefield floor in 1818, killed at the hands of the Ndwandwe's Zwide in the tall shadows of the Ngome Forest, Shaka filled the void left by his tutor. He absorbed the scattered Mthethwa forces within growing Zulu armies, implicitly announcing that his time as a protégé was now firmly concluded, the apprentice was to become the master.[39]

There's a satisfactory redemption arc bedded into Shaka's narrative, a figure who, despite abject rejection, endured and then returned to conquer. The fantastical and bleak conditions that moulded Shaka and his reign captured nineteenth-century European imaginations, as seen with the accounts of Western explorers like Nathanial Isaacs and Henry Francis Fynn.[40] The wandering and suffering of Nandi and Shaka culminating in the centralisation of power around the latter was a rousing tale, one ripe for retelling and embellishment.

Shaka's single-minded approach and military acumen earned him a host of titles. 'Shaka the Great', 'Shaka the Conqueror', 'Emperor Shaka', 'Africa's Greatest Commander', 'Father of the Zulu Nation' are words readily tied to his legacy.

There is another word associated with the Zulu ruler: *Mfecane*. And, in Nguni tongues, it means 'the great crushing', 'destruction' and 'genocide'.

'Mfecane,' says the museologist sombrely, its utterance bouncing off the plain walls of her brown-toned office. 'That's when the tribes were killing each other, it's how we even learnt about other tribes.'

As with much of his legacy, controversy and debate swirls around Shaka's involvement in the *Mfecane* which took place in the 1820s and into the next decade. Old states were defeated, annexed to others or forced to uproot their traditional localities and establish themselves in new areas. Whole village populations were taken in to captivity or bluntly annihilated as Shaka and the Zulu greedily swallowed the land of Southern Africa.[41] Shaka's desire to strengthen his kingdom – against the looming threat of the numerically superior Ndwandwe and a peripheral albeit encroaching white European presence – engulfed the region.[42] To what degree Shaka and the Zulu were the cause of the *Mfecane*, however, remains a bed of vigorous inquiry.

One historical position on the *Mfecane* is that the turmoil and violence in the region was the result of a complex mesh of factors. These included increasing inequalities within and between Southern African societies, a series of environmental crises which led to competition over natural resources and trade, resultant vulnerability to drought-induced famine, and vying over the remaining fertile land.[43] The stage was set for a leader, like Shaka, to soak up the weaker groups. Assimilation among the Zulu was the only proffered option; it could be chosen voluntarily or on the pain of death.

Interpretations of Shaka's life regularly highlight the terror and violence that have characterised his rule. Historians offer up details, sometimes seemingly with relish, that paint a bloodthirsty, despotic and authoritarian ruler. One historian says that he enforced a politic of exhaustingly long celibacy upon his warriors and was followed by an entourage of slayers who would crush skulls at the nod of his head.[44] Another posits that Shaka's soldiers were allowed to have sexual intercourse but were forbidden to impregnate their lovers, traced to the ruler's fixation with pregnancy. They suggest that Shaka would not allow any woman made pregnant by him to live and was said to have 'cut a pregnant woman open' to see how the foetus lay in the womb.[45]

All and any truth, however, is tangled in the imperialist agenda of the colonial historians who relayed these details. We must unpick the imperial interests that underpin the analyses before we can even attend to the historical actors. But often, the damage is enduring and malignant.

Despite their now largely disputed eyewitness accounts,

aforementioned British explorers Isaacs and Fynn – the latter to
a greater degree – have long been positioned as experts on all
things Zulu and Shaka. This is as a result of their travels and time
reportedly spent with Shaka himself.[46] When the pair laboured
over their manuscripts in 1832, in a letter, Isaacs offered his fellow
adventurer some advice: 'Make [Shaka] out as bloodthirsty as you
can... it all tends to swell up the work and make it interesting.'[47]

Isaacs' *Travels and Adventures in Eastern Africa* was published
four years later, introducing the British reading public to the Zulu
people and forming the basis for popular perception.[48] Meanwhile,
Fynn's manuscript – littered with inconsistencies, omissions and
inflations – was finished in 1840. It then underwent substantial
on-and-off editing between 1905 and 1942, before another round
of edits by a different editor in 1946 which spanned a further four
years. Finally fit for the printing press, *The Diary of Henry Francis
Fynn* was published in 1950.[49] South African historian Dan Wylie
asserts that the 'diary', since its publication, became 'the paramount,
and until recently largely unquestioned, source on Shaka's famous
reign.'[50] Alongside catapulting the two authors to prominence in
their field, accounts like these also underscored growing colonial
assertions: that only European intervention could restore peace and
security to the region.[51]

Shaka, his reign and the Mfecane come to us distorted and aug-
mented, but it doesn't diminish the displacement, destruction and
annihilation of Southern African peoples at his hands, in service
to his own security. Shaka was trying to become president, the
museologist would tell me. And if so, Nandi was his first lady.

Dark brown bodies, adorned with beaded regalia, anointed with
sweat and dust, gyrated in time to drumbeats. The striking of
spears – into the ground, against shields – also formed part of
the consuming cacophony. The gathered people absorbed the
reverberations and emitted them as chants from deep within. The
smell of cooking bull drifted between their moving limbs. This was
an annual undertaking, a yearly release, as they ushered in the first
days of the harvest season. During the *Umkhosi* – Festival of First

Fruits – congregants watched as crops were sampled by their chiefs.
They took in the might of their army, with every warrior required
to attend the ceremony. No Zulu would even dare to harvest their
crops in advance of the precise timing of the *Umkhosi*.[52] Together,
with one voice, they revelled in the power and wealth of both their
sovereign and nation before commencing the harvest.

What could a ruler like Shaka do but stand before them and soak
it all in? The weight and glory of the tradition had preceded him and
would long succeed him.[53] Behind him, year on year, overlooking
the parade and the fanfare, would've sat the royal court. Courtiers,
distinguished chiefs, Shaka's siblings would've been just a handful
of those present on a royal dais with Queen Mother Nandi.[54]

Looking out at the mass of Zulu, bodies electric with jubilance,
surely Nandi could not have foreseen that those crows of contempt
would one day morph into hoots of pride. That she'd own a herd of
thousands of bleating cattle, housed in her own great royal kraal at
emKindini.[55] That she, Shaka and her other children would move
from orbital obscurity to the centre of the nucleus.

Watching on as her firstborn fought and killed and expanded,
Nandi would later be understood as being wholly influential over
him.[56] She has been credited as a voice of moderation and stability
with her counsel, with her attempts to warn him of his mounting
enemies.[57] And blame has been placed squarely with her for Shaka's
shortcomings.

For example, Zulu scholar Jordan K. Ngubane cited Nandi as the
reason why her son would never marry. 'Nandi saw herself and her
children as the victims of the greed of the aristocratic families of
her time,' he wrote. 'She awakened a hatred for the aristocracy in
Shaka which made it impossible for him to want to leave behind
any heirs.'[58] Given the ways that lineage and tradition had defined
the contours of their lives, it's possible that, as some historians
have suggested, Nandi desperately craved the security of respect-
ability. That she actually wanted a married Shaka with a designated
heir to continue the monarchy. On this subject, however, Shaka
appeared unshakeable.

This aside, Henry Francis Fynn claimed that Nandi was able to

move her son with her tears. It's an assertion made all the more
stark given the ruthless brute of a conqueror he beguiled his
twentieth-century readers with.[59] An 1824 portrait of the Zulu leader was published in the book of his friend, Nathaniel Issac, and
is attributed to James King. Named *Chaka King of the Zoolus*, a
tall, muscular and dark-skinned man in feathered-trimmed cloths
props up a spear in one hand and a hefty shield longer than his
body in the other. That same image, claimed to be the most accurate
depiction of Shaka, hangs today in one of the dark ground-floor
rooms of the Campbell Museum.[60]

Meanwhile, nestled in the museologist's office chairs, the Bantu
woman had told me that Shaka was moulded by his mother, that
when he went back to claim his father's throne, that he knew who
he was and what he wanted – vengeance.

For her, the maltreatment of Nandi would have been pain-
fully obvious to Shaka – with or without her direct influence.
'Senzangakhona was supposed to at least acknowledge Nandi
and make her a wife, even if she was the one hundredth wife.
He should've built Shaka a home, given him his roots and a space,
but instead, he rejected them.'

With a pause, amusement in her eyes, the museologist had
continued, 'So when Shaka took over the throne, he refused to get
married because he could see that it was oppressive.' It was with a
snort that she had delivered her next words. 'What did you expect
coming from a scorned woman?'

Shaka does not just come to us in colonial tomes or portraits,
but in the voices of his people too, because wherever Shaka went,
imbongi followed. These court poets regularly shouted a string
of praise in his presence – the practice of *izibongo*. These poems
impart both admiration and admonition.

Izibongo stretches far beyond the royal kraal. While not everyone
in Zulu, Xhosa and related societies is an *imbongi*, everyone uses
the tradition in everyday life. Academic Somadoda Fikeni describes
the practice as one that pulls together strands of collective memory,
offering spiritually centred oral narratives steeped in indigenous
wisdom.[61] Through *izibongo*, individuals are connected to a galaxy

of ancestral guidance and recollection. The writings stand as both societal conscience and historical record.

Within the genre, criticism is just as crucial as encouragement, with *izibongo* serving as a means of social control. It cautions, it advises, it exalts. However, scholars like Professor Nompumelelo Zondi find distortion within the current *izibongo* writings under study: they seem to suggest *only* the negative connotations of the royal women in question. While royal male family members are lavished with honour and status as would be expected, those of Nandi, for example, cast her as no different from any other woman in the kingdom.[62]

Nandi's translated praises begin with the following lines:

> *USomqeni!* Father of laziness!
> *UMathanga kawahlangani,* She whose thighs do not close,
> *Ahlangana ngokubon'umyeni.* They close at the sight of her husband.
> *UGedegede lwasenhla nenkundla.* Loud voiced one from the upper part of the court.[63]

Zondi suggests that her praises were composed before Shaka's rise to power because, even taking into account their intended critical nature, they don't reflect the status Nandi acquires later in life as 'mother of the nation.' Instead, they embody a wave of disapproval directed towards the woman who had reached beyond her station and squeezed her way into the upper echelons.[64]

History books, journals and articles have echoed the malignment. Sightings of her are spotted in the footnotes of tomes dedicated to Shaka, brief glances in extended studies on her son. Even perfunctory mentions pass scathing judgement: Nandi was headstrong, improper and physically unattractive. It was she who had singled out Senzangakhona and impertinently led the courtship. It would be promiscuity – but also sexual frigidity – and a violent temper that forced her expulsion.[65] Her position is one of precarity, straddling being seen and unseen.

An analogy that the museologist used in our first conversation about Nandi has stayed with me since. As we stood before the drawn interpretation of Shaka, minutes after I had stepped through the museum entrance and introduced myself, the custodian had cocked her head in thought before comparing Nandi's positioning to that of Mary, mother of Jesus. She drew parallels between how these women are often engaged with as mere vessels for the greatly revered men they brought into the world. She required little documentation outside of her one great act. She had served her purpose, her destiny fulfilled.

Langazana, Senzangakhona's fourth wife, was said to retain a clear memory until her death in 1884. She was described as 'the richest living repository of Zulu history from before the rise of the nation's power to its zenith and final collapse.'[66] Her passed-on recollections paint a picture of the Zulu ruler and his mother in the 1820s.

Perhaps with hands that had begun to show signs of trembling and a sun-weathered face, a greying Nandi was hovering around sixty. Already tangled in grief over the passing of Mfunda, his maternal grandmother, Shaka concerned himself with Nandi's health and procuring elixirs for the means of extending her life.[67] Meanwhile, the throb and grind of her ageing joints may have underscored her own mortality, emphasising the need for an official royal grandson. The children of her second son, Ngwadi, simply wouldn't do. However, that heir would never come, although historians – Zulu and Western – allude to a son of Shaka's who would flee the kingdom.[68] Could the loss of this elusive grandson – the erosion of a coveted dynasty and secured bloodline – have contributed to her decline? Or had the malaise that had been threaded through Nandi's life finally taken its toll?

Zulu oral history suggests that Shaka – a man said to have put to death the women who fell pregnant by him – discovered that Nandi had allowed one of his lovers, a Cele woman by the name of Mbuzikazi, to flee with their son, sending him into a deadly rage against his mother.[69] Such a detail would have, surely, been picked up by Fynn with relish, however, the British explorer only attributed her death to 'dysentery', which is a type of gastroenteritis.

Historians have also since pointed to the possibility that Shaka killing his mother was a rumour spread by a rival to trouble the devotion of the Zulu people to their leader.[70]

Whether she died by Shaka's hands or subsided into a claiming coma as has also been suggested, Nandi would exhale her last on 10 October 1827.

Pained shrieks sliced through the air. Led perhaps by Shaka's own agony or remorse, bereft lamentations were offered up by the Zulu in their tens of thousands as they gathered to mourn. Those sorrowful expressions floated upwards as if to accompany Nandi on her transition from the earthly.

Day and night blurred as the cries became more frantic and the gathering's number swelled.[71] It shifted into frenzy, however, when Shaka ordered several men executed on the spot – their displays of grief had not been satisfactorily respectful of his late mother.[72] A performance of sufficient anguish was now required, and falling short was fatal. Historians believe that 7,000 Zulu were killed in the massacre that ensued.[73]

In the wake of Nandi's death, the mass slaughter was combined with a slew of repressive decrees. No cultivation of the land was allowed for a year. No milk was allowed to be ingested and if it was drawn from the cow, it was to be poured into the ground. All women found to be pregnant thereafter during the year of mourning would, with their husbands, be put to death.[74] The brutal excess of this grieving resulted in widespread starvation, and it would only be remedied when Shaka realised that they were, in fact, extreme. One historian suggests, however, that the mourning didn't arise from his own choices but from his counsel who had decided on which form the people's mourning should take.[75]

'I have conquered the world but lost my mother,' the young Zulu king purportedly uttered, lost in folds of sorrow. However, his grip on that world was becoming ever-tenuous. The furore around Nandi's passing was an early indicator of the instability of the monarchy. Coupled with the steadily building Boer and British presence that would soon engulf their lands, destruction loomed ahead. The Zulu Kingdom, as established under Shaka, would soon be no more.

And sure enough, just a year after his mother's death, Shaka was assassinated at the hands of his half-brothers, Dingane and Mhlangana, on 24 September 1828. The former took the Zulu throne for himself, with his brother's deadly manifestations of grief surely a welcome avenue for usurpation.

Despite a rule imprinted with blood, Shaka and his Zulu nation continued to garner popularity, particularly spanning the 1940s through to the early seventies. African writers understood him as a nation-builder, a man who unified his people, which only galvanised movements of independence and developing Black consciousness.[76] Léopold Sédar Senghor, Senegal's first president and prominent theoretician of Négritude, wrote a poem entitled 'Chaka' – pulling from Sotho novelist Thomas Mofolo's eponymous work – in which he understood Shaka as a martyr who died for the love of his people; a symbol of African defiance against European imperialism.[77] His cultural significance would continue through to the twenty-first century, with Durban's primary international airport named 'King Shaka' following its popularity at public hearings.

During our conversations, the museologist described a revamp of the 1986 Shaka Zulu film that the museum had been involved in. At a press event during the film's launch in Durban, she recalled a descendant from Nandi's family standing to accuse the parties involved with the remake of sidelining Nandi. Before he was shut down, he asserted that they continued to present her as little more than a flighty, promiscuous supporting act.[78] If Shaka is readily celebrated as a king, then what did that make the mother who bore him?

My time spent at the Campbell Collections has been necessary, its usefulness made starker by the little I gleaned at other locations. For example, when I couldn't find information at the Old Court House Museum in downtown Durban, the staff there directed me to the white neo-Cape Dutch style house. And when I would later travel just over an hour to the further in-land city of Pietermaritzburg, I'd find one inadvertent reference to Nandi in KwaZulu-Natal Museum's Animal section as a result of her royal title of *iNdlovukazi*: the great she-elephant. The kind and quiet librarian who oversees the Africana Library at the Campbell location also didn't think that they possessed much on the woman of the eLangeni people, piling books about Shaka before me. But it's here that I've been most able to stretch and reach for Nandi within the gaps.

And yet, I'm still curious about the family whose last name can be seen at every turn. Posters and portraits around the sprawling property – which she would donate to the University of KwaZulu-Natal alongside their materials – depict Killie Campbell at different stages of her life. Donning chaste nineteenth-century outfits and unsmiling expressions with her brother, William, in their youth. Gravity tugging at her features in old age as she poses behind a desk, heaving bookshelves in the background completing the tableau. The images give little away and, as the museologist and I wrap up our final conversation, I broach the topic of the Campbells.

'Marshall Campbell was a colonialist to the core,' she says firmly of the father of Killie and William and original owner of the house. Her words and gesticulations paint a picture of the man who emigrated from Britain, who history would remember as a senator for Natal, sugar cane magnate and, later, as a knight for services to the country. 'He was one of the founders of Durban and he wrote the segregation rules,' she says plainly.

She tells me of a township, just outside Durban, named after Marshall Campbell: KwaMashu. *The place of Marshall.* As white imperialists began rolling out their apartheid plans, Black people were relocated to the outskirts of sprawling cities. 'It was the whites on the good land, Indians next to the whites, coloureds [people with mixed Black Bantu, white European and/or Asian ancestry] in a hidden place and then it was the Blacks.' It's why she was initially impressed to learn that Campbell had built houses on part of his sugarcane field for Black South Africans, the newly formed township named for him as a token of celebratory gratitude.

There's a bashfulness about the museologist as she conveys her naivety. 'It took a white man to wake me up. I thought [Campbell] had fought apartheid.' For one day she had started talking to this man at a function, mentioning her line of work and her gratitude for Campbell Senior's contributions. He had told her that those tiny houses built on Campbell land were called matchboxes.

'Why?' she asks me, as she leans forward, as if my attention isn't already and completely hers. 'Because after five p.m., there were policemen who would go into the township every day to count the heads.'

She pauses, mild disgust pulling at her lips. 'The man asked me, "Was it out of love or was it a control system?"' The dots began to connect for the custodian and she repeats her fellow party guest's words to me. 'It doesn't matter how wealthy you are – you would never take your land and just give it away just like that.'

The revelations wouldn't stop there. The energy and warmth I've come to associate with the museologist dip further as she continues.

'If you walk the halls and corridors, eventually, you will find shackles.' Her voice is thick with sorrow. 'I almost cried. There are shackles in the museum right now.'

She had only discovered them a few months before we met. Those shackles, unforgiving metal edges for the purpose of restraining and cutting into tender Black skin, went hand-in-hand with her further examination of the museum basement. Never having come across information that even hinted at people being enslaved on Campbell property, the museologist had simply assumed that it was a storage space. That was, until she took it in for herself. The high walls, the outside locks, more shackles, the windows and doors that can only be opened from the outside.

'That's the sick truth about the museum,' she utters. Her words are heavy to say and difficult to hear, but it's harder to see it on her person. She carries a certain disbelief merged with betrayal that she has unknowingly spent so much time in a house that was a prison to her ancestors, and maybe even a final resting place.

It's coded into another bitter truth: that whenever you scratch away at official narratives, with intention and ferocity, you'll find accounts that you've long been persuaded to turn away from.

Below the Campbell legacy of nation-building and service, you find traces of enslaved Black Africans forced into servitude. Peeking within Shaka's glorified reign, you find hosts of displaced and massacred peoples. And couched under the celebrations of his legacy, you find a mother whose image has been warped by misogyny and sexual shame – Nandi, the woman who moulded him.

CHAPTER 7

Ranavalona I

The Anti-Imperialist Punisher

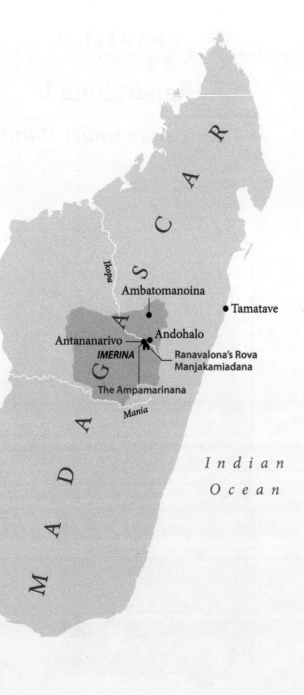

It was the cries outside that would alert them. The noise of gathered throngs baying for justice, blood or both, their raised voices pelting the accused's home.

'The guilty shall die, while the innocent will live,' they exclaimed with fervour. Whether facing charges of sorcery, treachery or simply the possession of bad character, the refrain would follow the accused as they were led away by a high-ranking spiritual leader. The charged individual would have little choice but to follow the practitioner to an isolated house.[1]

A plate of boiled rice, cooked on nearby flames, would be placed before the accused. Not eating was not an option: it was obligatory to choke the grains down throats tightened by peril. Meanwhile, the practitioner was busy preparing the *tangena*. The fruit of a shrub harvested in the coastal forests of present-day Madagascar, its *kebona* – the bitter, almond-like kernel within – is poisonous. Ground into powder or shaved like flecks of nutmeg, the *tangena* would be mixed with water.[2] This, alongside three pieces of chicken skin – each perhaps the size of a large coin – were placed before the accused. After the plain rice, they were to ingest the *tangena* and the chicken skins.

The premise was simple. As the practitioner lay hands on the charged individual, imploring the *tangena* to reveal all, there were only a few possible outcomes. If the poison seized hold of the accused, killing them, they were always guilty.[3] If they retched but all of the chicken skins did not reappear, they were still considered guilty, potentially a *mamosavy* – a person possessed by dark forces – and execution normally awaited.[4] The reappearance of all three skins was their only salvation. Vomiting the slivers of chicken was a sign that the *tangena* had seen fit to preserve their life and no further action was to be taken. They could return home, carried by the jubilation, singing, dancing, and imminent feasting of their companions. 'E tonga e he, tonga re ny soa tsy mandaingia.' *Oh, behold, here comes the guiltless one ... who tells no lies.*[5]

Before their families, their people and their ruler, they had proven their innocence. But there is one ruler in particular that the *tangena* method is most closely associated with. One ruler who

employed the practice liberally across her reign. And her name was
Ranavalona I, *mpanjaka* – ruler in Malagasy – of Imerina.

Hasina historically bound the people of Imerina and it's a belief
system that we in the West, particularly historians, have continu-
ously struggled to conceptualise.

Perhaps it lies in the intangible, unfixed nature of *hasina* which
flows as an energy – described as an electric current – which
circulates between places and people.[6] Although each individual
is believed to possess innate *ziny* (personality) they can also be
bestowed with *hasina*. The energy can be found in groves, springs
and all manner of natural sites that proliferate across the island of
Madagascar. It can be easily transmitted, whether radiated from
the earth, communicated in a look or a touch, or flowing through
speech.[7] Tombs belonging to a kinship group is where the most
hasina is accumulated, with the final resting place of the *razana*
(ancestors) buzzing with the *hasina* they all collected over their
lifetimes. As such, it is unequally distributed: because of their proximity to the ancestors, elders claim the most *hasina* in Malagasy
society.[8]

Any success a person experiences has been enabled by *hasina*.
They learn that the land doesn't belong to the living, it belongs
to the *razana*: it is they who are its owners, who approve and
disapprove of marriages, and whom the patterns of society are
dictated by.[9] Among the Merina people, all success was nurtured
by the collective and sanctified by *hasina*.[10] This was how the sacred
stream flowed – until it was diverted by the monarchy.

Mpanjaka Andriamasinavalona's (r. 1675–1710) Imerina Kingdom
was populated by *rovas* – fortified royal compounds – which sat
atop the hills of the island's central highlands. When it was time
to think about the future of the realm, he decided to divide it into
quadrants among his four favourite sons. We now know he made
a grave error.[11]

Whatever unity he had sought – some historians suggest he
believed four sub-kingdoms ruled by four brothers would be
better defended against outsiders than just one – was undone

by the decades of infighting and conflict.[12] Imerina wouldn't
be re-unified under a single ruler until 1785 with the advent of
Andrianampoinimerina's reign.[13] It wasn't just his conquest and
consolidation of the highlands that signalled winds of change. He
overthrew rulers through military campaigns and sought treaties
with others, he returned the political status to the conquered city
of Antananarivo by making it his capital and, crucially, Andrianampoinimerina sought to commandeer *hasina*.

The ruler placed himself at the top of the hierarchy and codified
the ways in which *hasina* were presented – primarily through him.
In return for the 'superior' *hasina* bestowed upon Merina peoples
from their ancestors, they offered 'inferior' *hasina* in the form of
material goods. These were intended for the ancestors but now,
they passed through an intermediary – the *mpanjaka*.[14] A trans-
actional relationship emerged, one that greatly benefited the ruler.
While the passing on of the spiritual offerings to the ancestors
is not in question, the material 'inferior' *hasina* offerings – rice,
cattle, muskets and piasters [units of currency] – remained in this
world under Andrianampoinimerina.[15] Not only did it strengthen
his individual power and political authority, but it also exacerbated class disparity and economic inequality.

I'd later to be told that the literal geography of Madagascar
reflects class status, built on a historic Merina caste structure rooted
in descent. The *racout, mainty* or *andevo* formed the lowest-ranked
caste and normally occupied the southern and coastal lands of the
kingdom. They were enslaved people – and their descendants –
who were transported to the island from the sixteenth century
onwards to work on plantations, mainly hailing from East Africa
including present-day Mozambique and the Kirimba Islands.[16] They
were referred to as *olona* – 'lost people' – because they did not have
tombs for their dead, burying them hurriedly within twenty-four
hours and under the cover of night 'like burying a dog', one *andevo*
person is recorded commenting.[17] Without tombs, their kinspeople
who passed away could not achieve ancestral status. And no *razana*
meant no downward-flowing *hasina* for descendants, compound-
ing the malignment of the *andevo* caste.

Meanwhile, the *hova*, or 'the middle of the mountain', secured their status at the expense of the *andevo*. Where the *andevo* were enslaved, the *hova* were free. They owned land and traded the goods produced from the labour of the unfree.[18] While a *hova* could be punished for a crime by being enslaved, they still remained set apart from *andevo* status. They became *zaza-hova*; enslaved yet shielded by protective privilege afforded them through lineage.[19]

And above both, figuratively and literally, sat the caste of nobles and royals: the *andriana* who occupied the highlands. Ranavalona I's caste. Ruling over their principalities, the *andriana* led ceremonial rituals and were the only caste allowed to become soldiers of the kingdom until recruitment was later widened to include the *hova*.[20] Largely characterised as being of Austronesian descent – descending from the Javanese or Malay – their presumed superiority over the other groups on the island ran across these ethnic lines.[21] Four centuries on, the depth of these divides are still visible in Madagascar today.

The cheerful driver who picks me up from the Ivato International Airport steers our way to Antananarivo's city centre, the car's tyres stirring up whirls of dust. He gestures at the sights of Antananarivo beyond the windows, offering me Malagasy words then asking how I would define them in English. On our way to the city, we pass cattle grazing next to rice paddy fields and tall piles of crops ready to be threshed.

Before Antananarivo was born, the locality was called Analamanga. *Anala* means 'forest' and *manga* translates as 'blue', reflecting the lush landscape that engulfs the island under cerulean skies.[22] Once, all that land had belonged to the Vazimba people.

We cannot separate the original occupiers of the land from Malagasy fear, projections and conjecture – the ideological accompaniment to colonising an indigenous population. We cannot be sure of their features or origins, as physical descriptions seek to extol the Vazimba's wickedness, ignorance and primitivity. Their 'level of culture' was claimed to be 'quite limited' and, despite having made a home of the Analamanga region, 'they did not know how to unite in a single kingdom.'[23] Such characterisations offer license for usurpation: settlers always believe that they can and will make better use of the land of the dispossessed. Therefore, when the Vazimba were forced out towards the west of the island, with their kingdoms in the highlands destroyed, it was simply the natural order of things.[24]

Their expulsion and subsequent expunging makes it possible to question if the Vazimba people ever existed. 'Myth or reality?' prompts the title of one article. One Malagasy man I met would tell me that there are no Vazimba that he knows of today. It's likely, however, that they intermarried with the incoming Merina popu-lation, particularly given that the ruler credited with driving out the indigenous population – Andriamanelo (c.1540–75) – is said to have been of both Vazimba and *hova* descent.[25]

The area became Antananarivo and grew into the beating heart of the Imerina kingdom. *Tanàna* – village or city – and *arivo* – thousand – gave the city both a name and a meaning, for it would be referred to as the city of a thousand warriors. Centuries later, it is the capital of Madagascar, affectionately shortened to 'Tana'.

The expanses of green open space shrink once our car joins queues of traffic snaking into the city. Street vendors weave in be-tween the cars, exhibiting sunglasses, fans and snacks for sale. Our vehicle crawls past gated and guarded institutions, like Western international schools and different EU residences. The imposing, sleek security around the buildings feels at odds with the dusty road that children are walking in with bare feet or sliders, the gates of metal keeping them at arm's length.

Today, Merina people are considered to be from or based in Tana but as a metropolis, there are many passing through, coming in and out of the city. Merina is just one of the eighteen established ethnic groups among the Malagasy. There are the Betsimisaraka on the east coast of Madagascar, who are often fishermen or vanilla farmers, and were said to emerge from the union of an English pirate and a princess from Anteva. A host of Sakalava communi-ties can be found from the south-west to the north of the island, descended from Bantu peoples on the continent, making them the second-largest ethnic group in the country. The small south-eastern Antanosy group who live on rice, cassava and fruit. The Bezanozano who are remembered for their role as slave traders but, today, are known as the island's coal producers. The Antefasy – which translates as 'those who live in the sand' of the hot and dry parts of south-east Madagascar – who were enslaved and killed by the Merina around the nineteenth century.[26]

The Merina were one of many on this floating rock but, through a ceaseless campaign of violence, displacement and enslavement, forced themselves to the top of the hierarchy. They stayed there through the introduction of social and political institutions which reinforced centralised rule. This included a council of twelve *sampy*, guardians of the state amulets which protect the power of the court.[27] Over time, the Merina established themselves as the island's true, divinely intended monarchs. Rabodoandrianampoinimerina – also known as Ramavo and, later, Ranavalona I – was never intended to be one of them.

Her ascendancy was set in motion when Radama I, the son of Imerina's great unifier in Andrianampoinimerina, died towards the end of July 1828. He left behind a number of wives, including Ramavo, believed to be his most senior wife – and one of his least favoured – out of the dozen or so women who called him their spouse.[28]

Their particular union had come about after Ramavo's father, Andriantsalamanjaka – who ruled over the village of Ambato-manoina to the north-east of Antananarivo – warned Andrian-ampoinimerina about an attempt on his life.[29] In gratitude, the latter adopted the young Ramavo, born in 1788, as a daughter and designated her as a future wife to his son (and her cousin), Radama.[30] Any offspring from the union, he ruled, would take precedence in matters of succession, perhaps aided by Ramavo's mother – Rabodonandriantompo – also being a royal cousin. On Andrianampoinimerina's orders, potential challengers were killed, including his eldest son by one of his wives, or enslaved.[31]

So Radama I's death left a vacuum. Who would mediate between Merina and their ancestors? Who would protect the island from those who would seek to destroy it? As it turns out, he also left behind a diplomatic quagmire.

The British occupation based on the island of Mauritius had set its sights on Imerina for some time. They saw an opportunity to expand their colonial stretch and outmanoeuvre staked French claims to the island. Nothing had made British designs more apparent than the first draft of the 1817 treaty put before Radama. It revealed that the British colonial governor of Mauritius, Robert Farquhar, sought to 'systematically... colonise Madagascar with British Mauritian settlers.'[32] Although Radama seems to have understood and would ultimately thwart these plans, it wasn't a deterrent to signing the treaty, nor the 1820 version that cemented the alliance.[33]

The treaty prohibited the export of enslaved people from Radama's island. This was problematic for him given that his realm had established itself as the major supplier to the nearby Mascarene Islands in the last quarter of the eighteenth century.[34] It had the potential to undermine the Merina crown's political support among leading Merina slave traders. Even so, the offer of compensation proved too tempting.

Military aid from the British to support Radama's mission of subjugating the whole island; technical assistance with 'legitimate' exports; supplying British missionaries to establish schools and teach the free population to read English; and crucially, personal compensation to the Merina crown for losses from the ban. These terms allowed the *mpanjaka* to sway his kingdom's elites. Honour and wealth through imperial expansion could be theirs, he promised them. There was more fertile land to be gained and a lifetime of luxury awaiting them if they forced enslaved people to cushion their lifestyles, instead of selling them.[35]

Radama also wanted to maintain Imerina's sovereignty. He envisioned a British alliance that would jumpstart the growth of an island empire, one that would stand as a peer to British and French powers. When it eventually became clear that wouldn't happen under the established free trade structure, Radama broke with the British between 1824 and 1826.[36]

Before his death in 1828, the ruler had rejected free trade and set about establishing an economic vision of self-sufficiency, one with limited or no international trade. Restrictions on the freedom of foreigners on the island including their rights to property, mandating ten-year resident permits for said foreigners (including missionary workers who were considered part of an 'official British presence' in Imerina), tax duties on European traders and artisans – these were just a few of the measures taken by Radama I. His passing, therefore, came at a febrile time for the nation.[37] The issues of succession that followed did little to alleviate such conditions.

Despite what his father may have wished for succession, Radama had designated Rakotobe, the son of his eldest sister, as his successor, given that his only son had died in infancy. However, the young heir's grip on the seat of power was short-lived as, in the same year of Radama's death, the thirteen-year-old Rakotobe was executed, alongside both his parents, in order to, as some chroniclers believe, clear the path for Ramavo.[38]

Under her throne name, she took power. A Merina kingdom, caught in perilous transition, was now Ranavalona I's to steer.

The fatigue, the nausea, the cravings, the forgetfulness, the back pain, the increased swell of her sensitive breasts, the persistent pressure on her bladder. After ten months of mourning for the late monarch, a heavily pregnant Ranavalona in her early forties stood before the people of Imerina in 1829.[39]

Together, the boom of fired cannons, the beat of drums and the song of trumpets had called the public and military factions alike to proceed to Andohalo for the national assembly. More cannons had heralded the ruler-in-waiting's departure from the palace, transported by the rock and sway of a gold-laced palanquin. Women singers from all corners of the island flanked her, alongside members of her family, lieutenants of the capital, heads of provinces and districts, lines of soldiers and shouting crowds numbering around 60,000.[40]

After *hasina* had been presented and collected, it was time for

Ranavalona I, clad in gold jewellery with layers of purple, white and scarlet silk draping her swollen stomach, to speak. With her hair arranged in the numerous small braids styled in the way of the *hova* and crowned by a *volahevitra* – a golden adornment with red stones and a mother-of-pearl shell – which twinkled above her forehead, she addressed the assembled masses:[41] 'I will not change what Radama and my ancestors have done; but I will add to what they did. Do not think that because I am a woman, I cannot govern the kingdom: never say, she is a woman weak and ignorant, she is unable to rule over us. My greatest solicitude and study will always be to promote your welfare, and to make you happy. Do you hear that, *Ambaniandro*?'[42]

Her *ambaniandro* – the subjects gathered before her, likely jostling to catch her every word – replied. 'Yes,' they responded. *We hear you.* The command was clear: whatever my appearance and outward presentation may suggest to you, do not underestimate me.

Much of what we know about her coronation is mediated through Christian missionaries determined to deliver the islanders from themselves and their 'idols'. The application of their Western, colonial worldview to Imerina and its people obfuscates, not only how their society functioned, but also the most basic of details – such as Ranavalona's title.

Scholar Stefan Amirell writes that 'queen' and its equivalents in other European languages (*rainha, regina, reina, reine, dronning* etc.) is often used in contemporary European sources and modern translations uncritically, with a host of potential meanings. It's not always clear whether a 'queen' was the sovereign ruler, the wife of a sovereign who inherited the throne, a queen mother acting as regent or an heiress to the throne with limited political function apart from transferring power to her husband.[43]

While largely gender-neutral indigenous royal titles like *mpanjaka* and others – such as *jumbe, mwana, raka* and *ratu* – are not necessarily more precisely defined, what outside observers often misunderstand are the local structures of power. Western societal models are projected onto societies like Imerina, where every political leader is a 'king' or a 'queen' even though, in some cases, 'it might have been more appropriate to describe them in terms of, for example, "chieftain" or "high priest/ess".'[44] Even these remain paltry substitutes for conveying the power, sovereignty and divine pre-eminence held by an individual like Imerina's newly honoured ruler.

Ranavalona's rise to power came through a military *coup d'état*, one that historians believe was organised by generals and officials who sought to exploit the establishment of a standing army. It turned out to be a canny manoeuvre, one that offset Ranavalona's personal lack of army experience while pointing towards a military-minded expansionist government.[45]

Credited as one of the principal figures who cleared the path to the throne for Ranavalona was the first prime minister of the Kingdom of Imerina, Andriamihaja. His role as a conspirator was rewarded following her ascension.[46] The *mpanjaka* elevated him to the ministerial position, bequeathing him with an ensemble of other titles like 'guard to the embassy', 'commander-in-chief' and 'royal confidant'.[47]

The pair's collaboration is one believed to have extended beyond governance. Given the unlikeliness of a pregnant Ranavalona carrying her late husband's offspring over ten months after his passing, many eyes have since turned to Andriamihaja. That said, there are claims that she had a clutch of lovers, and the commander may well have been among them. Her child would officially be recognised as the late *mpanjaka*'s progeny, even so, it would always be rumoured that Ranavalona had birthed the child of another.[48]

By her side, Andriamihaja would've watched on or, likelier still, influenced the way Ranavalona exercised her new powers. She immediately expelled the British agent at the imperial court and spilt the blood of potential rivals, including many of Radama's trusted coastal administrators, within a matter of months.[49]

The early period of political bloodshed was indicative of what was to come.

*

As the British and the French vied for access to Imerina shores, spurred on by dreams of an island rich with gold ores and other untapped resources, Ranavalona – like her late husband – was forced into defensive manoeuvres. For example, when French companies – made up of Wolof fighters hailing from lands in present-day Senegal – attempted to claim a portion of the island's eastern coastline around 1829, they were met with the armed forces of the Merina ruler.[50] In correspondence with a French colonial administrator in the lead-up to these conflicts, Ranavalona had warned him not to misjudge her: 'If it is because I am a woman that you have written in such an arrogant tone and you think you can make laws in my name in my own land, you are mistaken.'[51]

The French remained undeterred. A year later, their administration sent the Malagasy ruler a letter, demanding the cession of one third of the island to their authority. She responded with force. Imerina's military successfully repelled the Europeans – strengthened by her addition of reportedly 23,000 soldiers.[52]

Ranavalona's position was bolstered by the *hasina* she was now the latest to harness. Her domination over the masses was because the ancestors had willed it so, having endowed the *mpanjaka* with a divine mandate. Alongside the ancestral authority and material wealth it granted her, *hasina* was also reinforced by the way she administered her kingdom.

Radama's power had been visible, especially as he had often personally led his soldiers into conflict. In contrast, Ranavalona's authority lay in administration and bureaucracy. She wrote letter after letter, laden with directives, to military generals, port authorities, the chiefs of her provinces, European colonial officials.[53] She relied on the written word, with her daily administrative work placing political authority in the confines of offices, rather than in the din of public *kabary* conferences – spaces that her predecessors had relied upon to issue orders and garner advice.[54] Instead, she operated as the invisible hand of the kingdom. Her unseen management surely only strengthened the sacred will she was believed to channel.

Ranavalona's introduction of a professional army, bureaucracy and a massive industrial complex developed alongside the power of the *razana* she represented as ruler, the trappings of modernity interlocked with ancestral energy that ran through the earth.[55] However, perhaps one of Ranavalona's most notable contributions was her foreign policy, which rested largely on isolationism. Self-reliance, independence and limited foreign trade. She chose to expand on Radama's policy that Imerina should stand alone. Their shared vision was of an imperial Merina powered by its own economic growth.[56] The ruler was determined to shield her island from the rest of the world.

The early 1830s saw Ranavalona work to shore up Merina sovereignty. She wanted to increase Imerina's reserve of hard currency – currency unlikely to depreciate suddenly, making it a reliable store of value. In 1831, she encouraged foreigners along the coasts to pay for exports in munitions while she continually ordered her port administrators not to use money to pay for foreign imports. Alongside stabilising Merina currency, it allowed the ruler to stockpile munitions as she set the foundations for her own weapon-based industry. She wanted to wean the kingdom off high-grade European manufactured equipment. It would be a decade before the Merina were able to produce their own cannonry and siege guns.[57]

It didn't stop at weapons. Ranavalona ordered the regulation of imports in line with local production: she wanted no more imported soap sent to Imerina, for example, because local markets had plenty of soap supplies. A flooded market, she told her port governors, would mean that local sellers could no longer turn a profit and would unravel the city-state's soap industry.[58] As a result, she deemed record-keeping on Imerina's commercial activity of paramount importance and they were to be sent to her at regular intervals. The reports needed to be timely and accurate, she instructed, because she, their *mpanjaka*, would be meticulously checking each one.[59]

What Radama began, Ranavalona sought to finish. She built upon the budding legacy he left behind, which included restricting the movement of foreigners within the kingdom. Under Radama,

missionaries were told where they could live and had their evan-
gelisation plans rejected. The surveillance of all foreigners included
them having to apply for passports to travel any distance.[60] The
London Missionary Society, which had set its sights on the island
from as early as 1797 and began sending its missionaries over in
1818, had experienced restrictions under Radama yet laid all the
blame at Ranavalona's door.[61]

Radama's reign was one heaped with praise by the missionaries
and colonial administrators alike. To them, he was a ruler who
understood the 'superiority of European techniques', elevated the
'physical and moral condition of his own people'. They called him
'one of the most enlightened and... one of the most humane rulers
that the land has known.'[62] Meanwhile, Ranavalona, held responsible for the isolationist dawn over the Malagasy isle, was 'ignorant,
gullible [and] easily influenced' for breaking with European influence, seeking isolation and rejecting Christianity.[63]

In the eyes of the missionaries, fired up by their aims to 'spread
the knowledge of Christ among heathen and other unenlightened
nations', she was the smear on Radama's legacy. Additionally,
the *hasina* rituals Ranavalona participated in as the kingdom's
monarch were interpreted as a slight against the Christians. They
saw it as an insult to the work they were doing to convert the
Merina masses, translate the bible into Malagasy and erect mission
schools. These 'pagan rites' were a sign that 'the enemy was permitted to triumph.'[64]

To their minds, the most heathen of them all was resting on the
Merina throne. They were right to feel threatened by her because
Ranavalona was not done with them yet. She refused to sit still, to
be passive, and this extended to her romantic dalliances.

Whatever passionate caresses, smiling whispers or loaded glances
may have been shared between Andriamihaja and Ranavalona, by
1831, they were no more. Whether it was down to the sour demise
of a relationship or the cold cycle of the deposer becoming the
deposed, the truth sits beyond us.

It's said that the general was resented by other courtiers and
military officials. Among them were two who held a particular

dislike towards the well-connected paramour of the *mpanjaka*: brothers Rainiharo and Rainimaharo, leaders of the conservative faction in the Merina court.[65]

There was history here. Rainiharo had also been a lover of Ranavalona's and was reportedly jealous of the presumed father of her son, Rakoto.[66] This swirl of motives may be why the siblings used their influence with the keepers of the *sampy* and other divine leaders to sway the mind of Ranavalona. They suggested that Andriamihaja was plotting a move against her, an argument made more convincing by his recent conversion to Christianity.[67] He was charged with *mosavy* – witchcraft, sorcery or enchantment – and the people came for him. The boiled rice, *kebona* and chicken skins awaited. Andriamihaja, better than most, would've known that the hour of *tangena* was upon him and he refused to submit to the torture method. He was, instead, stabbed to death.[68]

The seat of royal consort to the *mpanjaka* now vacant, Rainiharo was on hand to fill the void. He became her lead paramour, commander-in-chief of the army and then, in 1832, Ranavalona's new prime minister. Given that Ranavalona and other high-ranking women could marry whom they pleased, as status was inherited matrilineally and rendered paternity of little import, she added another feathered title to his hat: husband.[69]

Together, they would usher virulently anti-Christian policy into Imerina, subjecting many to the same treatment as Andriamihaja. If the late commander's proximity to Ranavalona didn't spare him, there was little hope for the many others who would follow.

Nestled in my Instagram requests, Cathia's excitement at the announcement of my book and the inclusion of Ranavalona in 2021 stayed with me. 'Thank you for choosing to tell her story as part of your book,' the young Malagasy woman wrote.

Almost two years later, after I settle into my wood-accented hotel in the heart of Antananarivo, Cathia – delighted that I've safely made it to her home country and fuming that she is sat working at her kitchen table in north London – delivers one of the greatest treats a travelling researcher could hope for: a locally

based, multi-lingual family friend happy to be paid for his knowledge of the area and its history.

The friend shares his name with Ranavalona's deposed, possible
lover. Mihaja cheerfully sings over his shoulder as he brings me to
the *Rova* of Antananarivo by moto. Groups of Malagasy men and
boys stand around the main entrance to the compound, watching our approach. Mihaja exchanges quick words with one man
who peels off from the others, marked out as the lead guide of the
group. They will watch the moto, Mihaja translates, while we're led
around the historical heart of Tana.

We walk around the side of the complex, further along the tall,
spiked metal fence that marks the royal perimeter. In between the
metal bars, I catch a first glimpse of the Manjakamiadana, one of
the handful of palaces that sit within the complex. It was originally
built on the orders of Ranavalona I in 1839, earning it the colloquial
title of 'The Queen's Palace'.[70]

In keeping with the traditions of Merina architecture, there are
factors that set the *Rova* – and other buildings belonging to the
noble *andriana* caste – apart from other residences. Its superior
location on a rise which aided other defences like moats and walls
(with the latter normally reserved for the royal class); its size as
well as the decorative ornaments like the horns of oxen on cross
poles protruding from the roof; and lastly, its building materials.
They were unlike the ancestral tombs constructed of stone or
the houses and huts of lower castes made of unbaked clay, reeds
and grasses. Instead, the buildings of the *andriana* were largely
made of wood.[71] And when it came to the Manjakamiadana, it
was *fady* – taboo – to use any other construction materials to
build the royal house.[72] 'For Malagasy people,' our guide explains,
'when they build houses, they use only wood because it is for life.'
Before the nineteenth century, stone was forbidden as a material
for the living.[73]

It is also *fady*, I learn, to point your finger directly at the palace
itself, especially as the royal stone tombs lie within the *Rova*,
further sealing its venerated status. As one of the sacred sites
around the island, it has been commonplace to find offerings

around the compound in the form of sweet treats like bananas as well as blood from chicken and *omby* – known also as 'zebu', the humped-back cattle that is a symbol of royalty, sacrifice, wisdom and wealth among the Malagasy.[74]

My view from the metal bars is as close as I'll get to this compound. On 6 November 1995, a fire raged through the *Rova*, devouring traditional houses, chapels and much of the Manjakamiadana's interior, leaving behind a smoking carcass.[75] 'My staff were zombies the next day,' an unnamed diplomat told the *New York Times* a year later. 'One of them was in a panic because she was breathing the ashes of her ancestors.'[76]

Many, including our guide, suspect arson. 'It was a political fire,' he says adamantly to which Mihaja nods vociferously, murmuring his agreement. 'When you have something important like that? Political. Yes, we've lost some history but we've still managed to preserve it.' Although restoration work has been intermittently under way since 1996, at the time of my visit in early 2023 the royal compound is off-limits.

Sitting atop Analamanga, the highest hill in Antananarivo, the *Rova* gazes down on the region below which is also named by the since-expelled indigenous Vazimba presence. The hillsides, once overrun by verdant palms and bushes jostling for sunshine, are today densely speckled with the off-white, orange and blush roofs of Malagasy homes. Sun-worn stone paths wind around the hill and every step I take offers a new panoramic view that rebuffs my attempts to capture it with my phone.

In the distance sit the rest of the twelve sacred hills. Rising all around Tana, each hill – from Ambohimanga in the north to the south-westerly Ambohijoky – represents a small kingdom that once rivalled the central hill of Analamanga before Merina occupation.[77] Once the kingdoms were collapsed under Andrianampoinimerina, Radama's father, he designated a sacred hill to each of his twelve wives, our guide tells me and Mihaja. Other Malagasy people have recalled stories passed onto them in which the *mpanjaka* had fought his cousins, uncles and perhaps his own father who inhabited the other hills and were therefore obstacles. He set about replacing each of them with his spouses.[78] It's a steadfast cornerstone to Merina oral tradition, even though it is largely understood that there are more than twelve sacred hills and that Andrianampoinimerina likely had a lot more than twelve wives.[79] The sites are also the final resting places of Merina rulers, their tombs marked with stone slabs, their *hasina* flowing through sun-sizzled red earth.

The other hills watch on as we pick our way around Analamanga, aloof onlookers tracking us from every side. So expansive is Tana before us, at times, it feels like the view is falling away at our feet, that we are falling into it. Our guide, his faded red cap shading his face, tells me to look up. I reflexively squeal at the sight of a large black spider suspended between branches, its fine web near invisible against an azure sky.

'The snakes and spiders in Merina are not poisonous,' he informs me, perhaps with the aim to soothe. 'You should only be scared of scorpions, those are dangerous.'

At the end of one path, the Manjakamiadana looms into view again, this time from a different side. Once built entirely of wood that honoured life, it's now towers of stone that are visible above a high brick wall – we'll come to the once-banned stone later. The three of us turn past it, walking further into La Haute Ville d'Antananarivo – the Upper Town – and are greeted by a wall with a long bas relief, perhaps forty metres long, from the 1940s. It details Malagasy history, the viewer travelling through time as they walk from left to right. Engraved into the red terracotta are the Vazimba inhabitants with their fishing boats, fighters armed with spears to escort herds of zebus, the Merina royalty in their regalia, the first European occupiers with their parasols and guns, the first governor of a colonised Madagascar sat beside the island's last sovereign and the modern-day Malagasy person in Western garb.

I'm led a little further on to the Palais de justice d'Ambatond-rafandrana, named for a Vazimba ruler and Merina royal ancestor, Rafandrana. The old Justice Palace was built in 1881 as a granite, now concrete, Greek-style temple, its sixteen Doric columns representing the kingdoms fashioned together to form Imerina.[80]

'*Fitsarana*' – justice – is engraved into its front-facing pediment between a crown and crossed spears.

However, nearby, there was a different form of judgement passed. The palace stands next to a precipice from which Christians were thrown to their deaths. It's named the Ampamarinana. *The place of hurling.*

When the sultan who ruled over Oman and Zanzibar – believed to be Saïd bin Sultan – sent an ambassador to the Merina court around 1833, an aghast Ranavalona took some special measures.

The archipelago of Zanzibar was on its way to becoming a centre of Islamic scholarship. By the nineteenth century, it was ruled over by an Arab elite who developed clove plantation complexes which were toiled and tilled by enslaved Africans.[81] Islam and other foreign organised religions posed a large, looming threat for the *mpanjaka* and, like the Christian missionaries who spoke of alien ideological values, she wouldn't permit the sultan's ambassador to enter Imerina. She worried that he would bewitch her.[82] Ranavalona and other traditional practitioners feared any Merina person who converted. They believed them capable of *mosavy*; their fellow countryfolk were possessed by an alien god named Jehovah, manipulated by the foreigners spreading this doctrine.[83]

The religious dogma carried from distant plains ran counter to their own. The Malagasy believe, instead, in a Supreme Being known as Zanahary (the Creator) or Andriamanitra (the Fragrant Lord).[84] There's no Malagasy pantheon. Zanahary is the ultimate source of all beings and all order, and from this figure stems the power of the ancestors. If Zanahary belongs to the transcendent, unknowable realms, it's the *razana* (ancestors) who span both the worldly and otherworldly, given that they have passed from one to the other. Both of these divine presences are often coupled together in standard Malagasy speech patterns. 'Ho tahin' Andriamanitra sy ny razana anie hainao.' *May you be protected by the Creator and the ancestors.*[85] Part of that protection came in the form of *sampy*, the protective amulets of the Merina people, which, by Ranavalona's

reign, occupied a preeminent place in society as they were closely
linked to the life of a community.[86]

Therefore, to unseat the Creator with another was to unravel the
people. This was certainly how Ranavalona saw it. To offer *hasina*
to others severed the link between the *razana* and their living
kin. Plus, with its political sway, to offer *hasina* elsewhere, moved
beyond a matter of faith, as it was understood by missionaries. It
also became a politicised stance: one that was firmly against the
mpanjaka and the Merina state.[87] To her, there was no place for
Christianity – its worship or tolerance – in Imerina: 'As for me, I
will not pray to the ancestors of foreigners but to [Andriamanitra]
and my own ancestors, for each peoples has its own ancestors.'[88]

In a letter she'd later send to missionaries, Ranavalona demonstrated an awareness, and maybe even a tolerance, towards foreign
cultures – provided, of course, they remained beyond the boundaries of her realm:

> You Europeans may follow the customs of your ancestors for
> if there be a knowledge of the arts and sciences that will be
> useful to my country, teach that, for it is good; and I inform
> you, my relations and friends, of this that you may hear
> of it – God is not the God of one [nation] only but of all,
> for all nations have different words for God and all follow
> the customs of their ancestors – these are the laws of my
> country...[89]

However, the Christian mission in Imerina was growing. The first
Merina converts were publicly baptised in May 1831 with several
thousands more to follow, each adopting the teachings of 'the
ancestor of the whites: Jesus Christ.'[90] The makings of a Church
of Madagascar was under way and a material threat had emerged.

Ranavalona took action. Issues were ordered by her government that no soldier or mission school pupil should be baptised
or partake in communion – this was later broadened to apply
to every Merina subject. Enslaved people were prohibited from
learning to read, another attempt to curb the spread. Rumour and

accusation proliferated: Jehovah had actually been the first king of the English, Jesus Christ was the second, so the missionaries were trying to divert loyalty from the Merina sovereign to the English throne.[91] In 1835, the year after the Malagasy-translated bible was completed, printed and being distributed, the Merina court ordered the destruction of all books that contained the words 'Jesus Christ' and 'Jehovah'.[92]

At a *kabary* that same year, with all her people summoned to the capital, the *mpanjaka*, approaching her fifties, issued her special decree. Anyone who had been baptised, entered into Christian society or formed houses for prayer or worship was to confess to the public officers within one month. If they did not confess of their own volition within that period and instead, had to be found out and accused, the cost would likely be their life.[93] Ranavalona was determined to rip Christianity out of Imerina by the roots, using not only the Ampamarinana, but also the toxic *tangena* as favoured devices.[94] The poisoning method, understood as the most accurate means of detecting *mosavy*, was administered widely. Each district was required to use a ballot to select *mosavy* suspects as a means to '[cleanse] the kingdom'.[95]

The realm suffered huge loss of life. It was a combination of decades of unrelenting military campaigns, devastating smallpox epidemics, the spread of infectious diseases and famine, high death rates among enslaved people – particularly those subjected to forced labour – and Ranavalona's deathly scourge of the converted Merina.[96] The island's population is estimated to have fallen from 5 million to 2.5 million between 1833 and 1839; within the Imerina highlands, the population declined by over 80 per cent – 750,000 to 130,000 – between 1829 and 1842.[97]

What would've been most important for Ranavalona, however, was that by 1836, all of the LMS missionaries had either withdrawn from the island or been expelled.[98] The colonial powers were certainly still swirling, particularly the French, but at least one danger had been abated. Every execution, every body relieved of its breath through torturous, visceral and painful means, to her mind, brought her closer to the goal she had been chasing since she had ascended the throne, to eluding the threat that had haunted her days and nights.

Perhaps the ruler felt that, in time, the Merina people would understand her brand of justice. That her brutal governance would be read as a love letter by future generations. That maybe they would understand how, through blood, bile and terror, she was protecting their land, their people and their sovereignty.

Before exploring Tana, when I was being driven from the airport to my hotel, I asked my driver what he knew about Ranavalona I and he had chuckled. With his eyes on the road and one arm slung out of the window to enjoy the sun's attention, the man – somewhere in his sixties – directed his joking response over his shoulder. 'It's history and I'm young!'

Then, once I was settled at my hotel, comfortable under the cosy, wooden-beamed design that runs throughout, I had sat at its tiny bar and got chatting to three women staff members. I asked them the same. The shared blank looks told me that they didn't know much about Ranavalona I. One said that it was a very long time ago and that she'd have to check the internet while reaching for her phone. Later that evening, a different hotel employee, who was also a teacher of history and geography, told me simply that Ranavalona is loved by her people, she just didn't like Christianity and preferred Malagasy roots.

'Is Ranavalona loved by the Malagasy?' I ask our guide. We're walking over to the Andiafiavaratra Palace, the residence of the island's late-nineteenth-century prime minister, Rainilaiarivony, which holds an estimated 1,466 artefacts rescued from the 1995 fire in the nearby *Rova*.[99]

From under his faded cap, he speaks plainly. 'She didn't believe in God. She was killing Christian people, cutting their heads off at the Justice Palace and then throwing their body over the big cliff.'

Our guide fishes around one of his pockets and retrieves a weathered booklet with pictures of the Merina rulers. Among preceding and successive *mpanjakas* sits a portrait of Ranavalona I, one of the most widely deployed images of her.

'Look at her face,' he says, with measured distaste. With a white handkerchief in one hand and a weighty crown balanced upon her head, a stern-looking Ranavalona with furrowed brows and a set jaw stares out to the side. She's dressed in a dusty pink gown draped with a threaded cape; historians are often drawn to the fact that the ruler followed and held a preference for European fashions.[100] The guide taps her image with a weathered finger. 'Bad queen.'

A few months later, when I'm back in my London home, Audrey Randriamandrato speaks to me via video call about the averse, sometimes disgusted, reactions of local people towards their historic ruler. While the founder of the Malagasy Women Empowerment association (MWE) – an organisation working to improve the conditions of Malagasy women through education and community work – reads Ranavalona as a 'symbol of feminism' taking actions for the good of the country, Audrey understands why many don't hold her in that regard.

'We learnt when we were kids that she was a sanguinary, brutal queen – someone you'd refer to as a "rude woman",' she shares. 'However, when you begin to grow and learn more about French colonisation, you understand that the only thing she wanted to do was to protect [Imerina].'

For a long time, she didn't question the lack of archives and resources around the island, only to later learn that they were burnt by colonial forces. When Audrey reflects on how she was taught, for example, that globalisation was a good thing, she levels blame at the state of education in Madagascar. She describes an island split by two education systems: the colonial French system with schools and curricula modelled after those in France and then the indigenous schools for the Malagasy.

'If we are in the French system, we only learn about French history,' she explains. Those that seek out Malagasy history are made to feel like they are exhibiting animosity towards foreigners and often, whatever they can access feels hollow. 'When you learn about [Malagasy] history, you're taught the events and actions, rather than why things happened.'

With a wry smile, Audrey recalls when she began to do her

own research. 'One day, I was learning for a [high school] exam and I was like, it's not normal that I know more about French history and colonisation than my own country.' She tells me that she can reel off the European country's history by heart – the late eighteenth century French Revolution, the introduction and dismantlement of the monarchy, the German occupation of France during the Second World War, the rise of the present-day Fifth Republic. Meanwhile, she only had one class in Malagasy which was centred on the language and how to read texts.

After high school, Audrey started buying history books and visiting the island's historical sites with guides, a determined attempt to fill her brain with the knowledge of her people. This kind of education isn't a priority for all. In fact, the MWE front-woman has friends who have lived in Madagascar all their lives but do not speak Malagasy. 'They were in French schools, went to French churches and they didn't search around for our history.'

This decidedly hungry approach to Malagasy history, digging for morsels that have been purposefully scattered and buried, informs Audrey's favourable view of Ranavalona's reign. For her, it stood as a stubborn challenge to the West, a reign that had sought to thwart what would eventually become Madagascar's colonial reality. However, a 'means to an end' approach is little comfort to those who lost their lives on the sovereign's orders, persecuted for faith, nor to descendants whose bloodlines feature gaping holes.

Crucially, Audrey's insights demonstrate how the pervasive colonial legacy continues to mould the island today. Despite originating from faraway Western lands, the agendas they've left behind are interlaced in the lush fronds and blown along with the dust of the red earth.

Around February 1837, the six Merina ambassadors who stood in a cold Windsor Castle felt a chill in more ways than one. Not only was there a frosty bite in the air, but the men from Imerina – after a choppy voyage to London via Mauritius and the Cape Colony – carried a glacial message from their ruler.[101]

Across a near month-long stay at Radley's Hotel in London, the delegation had multiple conversations with the frail King William IV (who would die of heart failure four months later), Queen Adelaide, Foreign Secretary Viscount Palmerston and other state officials. At Ranavalona's behest, they insisted that Madagascar – as it was recognised by European states – would decide its own affairs, without British intervention. The ambassadors stressed their ruler's 'anti-European sentiments' and they weren't swayed by indulgent visits to the likes of the Bank of England, the Tower of London and the Zoological Gardens, all designed to overawe.[102]

'Tell the Queen of Madagascar from me that she can do nothing so beneficial for her country as to receive the Christian religion,' Queen Adelaide implored the embassy before they departed for Paris in March.[103] The delegation took home her words and a 'proposed convention' that the British Foreign Office held out little hope for. Even so, they felt they had to try. There were the 'treaties of friendship' with Radama that needed to be honoured and a strategically important Madagascar – which supplied both food and labour to the British-colonised Mauritius – to exploit.[104]

However, Ranavalona had made herself clear. In two letters to the declining William IV, hand-delivered by her ambassadors, she detailed that the law of her country would not became a playground for Europeans. 'She would not tolerate Christianity, admit a resident agent, allow Europeans to live in Madagascar, save prisoners of war from death, or encourage international commerce,' writes Arianne Chernock, a historian of monarchy.[105] These were the kinds of terms that the British stressed were key to friendly relations; stipulations the Merina ruler would not accept.

There was a buzz that had built around Imerina and its ruler. A slew of British colonial travellers were publishing their 'swashbuckling adventures' which detailed a Malagasy island population that lived among roaming lemurs, chameleons and giant rats. However, after Ranavalona's rejection, the humiliation and anger felt among British officials, missionaries and journalists metamorphosed this attention into something else, into assertions that rode waves of white, Christian superiority and antiblack, anti-African sentiment.[106] How could a nation they perceived as primitive scorn their righteous advances? What gave the Merina people and a woman who called herself queen the right to reject British civilisation? How dare an island alive with cultures and imagery that connoted 'barbarity' resist Western deliverance? Why would they – *she* – not simply acquiesce like they wanted?

As Chernock points out, all of the deeply offended British parties could've written off Ranavalona and her policies as 'a problem of queenship'. Quips like 'Sovereign, such as she is', never levelled at her first husband, meant misogyny certainly still bubbled under the surface.[107] However, discrediting the *mpanjaka* in such a way, and by extension all women sovereigns, had a clear drawback. In March 1837, a seventeen-year-old Princess Victoria was being prepared for British rule.

Criticism couldn't hinge on gender. How could it when Victoria would go on to become queen that June, a matter of months after the Merina embassy had departed? What state of instability could that place the Crown in?[108] Attacking women sovereigns was out, fixating on a dichotomy between a 'savage' and her 'civilised' counterpart was not.

The British political-media complex, alongside Christian commentators, quickly set to work. The communications of the Foreign Office regularly contrasted Ranavalona's 'practices abhorrent to humanity' with Victoria's own 'humane' qualities.[109] The same tack was employed by an LMS missionary in an 1838 letter to Palmerston: with the Merina sovereign's 'suffering nation' found wanting in comparison to that of 'Her Britannic Majesty', this surely offered grounds for a 'just and humane interference'.[110] A binary narrative was constructed around the two rulers. The morally upstanding versus the morally depraved. The good Christian up against the idol-worshipping heathen. Well-mannered refinery forced to contend with uncouth coarseness. Little would epitomise this better than the events of 1845.

In May of that year, Ranavalona, who had been reigning for almost two decades, passed a new law. It decreed that all foreigners on the island had to join in with the maintenance of public infrastructure, including labour that was reserved for enslaved people.[111]

Ordered by the Merina court to leave the island within eleven days after they refused to obey, the foreigners sent a cluster of letters to the British colonial governor of Mauritius.[112] It was like a struck match to kindling.

Resolved to teach the Merina a lesson, Britain partnered with France to attack the Malagasy port town of Tamatave in June 1845. They deemed it necessary after the Merina sovereign had refused the colonial requests that the settlers be given a year to dispose of their property and that the law be rescinded. However, the joint forces had underestimated the strength of the Merina who were well equipped with both firearms and military expertise. The military action lasted just four hours before a colonial retreat without capture.[113]

Fleeing the island for their vessels, the colonial forces left behind twenty Europeans in the process – the skulls of the four English and sixteen French soldiers were reportedly fixed on poles outside the Tamatave fort.[114] Although a long-standing practice among the Malagasy, it incurred the wrath of Westerners, their ire and humiliation inflamed by Ranavalona's absent contrition.[115] In a letter to the British naval captain, which he later conveyed to a Manchester newspaper in 1846, the *mpanjaka* noted how 'very odd' it was that European powers would 'interfere in her own affairs'; she pondered 'how Queen Victoria and Louis Philippe would take it if she were to meddle with their countries'.[116]

British hostility towards the ruler reached fever pitch. From the mouths and nibs of politicians, writers, missionaries and journalists, condemnations flew thick and fast. 'Monster of cruelty', 'female fury', 'heathen queen', 'an unscrupulous and energetic woman' and 'a woman combining in herself the worst traits of character of Jezebel, Athaliah and bloody Queen Mary'.[117] Contrasted against Queen Victoria's whiteness, commentators increasingly described the hue of Ranavalona's skin, relaying that she was 'dark, and very much pitted with small pox', underscoring her unsuitability as a monarch.[118]

One of those titles would stick. As is the British way, grappling with historical figures often requires a sensational Western frame of reference; only through this approximation does their ignominy bear relevance. And so, referencing the Tudor queen known for burning Protestants at the stake, Ranavalona became the 'Bloody Mary of Madagascar'.[119]

Of the British commentators baying for Ranavalona's blood, William Ellis was prime among them. The foreign secretary to the London Missionary Society and a well-regarded author, he was central to fashioning Ranavalona into the anti-Victoria, particularly in his acclaimed two-volume *History of Madagascar* (1838). Although he had not travelled to the island by the time of publishing, his extensive correspondence with missionaries was enough to make him an expert on all things Malagasy – including its sovereign.[120] Ellis portrays Ranavalona as deceptive, wily and tyrannical, a woman who was 'almost single-handedly responsible for the stalling of civilization on her lush, mountainous island'.[121]

The reach and impact of Ellis's assessments of Ranavalona and Imerina stretched far beyond the self-styled anthropologist's lifetime. *History of Madagascar* and other missionary accounts are cited in this chapter, with Ellis found in a number of appraisals of the kingdom. If I don't cite from these sources directly, there's a good chance that a secondary source might. As with the appraisals of Njinga, there is some value that can be found in their insights, given that figures like Ellis and missionary David Griffiths spent time with the Merina *mpanjaka*. The latter was considered a confidant by Ranavalona and spent years in her court prior to expulsion. It's through these sources that we have, for example, the vivid descriptions of attire and the order of public gatherings, processions and courtly forums.

They cannot be entirely discarded but a reader must swim through a deluge of entrenched and sincere belief in African inferiority, colonial deliverance and white superiority. It's these missionary sources, where Ranavalona is referred to as a 'Malasian Jezebel' whose actions '[legitimate] Britain's presence in Madagascar and beyond', which also offer estimates for how many people were killed by *tangena* across her reign – based on information compiled by other missionaries.[122] There is glee and revelry in the Merina

ruler's communicated madness. A quick online search will bring
you face to face with the tales that have emerged around her since:
that she tried to make a pair of giant scissors to chop invaders in
half; that when she wanted to go on a buffalo hunt in a location
with no roads, she had people make a road before her wherever she
went; that during Radama's mourning period, she made it illegal to
look in a mirror or clap your hands with a lifetime of enslavement
hanging in the balance.

Given tightly held Western prescriptions to racial hierarchy,
how much of Ranavalona's legacy has been shaped by fury and
the perceived impertinence of an inferior people? It's exacerbated
by a lack of access to Malagasy histories for non-French and non-
Malagasy speakers. We end up with an over-reliance on colonial
testimonies.

The same names crop up again and again, like the widely cited
French scholar Hubert Deschamps. A professor of modern and
contemporary history at the Sorbonne University in Paris in the
late 1960s, it was this scholar who understood Malagasy colonisation as a critical, necessary intervention. Their ignorant and gullible ruler had pulled the kingdom away from the light of European
technological superiority that Radama had been walking towards.[123]
His writing crackles with vim and fury, seemingly taken aback by
Ranavalona's audacity. Further research on my part yielded that,
before he entered the field of academia, Deschamps was a French
colonial administrator. Governorships of the French Somali Coast,
Côte d'Ivoire and Senegal were all positions he enjoyed from 1938
to 1943. Before that, he spent a decade as the colonial administrator for Madagascar, from 1926 to 1936. These facts barely feature
in appraisals of his work.[124]

Colonial historians and anthropologists like Deschamps tend to
be the rule rather than the exception. And like Njinga, the same
questions around cruelty must be asked of the historicising of
Ranavalona: how much has her capacity for cruelty and bloodshed
been garbled by a colonial paradigm, one that already indicted her
for rejecting European imperialism?

*

Although the 1850s were sprinkled with foreign attempts to unseat Ranavalona through plots and *coups d'état*, they were unsuccessful. In the end, the ruler departed this world unassailed. After a reign of thirty-three years, Ranavalona died on 16 August in 1861 at the Manjakamiadana. She was buried seven metres under the ground, as was customary, with her tomb bearing a red roof – unlike the black roofs for men rulers.[125] Before she died, she counselled her son and designated heir, Rakoto, who would go on to rule the Merina people as Radama II.[126] Whatever advice the frail woman in her eighties may have given him from her deathbed turned out to be wasted last breaths.

The freshly ascended Radama II quickly unravelled her life's work. He immediately abolished the *tangena* trial, openly identified with the Christian movement, dismissed the royal *sampy*, publicly disregarded *fady*, abolished the traditional Merina calendar, welcomed foreigners back to the Merina dominion, permitted Christian missionaries to undertake major church-building projects, introduced the Christian ban on Sunday trading, and re-established diplomatic links, concessions and privileges with Britain and France with both powers appointing consuls to the island.[127] The new *mpanjaka* had decisively broken with his mother's policies and was 'revers[ing] every feature of the queen's government', publications like the *British Quarterly Review* gleefully reported in 1863.[128]

Ranavalona's brutal Christian interventions had come too late. The foundations had been laid for a quickly growing, converted community who were so committed to their new belief system that they had defied the authorities. At the height of the Christian purge, they had illegally retained their holy texts – bibles, testaments, hymn books – that were 'considered to be more valuable than gold', some of which had been buried in the ground by LMS missionaries before they had been expelled.[129]

The rulers who followed – Radama II's widow named Rasherina, Ranavalona II and the kingdom's last sovereign, Ranavalona III – would only accelerate the split from the first Ranavalona's policies. Some completely departed from traditional cultural practice.[130] For example, under Ranavalona II, the 'idols' of the Merina peoples were confiscated and destroyed, the Manjakamiadana was entirely restored with stonework (making her the first ruler to do so) and the Fiangonana – a stone chapel which took eleven years to complete – was built on the grounds of the *Rova*.[131]

Ranavalona III's reign would administratively end under French bombardment of the kingdom and their capture of Antananarivo. It culminated in the French annexation of Madagascar on 1 January 1896. Her rule officially ended when she was exiled on 27 February 1897, never to return to her island again, with the monarchy dissolved the next day. A French colony, it would stay that way for more than sixty years, until the establishment of the Malagasy Republic in 1958 and full independence two years later.

There are tales of the ghost of Ranavalona I haunting the island. Her spectre was blamed for the plagues and cholera that wracked the Malagasy people. It seems fitting to some that the deathly acts of this ruler would continue from another realm.

You can't help wondering, if she floated above the lush, floating rock from on high, whether there might be pain, confusion, a sense of emptiness, or dare we consider, even remorse. The island on which she ruled, consumed by the goal of self-preservation, was swallowed by colonial rule anyway.

Rather than the saviour she believed herself to be, Ranavalona I instead remains one of Madagascar's greatest villains.

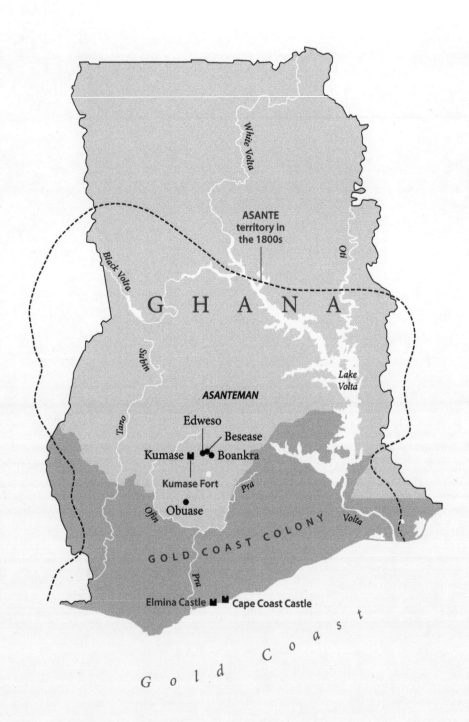

White Volta

ASANTE
territory in
the 1800s

Black Volta

Oti

G H A N A

Sabin

Tano

Lake
Volta

ASANTEMAN

Edweso

Besease

Kumase

Boankra

Kumase Fort

Pra

Obuase

Ofin

G O L D   C O A S T   C O L O N Y

Volta

Pra

Elmina Castle

Cape Coast Castle

G o l d   C o a s t

CHAPTER 8

Nana Yaa Asantewaa

The War-Leading Elder

When the lights flick off, she arises. Being swallowed up by darkness has become so commonplace now, she has a routine. Her feet know the way around the compound, even if light abstains from guiding their path.

As she walks, she gathers up children, calling their names and beckoning them to follow her. Once satisfied with her yield, she leads them to where they can sit at her feet or battle with one another for space on surrounding furniture. The older children might be reluctant – they've surely outgrown this, no? The younger ones are perhaps putting on a show of bravado because being afraid of the dark is for babies and they're not babies anymore, are they, Nana?

Time has bequeathed Nana with many stories and each time a blackout absorbs their village, she offers a new retelling. Some are folklore, like the many stories on the skilful trickery of Anansi. Others are historical, regaling children with tales of colonialism, independence and the building of a nation-state.

The elderly woman plants seeds. She's mindful that they might not all take. For some of these children, these stories will be just that: stories, where histories of resistance make for thrilling narrative devices. But for others, these impromptu moments with Nana will be a catalyst, held dear for the rest of their lives for the way they lit a fire.

The compound's unwilling generators grunt and sigh behind

the gathered congregation. Undeterred, Nana unwinds tonight's tale – its setting the land currently beneath them, its protagonists their ancestors – before her waiting audience.

What Osei Kofi Tutu I, the first *asantehene* (ruler in Asante Twi) and Abla Pokou's uncle, had sought to build, his successor, Opoku Ware, looked to expand. For example, it was under Osei Tutu that the Asante army, comprising of many factions, was established in the latter half of the seventeenth century.[1] However, it would be the second *asantehene* who consolidated the building blocks of an empire and pushed for more. Opoku Ware is described as the ruler who 'extended the Asante Kingdom more than any of his predecessors, or any of his successors'.[2] Asanteman's domination crept from inland to coast, greedily ingesting swathes of land and peoples into its empire, no matter which ruler sat on the throne.

As the nineteenth century reached its midway point, the reins of Asanteman were in the hands of Kwaku Dua Panin, the empire's eighth ruler. He ordered the construction of proper bridges across streams within and beyond the metropolis of Kumase, as well as paving newer, wider streets in the capital – namely for the convenience of his carriage.[3] When Kwaku Dua Panin had attained the highest seat of the kingdom in 1834, he became the latest in a carousel of rulers, both *asantehenes* and *mamponghenes* (the latter was installed as acting *asantehene* in the event of the late ruler passing away.) Somewhere between the reigns of Panin and his predecessor, Osei Yaw Akoto (r. 1822–33), Yaa Asantewaa was born.[4]

While the exact year and date of birth float beyond us, thanks to the Akan Kwa day naming system, we know one thing with certainty. She was born on a Thursday. With a day name of 'Yaa', the qualities she would exhibit had already been predetermined: a sense of discernment, guardedness, courage and diplomacy. Those bestowed with the name 'Yaa' are believed to crave freedom, no matter its form, with an innate skill to lead – including, if called upon, marshalling their people into battle.

Yaa Asantewaa grew up working the farmland, even though it was considered the work of boys, like her brother Kwasi Afrane

Panin, who had been trained by their fathers to till the land.[5] Born in Besease, a small village sat just beyond the hubbub of Edweso, the young labourer earned herself a reputation for single-mindedness and focus: Yaa ko afuom a onkra. *Yaa always leaves for her farm without bidding farewell to anybody.*[6]

It would have been a gruelling to-and-fro with the earth, a cycle of coaxing and tending until it surrendered its lot. Its tributes were on a mission to puncture and pierce, to rise above their confines and seek out the sweet kiss of the sun. They wouldn't breach the surface unaided. The sweat-laden rivulets that danced down the planes of her body and the aching pulse that kept time in her back would have been the proof. But it was a mission not without reward. The rough, dark-brown edges of cassava, the waving ears of rust-hued sorghum, and the bunched leaves extending long pods of cowpeas for perusal were likely among the vegetables pulled from the earth by Yaa Asantewaa.

The soil Yaa would've dusted off as she inspected the crops and the ground under her feet belonged to her father, Kobi Ampoma. However, stewardship of the land was a responsibility that belonged to every Asante person. In fact, the importance of the land played a defining part in the designs of the first Asante flag over one hundred years later. The trinity of colours in horizontal stripes sought to capture the essence of their people: yellow for the gold of the land, green marked its rich vegetation and the central black stripe denoted its people. 'The rich Black man living in his forest' is how the flag would be described to me across my time in the long-standing central hub of the Asante, today stylised as Kumasi.

Oblivious to the symbols and institutions she would eventually be central to, Yaa toiled under an unyielding sun. And after each day of cajoling the earth, she'd return to her home of red clay for respite before rising to attend to the soil once more.

Disruption to this routine Yaa had established came in the form of a man, one with a hand outstretched for marriage.

Given her aversion to perfunctory niceties, did the Asante woman view the customs that came with such a union as another exercise in performance? Did she struggle to still her tongue as permission was asked of her parents and gifts of fish, tobacco and gold dust were placed in the waiting hands of her family members? Perhaps she relished the fact that, once the customary bride-price had been paid, her consent was also required in order to set the wedding day. Or it could be that on the morning of the wedding, Yaa allowed herself to be swept up in the pageantry of it all, as she – adorned in tinkling gold and finery – followed her mother, Attah Poh, to her husband-to-be's home.[7]

After a whirlwind of thanking her bridegroom for his gifts, watching on as the village chief observed customary rites and jubilant celebration, the union was sealed. Yaa Asantewaa was now a wife, but she wasn't her husband's only. Owusu Kwabena was also married to Adwowa Kromo and Nana Atiaa – two women who formed part of Asante's elite classes as members of local royal and governing families.[8]

While polygamous marriage was a traditional social institution among the Asante and other Akan groups, scholars including Ghanaian historian Agnes Akosua Aidoo describe it as 'the most enslaving [tradition] for the African woman'.[9] The potential for jealousy, hostility and the absence of intimacy and trust with her husband all lay in wait for the new wife. She was thrust into a dynamic where more established wives held seniority. However, that very hierarchy meant that Yaa's co-wives would've had to have given their approval to her selection, while also receiving *mpata* – a formal and public compensation bestowed upon 'old' wives as a 'new' one took her place among them.[10]

Their husband, a man from Kantinkyiren – a village on the other side of Kumase from Yaa's hometown – had royal ties. He was a paternal grandson of the seventh *asantehene*, Osei Yaw Akoto, who had ruled from 1824 until his death just under a decade later.[11] It meant that four elites, their families and their lineages were intertwined through these unions, for Yaa had her own noble claim. She and her brother had been born into the Asona royal family of Edweso.

Even though the seat of power in the Asante Empire was based in Kumase, formerly Kwaaman, and still firmly in the grip of the Oyoko Dynasty, towns and villages had their own rulers who sat under the *asantehene*. The establishment of their authority dated back to the Akan migration across the seventeenth century. Like the Oyoko and many others, the Asona royals of Edweso had also settled in the Kwaaman area.

Banded together with other Akan peoples by Osei Kofi Tutu to fight off the Denkyira, the decisive Battle of Feyiase in 1701 had sealed their collective destiny – as well as Osei Tutu's place as their first ruler. However, before the fighting took place, Okomfo Anokye, his spiritual advisor and chief priest, called for a volunteer to sacrifice their life during the battle to secure victory. Into the vacuum stepped *Edwesohene* Duko Pim. In recognition of an act that would cost a man his life and Edweso their ruler, Osei Tutu swore a public oath. None of his successors in Kumase would ever execute or persecute the Edweso or any other Asona clan members. The battle was won, Duko Pim breathed his last and, with the Denkyira vanquished, Osei Tutu seized his new title before a newly formed Asanteman.[12]

As solemnly as that oath may have been uttered, time weakened its binds. Long after Osei Tutu was gone, successive *asantehenes* imposed huge fines in gold on Edweso. Knowing that the debts could never be paid, the people of Edweso were forced to transfer allegiance to those who could pay on their behalf. As intended, those who swooped to their rescue were wealthy Kumase chiefs. They settled the debts owed to the Asante seat and in return for the costly, manufactured favour, they snatched up Edweso lands and villagers. It was through this process that the state of Edweso lost thirty-seven villages from the eighteenth century onwards, haemorrhaging wealth, land and people to further the power of central government.[13]

Although Yaa's ancestors would be regarded as a core member of the initial Asante state, they understood their relationship with Kumase as one of sustained subjection.

*

Adekorato guides me through the sprawling Ghana National Cultural Centre. In the centre of today's Kumasi, here is where its historical heart beats. Artefacts and practices from across different periods coalesce, all threads that pull together a tapestry of Asante life.

Silver-painted statues, like that of the centre's founder Dr Alexander Attah Yaw Kyerematen, gaze out at passing visitors headed towards the crafts buildings where traditional *kente* weavers at work can be observed and their finished products purchased. The smell of peat hangs in the air. All of the various departments that make up the centre are shaded by lofty, thick-trunked trees reaching upwards to the thin clouds. The real reminder that the Asante kingdom was once a forest sits in the centre of the grounds. The hardy, centuries-old Indian rubber tree dangles wizened vines that my guide assures me will hold my weight as she challenges me (and likely every visitor taken under her wing) to jump up and hang from them. My cynicism dissipates into stunned excitement as I swing from the dark shoots.

My childish glee satisfied and my travelling purse sighing from overuse, Adekorato leads me towards a red and mint-coloured building that reads PREMPEH II JUBILEE MUSEUM. There, we dodge masses of chattering schoolchildren before she hands me over to her colleague Kobi and bids me goodbye. After my new companion makes it clear that I'm only permitted to take scribbled notes, he leads me into the museum space. Resembling a small courtyard, its four walls are lined with original war attire and weaponry, aged framed photos and ancient regal paraphernalia. Against the clamour of the nearby children also being shown around, Kobi launches into his well-practised script. He recites the names of Asante rulers as we gaze up and into the stern faces before us. Most of the sepia photographs show two rulers: an *asantehene* and an *asantehemaa*. 'The king's sister or mother can be queen,' says the guide. 'But never the wife.'

As with all Akan societies, descent is traced through the mother's lineage. She is understood as the link between future generations. It's her *mogya* – blood or life-force – which is transmitted to her children, determining their citizenship, rights of succession to office and inheritance to property.[14] Akan and wider African principles of inheritance assert that the 'biological heredity on the mother's [side] is stronger than the heredity on the father's side', ultimately leading many to conclude that 'a child is wholly that which its mother is and only half of what its father is.'[15] Akan mythology points to the belief that 'a man is supposed to derive his blood from his mother, one soul from God, [and] another soul or spirit (*ntoro*) from his father.'[16] Professor Simphiwe Sesanti writes simply that paternity is a probability, while maternity is a certainty. As a result, Akan customs have historically demanded that the successor be the son of the ruler's sister: 'The sovereign can be sure that his nephew is indeed his sister's son; but nothing can assure him that the son he considers his own in actuality is.'[17]

Mothers form the backbone of Asante society. The viability of an Asante village is established by a 'core of women ... who have children there, and whose daughters there give birth to other daughters who will continue the matrilineage.'[18] Meanwhile, the right to rule has consistently run through the *ahemaa* – women rulers (plural of *ohemaa*)– of the state. As one *ohemaa* reportedly told anthropologist R. S. Rattray, 'if my sex die in the clan then that very clan becomes extinct'.[19]

Blood figuratively and literally pumps through these matrilineal codes. Traditional Asante thought promoted the belief that only women could transmit the blood of a lineage. Their proof was a combination of the visibility of menstrual blood, how it could indicate fertility, and pregnancy (including the loss of one), and the value placed on the role of cisgender women as vessels for new life. Together, they induced awe and esteem, particularly among Asante men.[20] Women and *mogya* also sparked fear, which left its imprints on social customs.

As we slowly make our way from one weathered wall of the museum to the next, Kobi explains that the *asantehene*'s wives don't cook for him when they're menstruating and he puts it down to them being 'dirty and jealous', adding that 'he has many wives, what if one puts charms in the king's food to make him favour her more?' However, the perceived potency of a woman's blood – especially if it signifies menstrual and reproductive capacity – speaks to a more deep-seated fear.

One early-nineteenth-century *asantehene*, referred to as Osei Bonsu or Osei Tutu Kwame, was said to have been greeted at the outer gate of the palace by several of his wives. He was returning from a campaign against the insubordinate northern vassal kingdom of Gyaaman, but the women were fleeing because of a coup that had taken place in their husband's absence. In fact, the uprising was still being crushed when he arrived. In their distress, they rushed to embrace the *asantehene* in front of captains, who accordingly covered their faces with both hands and dispersed with speed. His wives' violation of gendered codes of decorum earned sharp words from the monarch but he returned their embraces. His begrudging affection tipped into anger, however, when Osei Bonsu later learnt that the women were menstruating. The monthly flow of blood that made them ceremonially 'unclean' meant that women ate separately, were kept out of men's social activities within the community and, most importantly, were kept away from military activities and personnel until they no longer bled. To avoid 'menstrual contamination', chiefs and captains going to war sought to leave town as soon as they had taken the war oath to the *asantehene*. Disregarding these rites was not permissible, and the perils taking place in the palace were not enough to save the royal wives. They were reportedly ordered to be cut into pieces, their remains cast into the depths of the forest.[21]

After all, the *asantehene* is understood as inherently vulnerable. He's not allowed to walk around barefoot and when seated, would traditionally rest his feet on ivory tusks. His fingernails and toenails are collected by royal staff lest they be used in charms against him. If it rains, the ruler must stay indoors. However, for all those precautions, it was feared that a woman, specifically a menstruating one, could be his undoing.

With blood binding a mother to her offspring, children – including those of the king – belong to the woman who bore them. It follows, then, that Asante people belong to the *abusua* (the great family) of their mother, a group linked by common matrilineal ancestors, an extended maternal family.[22] While largely used interchangeably, 'abusua' and 'clan' aren't equal terms. Where abusua defines a group of people descended from one great-grandmother on the maternal side, a clan can be the accumulation of different groups of abusua. Marriage between members of a clan is permissible; the same within an abusua, an act akin to incest, was historically not, although the passage of time has since worn away at its taboo status.[23]

The Asante form one Akan tribe and though the number fluctuates depending on who imparts the information, like other Akan tribes, each individual belongs to one of the seven or eight abusua.[24] Kobi is of the Ekoona abusua, he tells me as we study wooden plinths and inscriptions that detail each great family's totems, symbols and key contributions. The schoolchildren and their babble have since filtered out, leaving the pair of us and a few individuals perusing the collection. My guide's totem is the buffalo, symbolising strength and uprightness. The dog – representative of hard work, humility and service – belongs to the great family of Aduana, while the bat of the Asenie abusua speaks to adjudication, diplomacy and bravery. Cleanliness, beauty and stamina are evoked by the vulture of the Asakyiri, multitude and unity and eloquence by the parrot of the Agona, while aggression and exceptional bravery mark the Bretuo abusua, represented by the spotted leopard. The latter family group also yields the Asante state's second-in-command, the often fur-clad mamponghene. The totem of Yaa Asantewaa and her Asona abusua is the crow, yielding qualities of wisdom, purity of heart, peace and statesmanship.[25]

The final great family, the Oyoko, belongs to that of the Asante monarchy. The eagle, falcon and hawk are all presented as their totem, the birds of prey ushering in self-confidence, might and patience – qualities that only bolster the enigma that lines the asantehene's station. A station handed to him by a woman in his family. 'The asantehemaa selects the next king,' Kobi tells me as we continue our slow ramble around the small museum. '[After the first asantehene, Osei Kofi Tutu] they wanted to know who would be next,' he adds with a wry smile. 'He had married so many wives, there would've been conflict.'

The delicate nature of balanced power between the two rulers is highlighted further at my next site visit, this time the time-worn yellow and dusty red façade of the Manhyia Palace. About a kilometre away from the leafy Centre for National Culture, the palace was built by the British in 1925 and is technically the second Manhyia Palace. The first was demolished with explosives, also by the British, in 1874. In 1995, it was turned into a museum and it's this threshold I step across.[26] I join a group of fellow tourists and foreigners as our tall and effusive guide leads us through corridors, across the great hall, past life-size effigies of bygone rulers, in front of cases displaying medals from Britain, Ethiopia and Liberia bequeathed to whichever *asantehene* was in power.

As he leads us from one stately room to another, the guide emphasises the nature of dual Asante rule and social dynamics. 'The woman is the blood or life of the family,' he says. 'The man is the strength or spirit.' It's why, he adds, that women are seen as continuity and it is only those who come by the bloodline who are entitled to power.

'Is that why women are always forced to have a daughter?' asks a member of our group, a jovial large Black man with a West African accent I can't place. 'They can have ten boys but will still look for a daughter.'

Laughter punctuates the guide's response. 'When a mother gives birth and they are only males, we like you and you are part of the family, but we won't see you as the future of the family because when you all die, the legacy will be ended.'

Within the monarchy, power is so tightly controlled by the *ohemaa* that she can remove her counterpart at any time she wants but he is not permitted to do the reverse. With that in mind, I ask the guide steering our visit why the *asantehene*'s feet cannot touch the ground but the same isn't true for the *asantehemaa*. My answer comes in the form of a proverb: 'When a woman buys a gun, it's the man that fires it but the man should know who the gun belongs to.'

He continues with an explanation. 'You might be controlling the power but you must know its source. Therefore, in the public space, power is controlled by the king, so everything that happens in the public space comes to the king, protecting the woman.' It's why, for example, when the pair are seated, it's forbidden to greet the queen but the king can be interacted with by all – through his personal linguist, of course. The shield he offers his *ohemaa* – whether his sister, mother, or even niece – necessitates his own vulnerability and measures, like resting his feet on a footrest 'made of voodoo power', are taken to protect him.[27]

However, the status of the queen mother is never forgotten. When the ruling pair head out for public engagements that require a palanquin, the *asantehene* is carried by four strong men, the poles resting on their shoulders. The weight of the *asantehemaa*, however, is borne on the bearers' heads.

'The women carry the kingdom,' our guide notes simply. 'But the men are the strength of the kingdom.'

In a kingdom where women and 'the female principle' were central, where men were thought – and spoken of – as 'male mothers', it was by no means a matriarchy.[28]

In Yaa Asantewaa's Edweso, as in the other Asante central hubs, men almost exclusively occupied primary positions of power, despite having their status conferred by women.[29] While there may have been some gender parity among the elite classes, it was not reflective of the experiences of an Asante woman whose lineage did not afford her, or her descendants, inheritance and prestige. Meanwhile, prevailing beliefs around public behaviours of aggression specifically in women could see them put down sharply as *obaa-barima* – a 'he-woman' – while menstruation routinely restricted them from engaging in public life.[30]

Yaa's brother, Kwasi Afrane, would take up one of the coveted positions of power. In the early 1880s, through his birthright, he was elevated to the position of *edwesohene*. He came to rule Edweso during a fractious period for the monarchy, which saw two candidates locked in a struggle for the coveted *asantehene* title. Ruling over a division that commanded untapped military manpower during a Kumase civil war, Afrane occupied a lucrative position – one that saw him lay out terms to *Asantehemaa* Yaa Akyaa who wanted to secure her son as the next successor. Extracting oath after solemn oath from weakened Kumase royals in the presence of other chiefs, the Edweso ruler not only demanded the liberation of his people in *awowa* – held in pawn – but also the return of seized villages and lands. Their agreement procured the aid of Edweso and other states in defeating Prempeh's rival, earning the *asantehemaa*'s son – believed to be around eighteen at the time – the kingdom's highest office by July 1888.[31]

The manoeuvres of Edweso, and the similarly positioned Ofinso state, saw them raised up in prestige, meaning that these divisional rulers now had enhanced powers and privileges, as well as greater status in deliberations whenever the *Asantemanhyiamu* – Asante assembly – met.[32] Some historians have since claimed that Kwasi Afrane became the single most powerful chief in Asante, elevated to general of the *asantehene*'s armies and the custodian of the royal arsenal.[33]

Within the matrix of Asante political machinations, there was only one office that women could hold in the typical Akan state – and it would be this station that Yaa Asantewaa would be raised to by her brother before the close of the 1880s: *ohemaa*. A coruler with her sibling, she held joint responsibility for the affairs of Edweso. In the absence of a male counterpart heir, she could rule alone as the division's monarch.[34] The formation of rule followed the Asante model of social organisation: an *abusua* would be headed up by a male and female elder respectively. The roles of the *ohene* (male) and the *ohemaa* (female) reflected these precedents on a state level.[35]

Growing into her role alongside her brother, Yaa Asantewaa, now somewhere around her forties, shouldered the same weight of expectation that had been borne by every *ohemaa* before her. The male mothers around Asantewaa looked to her to bring balance to the rule of Afrane. As his counsel, she was perceived as his moral compass, leaving him with sage words of wisdom and emotion;

her reason completing his bravery, compassion countering inflexibility. These were qualities seen beyond the remit of the men who gathered around her and the *edwesohene* holding court, musing and pontificating in the midst of their thatched homes, resplendent robes trailing in warm dust.[36]

An *ohene*'s successes were naturally also credited to his *ohemaa*, but so too were his failures – perhaps even more so. The disastrous rules and subsequent removals of Kofi Karikari (r. 1867–74) and his successor and younger brother Mensa Bonsu (r. 1874–83) – the former deemed incompetent, the latter gratuitously punitive – was blamed on their mother and *asantehemaa* Afua Kobi. Though both around thirty-five years of age when they took up the mantle of *asantehene*, oral traditions point a quivering finger of blame at their mother for failing to provide them with 'good counsel'.[37]

Some historical and anthropological literature has placed emphasis on the office of *ohemaa* as a symbol of motherhood, characterising the role as little more than 'an elevated domestic position.' But, to do so, is to hollow out its complexity. While Asantewaa's role involved providing guidance, there was nothing ceremonial about her duties. Her presence was required when there were critical matters of state to be decided, or when judicial cases involving sacred oaths of state needed to be heard. The knowledge of the *ohemaa* traversed divinity, law, history, politics and affairs of the everyday.[38] She held her own separate court, assisted by counsellors and functionaries of different genders, where her independent jurisdiction covered all domestic matters pertaining to women and other royals. It wasn't just an expectation for the *ohemaa* to advise, criticise and rebuke the *ohene* in public – it was her constitutional duty. Failing to carry it out satisfactorily could see the sovereign deposed by an assembly of chiefs.[39]

Beyond the buzzing activity that swarmed her each day, an enveloping swirl of urgent requests and indignant complaints and fawning praise, there was yet more asked of Yaa Asantewaa. As *ohemaa*, she was also the in-house royal genealogist, called into action to determine the legitimacy of competing claims should her brother or future *edwesohenes* vacate the office.[40] No man could ascend without her say.

The *edwesohemaa*, commanding respect and deference, earned a new designation – an Akan honorific that prescribed high status to its wearer. Rulers and community elders alike are connected by a title that presents them as wise before their name is even invoked. In keeping with tradition, the Edweso queen mother took the honour that was hers to claim.

She became Nana Yaa Asantewaa.

Asantewaa and her husband had one child. Alongside celebrating the birth of their daughter with the people of Edweso, there were many other key moments to be commemorated as Ama Sewaa Brakatu grew – an individual who would also come to be known as Ama Sewaa Boankra, after the farmlands that had collected her mother's toils.[41]

When the infant, likely under the watchful eye of her parents, began to crawl on tiny hands and chubby legs, Ama Sewaa would've received a wooden stool, like all other children who survived the dangerous period of infancy. Years later, when she underwent *bra goro* – the puberty rite observed for girls – she would've been ceremoniously placed on another stool, symbolising her admittance to womanhood. When, even further down the line, the *edwesohene*'s daughter was joined in marriage with Kwadwo Frimpon from a town near Besease, her new husband would've presented her with a stool to seal the permanency of their union. And when Ama Sewaa herself became a mother, bearing eleven children, it would be her turn to mark the rites of passage for each child with their own stools.[42]

The meaning and function of the stool among the Asante, however, extends far beyond the domestic. Normally fashioned from the white, fine-grained wood of the Osese tree – a supernatural bark that required poured libations to pacify the spirit and ensure the safety of the carver – the *dwa*, or stool, itself is a sacred object. On an individual level, a *dwa* is imbued with its owner's essence, and the more they sit on its smoothly carved crescent seat – symbolic of a mother's embrace – the more potent its sacred nature becomes. When the stool is not in use, it is placed on its side to thwart another person's spirit entering it.[43]

The *dwa* is also sacred in that it is a conduit to a society's ancestors, embodying the soul of their people. Through blackened – or ancestral – stools, the Asante and other Akan peoples commune with their ancestors, the *dwa* a channel to unseen realms. The stools that were frequently used by admired elders and chiefs with lauded reigns are preserved and blackened with a mixture of eggs and soot. Kept in designated stool rooms, each blackened *dwa* is ripe with inhabiting ancestral spirits and, as such, reverence and respect are paid through offerings (originally of the sacrificial nature), the performance of religious rites and requests for protection and blessings.[44]

However, alongside its entangled utilitarian, domestic and sacred functions, the *dwa* is also a political symbol. Every *ohene* has one or more stools that denote and validate his rank, with the stool an emblem of social, judicial and political power.[45] Alexander A. Y. Kyerematen – the Ghanaian social anthropologist who would go on to establish the Centre for National Culture in Kumasi and serve as its first director – described stools as 'the most important of the chief's regalia and the *sine qua non* ("without which, not"; an indispensable ingredient) of his high office.'[46] While the *ohene* also has stools for eating and bathing, it's the ceremonial stools used in public rites that are most important, standing apart with more elaborate designs and repoussé metal plating. The middle of these stools bears the most creative and artistic expression, motifs and patterns carved into tree flesh that will one day house the spirit of its owner.[47]

There are connotations with each design, delivering verbal, visual and divine messages, each chosen and communicated by the patron to their carver. Animals, human figures and abstract geometric forms are frequently used and offer boundless interpretations.[48] The *obi-te-obi-so-dwa* is a typical ceremonial stool, translating as the 'one-sits-atop-another stool' with its two-tiered design speaking to the hierarchical societal order. It means that even among chiefs, priests and elders, there is an order of precedence to be observed by all for community cohesion.[49] The rainbow stool emerges from the Akan proverb 'kontonkurowi eda amansan kon mu' – the rainbow is around the neck of every nation. It both conveys the authority of the ohene over all his citizens, and that death is the lot of everybody, including the area's paramount, and therefore he must temper his pride and ego.[50] Meanwhile, the kotoko dwa – porcupine stool – with its spiked middle is associated with another adage which roughly translates as 'if you kill a thousand, a thousand will come', a defiant message to underscore a chief's invincibility in battle.[51]

Additionally, the dwa becomes a linguistic vehicle. 'Stool' denotes the office of an ohene and other officials, but it also names a governed area, such as the stool of Edweso. After a successful ohene candidate has taken the oath and has been installed, he is said to be enstooled in the office. When referencing his ongoing reign, the chief sits upon the stool. If, like the unfortunate asantehene brothers, any ohene is deemed unfit for office and it results in his removal, he has been de-stooled. And when the ohene dies, whether with the roar of battle in his ears or surrounded by palace comforts, the Asante say, 'the stool has fallen.'[52]

However, above even the most paramount of Asante divisional ahene (plural of ohene) sits the asantehene. And above even the most intricately carved or ornately plated ceremonial stool rests the Sika Dwa Kofi. The Golden Stool. Its full title? 'The Golden Stool born on a Friday.' Its origins are credited to divine means.

Like their extended Baoulé kin, the Asante have long understood their world as a material one underequipped to explain the breadth of existence. Historians Emmanuel Akyeampong and Pashington Obeng describe a universe where spirits, humans, animals and plants made up just a few of its contributors: 'It was a universe of experience in which some of the participants were invisible [...] [the universe] was one in which humans coexisted intimately with spirits: no human pursuit could be accomplished without it being secured successfully first in the spiritual realm.'[53]

That universe, created by the supreme and omnipotent deity of

the Akan known as Onyame, was imbued with their *tumi* – power
and the ability to bring about change.[54] Therefore, those who knew
how to harness that power could make use of it, whether for good
or nefarious purposes. Accordingly, divine activity was shrouded
in secrecy, with most Asante people not expecting to know much
about their own gods. Knowledge – and with it, power – was
soaked up by a select few.[55]

It was against this backdrop that Okomfo Anokye emerged, a
figure cloaked with historical silences but who maintains a preeminent status for his role in bringing an Asante national identity
into sharp clarity. While victory over the Denkyira in 1701 brought
elation and an end to the reviled overlordship, it also saw chiefs and
rulers – brought together as a union by Osei Tutu for the purpose
of war – prepared to leave the alliance, their most pressing matter
now concluded. In the relative calm that followed, Anokye, the
union leader's high priest and counsellor, and Osei Tutu sought to
harness the unity of war and channel it towards the new kingdom.
Their solution came in the form of the Golden Stool.[56]

According to oral traditions, the priest promised his ruler that
he would conjure a *dwa* from the heavens which would serve as a
divine symbol of both the nation's soul and Osei Tutu's authority
to lead them. With the following events believed to take place on
a Friday, Anokye gathered all the chiefs of the kingdom, including Osei Tutu, by the banks of River Bantama where he insisted
that they all surrender their regalia. Each chief's spears, swords
and stools were buried under the earth, their interment followed
by a flow of incantations from the mouth of Anokye. Clapping
thunder and streaking lightning – cacophonous rapture for the
ears and eyes – heralded the descent of the Golden Stool from the
sky, a solid-gold mass that would drop into the lap of Osei Tutu.
To demonstrate that the heaven-sent *dwa* belonged to the nation,
and not just the man who would become their first *asantehene*, an
ointment made with the nail, head and pubic hair clippings of each
chief was smeared onto the stool.[57]

The Golden Stool's arrival came with conditions, Anokye warned
the Asante when he laid out a number of laws – seventy-seven,

it's believed – to the nation. There were rules for both the people and the Asante ruler – for example, only the king had the power of life or death, making manslaughter and murder punishable by death – but there were also specific codes around the *Sika Dwa Kofi*. It could never rest upon the bare ground and later, Osei Tutu would make two chairs for public assemblies – one for him, and one for the sacred stool. To actually sit on the Golden Stool would be sacrilege. Treated like a living being, and named like any Akan child, it also had to be fed at regular intervals, its nutrition coming in the form of brown sheep, yam and liquor. If left to go hungry, the stool and its nation would be in grave, even fatal, peril. It was also blasphemous for another to create a Golden Stool or decorate any other *dwa* with gold: before Osei Bonsu put his menstruating wives to death, the campaign he had waged against Gyaaman was due to the *gyaamanhene* making his own rival golden stool. Lastly, should the Asante ever lose the Golden Stool, they risked the kingdom falling apart.[58]

As decades stretched into centuries, with each newly enstooled *asantehene* raised and lowered over the Golden Stool three times without touching it, Anokye's vision was realised.[59] The revered symbol, made of the most precious metal to the Akan, sealed the union of the Asante and the formation of Asanteman. Unified, they were a people galvanised to conquer, expand and vanquish.

Unforgiving ground lends itself to fidgeting fingers and half-asleep behinds. A barely disguised yawn might pull an almost imperceptible smile from Nana's lips or unlock an impatient call to sit up and pay attention.

There will be others she doesn't need to chide. Those children are already lost to the story's grip, beguiled by tales from a world that once was. More importantly, it once was *here*.

Imagination always feels more potent in the darkness and as it continues to engulf the compound, Nana knows which words will paint vivid tableaus, elicit shocked gasps or invite a crop of follow-up questions.

*

Perhaps there's an urgency to her storytelling. The older she gets, the less time she has to pass on fragments collected over a lifetime. She presses on.

All her life, Nana Yaa Asantewaa had never known an Asante kingdom free of the British. It was one of the colonial presences which had loomed around her people long before her birth. Over a century before her time, when Osei Tutu and the Asante union overthrew the Denkyira, who had dominated trade routes between the inland territories and the separate Gold Coast, they had effectively cut out the middleman. The Asante began commercial contact with the European trading companies on the coast.[60] The British and the Dutch – the latter who had been trading along the Gold Coast for more than a century – competed for Asante commerce, where their offerings of guns, gunpowder, cloth and brass could be weighed up against Asante gold and the lives, bodies and labour of enslaved Africans.[61]

By the 1800s, the Asante Empire had reached blistering heights and was weathering consuming lows. Asanteman had swelled to what would be its maximum. It enveloped most of modern-day Ghana and south-eastern Côte d'Ivoire and its expansionist campaigns were continued by successive rulers.[62] Trade gathered momentum, particularly the business of enslaving Africans, including potential dissidents removed after inter-state warfare. This led to conflict between the Asante and the Fante, an Akan people inhabiting the coast and who were accruing their own power as acting intermediaries. The best part of a decade – 1806 to 1814 – would see wars and skirmishes between the two groups as a result.[63] In spite of this, during the Atlantic enslavement complex, the Asante Empire went on to become the state in today's territory of Ghana that both owned and traded the most enslaved people.[64] This was a problem for the British who, in 1807, passed the Slave Trade Act which abolished trading enslaved Africans across the empire. Not only was enslaving kidnapped Africans becoming morally and religiously distasteful, but it was no longer economically profitable.

The Act didn't abolish slavery itself, just the trade, as Britain moved towards wage labour and 'legitimate trade'. Even so, illegal trading continued for a further sixty years and many enslaved people were not freed until their slave-owners had received compensation.[65]

It wasn't long before the British, who had allied themselves with the Fante throughout the Asante raids on the coast, began waging their own wars in the 1820s. Taking advantage of the desire of Fante, Wassa, Assim and other Akan societies to rid themselves of Asante hegemony, opportunity glittered in the eyes of the British.[66] Having colonised the Gold Coast in 1821 in the name of the ruling Queen Victoria, the British wanted to strengthen and expand their influence inland. Riding the frustrations of the coastal peoples now sheltered under their protection made for a worthy vehicle.[67]

And so began a series of major conflicts that would come to be known as the Asante–Anglo wars. Or rather, to the British, the Anglo–Ashanti wars. Back in the Manhyia Palace on my tour, when I query the two different spellings, the tall, lithe man guiding us confirms my suspicions. 'Ashanti' is what the British heard and it would be this anglicised version that would make it into all their historical documents. 'In our own [historical documents], it reads "Asante", the original word,' our guide explains, 'which, of course, means "because of war".'

Another difference is the number of conflicts believed to have taken place between the two empires during this period: a number of British sources refer to five, but my guide refutes that. 'The Asante fought the British colonial powers seven times, with the wars lasting one hundred years.' His words bounce off the cream walls of this rebuilt Manhyia Palace. After Asante forces invaded the Gold Coast in 1873 and took several of their missionaries hostage, the British defeated the Asante army and set Kumase ablaze, the same flames that would engulf the original palace.[68]

The inexperienced *Asantehene* Kofi Karikari was overwhelmed by Asante military generals who forced him into the disastrous 1873–74 Sagrenti War. And though *Asantehemaa* Afua Kobi would later be blamed by Asante traditions for her son's infamous rule, she had correctly judged that a full-scale campaign against the

British would end in Asante peril. She had even argued such before her son and his assembled chiefs but her counsel went unheeded. The war was lost and Afua Kobi was faced with no choice but to de-stool her indecisive son for the ruin brought to Asanteman.[69] In late September 1874, the dejected mother, in the traditional way, took her sandal and hit it on the head of Karikari. His reign was no more. 'It's a sign that you are fired,' my guide laughs.

There is a blurring between when Karikari's reign ended and that of his replacement and younger brother, Mensa Bonsu, began – both in 1874. As such, sources name one or the other as the *asantehene* who oversaw the end of the fighting by entering into a dangerous deal with the imperial colonising force.

'The British powers signed an agreement with the Asante that at the end of every month, [the Asante] were supposed to pay [the British] thousands of ounces of gold,' the guide explains. Among other terms, like the *asantehene* denouncing his claim to Denkyira lands and other tributary states and withdrawing Asante warriors in the south-west, the Treaty of Fomena outlined that the Asante were to pay an indemnity fixed at 'the impossibly high figure' of 50,000 ounces of gold.[70] The Asante handed over gold beads and other worked jewellery in attempts to pay it off – some of the gold was auctioned off by the London Crown Jeweller, Garrard, with thirteen of these items acquired by the Victoria and Albert Museum in June 1874.[71]

As chaos and upheaval engulfed the Asante, Mensa Bonsu and Afua Kobi faced a new challenge: one from his sister and her daughter, Yaa Akyaa. From the late 1870s, she worked to build up a powerful political base, one that advocated the claims of her own children to the Golden Stool. The politically astute Yaa Akyaa was also against the indemnity levied upon her people. Ending Mensa Bonsu's rule, she believed, could eradicate that debt.

The resultant civil war – the same one that Nana Yaa Asantewaa's brother Kwasi Afrane would leverage for the gains of Edweso's people – saw Yaa Akyaa, Afua Kobi's eldest daughter and now rival, oust her mother from office. Both she and Mensa Bonsu were banished from Kumase in 1884. The new *asantehemaa* – who would earn that disparaging, gendered title of *obaa-barima* in Asante historical traditions – had political ambitions that even the death of her son, *Asantehene* Kwaku Dua II, forty-four days into his reign would not derail. She turned to her next son, Prempeh I, and the administrative matters of building his support. This second round of internal political strife – heightened by a challenge from a maternal uncle – would prove far more testing, reflected by the four years it would take to secure the kingship for her son. So embittered was the contest, the *asantehemaa* took personal possession of the Golden Stool to ensure that none of her opponents in the royal clan could be physically enstooled even if they triumphed.[72]

Though Prempeh I would emerge victorious, Yaa Akyaa was the power behind the throne of the teenage ruler, believed to be around sixteen or seventeen years old when enstooled. In 1888, he became the thirteenth *asantehene* of the empire, taking the proper stool name of Nana Kwaku Dua III (however, he is usually referred to as Prempeh I). His ascent aligned with the elevation of Nana Yaa Asantewaa to Edweso's *ohemaa*. Unbeknownst to them both, the Asante were headed towards a critical juncture – one in which both historical actors would play defining roles.

When the *edwesohemaa*, approaching her fifties, watched on as the newly elected *edwesohene* undertook his rites in 1894, was she fearful? Not only had her brother, a man who would be described as the 'architect of Edweso's resurgence in the new order', passed away, but there was also the steadily mounting British threat that was proving difficult to shake.[73] Or, as Asantewaa appraised the man – her grandson – nominated as the Edweso chief, was she resolute in the decision she'd taken?

Following in his great-uncle's footsteps, Kofi Tene was next to occupy the Edweso *dwa*. In fact, to his grandmother, he was doing much more. Nana Yaa Asantewaa believed him to be a *kra pa* – reincarnation – of Kwasi Afrane.[74] Like the man who had ruled before him, there were tough decisions lying in wait. But unlike his predecessor, Kofi Tene (who was also known as Afrane *kumaa* – the younger) wouldn't enjoy as long or successful a campaign.[75]

Enstooled as ruler of Edweso, a now powerfully positioned state, Kofi Tene was an important cog in the assembly of chiefs reporting to an *asantehene*, Prempeh I, coming under intense pressure. It was a quandary that my Manhyia Palace guide summed up with frank panache. 'When Prempeh I became king, the British hurried to him to pay the gold, but he knew that this was why his uncles were de-stooled and he was not willing to do it.'

He had paused for effect before continuing, taking in his assembled audience of tourists. 'Prempeh I told them that he would not pay the gold because one, it was not him who signed the agreement, it was his uncle and, because he was dead, the agreement was dead. And two, if the British powers wanted their money, they should go to the cemetery and collect the money from the ghost of his dead uncle.'

It rather captures the firm opposition that the *asantehene*, steered by his mother whom British agents would recall as a 'frostily dignified old lady', held towards the Western imperial project and whatever designs it had for the Asante.[76] British official records documented the situation in far more passive terms, presenting what would happen next as a result of Prempeh I's failure to pay the gold in question. However, some historians, like Ghanaian academic Albert Adu Boahen, understand what would befall Prempeh I as merely a political weapon in the colonising power's arsenal.

Given the preceding fractious civil war, Prempeh I was expected to have limited success in his efforts to reunite and strengthen the Asante Empire – so much so that three years into his reign, in 1891, the British offered to take his kingdom under their protection.[77] The *asantehene*'s response was firm: 'I may say this is a matter of a very serious consideration and which I am happy to say we have arrived at this conclusion, that my kingdom of Ashanti will never commit itself to any such policy; Ashanti must remain independent as of old, at the same time being friendly with all white men.'[78]

When he was finally successfully installed as *asantehene* at a ceremony in June 1894 before all but one of the great rulers of Asante, alarm bells started ringing for the British. Prempeh I's attempts to seek military aid elsewhere and polite but firm, repeated refusals of accepting a British resident (a diplomatic government official exercising a degree of indirect rule) would've, by 1895, set off an almighty clamour. The ruler's vision of a transformed and independent Asante economy - with centralised gold mining, timber concessions, factories, public works and infrastructure like schools – was 'incongruous' with the advent of European imperialism.[79]

Using the largely unpaid indemnity as justification, an army was dispatched to Kumase and, despite Prempeh I's attempted negotiations, he was deposed by the British. That wasn't enough for the Europeans, though. Together with his mother and *asantehemaa*, his father, his brother and a host of principal *ahene*, the *asantehene* was arrested and, after months of imprisonment at the coastal Elmina Castle, exiled to the British-administered Seychelles Islands. Among the exiled chiefs was Asantewaa's grandson, Kofi Tene.[80]

Nana Yaa Asantewaa became the sole ruler of Edweso in 1896, as the dawn of British colonial rule rose over Asante, a kingdom bereft of its king.

Small though it may be, the courtyard-like walls of the Prempeh II Museum heave with original Asante artefacts.

There's the worn-looking *sanaa* (treasure bag) made by Okomfo Anokye in the 1600s from elephant skin, believed to contain valuables that have never been seen. The high priest's prophesy that the Asante kingdom would fall should it be opened was enough to halt any curious fingers. There are *etwie* (war drums) proudly presented on stands, each covered with leopard skin and used to frighten enemies during the throes of war. My companion Kobi demonstrates how, when many of these drums are scratched at once, they sound not dissimilar from the animal that adorns them. Firearms like flint-lock guns and blunderbusses line one wall, sixteenth-and-seventeenth-century French and British guns captured by the Asante during the Sagrenti War.

Among these weapons of war and protection, there are also items that trace the Asante way of life among the kingdom's elite – with royal funeral urns and stools and palanquins used by various *asantehemaa*. Walking from wall to wall, scribbling words into my fraying notepad, there is one item that catches my eye.

Small, delicately hammered with engravings all around it, it's the spitting image of the hallowed Golden Stool. The museum fixes no known time period to it, but its purpose is clear. This false Golden Stool was given to deceive the British in their request for the original *Sika Dwa Kofi*, the replica made of copper and heavily coated in gold. Today, however, it's just copper.[81]

'The British returned the stool,' laughs Kobi. 'Just without the gold.' While the unabashed gold-lined greed is laughable, it was only a symptom of a more ominous and much deeper problem.

By the late 1890s, the British had linked the political conquest of Asante with ownership of the Golden Stool. They had become attuned to its symbolic centrality to the nation.[82] British governor of the colonised Gold Coast, Frederick Hodgson, realised that it was the Golden Stool itself, not the person who occupied the station, that the Asante owed allegiance to. As a result, he believed that any person in possession of the golden mass would, by rights, be entitled to the acquiescence of the nation's people.[83] For the British, the Golden Stool was the key and if they 'surrendered' it, 'it meant that they ceased to be a nation, and became a scattered number of tribes.'[84]

After sending his private secretary on a fruitless secret expedition to capture the Golden Stool in 1899, Hodgson took it upon himself to travel inwards from the coast to the Asante capital.[85] When he reached Kumase, he summoned the leaderless chiefs of the kingdom to meet with him on 28 March 1900. They came, surely beleaguered and suspicious of what the British would be demanding of them this time.

Among the paramount chiefs sat the 60-year-old Nana Yaa Asantewaa, time and loss likely having etched themselves on her face, across her skin, in her bones. It had been four years that her grandson had been missing, spirited away to islands floating in the Indian Ocean. If she had entered the meeting room with hopes of his – and the others' – speedy return, Hodgson quickly put that to bed.

Before the assembly of Asante's political elite, Hodgson announced that their *asantehene* would 'positively never come back' and that they would have to pay a heavy tribute to the tune of 4,000 ounces of gold annually – a small, even generous, offer to the minds of the British.[86] It would offset, he alluded, the expenses that the British had incurred over the costly 1896 deposition – maintaining a residency in Kumase over the four years since was not a cheap endeavour and now it was time for the British to collect their dues.[87]

The Englishman was, by no means, finished. He launched into the next, most crucial order of business. Addressing the Asante congregation, he raised the issue that continued to plague his administration:

> Now Kings and Chiefs... What must I do to the man, whoever he is, who has failed to give the Queen who is the paramount power in this country, the stool to which she is entitled? Where is the Golden Stool? Why am I not sitting on the Golden Stool at this moment? I am the representative of the paramount power; why have you relegated me to this chair? Why did you not take the opportunity of my coming to Kumasi, and give it to me to sit upon?
>
> However, you may be quite sure that although the Governor has not received the Golden Stool, it will rule over you with the same impartiality and the same firmness as if you had produced it.[88]

Hodgson was met with silence.[89]

Before Nana Yaa Asantewaa's brother's death, he had taken possession of Obuase, a gold-bearing area that was some way from Edweso and was already being exploited by local Asante miners. The newly enstooled Kofi Tene had, around 1895, granted a concession over the 'Obbuassi Mines' and following his exile, the concession renewal rent was owed to Nana Yaa Asantewaa. However, the gleaming promise of the mines had caught the eye of the new British occupiers in Kumase and they were determined to regulate and maximise profits from Asante gold-mining. The British resident in Kumase had travelled to Edweso to speak to her in late 1896 and, while she argued her case and stressed her dissatisfaction with the lease's income, it would be all in vain. The concession was considered null and void, particularly as Obuase had been claimed by a pro-British *Kokofuhene*. And regardless, the *edwesohemaa* was told, under new regulations, Asante leasers would now only receive concession rent and no share in mining profits. By 1900, Edweso had lost all claim and title to Obuase.[90]

This treatment by the British had echoes of how Kumase had dealt with Edweso in the past. With yet another repudiated oath to her people surely ringing in her ears, fury – righteous and bubbling – guided her feet, and those of her fellow chiefs, to a secret Council of War just hours after that fated Hodgson speech. There, the leaderless paramounts quibbled and argued among themselves, weighing up the pros and cons of taking on the British, perhaps some even quietly – or loudly – considering the demand for the *Sika Dwa Kofi*.[91] So much so, Nana Yaa Asantewaa rose above them, not only to urge them into a fight for Asante freedom, but to sneer at the indecisiveness on display:

> How can a proud and brave people like the Asante sit back
> and look while whitemen took away their king and chiefs,
> and humiliated them with a demand for the Golden Stool.
> The Golden Stool only means money to the whitemen; they
> have searched and dug everywhere for it. I shall not pay one
> *predwan* [common Asante term for eight pounds] to the
> governor.[92]
>
> If you, the chiefs of Asante, are going to behave like cowards
> and not fight, you should exchange your loincloths for my
> undergarments *(Montu mo danta mma me na monnye me tam)*.[93]

As the elderly, slight woman embodied – maybe even revelled in – the loathed *obaa-barima* figure, did she peer into the faces of the men around her as she taunted them with male impotency?[94]

Did anger and contempt curl her lips as spittle and fiery words reminded them of the indignities the Asante had borne under the British? Or was her fury more implacable, wrought with chilled disgust and an air of finality? To punctuate her point, Asantewaa seized a gun and fired a shot before them. With that, her challenge was taken up. That night, the *ahene* 'drank the gods', bound by oath to rid the Asante of their British overlords.[95]

The kingdom braced for war under the leadership of Nana Yaa Asantewaa. Of course, there were those who had no intention of taking on the whitemen: the *dwabenhene*, *mamponhene* and *kumawuhene* were but a few chiefs to incur the ire of the Edweso ruler with their indecision.[96] However, with the Golden Stool secured and buried in the Aboabogya area, where it would stay hidden for over two decades, elsewhere in the kingdom, attention turned to strategies of battle.[97]

In April 1900, Asantewaa's Edweso became a hub of strategic activity. Blockades were built and troops were raised, organising 20,000 Asante warriors into a centralised fighting unit. Armed with weaponry, *suman* (leather amulets) containing safeguarding charms, protective animal-shaped pendants and warrior smocks, the Asante forces set about erecting stockades in front of their villages.[98]

Everyone had their part to play in warfare. Though ritual disqualification and the fear of menstrual contamination prevented many women from serving in the army, there were other arenas of battle that even pre-menopausal women could not be excluded from. As Akyeampong and Obeng write, 'If Onyame (the Supreme Being) had granted women the capacity to bear life, that same gift made them the best defenders [of it].'[99] The practice of *mmomomme* – a distinctly women-oriented form of spiritual combat – would see village women perform daily ritual chants until the warriors returned, urgently pounding empty mortars with pestles to spiritually torture their enemies while walking half-naked from one end of the village to the other.[100]

Now past the age of menopause, Nana Yaa Asantewaa joined the ranks of older women seen as 'ritual men'. They were afforded elderly privileges like wearing their cloths like men did, drinking liquor, and *dansikra* – the right to cut their hair short.[101] It was therefore fitting, that as commander-in-chief, the *edwesohemaa* was said to have donned the *batakari kese*, a war dress worn by Asante kings as they headed into battle since the inception of the kingdom. A tapestry of stitched pouches made of leather, cloth, silver and gold, they carried more hallowed charms to keep the Asante tactician protected as she strategised decoys, developed musical sounds to alert her troops of approaching enemies and instilled the use of snarling, foreboding drums to terrorise the British.[102]

Amid the galvanising efforts, a teacher who fled 120km west of Kumase to the town of Abetifi told Basel missionaries there the following:

> An old woman called Yaa Asantewaa lives in Adweso, the mother or the aunt of the chief there, a man who was sent into exile with Prempeh. Since then she has ruled the town. She has much influence in the whole of Asante, and is the soul and the head of the rebellion.
>
> When the Governor invited the chiefs to negotiate with him, she sent to tell them 'I have loaded my gun, and not for nothing.' She is in fact sitting quietly at Adweso, but sends her orders out from there to the different camps around Kumasi.[103]

The aging ruler's military forces blockaded all routes leading to Kumase, staving off British efforts to capture the capital.

Meanwhile, for the British governor Hodgson, his wife, the several hundred British officers, missionaries and their wives, and the hundreds of Hausa troops fighting under Queen Victoria's banner, the Kumase Fort they had sought as refuge in early April 1900 was no longer a shield. It was a cage.

Cape Coast Castle was the original, one of the dozens of European-built forts that lined the edge of the Gold Coast. Deep in its bowels, in a network of underground dungeons, the moans of the sick, the famished, the terrified, the delusional, the young, mingled as

hundreds of enslaved Africans awaited their fate. Forced incarceration in these cold and dark cells often marked the beginning of
unimaginable suffering as these people were exported across the
Atlantic like gold or mahogany, except they weren't deemed as
valuable. When they were packed into ships and the western coast
slipped from view, the passage brought an end to the life they had
known, the bonds of kinship they had formed, and ownership of
their own bodies – should they survive.[104]

Kumase Fort was built by the Asante as a replica of the castle
on the coast. Although the British destroyed it in the 1873–74
war, it was rebuilt in 1897 and they begin using it as 'a military
launching ground for the final offensive to incorporate the Asante
Empire into the expanding British Empire.'[105] Today, it only exists
for educational purposes.

I'm led through the fort grounds which have since been converted into Kumasi's Armed Forces Museum. Lined with outhouses
with rusted metal roofs, brilliant blue trimming and faded pink
walls that were once the shade of deep orange rust, Governor
Hodgson's besieged predicament looms into view.

I walk up the cracked stairs of the observation post, each worn
step displaying its own version of decay in the form of weeds,
small holes and exposed brick. My reward is not only a view of the
former military compound, its many rooms home to military artefacts, armoured cars, medals and photographs from Asante–Anglo
wars and the Second World War, but over the wall that separates
it from dense, thriving, forest-green foliage. Its leafy abundance
hints at the cover the Asante had when they positioned themselves
around the fort. With the post close to where the British stored
their rifles, I'm told that Asante fighters brought ropes along with
them and tied them to the branches to deceive the British into
thinking they were nestled among them while laid on the ground.
After the British spent rounds and rounds of bullets slicing the air,
with whatever ammunition they had brought along, the Asante
would start firing back.[106]

Asantewaa's forces and their innovative battle techniques could
only pen the British in for so long. July 1900 brought Hodgson's

escape, following months of a siege that would claim a number of lives among his entourage.[107] It also marked a tipping in favour and it was not towards Asantewaa. Kumase hadn't seen the last of Hodgson and when he returned, it was with bigger guns and reinforcements from the Gold Coast, Lagos and other British colonies. With Edweso and only a few areas around Kumase leading the charge, the swell of additional British troops left them greatly outnumbered and Asante capitulation imminent.[108]

This final Asante–Anglo war is primarily known today by two titles, each with their own framing and emphasis. In the 'War for the Golden Stool', the Asante emerged triumphant in their aim of keeping the *Sika Dwa Kofi*, the soul of the nation, out of British hands. But in the 'Yaa Asantewaa War', where its namesake fronted the resistance to British rule and sought the safe return of all the taken Asante elites, in November 1900, the elderly Edweso ruler tasted defeat.

The loss came with capture, and many different interpretations of Nana Yaa Asantewaa passed through the Kumase Fort's 'Gate of No Return'.

Much like the 'Door of No Return' featured at forts like Cape Coast Castle, Elmina and Fort Christiansborg, for those who crossed through these doorways, their fates were often sealed. Perhaps there's a theatrical, villainous edge to the way these portals are referred to today, as if issuing a challenge to curious visitors and tourists, but there's little to find novel or jovial. It often marked the final experience of their homeland before enslaved Africans were eventually bundled onto ships headed away from all they'd ever known. At Kumase Fort, it was no different.

There was the Asantewaa who was led through the heavy, thick, black wrought gate after her daughter was kidnapped, forcing her surrender, I'm told as I peer up at the doorway. Upon her capture, an examination of Asantewaa's chest was required in order to believe that she was a woman.[109]

There was Nana Yaa Asantewaa the war general, aged around seventy, who all during the war, never left the stool of Edweso, organising and strategising from her seat of power.[110] Forced to flee, she was eventually returned to the Kumase she'd recently had surrounded.

Conversely, we're told of the Asante grandmother who took to the battleground herself from the April day it began. This Asantewaa and her hand-picked bodyguard of troops, would be described as 'the best organized and most determined soldiers the British Empire forces had to face.'[111] She was slightly more reserved than the Asantewaa who fought at the head of the troops, tall and imposing in her trousers and battle dress, a smoking musket in her arms.[112]

Another Asantewaa, captured in the memory of a woman who witnessed her detainment, expressed fury at the Asante men who did not join her cause, with some supporting the British and others attempting neutrality. Relayed by the woman's son, Asantewaa's seizure went as follows: 'When she was being taken into exile, my mother told me she turned round as she was being escorted and said: "Asantefoo mmaa, me su mo" (Asante women, I pity you). Someone asked: "What about us, the men?" Yaa Asantewaa replied: "Which men? The men died at the battle front." She turned and walked off.'[113]

On 3 March 1901, all of these versions of Nana Yaa Asantewaa are said to have been led through the gate to the fort cells that held the condemned. There, a lack of light, food and ventilation awaited her. Though, the man leading me to her cell says, of all the principal war leaders detained, Asantewaa was the only one fed – a daily meal of two spoonfuls – as the British applied pressure for the location of the Golden Stool.[114]

When she wasn't being pressed for information or breaking her imposed fast, the clang of the heavy cell door and retreating footsteps left her alone once more in the belly of darkness. It was a pitch-black abyss that swallowed my vision and threw doubt over whether my hands were actually in front of me for the few seconds I stood in the tiny cell that would often be used to hold ten people at a time.

A month later, Asantewaa and her war council were sent on to Elmina Castle before being banished to the Seychelles, to join their exiled *asantehene* in June 1901.[115]

NANA YAA ASANTEWAA   229

*

In spoken Asante Twi, history means many things. It is *abakosem* or *nsem a abo ko* meaning 'a story of past things'. It is *abasem*, 'something that happened'. It is *tete ka asom* which translates as 'old things that remain in the ears' or the more succinct 'tradition survives'.[116]

Asantewaa has also become many things, beyond an old woman who lived out the rest of her days in exile on an island where there is scant evidence that she was reunited with her grandson. Beyond a ruler whose kingdom was never free of colonial interference across her nearly ninety years, and after her death on 17 October 1921, it would be nearly another forty years before it knew independence. Beyond the military orchestrator of a leaderless people, whose exiled Prempeh I would be allowed to return to Asante in 1924, and later negotiate the return of her remains and those of the other exiled Asante for royal burial, but as a demoted *kumasihene*, a position he held until his death in 1931.[117]

Nana Yaa Asantewaa is a title, one that could be worn by other women who followed her as *ohemaa*. A future *edwesohemaa* would be led into the sacred stool room containing the black stools of the rulers of Edweso in order to receive her stool name. Unable to rule under the name she was given at birth, she had to catch a name from her ancestors. The first black stool her hand trailed over, the adjoining name would be given to this queen-in-waiting, becoming the second, third, fourth of her ancestor's name. The presence of an ancestor's black *dwa* is necessary for the ritual – except Asantewaa's had been taken. The British had spirited it away, I was told at the Manhyia Palace, to the British Museum before the current *asantehene*, Nana Osei Tutu II, had it returned, blackened and safely stored in the *Edweso* royal stool room. It was only then that her name could be worn by future *ahemaa* of Edweso.

Nana Yaa Asantewaa is a cultural artefact, one worthy of her own locations, tourist destinations and events around Ghana. With museums and schools named for her, their overarching messaging homes in on female strength and leadership, self-sacrifice, and loyalty to one's nation, among others. The less pleasant facets like enslavement and the realities of warfare feature in the margins, if at all.[118] These tensions swirled around the Yaa Asantewaa festival launched in 2000, a cocktail of centenary events around the historical figure which also served as a travel boon for a country where tourism, at least then, was the third-largest foreign-exchange earner. The event planning sparked messy questions like, 'What do we do about the districts and chiefs who did not join Asantewaa's movement? How do we talk about traitors who shared her secrets with the British? What about any claims that she might have owned enslaved people?'[119] *How much do we keep and how much do we smooth its edges?*

Nana Yaa Asantewaa is a state emblem, a coat of arms, an anthem for the Ghanaian nation-state. The specificity of her fight for a liberated Asante empire and the recorded maltreatment of the stool of Edweso are blurred in favour of a galvanising national cause.[120] Her story has since been adopted by African nationalists, turned into a tale of a heroic Pan-African and anti-colonial military general who embodied the kind of exemplary values that other women should admire and emulate, particularly when Ghana was established as a new nation-state under its first prime minister, Kwame Nkrumah.[121]

It seems that we dictate who Nana Yaa Asantewaa becomes and what drove her.

'She was in a polygamous marriage, she was a farmer, she wasn't just a woman who picked up a gun and went to fight,' Shakia Ama Bonsu Asamoah's voice declared through my laptop speaker. 'I think learning about these different parts [of Asantewaa] is actually why I stopped looking at her like a feminist hero and, more so, a woman who had conviction. She cared about the people she lived among and we do ourselves a disservice by not telling those parts of a person or a story.'

The softly spoken PhD candidate studying at the University of Maryland spoke enthusiastically on my screen. Having followed one another on Twitter (now X) for a few years, it was normal to be greeted by Shakia's observant tweets around African, Black and queer feminist epistemologies all published under her @YaaAsantewaa handle. Yet, this was our first face-to-face meeting.

Despite her American accent, the education policy scholar was raised between Kumasi and Bekwai in the heart of the Asante region, regularly moving between her parents' and her grandmother's homes. It was during this formative period that she first received an education in Asante anti-colonial resistance. She recalls a school lesson on colonialism and its main focus on how it introduced civilisation and the Church, before touching the different resistance movements that emerged in response. 'This is when I remember officially learning about Yaa Asantewaa but I feel like I had heard more from family members just because we're extremely Asante people.' Her mouth widened into a smile. 'These are just the things my grandmother would bring up.'

When I asked Shakia how she would do this, she transported us both to one of the many nights of her childhood where severe supply challenges meant that electricity across Ghana would be switched off. Often when rain threatened to fall, villages would be – and often still are – blanketed into darkness. Each time this happened, her grandmother collected the children of her children and regaled them with all manner of stories to stave off boredom. 'My grandmother was really political for an "uneducated person".' Shakia's gestured air quotes flash on my screen. 'She would talk about colonialism and how people tried to resist it. She would tell us about how that translated to the independence movement and how, you know, Ghanaians lost sight of this goal of self-determination after independence.'

One of these story-time sessions proffered the tale of Yaa Asantewaa, whose actions remained just as galvanising for the young scholar two decades on from her first introduction. 'This is kind of petty,' Shakia emitted with a giggle, 'but I just like that she didn't take shit and was willing to fight for what she believed in.' She sobered slightly before saying, 'At some point, just talking about our politics isn't enough. At some point, somebody has to be the person who picks up the gun and says "I'm going to defend my people until I can't anymore."'

Her words stayed with me long after the call, one that ends with laughter, Shakia spelling the names of her family's villages, and excitable chatter – largely on my part – about our second call, that was to happen after my research trip.

It's a call that never comes. Less than a year after our call, I'd learn of Shakia's passing, aged just thirty-one. A feminist organiser and political educator whose impact rippled through Ghanaian, African and Black feminist communities gone, just like that.

I wish I had asked more questions, better questions, recorded every minute, date, location and event that Shakia was willing to share. I wish I had asked her what she had felt when the village would go dark, knowing her grandmother would come for her. I wish I had asked her for more of her thoughts on the modern feminist movement in Ghana. I wish I had probed her more on where she saw Nana Yaa Asantewaa fitting into the contemporary Ghanaian cultural tapestry and its nation-raising mission. I wish she got to hold a copy of this book in her hands.

I wish, I wish, I wish. This is the thing about history: it is, all at once, lasting and fleeting. Somehow entrenched yet ephemeral.

Shakia, her grandmother and Nana Yaa Asantewaa were all stewards of history. Their methods differed, from painstakingly tracing lineage to relaying historical accounts by mouth. And, through these women's committed guardianship of time, their people and their legacies, their voices live on.

Maybe it's with a hum, or even a buzz. Slowly, the lights blinker on.

Some will scatter like a shot, resuming their activities before the unplanned interlude. Others will drift onto something new, their attention snagged by a fresh distraction.

But a few might stay with Nana, more questions have bubbled up and they need answers. Whenever she's greeted with animated chatter stoked by her storytelling, does it coax a smile from the old woman?

Darkness has its own kind of beguiling magic but these stories also belong among streams of light.

CHAPTER 9

Muhumusa

The Spiritual Avenger

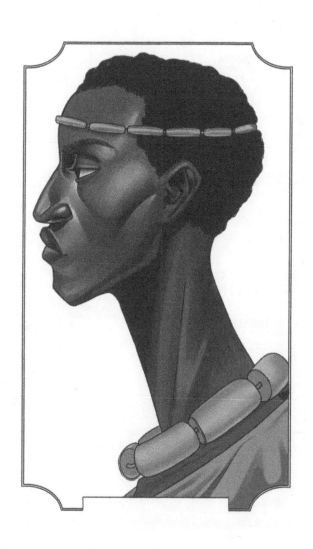

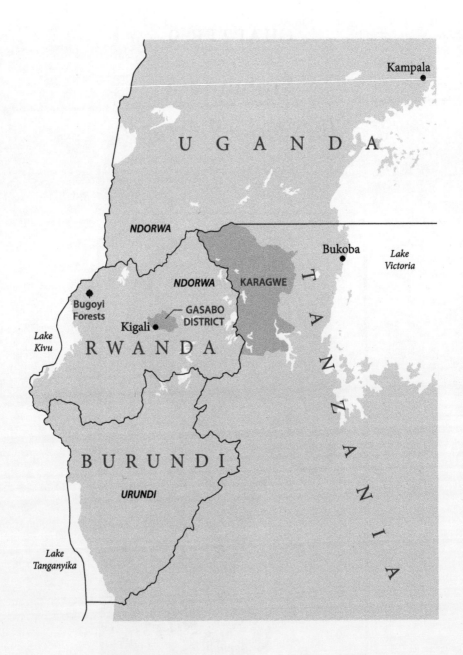

Like many museums, you can't take pictures inside the Kandt House. Not only is it named after Richard Kandt, the German physician-soldier-poet who was appointed the first colonial governor of Ruanda in 1907, but it was also his official residence.[1] The institution established in 2004 under the leafy boughs of Kigali was intended as a museum of natural history – in line with Kandt's interests as an 'avid naturalist' – but by 2017, this was expanded to the museum's current remit.[2]

Today, the Kandt House Museum commits to presenting Rwandan life in all its aspects before the colonial period, during occupation and following independence, with specific focus on Kigali, which was made the country's capital in 1962.[3] Split into corresponding sections, the building's white walls hold plaques, pictures and artefacts that hint at the origins of today's Rwanda. Kandt's life and personal items are scattered throughout, eternal reminders of the colonialist who laid these foundations. Even so, standing before images that cannot be replicated, that cannot be removed from these rooms, allows us to imagine what once was – and what continues to be among the indigenous communities who have preserved their ways. Like the rest of my time spent in the Land of a Thousand Hills, I walk through the exhibit seeking out the communities who have long inhabited present-day northern Rwanda and southern Uganda. A picture of an early 1900s northern settlement emerges.

Children giggling as they dash between huts with thatched roofs and woven walls. The mischievous expressions poorly hidden behind their *ibisage*-styled hair (Kinyarwanda for a hairstyle for children of small locks coated in butter and adorned with pearls, cowries and other pendants) as they are chided by an elder.[4] Maybe they veered too close to one of the large sticks supporting the brown hut's structure or played too enthusiastically next to the granary where crops, particularly sorghum, are stored. Their laughter would be just one of the layers in this soundscape.

The chuckles of elders sated by the bubbles of *urwagwa* (banana beer). The chatter of women doing wicker work, bare chests and double crescent-shaped *amasunzu* hairstyles denoting which of them are unmarried. The grunts that accompany hoisting a full fish trap onto one's back, its contents soon to be bartered and devoured. The unmistakable sound of blade slicing through stalk as a community of farmers thresh the crops in the heat, their *impuzu* (clothes made from pounded bark or animal skins) damp from their efforts. The low mooing of grazing *inkuku*, the common breed of cattle. (The special long-horned *inyambo* breed belonged exclusively to Tutsi rulers and chiefs.) The solemn tones of a *gacaca* court where the accused always holds a squatting position as they're surrounded by those that will judge them – this is how the community hears local disputes, acknowledges harm and disseminates justice. Of course, there's the call of the *inanga*. The plucked notes of the slightly concave zither unlocks hips and greases knees, cajoling dances like the *ikinimba* from tired bodies. Music proliferates in all its forms.

But before there were settlements, there was the Twa. Although their existence is sometimes neglected in histories of Rwanda, the Twa people, noted for their small statures, have inhabited its dense forests from time immemorial.[5] Ruled over by their kings, chiefs and councils of elders, the forest people brought down small game with their arrows and spears and gathered rainforest fruits and plants.[6]

Then Hutu agriculturalists arrived from regions near Lake Chad, as early as the first century CE according to some historians and as late as the fourteenth say others.[7] The Twa had an accord with the new settlers, '[providing] the farming [Hutu] population with game in exchange for agricultural goods.'[8] Retreating deeper into the forests, the Twa watched on as the Hutu established *ubwoko* (clan systems) and small kingdoms ruled over by Hutu rulers known as *abahinza*.[9] The transfer of land from the Twa to the Hutu took place through an exchange of gifts including beer, goats and sheep.[10] 'The Twa and Hutu kingdoms lived side by side, but were separate,' writes scholar Dominique Uwizeyimana. 'Their neighbouring kingdoms each had its own territory, citizens, and leadership.'[11] For centuries, they stood independent of one another, unless they deigned to trade.

Believed to be from 'Abyssinia' – the European exonym for present-day Somaliland, Djibouti, Somalia, Eritrea and Ethiopia – the Tutsi arrived around the fifteenth century.[12] Driving their cattle herds westwards, they gradually settled in Gasabo, the site of the today's Gasabo district in Rwanda.[13] Having lost land, forest and resources to Hutu farmers and Tutsi herdspeople, the Twa turned to making pottery for trade and money. They observed as the new Tutsi settlers established the *Nyiginya* dynasty, the ruling clan of *abami* (male rulers) that would last for the next 400 years.[14] In the late nineteenth century, the latest *mwami* was Kigeri IV Rwabugiri, the husband of Muhumusa.

After he took the reins of the Ruanda kingdom in 1876, Rwabugiri established himself as 'the great warrior-king of the late nineteenth century'.[15] And like many regents on the continent, including within the *Nyiginya* line, his claim to power was steeped in controversy and suspicion.

When an *umugabekazi* (queen mother) is named, the *mwami* is also indirectly named. Together, the mother and son would be presented to the kingdom as co-rulers, bringing the freshly named *umugabekazi*'s kin into the fold of power.[16] Therefore, conflict over which of the predecessor's wives would be named spelt trouble for dynastic succession and the wider kingdom. Rwabugiri's claim to the throne was – and is – disputed but even so, he quelled any complaints with bloodshed, plots and internal machinations.[17] The ruler had his mother, already elevated to *umugabekazi*, assassinated, among other family members. Although they weren't murdered, his brothers didn't escape Rwabugiri's measures, both mutilated to prevent dynastic challenges down the line. Threats eliminated, the *mwami* turned his attention to the kingdom.[18]

Since their arrival, the Tutsi had gradually settled among the preexisting population. Relations between themselves and the Hutu were primarily of a commercial nature, including exchanging cattle for agricultural products.[19] This accord wasn't to last. The Tutsi, many of whom lived in warring bands, used their advanced combat skills to acquire more grazing land from the Hutu. It set precedents for brutal encounters, the desire to conquer and pacify autonomous Hutu communities and establish military rule.[20]

The Tutsi ushered in *Ubwami* (feudalism) and the region's administrative system was built upon it. By the early nineteenth century, Ruanda was divided into around eight provinces, each overseen by two chiefs. One was in charge of the land and collecting tributes from the Hutu farmers; the other was in charge of the pastures, holding jurisdiction over other pastoralists – largely Tutsi – who owed tributes of meat, milk and dairy products. Under these two chiefs were the lower-placed hill chiefs and neighbourhood chiefs, 95 per cent of whom were of Tutsi descent.[21] Those officials sat under the Tutsi army chief, charged with protecting the kingdom and extending its borders through conquest of neighbouring kingdoms. All of Ruanda's subjects – Hutu, Tutsi and Twa – were understood as belonging to the army and therefore within the army chief's purview.[22] Above them all was the supreme authority of the *mwami*.

The inequality between the ethnic groups was exacerbated by Rwabugiri, namely because of the introduction of the *Ubuhake* (bondage) system. It's suggested today that the system was a 'client-patron contract' which, at first, meant that Hutu could use Tutsi cattle in exchange for personal and military service.[23] Even if those were indeed its origins, *Ubuhake* morphed into something else. Midway through the nineteenth century, land and cattle belonging to Hutu farmers were seized by the Tutsi, transferring power entirely to them.[24] 'The Hutu majority (85 per cent of the population), who previously owned land, worked on it, and lived on its produce, were turned into landless labourers for the Tutsi lords,' writes one scholar; there was little alternative for them but to indenture themselves to Tutsi lords to make a living.[25]

Alongside the confiscation of their land, cattle and means of production under Rwabugiri, the Tutsi forced the Hutu to supply free labour. A Tutsi landowner might promise some of their flock to their Hutu serfs but there was no limit set on how many years it would take to earn a cow nor any guarantee that a cow might be given at all. It all hinged on the whims of that particular Tutsi overlord. Even after giving a cow, the Tutsi could change their mind if they found themselves unhappy with the serf. Hutu peasants who later shared their experiences with journalists frequently told them that 'Tutsis look down on them as "subhumans"'.[26] Meanwhile, both Hutu and Tutsi cast marriage with Twa people as taboo, refusing to share food or drink with them.[27]

Muhumusa's spouse Rwabugiri – as of yet, it's not clear when they married – ruled over a nation of Tutsi masters, an enslaved Hutu population socially and economically excluded from his hier-archical society, and a smattering of disappeared Twa. Parricide (killing one's parents and/or other close relatives) had set the tone of the *mwami*'s reign, while military campaigns occupied his time. As power became increasingly more centralised to Rwabugiri's court, the kingdom structurally transformed under his hand.[28] It would be this Ruanda, organised by violence, inequity and subor-dination that Europeans would soon set foot in.

The conference about Africa took place within Berlin walls. Around a horseshoe-shaped table in German chancellor Otto Von Bismarck's official Wilhelmstraße residence, the international gathering was officially opened on the afternoon of Saturday, 15 November 1884.[29]

There were fourteen empires represented around the room. Noblemen from Austria–Hungary rubbed shoulders with parlia-mentarians from the United Kingdoms of Sweden and Norway. Diplomats from the Danish, French, Russian, Spanish and British empires all jostled for space. The future prime minister of Portugal made himself available. Leopold II of Belgium's 'International Congo Society' also secured a seat, making sure the interests of his new empire in the resource-rich Congo would be on the table. The Dutch, Italian, Ottoman and American colonial empires also made sure they had plenipotentiaries in the mix. Bismarck, who represented the recently formed German Empire, hosted the pro-ceedings.

The men gathered in a room overlooking verdant gardens. A large drooping map of Africa hung from one of the walls, signalling the purpose that had drawn them together. They were here to banish confusion and protect commercial interests, to 'manage' the ongoing process of colonising Africa – but in such a way that would ideally bypass the unsavouriness of armed conflict between rival powers.[30] A heated rivalry between the British and the French over the west of the continent, for example, required intervention. As the 1870s and early 1880s brought about European industrial booms and the age of the factory, the empires were on the hunt for natural resources and Africa glittered.[31] Surely, the colonists might've thought, there was a way to soothe any fissures – and safeguard their claims to African territory – in a civilised, dignified fashion?

Across the three months that the conference spanned (although they took a short break for Christmas and the New Year), the congregants – none of them African – set about regulating their colonisation.[32]

'In the popular imagination, the delegates are hunched over a map, armed with rulers and pencils, sketching out national borders on the continent with no idea of what existed on the ground they were parcelling out,' writes Kenyan journalist Patrick Gathara. 'Yet this is mistaken. The Berlin Conference did not begin the scramble.'[33] Occupation was already well under way: by the early 1880s, European colonies in Africa were largely concentrated along the coast with the majority – a suggested 80 per cent – of the continent under indigenous control.[34] Rather, this international gathering set out to formalise the rules of colonial play. These would be enshrined in the signing of the General Act of the Berlin Conference on West Africa on 26 February 1885.

According to them, the Congo Basin would be a region of neutrality, free navigation and trade. As the men stroked their whiskers, they pledged to end the trade of enslaved Africans on the continent and agreed that it was their responsibility to protect the interests of the indigenous populations.[35] They established principles of 'effective occupation' in order to demonstrate to other powers that they could effectively administer their claimed African territory: had the colonial power made treaties with local leaders? Was there paper evidence of these? Had the colonial power's flag been flown there?[36]

The game of plunder had new codes. The agreed terms wouldn't be stuck to – indigenous people were violently exploited and brutalised, the threshold for the 'effective occupation' of land often wasn't met – but even so, imperialism took on a refined and suitably buffed veneer.[37]

In the years that followed, Africa became unrecognisable. European landgrabs pockmarked its surface. Lines etched into the surface of maps cut through regions, kingdoms, villages and kin. While Africans – Njinga's Mbundu people, Hanbgé's Fon, Nandi's Zulu – wandered their homesteads and readied their goods for market, they were being organised into units that were legible to the colonists. Their new overseers had to make sense of the 'confusing milieu of fluid identities and cultures and languages' that stood between them and untapped economic potential.[38] Traditional kinship structures were co-opted into colonial constructions of 'ethnic groups' and a territory's governance was constructed around them.[39] Kingdoms that had been locked in conflict for centuries were bandied together as a sole territory to be ruled by foreigners; communities that shared tongues and customs straddled different sides of human-made borders.

France swallowed much of the North and West, with the British holding onto the Gold Coast and swathes of Eastern and Southern Africa. Portugal, Spain and Italy also held sizeable chunks of the continent. Leopold II's 'International Congo Society', which masqueraded as humanitarian work, paved the way for the establishment of the 'Congo Free State', which was privately owned by the Belgian sovereign, unlike the other European powers.[40] During his period of absolute rule, it's estimated that ten to fifteen million people were killed as a result of the actions – and inactions – of Leopold as he extracted resources like rubber and ivory from the Congo region. Forced labourers, many of them children, 'were seen as expendable, and were mutilated or murdered for failure to meet quotas; severed hands even became trophies or determined the wage bonuses of European soldiers.'[41]

By 1914, 'Abyssinia' and Liberia were the only two territories unclaimed by a European coloniser. 'German East Africa' was one of the many specially created occupation states the Great Lakes region greedily seized. The area claimed by the German emperor and king of Prussia included the territories of present-day Tanzania, Burundi and Rwanda, as stylised by Europeans.

When Rwabugiri died in 1895, succession noise reached deafening heights. While still alive, the *mwami* had taken the (unusual but not unheard of) step of establishing his son, Mibambwe IV Rutarindwa, as a co-ruler and, therefore, his designated successor. Following the passing of Rutarindwa's mother, Rwabugiri had named another of his wives, Kanjogera, as the heir apparent's *umugabekazi*.[42] The trouble was that Kanjogera of the powerful Abakagara lineage, the biggest political rivals to the royal family, had a son of her own.

Upon the death of her husband, Kanjogera and her brothers instigated a blood-drenched coup which stretched into late 1896. In the Coup of Rucunshu, Rutarindwa was overthrown and died alongside many members of the royal family and his supporters – whether they were killed or died by suicide remains contentious.[43] Described as a holocaust, the *mwami*'s forces were definitively overpowered by those fighting under the orders of his own *umugabekazi*.[44]

Instead of guiding Rutarindwa's rule, Kanjogera directed power into the hands of her young son, Musinga. Until he came of age, his mother and her brothers ruled in his stead. With customs disrupted and the Abakagara strengthened, the kingdom had become a dangerous place for anyone who wasn't aligned with the *umugabekazi* and her son – including Rwabugiri's other wives.[45]

One of those wives was Muhumusa. Muhumusa is a woman who bears different names, each tied to their own exploits. Many traditions take note of how she fled north, driven out of the royal court as massacres erupted around her. From there, however, the details unravel in different directions; the nuggets of Muhumusa's life scattered by word of mouth like flurrying grains of sand whipped up by Saharan winds.

She's Muserakande, the wife of Rwabugiri from Buha, who was saved by the Abateke people alongside her son Biregeya while she was pursued by the royal court's troops. Some question if they survived the coup at all or fled beyond the Great Lakes region.[46] Some whispers named her Nyriagahumusa while others claimed she was actually Nyakayoga, the former wife of Rutarindwa and the mother of *his* son.[47] Elsewhere, Muhumusa is read as a completely different person to Muserakande. Countless questions about her – or their – emergence hang unanswered.

To the locals I speak to while in Burera in Rwanda's Northern Province, she is simply Muhumusa. The wife of the former *mwami*, they say she had her child in the north of the kingdom, that she fanned growing flames of rebellion that charged Musinga, Kanjogera's son and the next *mwami*, with being a usurper.[48] As the cries grew in volume, the *Nyiginya* royal court was increasingly unsettled by the noises that made their way southwards. Whatever name she went by, all the people knew was that there was a Tutsi woman in the nearby kingdom of Ndorwa who claimed to be the mother of Rwabugiri's legitimate heir.[49]

Since the 1890s, the British and the Germans had been manoeuvring for control of the Great Lakes region but it was the latter who brought their vision of a 'German East Africa' to Ruanda.[50] In May 1894 – nine years after the Conference of Berlin and a year before he died – Rwabugiri, the first *mwami* to make contact with Europeans, met with Gustav Adolf Graf von Götzen, a military officer and the first German to step foot in the territory.

While Muhumusa fled to the north and turmoil roiled around the kingdom, the colonist had propped the door wide open for his fellow countrypeople. Richard Kandt, the German Jew whose name sits over the Kigali museum, became the first European to meet Yuhi IV Musinga, the 18-year-old *mwami*, in October 1900.[51] Missionaries followed soon after, with Protestants and Catholics jockeying to establish themselves first, both attempting to stem the influence of Islam while making conquests in the name of the Lord. They set out to 'save' the people of Ruanda who already had a belief system which centred on the omniscient Imana.

Missions popped up across the kingdom in Muramba, Rwanza, Zaza and more. The missionaries, many of them priests, came accompanied by their wives and children, certain that the kingdom's people would see their nuclear families as an instructive model to be replicated. Their practice was largely conducted with force. After all, a number of priests were also soldiers, their guns useful for interactions with an African population that white occupiers both feared and scorned. Not only did missionaries claim that it was their right to use the forced labour of Ruandi people to construct their buildings or supply them with food (some demanding 800–1,000 men per day), many – if not all – were chasing out locals and settling on their land.[52] Missionaries like the White Fathers, a Roman Catholic society, had established schools on seized ground by 1903. Many took it upon themselves to teach the local population how to count and how to make bricks and form them into European-style houses.[53] Meanwhile, as the Christian conquest took hold, traders were surging in en masse, the smell of untapped resources – minerals, livestock, trade route opportunities – flooding their nostrils.[54]

Musinga and his court were no helpless pawns, some historians assert, but rather 'real players in the game of [colonial] administrative reform'.[55] Alongside turning a profit from new colonial requirements, like the building of roads and planting of crops, Musinga played the German colonials off against the missionaries, although never enough to completely sever ties with either.[56] After all, the Germans had already proved useful to the *mwami*. For example, when the people around Gisaka rose up in 1901, Germans crossed the occupied Ruanda kingdom to tell the population to obey Musinga's court, using their military strength and punitive expeditions as incentives.[57]

The nature of the relationship between the Tutsi sovereign and the German occupiers was quickly established. The *mwami*, decried by many of his own subjects, clearly didn't have the manpower or

weaponry to oppose the foreign powers, but he was also struggling with the different resistance movements springing up across
the realm. These included the uprisings headed up by a Twa man
known as Basebya whose raids in north-central Ruanda had
become feared and influential. Many Hutu and even Tutsi people
joined his forces to increase their herds and protect their own
land.[58] European backing was, therefore, a huge benefit to Musinga.
The German authority neutralised a host of resistance movements,
bringing them back under *Nyiginya* authority.[59] Indirect rule suited
the colonisers. It made sense to them to simply use and manipulate
the political structure they had been met with, one that placed the
Tutsi sovereign and his dynasty at its precipice.[60]

As far as they were concerned, the Tutsi were suited to rule. With
their 'fine hands, with well-shaped feet', the Tutsi elites 'depicted
a noble character that made us believe that we were not among
Negroes'.[61] It was their unmatched intelligence, the latest settlers
argued, that had propelled the Tutsi into becoming dominant
masters despite their small numbers.[62] Unlike the nearby occupied
Urundi kingdom which also had Tutsi, Hutu and Twa populations,
the Germans reasoned that this Tutsi supremacy was why Ruanda
was supremely 'disciplined and peaceful' under the *mwami* and his
father, Rwabugiri.[63] 'It is in the interest of our colonial policy to
have the king on our side and to maintain the rule of the Watussi,
with total subjugation of the masses', Kandt surmised.[64] In June
1906, a protectorate was declared on Ruanda – separating it from
Urundi. Although he had been active in the kingdom since 1898,
Richard Kandt was officially in place as the 'Imperial Resident to
Rwanda' in 1908. He chose the Nyarugenge district – with Kigali at
its heart – as the administrative centre of the 'Imperial Residence'.[65]

Musinga, effectively a colonial administrator, watched on as the
colonial operation took hold. While he did target practice with
the occupiers, trying out their German guns, the kingdom was
being remoulded, purged of its traditions as Christian puritanical
zeal spread throughout. For example, the Germans supplanted
the *gacaca* courts, offering up their own kind of punitive justice.
Before, the punishments issued by the traditional courts would take

the form of owing the aggrieved party beer or cattle; the Germans switched this to whippings and imprisonment.[66]

The *mwami* relied on them to subdue his subjects, not least because there was a movement picking up speed against him in the north and it was one rooted in the spiritual.

Among the people of Ruanda, things aren't simply considered 'good' and 'evil'. Instead, sacred power either sustains life, or extinguishes it.

If, for example, a person has sacred power, they cannot die. When they die of old age, it is therefore normal because their power has been exhausted. However, when a young person passes away, especially suddenly, a diviner or spiritual practitioner is suspected.[67] 'Thus, the concern over the *presence or absence* of power is much greater than the concern of the triumph of good over evil, which plays such an important role in the Judeo-Christian tradition,' writes one observer.[68] Powerful deities, like Imana, replenish sacred power and protect their devotees. Nyabingi is one such force.

Some scholars say she was once a woman named Kitami, a queen of Karagwe, who was abused and murdered by a husband who had sought access to her realm, including the region of Ndorwa, a gift from her brother Ruganzu.[69] According to the Songora people of present-day Uganda and the Democratic Republic of the Congo, Kitami cya Nyawera was their ruler who died after a bee sting and toxic shock claimed her around 1725. Rather than being Nyabingi herself, it was claimed that Kitami had been a priestess of the deity.[70] Elsewhere, colonial historians describe Nyabingi as a 'female spirit' that lives underground but walks among humans, assuming different feminine appearances, from a child to an elder. 'This spirit is usually malignant, and causes death, illness, etc,' penned E. M. Jack in 1913, a writer aligned with the Royal Geographical Society in the UK. 'One of our party suffered from a series of sores on the legs, which we were told by the natives was the result of expressing doubts as to her existence.'[71]

Nyabingi (or Nyabinghi), like Muhumusa, means, literally, many things: it's what the deity's name translates as in both Kinyarwanda and Swahili as well as 'abundance', 'rich', 'providence'. Accordingly, the legends and details of Nyabingi's power are plentiful and varied. During my time in Rwanda, every person I ask about her has a new dimension to add. I'm told that in times of rain, drought and strife, the people, laden with their offerings, would ask Nyabingi for relief because she was seen as a mediator between Imana and humans. That people who struggled to get pregnant sought out Nyabingi who was a healer, a rainmaker, a miracle-worker. That she was the medium through which Imana spoke, delivering prosperity, peace, fertility and happiness. That her power emerged only after her death, when she was beheaded and thrown into a lake which would later turn into a boggy wetland. For locals, there's no equivocation around whether or not this figure from the fifteenth or sixteenth century existed: 'What we're taught is that she was a bad spirit, rather than a person from a palace who lived.'[72]

Nyabingi became the face of a spiritual movement, another belief system missionaries would present as evil, demonic and a bad omen. The validation of Christian missionary work and ideals necessitated the denigration of the divinities they encountered. However, devotion to Nyabingi endured in spite of colonial purges against 'witchcraft'.

At the turn of the century, shrines began appearing. Large huts were erected in the deity's honour. The outer compartment homed four or five *abagirwa* – normally traditional healers who act in her name – while the inner contained a bed and food laid out for the sacred figure.[73] The disciples of Nyabingi were 'almost invariably women' but *abagirwa* of all genders wore feminine-coded clothing.[74] Not only did they speak as her representatives on earth, but they also channelled Nyabingi. Shrouded in veils made of bark cloth, the *abagirwa* trembled and spoke in high-pitched tongues as they held divine dialogues with their *emandua* (powerful ancestor).[75]

Their intercessions permeated the earthly realm too. As vessels for Nyabingi's might, each *mugirwa* possessed the power to cure the sick and distribute cattle and beer among the people. In return, they expected allegiance and tributes from chiefs, disrupting tribute patterns in the kingdom. They were divine figures but also community leaders; their political authority flowing from their prophetic status.[76] The *abagirwa* built a reputation of leading rebellions and amassing followers who spurned Musinga's authority. Unlike the royal court, they were not beholden to the colonial powers. In fact, during the colonial period, sacred power was seen to have been withdrawn from Musinga, a *mwami* who could not vanquish a foreign entity that had subdued his kingdom while disease and pestilence ravaged it. Falling out of favour with the sovereign had once been seen as the worst thing that could befall a Ruandi subject. However, as the twentieth century dawned, rejecting Musinga in favour of another sacred power had become a necessity for some. What earthly power, especially a weakened one, could contend with the feared supernatural forces that would punish those who ignored Nyabingi's demands?[77]

By 1903, Muhumusa had already built up a powerful following. Her influence wasn't steeped in her association with the royal court but, rather, because she, too, served Nyabingi. Some colonial historians suggest that she eventually 'proclaimed herself as the full personification of the Nyabingi'.[78] Her claim to spiritual authority was a growing threat to Musinga. In 1905, Muhumusa started encouraging her followers to attack the central kingdom, unseat the usurper and crown her son. It was taken so seriously, in fact, that Musinga implored the Germans to attack her.[79] They refused. However, the following couple of years were marked by raids and organised resistance against the *mwami* and the elite classes. The Germans, busy organising a 'native government' in Ruanda that would run in tandem with their own administration, were beginning to appreciate the challenge that Muhumusa, and others like her, posed.[80] By 1907, she began to trouble the British occupiers of Buganda too. One colonist notes that she 'made herself obnoxious' to their commissioners.[81]

Sooner or later, they contended, she would have to be dealt with.

'We are now in the Burera district!' Christian enthuses before seizing my phone and gesturing that I stand next to the roadside sign for pictures. Sweaty, muddy and aching, I flash him a big smile.

WELCOME TO THE ROOTS OF NYABINGI HERITAGE CENTER, it reads. We've finally arrived.

It's not the first time my guide has assumed the position of photographer and artistic director today. If anything, they're roles that should sit alongside his actual jobs: the founder of Burera Youth Community (BYC), a youth organisation promoting cultural tourism and conservation in the area, and the managing director of the centre. A two-hour journey from Kigali with the centre's quiet, gentle driver Marc had delivered me into Christian's hands in the north of the country. Our morning activities had been a kaleidoscope of remarkable sights, admiring Christian's extensive historical knowledge and following his instructions to stand on, next to, behind or in front of various things as he snapped pictures and videos worthy of any content queen.

I posed by the roadside in Musanze with the Virunga Mountains looming in the background, their summits hidden by thick clouds. 'They're mostly inactive volcanoes,' Christian had explained. Because the chain of volcanoes sits in an area where Rwanda, the Democratic Republic of the Congo (DRC) and Uganda meet, a monument for each country can be found at the peaks of the volcanoes. I trailed my hand in the clear waters of Lake Burera while we shared roasted corn on the cob and Christian regaled us – Marc, the captain and myself – with stories of the *abami* who had once ruled from the ten little islands we slowly cruise past. The people who still inhabit some of these islands aren't allowed to date one another, Christian had added with a laugh. 'They're all descendants of one father. If you want to date someone, you take a boat and you cross from your island to another.'

Heavy rain, mudslides and freeing vehicles from squelchy red-brown earth had delayed our arrival at the centre but finally, we're here in Butaro, so far north that Uganda is a mere 10km away. Before getting out of our mud-splattered 4x4, I can hear the drums and the singing that herald our arrival. In front of the centre, its walls covered in vibrant mosaics and its pillars adorned in bright colours, are dancers, drummers and singers. The colours stand out against the green growth and towering trees around the centre's site. Adorned in red, blue and yellow shimmering fabrics over their everyday clothes, they skip, hop, twist and twirl to the beat. The stamping of their feet meets the jingle of cymbals. The ability to jump, to propel yourself upwards with your own strength, holds a place of import in Rwanda. *Gusimbuka Urukiramende* – or high-jumping – has been a respected sport since ancient Ruanda. Curving their bodies over a wooden stick placed between two makeshift posts, trained warriors could jump higher than 2.5 metres.[82] The jumping *Ikinimba* dance before me, particularly known among northern communities, is one link in a chain that stretches back centuries.

Although I had stopped to watch by the fence with other local onlookers, Christian – who is reliably filming on my phone, swivelling the camera to catch my reactions – insists I come inside and step closer. Marc, also filming, at one point stops to join the dance. My personal unease – at being another Westerner whose arrival requires performance – must take a back seat to the excitement of my guide showcasing his culture. 'Paula, you are most welcome,' he says. The words are echoed by a large smiling man who introduces himself as Jean, who handles the day-to-day running of the centre. When we greet each other, we both notice our almost identical gap-toothed smiles, our new-found friendship already sealed.

As we head towards the museum held within the centre's walls, Christian succinctly explains his motivation for the community work he is leading. 'It's an initiative we started because we saw that our culture and history was going to be forgotten.'

As I'm led around a corner, we're immediately met by the woman I'm pursuing: a larger-than-life rendering of Muhumusa graces a wall, her head adorned with beads and her shoulders wrapped in blue cloth. The men tell me more as we walk between the different rooms of the museum, filled with axes and machetes, calabashes and cups, herbal remedies and ancient board games. Present-day Burera sits within the historic Ndorwa kingdom that Muhumusa, in the name of Nyabingi, held authority over. The trees in the area are protected among the local people, particularly the huge Nyabingi tree next to the centre; it is not to be touched, let alone felled.[83] Christian explains that it's believed that blood will spurt out of the tree, with a curse cast over the cutter foolish enough to acquaint blade with bark.

When Catholic priests had first entered the area, their aim was to uproot the entrenched belief in Nyabingi's powers. Through demonisation, punishment and fear, they hoped to extinguish the influence of the *abagirwa* while instilling Western values. They burnt down houses, desecrated sacred huts, removed ritual symbols and purged anything that hinted at their cultural traditions. This included, for example, names.[84]

'You see my name?' Jean asks as we take a break from the tour, perched on wooden stools in one of the rooms. 'When we used to go to our local schools, your teacher would ask you, "What is your pagan name and what is your Christian name?"'

His birth name, he tells me, is Ntyeka. *God is a reader.*

'The name I was given by my father, they said it was pagan,' his sentence punctuated with a snort.

The local population was faced with moving away from the region or pulling back from the rituals they'd known all their life. Some would turn to Catholicism, Protestantism and Islam. But others would stay steadfast in their faith in Nyabingi, and their ways have survived through to the present day, kept alive in this region.[85] For the people who inhabit the hills today – that live dotted around the Roots of Nyabingi Heritage Center – are descendants of the deity's most fervent priests.

They are the children, grandchildren and great-grandchildren of the *abagirwa*.

She scared them. Maybe the local chiefs, the ones she demanded tribute from, felt Nyabingi was near when in her presence. Her high falsetto voice, achieved through years of training, and the way she moved – on her tip-toes in a crouching position with two sticks for walking aids – unnerved them.[86] Muhumusa's formidable reputation as a Nyabingi leader was so widely known, colonial administrators claimed that 'the chiefs with scarcely an exception trembled whenever her look was directed toward them.'[87]

However it was that she commanded support, people followed Muhumusa as she fought for her son's claim to rule. Ndorwa, a kingdom just north of Ruanda that had resisted its neighbour until the late eighteenth century, was fertile ground for her messaging. In her hands, divinity became a form of anti-royal, anti-elite action; a tool for galvanising farmers to rise up against 'both the old imperialism of Rwanda's central court and the new German imperialism.'[88] The movement would survive many decades, with triumphs and challenges – including the capture of Muhumusa.

Some say that, while visiting the home of an affluent fellow Nyabingi devotee, she was arrested by the German authorities in 1908.[89] Others suggest that, actually, a combined force of Germans and Musinga's troops brought Muhumusa to Kigali in the summer of 1909. There, Kandt wanted to keep her temporarily under his supervision – perhaps inclined to see whether she would acknowledge Musinga's authority. These accounts claim that her arrival brought a rash of rumours every few weeks with talk of Biregeya, Muhumusa's son, or another leader being named *mwami* by the Germans. Uprising lingered in the air alongside suggestions that Biregeya was in the kingdom once more. As a result, Kandt made the decision to send Muhumusa to Bukoba, found in present-day north-west Tanzania.[90] Out of sight, out of mind and out of trouble was the hope. One thing they didn't plan for was her escape in early 1911.

She hurried back to Ndorwa to re-establish her authority and realise one of the royal court's biggest fears: Muhumusa joined forces with the notorious raider Basebya of the Twa.[91] As the British, German and Belgian administrators erected borders through the centre of Ndorwa, Muhumusa's forces took up attacks across the kingdom, raiding, looting and burning lands of those who had sided with the Europeans. She sent messengers as far as the forests of Bugoyi to instruct the Twa to rise against the Europeans while missionaries spoke of their worries that Muhumusa would drive them all from the kingdom. The lands of her people sat in the crosshairs of vying European occupiers, staking claim to different areas. Kandt led another force north to capture her but to no avail. However, the British and the Germans remained undeterred.[92]

On 29 September 1911, Muhumusa was surrounded and captured through a joint British–German operation. It was the element of surprise that unravelled her and her forces, historians suggest. 'The battle that ensued was short and sharp... while her men who had trusted her to turn aside the enemy bullets [through divination], quickly gave in when they found their faith misplaced.'[93] Instead, bullets found their targets, killing around forty of her fighters and wounding their leader in one of her feet. Little is known of what became of Biregeya, who would've been around sixteen years of age. Once a child who sat between his mother's feet as she was carried around in her travelling litter, historians suggest that he was not present when Muhumusa was captured for a second time and, later, joined forces with Basebya to trouble Tutsi cattle and homesteads in German-occupied territory.[94] Some Rwandans today, however, believe that he was killed by the Germans around the time of his mother's capture.

Meanwhile, Muhumusa was detained under British authority and removed to their occupied territory known as Uganda today in 1913.[95] After more than a decade of trying to enlist the Europeans to take the threat of the Nyabingi leader seriously, finally one of Musinga's greatest problems had been alleviated. He must've been particularly heartened with the British introduction of the 'Witchcraft Ordinance of 1912' – a year after Muhumusa's capture – which criminalised the Nyabingi movement, promoted Christianity and encouraged indigenous anti-Nyabingi groups.[96]

But both he and the Western powers would discover an immutable truth: you can't kill an ideology with a gun and, when a movement's leader is incapacitated, more will rise in their place.

While we were sat on our boat, bobbing on the blue waters of Lake Burera, Christian had painted a vivid picture. It was one of the detained soldiers of Muhumusa, removed to the Caribbean by Europeans, who began teaching the islands' populations about Nyabingi there.[97] It echoes the transit of the Kimbanda tradition which migrated from Njinga a Mbande's kingdoms of Ndongo and

Matamba to Brazil and beyond. However, this is surely just part of the picture.

The famous prophesy by Jamaican Pan-Africanist Marcus Garvey rang out in the 1920s: 'Look to Africa when a Black king shall be crowned, for the day of deliverance is near.' Among a number of Garvey's followers in Jamaica, the working class and rurally poor being crushed under the thumb of British rule and struggling for land and economic independence, 'Africa' narrowed to Ethiopia.[98] A street preacher named Leonard Percival Howell 'followed Garvey's arrow back to the Motherland and found Haile Selassie, the emperor of Ethiopia, the only African nation never to be colonized, and declared that God had been reincarnated, walking among them in the form of a Black man, born Ras Tafari Makonnen.'[99]

On 23 Tekemt 1923 (or 2 November 1930), Haile Selassie I accepted the symbols that came with crowning the ruler of the Ethiopian Empire, as he sat on his throne, soon to be joined on the dais by his empress, Menen Asfaw. An imperial sceptre of ivory and gold, a diamond-encrusted ring, twinkling imperial vestments and a towering golden crown were among the bestowals to the 'Conquering Lion of the Tribe of Judah'.[100]

The following jubilation in Addis Ababa – booming cannons, blaring trumpets, ululating women – rode the waves of both sea and radio, reaching Jamaican lower classes who were agitating against their colonial overlords and organising labour rebellions.[101] The coronation of Selassie was, all at once, the second coming of Christ and the signal that Black liberatory futures could be closer than once imagined. Ethiopian resistance to the 1935 Italian invasion led by Mussolini only cemented this view, even though Selassie would be forced into temporary exile and his empire occupied until 1941. Jamaican papers printed front-page stories on the atrocities carried out by Italy in Ethiopia during the six-year period: the poisonous gases, aerial bombardments and creation of concentration camps.[102]

The Rastafari movement, which had long been rooted in the overthrowing of enslavement, began to emerge with the emperor at its core. C. L. R. James's 1964 appraisal of the group is one worth quoting at length. The Trinidadian historian describes the Rastafari as: '... the sect of Jamaican Negroes who reject the bastardised version of British society which official and educated Jamaica seeks to foist upon them. They have created for themselves a new world, in which the emperor of Ethiopia, Haile Selassie, is God on earth. His kingdom in Africa is the promised Heaven to which all the Rastafari elect will go, not when they die but when they can raise the money for the passage.'[103]

The revolutionary spirit of Rasta – a class and racial revolt against the colonial status quo – was expressed through hair, dress and ways of living off the land.[104] There was no overarching doctrine, but rather the passing on of wisdom from elder Rasta bredren and the teachings of radical Pan-Africanism around drum circles.[105] The colonial authorities on the island grew nervous and attempted to infiltrate meetings, because not only were the Rasta linking themselves with Ethiopia, but they also identified with the anti-colonial Nyabingi movement sweeping through the Great Lakes territories.[106]

Rastas referred to themselves as 'Nya men' while the 'strictest and most radical sect of Rastafari' was named the Mansion of Nyabinghi.[107] They attributed new meaning to the name 'Nyabingi'; to the Rastas, it was a rallying call for 'Death to Black and White Oppressors'.[108] Revered gatherings – which saw Rastas chant, drum, dance and reason with one another, smoke the holy herb of marijuana and give praise to Jah Rastafari – were known as a 'Nyabingi' or a 'Binghi'. It's described as the most important meeting of the Rastas and can last from a few days to a week.[109]

Rastafari ideologies were indivisible from the working-class and rural poor Jamaican communities from which they emerged. They ran counter to Garveyism which focused on a form of Black nationalism that was pro-capitalist: for Garvey, capitalist ventures were necessary for the advancement of the African diaspora industrially and politically. Within such a framework, built on colonial familial ideals, women were to stay at home and promote 'proper family life' while their male breadwinner advanced the cause of male migration and reduced the rates of unemployed local men.[110]

'Garveyism forged a link between capitalist men, Black and

white, at the expense of Black women's historical solidarity with Black men ... [it] emphasized race consciousness but the anti-racism insisted on a place for Black men alongside white men in the capitalist system,' writes scholar Terisa E. Turner.[111] The same promises of Black men's precedence over subordinated women can be found, in abundance, within Rasta doctrines.

Rather than being termed 'Rasta women', women in Rastafari were instead 'dawta' or 'sistren'. Recalling her early days in Rastafari, Trinidadian writer Lisa-Anne Julien notes that 'my then boyfriend told me that there is no such thing as a Rasta woman.' She could, instead, be a 'Rasta man's woman.'[112]

It was why women were maligned at Nyabingi gatherings, couldn't cook if they were menstruating, could not join men in 'reasoning' nor partake in the chalice (smoking marijuana). Despite the leading role played by women in the revolutionary uprisings that led to the establishment of 'Free Villages' across Jamaica in the 1830s – where bankrupt plantations were absorbed by the peasant classes through land seizures – the ideal Jamaican woman, in the eyes of the Rasta, was one that was domesticated and silent.[113] It mirrored the way that women in the Great Lakes region would also be disempowered through land loss, which eroded their self-sufficiency and ability to trade, but also the 'anti-witchcraft' crusade which 'delegitimised Nyabingi women's work as healers and seers.'[114] When Rasta women like Julien raised their critiques of the subordinate position of women in the movement – pointing to the likes of Empress Menen and Muhumusa – the arguments didn't move the men she came into contact with. They, instead, sought to placate her: 'I was not to despair at the impossibility of being God, but in fact as a woman, I could be God's mother.'[115]

It was a movement that would eventually see Rastas feared and reviled within an extremely Christian Jamaican society under British rule: they were viewed as unemployed and unemployable pariahs whose bodies deserved the brutality of the state; they were jailed and forcibly shaved by the government with their farmlands seized. When Jamaica's prime minister Alexander Bustamante called upon the military to 'bring in all Rastas, dead or alive' in

1962, they acquiesced by burning Rasta communes island-wide with an untold number of Rastas slaughtered, while others were imprisoned and tortured.[116] A bleak, painful future awaited those who adhered to the tenets of a faith that rested on Nyabinghi and their saviour, Haile Selassie.

However, in the 1930s, as the Rasta ideology was growing in influence and numbers, it was erasing a focal part of the eastern African movement it took inspiration from. In its transfer from East Africa, the Nyabingi movement lost its woman-centred essence. The faith-based resistance, named for one woman and preserved by many more, had been hijacked by men.

The people who served Muhumusa during her detainment in Kampala were loyal to her, Christian told me. According to local traditions, fighting strategies for the Nyabingi resistance were disseminated through them and they passed messages from the *mugirwa* to her army. Once the occupiers realised that she was in communication with her forces, Muhumusa was no longer granted servants. She's said to have spent the rest of her days alone, confined to a palace under British authority, until her death in 1945.[117]

Three years into her exile and isolation, would Muhumusa have been cognisant in 1916 that the land she had known had been renamed 'Ruanda–Urundi'? Or that occupation had switched from German hands to Belgian ones?

Following the departure of her servants, how would the resistance leader have learnt, if at all, about the way her fellow Nyabingi disciples continued to rise and rise again? Who would've made her aware that the Bakiga people in Kigezi – situated along Uganda's borders with Congo and Ruanda – would take up arms against the British in 1916, 1919 and, again, in 1928 in the name of the deity? [118]

What might she have felt, should she have received the news that the women-led movement, forced underground, continued to battle against – and kill – the foreign African Ganda intermediaries installed by the British to oversee them? That they didn't stop, even when those puppet chiefs were later replaced by Christian Bakiga men? That they refused to accept colonial conditions – including poll tax on land, labour, food and money – despite British efforts to crush them?[119]

Could the Tutsi woman have foreseen how far the spirit of Nyabingi would travel? Not only did it spread across the Great Lakes region, but the resistance lapped at the shores of Jamaica, Britain and beyond. 'Nyabingi' was a name worn by 1950s Rasta musicians who developed the 'Nyabingi drumming' style that would inspire the likes of Lee 'Scratch' Perry and Bob Marley.[120] The style spread globally, with Nyabingi drummers regular fixtures at carnivals, as well as Caribbean festivals across the diaspora. For example, alongside mas bands and steel pan orchestras, Nyabingi drummers were billed as performers on flyers advertising the 1987 St Paul's Carnival in Bristol, UK.[121]

She endured her incarceration for over thirty years, her own thoughts likely her closest companions. But even if she'd been detained for a further thirty years, in all that time, would Muhumusa even been able to hazard a guess at the horrors, genocidal in nature, that awaited Ruanda?

While Muhumusa was incarcerated, the kingdom that her husband, the late Rwabugiri, had ruled over was being morphed into a society that was more amenable to its Belgian occupiers and the Tutsi elite. Of course, the traditional administrative structure the Europeans encountered already favoured Tutsi dominance and the systematic oppression of Hutu and Twa peoples, however, the Belgians set about guaranteeing Tutsi privilege.[122]

Originally, Rwandans had primarily identified with one of eighteen different clans; 'Hutu', 'Tutsi' and 'Twa' developed as socio-economic classifications within those clans. However, they were solidified as hierarchical ethnicities when the Belgians introduced a mandatory identity card system by 1933. All Rwandan citizens had to carry an ID card which stated their name and one of the three ethnic identities. The colonists identified anyone who owned ten cows in 1932 as a Tutsi; anything less designated an individual as a Hutu or lower.[123] An even more rigid hierarchy emerged. The Belgians relied on the Tutsi to maintain their indirect rule over the territory, while the Tutsi aristocracy's control over the land and, in particular, the Hutu, expanded.[124]

Tutsi village chiefs often forced the Hutu, toiling to produce coffee, to work more days than had been set by the Belgian administration. The extra days were used to do private work for the Tutsi. Public flogging and other corporal punishments for not meeting requirements were administered by Tutsi chiefs, in front of the accused's family members, neighbours and wider community. They also enforced the payment of tax on behalf of the Europeans – according to Hutu accounts, they often exacted more than the official taxes mandated.[125]

The physical and financial subordination paired well with the general exclusion of Hutu from education, public administration, political posts and the shaping of society at large. The death of Musinga in 1944 and the succession of his son, *Mwami* Mutara III Rudahigwa, underscored the occupied kingdom's fate, particularly when the latter consecrated Rwanda to Christ in 1946 and gave the Belgians his assent to continue reshaping the realm.[126]

In 1957, the *Bahutu Manifesto* appeared, prepared to highlight the issue of race relations to a United Nations visiting mission. Signed by nine members of the Hutu counter-elite, it highlighted a range of issues facing Rwanda – the land ownership system, inequitable access to education, the rigged political system – that rested on fundamental ethnic components.[127] It denounced the 'political, social, economic and cultural monopoly of the Tutsis' and demanded greater equality for the Hutus.[128]

Translating these into political aspirations shortly followed with the emergence of the political party Parmehutu (Parti du mouvement de l'émancipation des Hutu, or Party of the Hutu Emancipation Movement) in 1958. APROSOMA, another party for 'the promotion of the masses' also took shape that year. That April, the Hutu leaders were invited to air their grievances before the *mwami* and his council, although these were 'ridiculed by Tutsi dignitaries.'[129] The rift deepened when the governor of Ruanda–Urundi openly declared the Belgian administration's 'sympathy' for the Hutu claims and, in response, the Tutsis formed the UNAR

(Union nationale ruandaise) party to advocate for the maintenance of their privileges.[130]

The sudden death of the *mwami* in July 1959 brought the country to the edge of a precipice. The freefall came after some Tutsis took the opportunity to elect Mutara III's brother, Kigeli V Ndahindurwa, as his successor, beginning what is remembered as the Hutu Revolution. The murder of a Hutu leader by a gang of Tutsis was responded to with the burning of Tutsi villages and the murders of their chiefs. Given that they only made up about 15 per cent of the population, the outnumbered Tutsis fled to the Congolese province of Kivu, Uganda, Urundi and other neighbouring areas. By November 1959, the Belgian occupation announced its intention to hold both communal and legislative elections in Ruanda and Urundi, alongside increasing autonomy in preparation for independence in 1962. While the new *mwami* and his advisors left the country to rally international support for their cause, the Parmehutu party stomped to victory in both, aided by the UNAR boycott of the elections. In 1961, *mwami* Kigeli V was deposed, the Rwandan monarchy abolished and Grégoire Kayibanda – founder of Parmehutu and one of the *Bahutu Manifesto* contributors – became the first elected president of the Republic of Rwanda.[131]

The stage was set for the advancement of Hutu Power in the country, particularly after Kayibanda's army chief of staff and minister of defence, Juvénal Habyarimana, overthrew the president in 1973 through a *coup d'état*. Two years into his reign, he founded what became the country's only legal party from 1975 to 1994, MRND, which replaced the banned Parmehutu party.

For twenty-one years, Habyarimana oversaw a totalitarian state rooted in Hutu supremacy which flowed through every arm of government. He, and his popular militia groups, stood for expanding Hutu-ness in all its forms and ethnically cleansing the land of the Tutsi, messaging that was reinforced by the country's media.[132] All of these elements were fundamental to the Rwandan genocide of 1994.

*

During our drive from Kigali International Airport to the city centre, my driver and I spoke in French – or Paul spoke and I tried. As he steered us through the wide roads of Rwanda's capital, lined with abundant trees and manicured grass, Paul explained how the nation is only now largely reacquainting itself with the language. After the genocide and the part France played in it, Rwanda had broken diplomatic relationships with the European power, including shutting down French institutions in the country.

'[The taught language in schools] switched to English and they removed French for about twenty-eight years,' he said, eyes on the road. 'We're now learning it again after the French formally apologised for their role.'

Paul was born in Uganda after his parents fled there as refugees, only returning to Rwanda when he was five. Other family members, including his grandparents, stayed across the border in the Southern Province, never to return to the country that had, for all intents and purposes, exiled them. They were but a handful of the hundreds of thousands of Tutsis living in displacement.[133] Some joined the Tutsi-dominated Rwandan Patriotic Front (RPF) founded in Uganda which sought to restore their rights and privileges. On 1 October 1990, the RPF's army force – the Rwanda Patriotic Army (RPA) – invaded Rwanda. With the RPF taken over by Paul Kagame, the RPA seized much of the north of the country through guerilla attacks and multiple massacres of the Hutu living in the region by 1992.[134]

Meanwhile, the stance of the Hutu Power movement had been made clear in 1990 when they published their founding principles, the 'Hutu Ten Commandments' in *Kangura*, an anti-Tutsi newspaper. 'Every Hutu should know that a Tutsi woman, whoever she is, works for the interest of her Tutsi ethnic group. As a result, we shall consider a traitor who marries a Tutsi woman, employs a Tutsi woman as concubine [or] employs a Tutsi woman as a secretary or takes her under protection,' read one. 'All strategic positions, political, administrative, economic, military and security should be entrusted only to Hutu,' outlined another. Hutus were traitors if they did any form of business with the 'dishonest' Tutsi.[135]

Although a ceasefire would be negotiated and the Arusha Peace Accords between the government and the RPF would be signed in August 1993 after a year of talks, it was far from resolved. A transitional government was meant to follow, eventually leading to democratic elections. However, President Habyarimana saw the accords as surrender to the RPF. Behind the scenes, he had entered the then-largest Rwandan arms deal with a French company for $12 million. The loan was guaranteed by the French government.[136]

A few days after he picked me up from the airport, Paul drove me to the Kigali Genocide Memorial, complete with its own Rwanda National Police checkpoint and body, luggage and vehicle scans. No matter what you may think you know about the Rwandan Genocide, little can prepare visitors for the horrors that await inside the sleek exterior of the education centre. The carefully curated exhibit pulls together the painful strands that mark the country's very recent history; it details the events that led up to, occurred during, and came after the 100 or so days of bloodshed in 1994 where it is conservatively estimated that 500,000 and 1,000,000 Tutsi and Hutu respectively were slaughtered.[137]

As you walk around the darkened exhibit, each wall, dedicated to a specific facet of the genocide, bears more violence than the one before. How the assassination of Habyarimana and President Cyprien Ntaruamira, the Hutu Burundian president, on 6 April 1994 lit the fuse. Within hours of their aeroplane being shot down from the Kigali sky as it prepared to land, killing everyone on board, roadblocks were quickly constructed and houses searched. The way machetes, clubs, guns, any blunt tool became an executioner's instrument and roadblock checkpoints another sadistic way to humiliate, rape and murder the Tutsi. The elderly, considered the pride of Rwandan society, were slaughtered without mercy. The hallowed ground of churches, convents and schools offered no reprieve and they, too, were the sites of systematic sexual violence and bloodshed. The genocidal intent of the Hutu was laid bare. They wanted to ensure that a new generation of Tutsi would never emerge and, as such, bodies – particularly those of women – formed part of the earth to be scorched.

Neither the UN nor any foreign government showed an inclination to intervene in what was labelled as 'civil war' or 'ethnic strife'. France stands accused of (and has denied) playing an active role in the genocide by arriving to train Rwandan armed forces and Hutu militia.[138] Israeli sources also point to the selling of arms to the Rwandan government and aligned militias by either the Zionist occupation itself or Israeli private arms dealers.[139] This, too, is denied and the records which document the regime's arms sales to Rwanda remain sealed, thanks to a ruling by the Israeli Supreme Court.

In lieu of help from the international community, it was the RPA forces who, by July 1994, had secured much of the country. Slaughtering thousands of Hutu as they went – during the genocide and the months following – Kagame's RPF held control of most of the country by the end of the month.

With many government officials and genocidaires forced into Zaire – now, the Democratic Republic of the Congo – the genocide was declared over on 19 July 1994. It's a genocide with deep roots, roots that curl around the decisions made by Europeans poring over a map, Belgian-introduced classification systems and self-interested African elites who allied with colonisers to preserve personal power and crush popular movements, like Muhumusa and her followers.

'This man told me how he murdered my father,' the 70-year-old Celestin Kayijuka tells the *Guardian* for a piece on the reconciliation processes in Rwanda. He's seated on a small sofa next to Jean Marie Mukyemrwari who spent ten years in prison for his crimes during the genocide. 'He killed him in front of the house, with a single blow of a shovel. After that he dragged the body inside.' Celestin later buried the remains in his banana plantation.

Jean Marie adds: 'My children know I participated in the genocide. I have never told them exactly what I did. I'm not that brave.'

'I am the only one from our family who survived the genocide,' Marianna Nyirantagorama recalls. The 58-year-old's mother, two brothers and four sisters were buried in a mass grave. 'I was one of the few survivors in the midst of a crowd of dead people in the church where most of my family were murdered. I played dead among the bloody corpses.'

The man sat next to her on the wooden bench, whose hand she grips, killed her eldest sister. Released after spending almost seven years in prison, now sixty, Marc Nyandekwe couldn't face her. He barricaded himself in his home at first, then worked outside of the area and only returned to his family every once in a while.

'Marianna told my wife I no longer needed to flee. I was convinced it was a trap. She brewed banana beer and offered me a bottle. I refused. I was afraid she wanted to poison me. But she lent us money. She saw how poor our family was. She gave me jobs. The woman whose sister I killed kept me alive.'[140]

As we had floated on Burera waters, Christian explained that, today, Rwandans are simply Rwandans, 'Hutu', 'Tutsi' and 'Twa' had fallen away as descriptors. 'We don't have ethnic groups anymore. They used to be on the Rwandan national ID and now it's just your name.'

This was just one small facet of the reconciliation efforts that followed a genocide that, alongside its many dead, left two-thirds of Rwandans displaced. AVEGA Agahozo was founded in 1995 to support widows and their dependants whose lives had been devastated by poverty and sexual violence, providing medical services, counselling, education, housing and more. The traditional *gacaca* courts – the courts that Muhumusa would've known all her life – made a return in 2002, this time to bring together genocide survivors, perpetrators and witnesses before locally selected judges. Not only did they establish a forum for confrontation and confession, but many survivors were able to learn of the fates of their loved ones, locate their bodies and bury them with proper rites and dignity. Perpetrators who confessed could choose to serve half of their sentences in community service, building roads, making bricks and rebuilding houses.[141] Community-based therapy run by local volunteer therapists, known as *Mvura Nkuvure*, was completed by over 64,000 Rwandans. It means, 'I heal you, you heal me.'[142]

As its people attempted to make sense of the trauma, the cogs of

Rwandan governance ground on. After an internal coup, Kagame took the office of president in 2000 and has overseen Rwanda ever since. He is credited with 'much of the country's present-day development and stability'.[143] Kagame has since received a host of awards, many for his role in ending the genocide, although even his staunchest defenders cannot deny the way dissent has been cracked down on with opposition members and sceptical journalists suppressed. Kagame and the RPF have continued to win every one of Rwanda's last three elections with more than 90 per cent of the vote.[144]

However, until I met Shema just a day before I was due to depart the country, I could not have fathomed how fragile Rwanda's veneer is nor what oozes between its cracks.

'One of the biggest problems for me is that citizens are disempowered to speak up,' Shema explains from across the table of my hotel's breakfast area. 'Most of the bloggers and YouTubers who speak the truth are in jail, disappear or have been killed. Rwanda is one of the most ridiculous and repressive states but, on paper, it's perfect. It looks perfect, it's clean, everybody comes to visit.'

Shema is an African journalist, an identity it has taken her a long journey to claim but one that fits. Her goal has always been to attempt change within her communities. Today, she works across civil societies and women's rights organisations in Rwanda, Uganda and the DRC.

Shema is not her real name. She hopes that one day, she can attribute her own words to her name but, for now, she's just Shema. And the more she speaks, as her daughter plays on an iPad beside her after a long day at school, the more founded her fears become. 'A lot of websites and bloggers who have voiced [dissent], they're either in exile or refugees in Europe or America. Most of their websites are not even accessible here.'

She tells me about the Israeli spyware, Pegasus, and its growing appeal to the very small group of Rwandan military intelligence that she says holds the most sway in today's government. 'It's very expensive and usually this application is sent to people's phones so that they can tap the conversations they're having. YouTubers and political dissidents, even those outside the country, are always being spied on. There's a huge control of the narrative so a lot of young people don't have the information unless you have a VPN or you openly want to access the information on YouTube. In fact, the government has been working to shut down the accounts of YouTubers to which YouTube said no.'

She chuckles as she recalls her parents' words when she had finished her studies outside the country. 'I remember telling [them] I wanted to come back to Rwanda to work and my parents said, are you crazy? I didn't understand. Flash forward, I see what they meant and I think the situation is getting worse, particularly in April.

'[Every April] we have the Genocide Memorial Week. Part of what happens is that citizens are terrorised by the military intelligence. They throw stones on their roofs, they kill people so that they can actually show that things are worse, that there's no unity but still fear. There's a deliberate attempt to keep people silenced, afraid and traumatised so that they can keep leveraging them. So that they feel like they need to be saved by the government, police and military. They terrorise particularly those who survived so that it looks like there's still conflict between two ethnicities and the citizens think it's being done by the same people who were tried [in court]. A lot of people were tried, they went to jail and they came back into the community so there's always that thinking that [they] have never gone away.' A week later while in Burundi, I spoke to a senior employee at an international humanitarian organisation who did not want to be quoted but recognised and confirmed some of the intimidation tactics Shema refers to.

Shema and I are meeting in May so the memorial events have been and gone. And, like every April, according to Shema, there were bodies discovered with little attempt to explain their origin. 'Because there are no citizens asking for proper investigations, nobody knows [the causes of their deaths], but the media will say that they are genocide survivors. Things are worse than people think and know.'

Elections, for example, emerge as a test of loyalty, with conditions of extreme duress. 'You enter a ballot room and there's someone standing there watching what you're about to vote so you wouldn't dare vote for anybody that's not the right person. And it's not just anybody, it's military with a gun. It sends a clear message. Those found to have voted for the wrong person are followed and terrorised in their own communities. Next time, you know who to vote for. [Opposing] political candidates have been terrorised, going to jail for fraud and embezzlement, there's always a reason.'

We pause as I offer her daughter, still donning school uniform, the hotel's Wi-Fi password before she returns to poring over the tablet.

'The president has portrayed a positive image of African leadership, meanwhile sending troops into the Central African Republic and Mozambique to guard French interests [in mineral resources].' There's also the Democratic Republic of the Congo which Rwanda, with Uganda, invaded in 1996 and 1998 with claims that Hutu rebels were hiding in eastern DRC – this is considered a pretext for looting the DRC abundant resources. Widespread displacement and the mass slaughter of Congolese civilians – accused of supporting the opponents of the Rwandan forces and Congolese militia forces – continues to abound.[145] 'There's all sorts of evidence that Rwanda is equipping the militia groups in DRC but there are no reports produced on how the ruling parties are using the resources. For example, as we speak, there are people who are not getting their monthly pension fund because nobody can account for where the money went and they have no right to question it.'

In fact, as I tinker with the final version of this book in late January 2025, there have been alarming developments. At the time of writing, the March 23 Movement (the M23) – a Congolese Tutsi military group who broke away from the DRC's armed forces – have just claimed to have taken the key city of Goma, marking a huge escalation in their decade-long conflict with the DRC government. Hundreds of thousands of people have already fled their homes, while the M23 seize more territory than ever before, killing local civilians as they go.

The DRC and the UN say the Tutsi group are backed by Rwanda, with claims that at least three thousand Rwandan troops are operating alongside the M23. The military group claim their existence is for the protection of the Tutsi people in the country; however, the fact that the area they control in eastern DRC is rich with deposits of coltan (a mineral used in smartphones) and is believed to be worth $800,000 per month to the rebel group, is surely a determining factor. The DRC has severed diplomatic ties with Kagame's country, which borders the M23-controlled region.[146] It seems that we are watching a Rwandan invasion and, given the devastating recent history that precedes it and the ethnic divides that underpin it, the only thing we can be sure of is that the people caught between warring factions will suffer the most.

Rwanda's future appears finely balanced, resting on deeply painful histories that threaten to repeat in new forms. Nonetheless, for Shema, it is necessary to look backwards, to the figures who resisted colonial agendas and the overtures of a self-interested administration. Historical actors like Muhumusa are crucial reminders that the roots of political dissent and uprising in Rwanda run deep. That said, she only learnt about the Nyabingi leader in passing. 'There was an attempt to talk about the different kings that ever existed – those who fought colonialists and expanded the region – but that's mostly the information we're given. The focus is on those kings and barely their wives.

'Muhumusa represented passion and courage. Often, I look at the history of witchcraft and magic and the way that women who refuse social norms will often be labelled a witch. They'll be told that "these things you cannot control or understand". Women were assumed to not have enough intelligence so any woman who exhibited some had to be branded something.

'When you have so much power to mobilise people or to speak up, you're either a witch or worth being followed.'

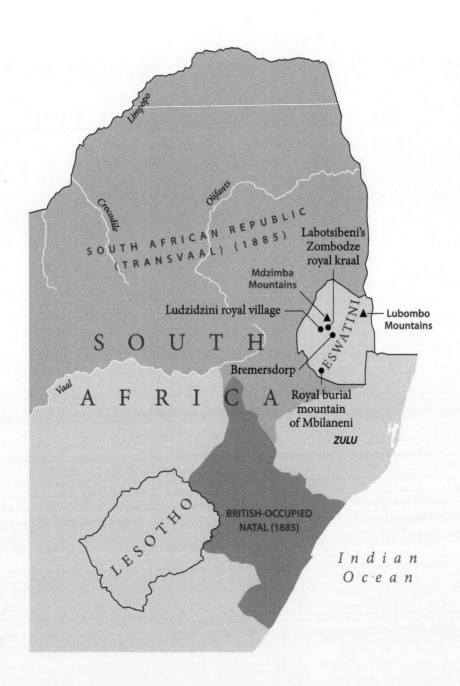

Limpopo

Crocodile

Olifants

SOUTH AFRICAN REPUBLIC
(TRANSVAAL) (1885)

Labotsibeni's
Zombodze
royal kraal

Mdzimba
Mountains

Ludzidzini royal village

Lubombo
Mountains

E S W A T I N I

S O U T H

Vaal

A F R I C A

Bremersdorp

Royal burial
mountain
of Mbilaneni

ZULU

LESOTHO

BRITISH-OCCUPIED
NATAL (1885)

Indian
Ocean

CHAPTER 10

Labotsibeni Mdluli

The Swazi Arbitrator

Although the KaNgwane people had inhabited the territory of present-day eSwatini before Shaka of the Zulu's genocide (the *Mfecane*), they truly emerged during and after the region-marking brutality. KaNgwane is the name given to the burgeoning nation made up of Swazi settlers, a group of a blend of Nguni, Sotho and Tsonga heritages.[1] The establishment and expansion of a Swazi domain is largely attributed to Sobhuza I – an *iNgwenyama*, a siSwati word translated as 'male monarch', who ruled from 1820 to 1836.

Through military and diplomatic manoeuvres like absorbing nearby chiefdoms into KaNgwane, Sobhuza I laid the blueprint for a future Swazi kingdom.[2] Consolidation was left to his son, Mswati II (r. 1840–1865), the 'fighting king' who continued shaping the Swazi realm. Nation-wide regiments were formed, bringing together young men throughout all the chieftaincies.[3] Crucially, Mswati II produced citizens who pledged their allegiance to him rather than their clan.[4] The fact that the Swazi would take their name from this ruler signalled a successful mission in nation-building. The individual and their kinship ties were both secondary to the survival of the kingdom.[5] A kingdom steered by the Dlamini clan, the ruling Swazi dynasty.

For one little girl named Labotsibeni, born towards the end of Mswati's reign at her eLuhlekweni homestead, political and societal transformations were taking place on the land she knew.[6] So young, the daughter of Matsanjana Mdluli – a regiment man under Mswati II – didn't know what these transformations entailed nor what they would mean for her future.[7] The same could be said for the way her family life would change, namely after the death of her father.

We don't know the name of Labotsibeni's mother, just that she was of the Mabuza people – one of the seventeen *bemdzabuko* of the Swazi people. Like the Mdluli, the Mabuza were among the founding groups to claim the land in the name of the Swazi. Her mother only appears tangentially following Matsanjana's death, after which she moved her family to the kingdom's capital of Ludzidzini (found in the present-day city of Lobamba, one of eSwatini's two capitals).[8]

There, waiting to assume his new responsibilities as 'father', was Labotsibeni's uncle and chief of the Mdluli lineage, Mvelase. As an *indvuna* (governor or headman) under Mswati, his regimental residence was located in the capital.[9] However, Mvelase wasn't Ludzidzini's only titled, elite resident. The little girl's new home also belonged to a senior widow of Sobhuza I and the mother of Mswati II. Her name was Tsandzile Ndwandwe – or laZidze – and she was the *iNdlovukazi* who ruled alongside her son.[10]

Growing up in the royal village of Ludzidzini, with its thatched homesteads made of dry grass against the backdrop of the sacred Mdzimba mountain range, would have been an education.

Leaving her formative years behind coincided with Labotsibeni's introduction to the cogs of the royal house of Dlamini. The politics, like codes of court etiquette, and history of the period were laid out before her like a new pasture for her to traverse. Holding her hand, guiding her through the landscape, was laZidze. Historians would refer to the lessons from the ageing royal as an 'early apprenticeship', with Labotsibeni unable to have had 'a better and more experienced mentor.'[11]

However, the royal homestead she became a part of was one being wrenched apart by the different bloodlines that laid claim to it. The death of Mswati II – 1865 according to some historians, 1868 say others – set off a chain reaction, one that gorged on combustible familial ties and loyalties. Under the joint regency of laZidze, who reigned until 1875, and one of Mswati's younger brothers, tensions manifested in a series of dynasty-defining acts.[12] The son of Mswati and the kingdom's next intended ruler, Ludvonga II, was killed in 1872, ensuring that he would never be installed as *iNgwenyama*. The suspicions of the Swazi royals hung heavily over the head of laZidze's unnamed co-regent, believing that he stood to gain from collusion in the murder. He was quickly put to death on the royal council's orders.[13]

When the next occupant of the Swazi seat of power was unveiled around 1875, it was within a febrile environment. During years of infighting, rival factions were determined to bend the opportunity for power in their favour. It appears that laZidze held some sway over who would become the next Swazi ruler and his name was Mbandzeni, the son of Tibati Madsolomafisha Nkambule and Mswati.[14] By the time of his ascension, his mother had died, leaving a gap for Ludvonga's grieving mother to step in as his *iNdlovukazi*. This was, however, short-lived. Mbandzeni had her executed after the new ruler uncovered her plot to murder him.[15]

Somehow, somewhere, in this web of fatal manoeuvres, Mbandzeni and Labotsibeni found one another. And eventually – after Labotsibeni would've signalled her betrothal with *wacola* (putting her hair up), after she'd made and bought presents for her prospective in-laws, after libations had been poured and meat shared, after the bridal party sang the song of the Dlamini as Labotsibeni likely stood with her face hidden by a heavy veil of beads, large fringe of pink wool and two dropping bunches of royal *sakabula* feathers on either side of the head – they were married.

Across their union, Labotsibeni would've surely learnt quickly that unrest and whispers followed her spouse. They were stubborn stains that clung to Mbandzeni and his thirteen-year reign. And when he died in October 1889, the unease only ratcheted up further. For, before his death, the ruler of the Swazi had yielded huge swathes of their kingdom – one of the most fertile, best-watered and mineral-rich areas in Southern Africa.[16] Land that the Swazis had taken for themselves had changed hands once more – this time claimed by white settlers.

However, Mbandzeni wasn't the first to cede Swazi-claimed land. Voortrekkers – descendants of Dutch, German and French Huguenot settlers who arrived in the Cape of Good Hope in the mid-seventeenth century and migrated throughout modern-day South Africa – had approached his father, Mswati II.

Priding themselves on being 'pioneers' ('voortrekker' translates as 'fore-trekker' or 'pathfinder'), these Afrikaner groups were the building blocks for what would become autonomous Boer ('farmer' in Dutch) republics. Their travels were a form of conquest, but before this form of systematic colonisation could take hold, the Boers first needed a base. In 1846, Mswati had signed a treaty with them and the terms were simple. In return for a herd of one hundred cattle, the Swazi relinquished to a group of Boers their claim to land between the Crocodile and Olifants rivers. More land was ceded to the Afrikaners in 1855, this time alongside the Pongola River through to the Lubombo Mountains.[17]

There was more than met the eye with these concessions, some historians have argued. Academic Hamilton Sipho Simelane points out that all the concessions were concentrated in the south of the Swazi kingdom, creating somewhat of a buffer zone between Swazi territory and the roving Zulu forces who often attacked at will. There was a diplomatic edge to this strategy, but so, too, an absence of wariness: the Swazi did not appear to be threatened by a Boer presence just beyond their territory. As far as they could tell, their militarily weak new neighbours were in no position to wage an expansionist campaign against them.[18]

Things had changed when Mswati died. With the legendary Swazi military man no longer around and a barely teenage Ludvonga being readied within an unstable royal class, the Boers had paid attention. When the youth's assassination soon followed, they assessed that it was time to make an advance – in the direction of Mbandzeni.[19] It's even murmured that they may have had a hand in his selection as successor.[20] At the ceremony of Mbandzeni's installation, dozens of Boers were in attendance, watching on as the eyes of the Transvaal Republic's government.[21]

This Boer republic, established in 1852 after formal British recognition of their independence, represented the Afrikaners who had settled north of the Vaal River. Their presence at the ceremony was significant. For the Swazi, it sealed their accord: clearly, the Transvaal Boers acknowledged Mbandzeni's sovereignty over their territory. So when it came to signing a treaty in August 1875, the Swazi had no problem with recognising Boer sovereignty over the concessions made by Mswati. They also agreed to give the Transvaal military assistance when called upon, extend the freedom of commerce and industry to Europeans already living within their territories, and provide physical protection if required.[22] The house of Dlamini saw the treaty only as 'a confirmation and consolidation of the co-operation' which existed between them, 'a reciprocal agreement in which each party retained their sovereignty.'[23] The Boers held a different interpretation: the land of the Swazi was under their protection, and its people their subjects.

The land concessions were further complicated by the introduction of 'land grants'. Europeans had brought with them principles of tenure like 'leasehold', 'freehold sale' and 'private ownership' – philosophies crafted in lands that were not Swazi. While the Boer understood the exchanges as a procurement of the land rights they craved, Mbandzeni and his royal cluster considered payments as a tribute to the *iNgwenyama*.[24] Rather, the reverse was true: the loss of land undermined the Swazi ruler's political authority and sovereignty.[25]

The territory that would become eSwatini was well and truly ensnared within the era's 'paper conquest'. With his advisors, Labotsibeni's husband signed away the kingdom and its rights.[26] His death in 1889 marked the beginning of a new chapter in the Swazi nation's story: the struggle to preserve its very existence.

As she padded around the cantaloupe-hued ground of the royal homestead, perhaps Labotsibeni compared herself to her fellow wives as they passed one another, all holding the same question in their minds.

Maybe she retreated to the coolness of her thatched home to make sense of the void that had cracked open her family, cradling the four small heads she bore the responsibility of guiding. When she and her children lay on grass mats at night, warm under a cowskin, questions and a lack of answers might have prodded her mind. Was Labotsibeni present while the royal council debated vociferously, flying spittle punctuating their remarks? If she wasn't, did her skin still prickle with the knowledge that her name was being invoked, thrown down as a staked claim? Which of the wives would be chosen?

The next *iNgwenyama* is only ever chosen after the death of their predecessor. It's a selection process that hinges on the incoming ruler's mother, picked from among the many wives of the deceased ruler. Key precedents guide the process, including that the *iNdlovukazi*-in-waiting should only have one child – a son – and that they normally came from 'queen bearing clans'.[27] Although the Mdluli were known for military prowess, they weren't considered one of the clans that usually proffered royalty. Additionally, with her three sons – Bhunu, Malunge and Lomvazi – and one daughter by the name of Tongotongo, Labotsibeni should have been disqualified.[28] In fact, when I spoke to locals during my time in eSwatini, they admitted that adherence to succession protocol isn't always strictly observed and, as a result, confusion abounds. 'It's why there's always infighting, ending up with illegitimate kings,' one said bluntly.

It shouldn't have been her and yet it was. The compliments that have been rained down on Labotsibeni by way of explaining her selection – highly intelligent, strong character, experienced, wise, perceptive, witty, determined – suggest that there was simply no other alternative. Historians assert that Mbandzeni himself had indicated that he favoured his tall, full-figured spouse for the position of *iNdlovukazi*. On 3 September 1890, before the year of mourning was complete, she was publicly acknowledged as such: the mother to the next ruler. Presented to the nation by her side, a 14-year-old Bhunu appraised the people he had inherited.[29]

Like the Asante, the Swazi monarchy operates on the understanding that two halves make a symbolic whole in the highest office of the land. The *iNdlovukazi* rules beside the *iNgwenyama*.[30]

They are distinct but the same. And, like the Asante, the Swazi woman monarch is seen as a safeguard for her royal counterpart. Built into her position is the idea that she exercises a 'restraining influence' over the man that is usually her son. While the *iNdlovukazi* holds no executive powers when ruling beside a living *iNgwenyama*, counsellors have historically appealed to her to change his attitude as she is kept abreast of important developments from his office.[31]

In Labotsibeni's time, the two lived apart. The village of the *iNgwenyama* was the administrative headquarters; his mother's was the Swazi symbolic and spiritual centre.[32] Similarly, there were two Swazi courts, one headed by each monarch. The *iNgwenyama*'s was the highest court in the land as the final destination for criminal and civil appeals, once more reflecting the imbalance of power between the pair.[33] That said, the residence of the *iNdlovukazi* would often become a refuge for political targets trying to outrun death sentences handed down by her son.[34]

In her new position, Labotsibeni would understand that, when he was of age, her son would hold the true power. She was a symbolic figurehead. For example, both monarchs had their respective military regiments. Even so, the *iNdlovukazi* force was not under her direct control. Rather, they answered to the princes who lived in her village who would, in turn, defer to Bhunu.[35] However, in the meantime, she was subordinate to another sovereign. Since the death of Mbandzeni, it was Tibati Nkambule – Labotsibeni's mother-in-law, so to speak – who served in her son's place as the regent of the land.

As was custom, his death was followed by a period of regency. Historians assert that the joint regents were normally the widow of the deceased ruler and an uncle of the next king.[36] It was they who shepherded the nation during the next *iNgwenyama*'s minority, waiting for their young royal to reach the age to rule. Tradition was broken with, though. Tibati, Mswati II's still living widow, was the one who took power in 1889 with one of his sons, Logcogco, and swarms of advisors.[37]

It's unclear what pushed the departure from their succession customs. Maybe Tibati, a known and respected old ruler, holding power once more reassured the Swazi people navigating the new shift that rumbled from within the Dlamini dynasty. Tremors of factional division emanated from the royal house, much of it circling on one persistent issue: what do we do about the British?

By the 1880s, the Swazi had recognised that Boers were a genuine threat to their sovereignty. The realisation was forced by attempted Afrikaner penetrations of their territory in addition to demonstrations of Boer military effectiveness elsewhere as they subjugated other indigenous peoples, like the Nzunza Ndebele people in 1883.[38] A decade before his death, Mbandzeni would have been aware of the Swazi's growing military and financial disadvantage, as the Transvaal's ranks and coffers swelled. It seems that he was also well aware of the animosity that existed between the Boers and the British.[39]

The Dutch East India Company had established their colony around the Cape of Good Hope and present-day Cape Town in the seventeenth century, quickly building a re-supply port for their trading vessels. In 1795, however, the British forces invaded and took control of the territory, as part of their endeavour to stave off French attempts to reach India.[40] After all, France had occupied the Dutch Republic that same year, with the Dutch populace eventually forming part of Napoleon Bonaparte's French Empire.

Aversion to British dominion was a key factor in Boers moving inland, in search of new lands to subjugate and settle. There were a number of other issues that spurred the Boer trek of conquest in the 1830s like taxation, cultural differences and more. A key sticking issue was that, after the British officially occupied the Cape of Good Hope – which became 'Cape Colony' – the British abolition of enslavement stoked resentment among the slave-owning settlers.[41] Relations between the colonial parties certainly didn't improve when the British moved to annex the Transvaal in 1877. They absorbed the Boer territory within their own, a combination of the discovery of valuable resources and the perceived economic threat of the Transvaal to colonies claimed in the name of Queen

Victoria. With the Boers seeking to reinstate their independence, the stage was set for the first and very brief Anglo–Boer War (1880–81) which resulted in British defeat and their quiet withdrawal.[42]

Somewhere in the wake of this, the British had passed the 1881 Swaziland Convention which recognised Swazi sovereignty while, along the way, surreptitiously reducing the size of their territory. Perhaps feeling somewhat encouraged, Mbandzeni sought to shrewdly exploit the enmity between the British and the once-again independent Boers. In fact, between 1882 and 1886, playing the imperialists off against one another was the main Swazi diplomatic approach.[43] It saw the late *iNgwenyama* plead for British protection against Boer encroachment, reporting to them each time that the Afrikaners penetrated their territory. The hope was that the British would take any Boer advances as a threat. 'Much as the British were reluctant to commit themselves on Swaziland, they were prepared to play the watch-dog role,' notes Simelane.[44] Each time Mbandzeni complained, the British demanded an explanation from Transvaal officials who issued denials. They were forced to tread carefully with the Swazi but the Boer pressure didn't wane, whether it came as sheer aggression or attempts at persuading the Swazi to accept Transvaal 'protection'. Labotsibeni's spouse had refused; the only government he would defer to sat in the British Isles.[45]

Diplomatic manoeuvring could sustain the kingdom for only so long, particularly given the further concessions made under Mbandzeni. The 1882 discovery of gold in north-western Swazi territory had brought European concession-hunters running but, even though they curried the ruler's favour, they refused to submit to his authority. The *iNgwenyama* turned to the British and requested an advisor to aid with the rate of granted concessions; in 1887, 'Offy' Shepstone was appointed 'resident advisor' and agent of the Swazi nation. From 1887 to 1889, the Englishman approved the greatest number of concessions across any two years, including at least six in his own name, before being dismissed.[46]

Beyond the widespread occupation of land which forged a dispossessed Swazi class with no rights to land, there was a glaring policy problem. The concessions made it impossible for any effective governance of Swazi territory without Boer involvement. The rights of the Transvaal government operating in the Dlamini-headed kingdom were, more or less, the powers of government.[47] It's why, by 1890 – a year after Mbandzeni's passing – the British concluded that extending their protection over eSwatini was 'not only legally impossible, but also politically and economically undesirable.'[48]

The Swazi were slipping deeper into the Boers' grip and they knew it all too well. Before he died, Mbandzeni lamented, 'I have white men all around me. By force they have taken the countries of all my neighbours. If I do not give them rights here, they will take them. Therefore I give when they pay. Why should we not eat before we die?'[49]

During the fractious regency period, Labotsibeni and Tibati stood divided on the land-grabbing Resident Advisor Shepstone and all that he represented. A pro-Shepstone cluster in the Swazi council, headed up by the old regent, favoured his eventual reinstatement. Labotsibeni's contingent was staunchly against the move. It epitomised the power struggle between the two women who lived in different villages with their own separate regiments.[50]

It's said that the elderly Tibati was suspicious of the new iNdlovukazi's intentions: here was her son's wife, seemingly eager to depose her to ensure that Bhunu would safely reach his seat of power once no longer a minor.[51] Despite officially holding no powers of governance, Labotsibeni was always in the conversation, attending discussions and playing an active part in decision-making. She was emerging as the face of a new national identity, one that would not rest under white control of the kingdom. Meanwhile, as the hub of Swazi activity swung to Zombodze where Labotsibeni had established her royal kraal, Tibati was fading into a symbolic figurehead. By the time of her death in 1894, she had been well and truly outmanoeuvred by her younger counterpart.[52] As if to rubberstamp the new direction the kingdom would move in, that same year, power finally fell to Bhunu. He became Ngwane V.

Much to his mother's frustration, the newly installed *iNgwenyama* wasn't a fan of matters of state. Rather than joining councils and absorbing the seemingly endless words of advisors, Ngwane spent his much-coveted time with soldiers from his Ingulube regiment.[53] The kingdom's perils could wait until after they'd had their fill of hunting and shooting. He seemed sure that Labotsibeni, who still held considerable authority, could handle it. Traditional Swazi bards opined over her frequent travels around the kingdom, with her feet described as red from the dust accumulated from her voyages.[54]

It was a tense relationship between the pair. She held suspicions about what went on at Mampondweni, Ngwane's Mdzimba mountainside retreat. He saw her preference for her younger son, Malunge, as both obvious and something to fear.[55] He'd discover that there were more urgent threats crouching in wait.

Before Tibati's death, colonial collusion driven by new officials in post had brought the British and the Boers into alignment in 1893. Together, they signed the Second Swaziland Convention, this time, bringing the Swazi under Transvaal governance. Recognition of the convention rested on the 'freely given assent' of the Swazi rulers on behalf of their people. They refused, hopelessly petitioning the British while trying to withstand surging Boer pressure. It turned out that Swazi cooperation was no longer a required component. On 6 December 1894, the ink dried on the signed Third Swaziland Convention. The historic KaNgwane, the kingdom that had emerged from the bloodshed of Shaka's *Mfecane*, was a protectorate of the Transvaal.[56]

As far as the young ruler Ngwane was concerned, liberation from Boer occupation could only come from the Swazi. Part of that was resisting as many forms of Transvaal governance as they could. He vigorously opposed the establishment of Boer courts of justice in his realm. It flew in the face of what the 1894 convention had approved and what he considered irrefutable: that Swazi people were only subject to Swazi laws.[57] When Swazi complaints – the floggings administered by Boer officials, deprivation of property by the settlers without redress, attempts to impose taxes on the

Swazi – were ignored by the British, Labotsibeni's son increasingly recognised military resistance as the only answer. It was reportedly only the staying hand of the *iNdlovukazi* that averted a wave of hostilities.[58]

The split between the co-rulers was beginning to yawn. While her son was of the mind that the Boer hut tax collection should be resisted by force, Labotsibeni and one of her chief *indvunas* – Mbhabha Sibandze – believed that they should just agree to pay; their logic was that it might bring them closer to some sort of peaceful co-existence.[59]

In 1898, the crack widened into a canyon. That April, Mbhabha was killed and the main suspect was Ngwane, his *iNgwenyama*.

When the ruler was implicated in the murder, was there any doubt in Labotsibeni's mind or did it only confirm what she suspected about her reckless offspring? When her son was summoned for trial before the Landdrost's Court in Bremersdorp – the seat of the Boer administration in eSwatini – perhaps she felt the insult laced in the demands of the court.[60] Likely she may have felt it was incredulous that a Swazi ruler could be expected to explain himself before a foreign power in his own lands. Although, it could be that she felt quiet appreciation for how her own position had been strengthened.

What we do know is that Labotsibeni appeared to have washed her hands of responsibility for her son, particularly when asked about his militant approach: 'I have long said that I am a woman without a husband. The three children were small, I took care of them and now they can do as they wish. What they do now I do not understand.'[61] (Although Labotsibeni had four children with Mbandzeni, it's possible that she might be discounting her daughter, Tongotongo, and refers here only to her three sons.)

The explanations for Ngwane possibly murdering the chief *indvuna* are numerous; it may have been because he had collaborated with Labotsibeni to frustrate the *iNgwenyama*, because he was said to even be cohabiting with her or because he had stolen the leg of an animal sacrificed to the ancestors. The consequences remained the same no matter the reason why. After allegedly killing

Mbhabha, Ngwane refused to present himself before the Boer special commissioner.[62]

It was only the pressure of the Swazi National Council, a month after the killing, that forced Ngwane to engage with the Boers. Even so, he appeared in Bremersdorp flanked by his warriors in full regimental regalia for a meeting that would bear no fruit. After the ruler refused to appear before the court again, the stage was set for all-out war. By June 1898, the Boers had been mobilising, calling in volunteers from Pretoria and further afield to support the Transvaal in subjugating the Swazi.[63] Although there are suggestions that Ngwane and his followers felt equal to it, calling for *sinike* – 'Give us war' – the Swazi council again made its will known. July would see Ngwane cross the border into British-occupied Natal. He was returned to Swazi territory under British protection, with one occupying power reminding the other of eSwatini's status and that Ngwane should still be recognised as their ruler.[64]

Along the way, the status of Labotsibeni's son was reduced – in the eyes and minds of the settlers – from 'king' to 'paramount chief'. Imposing fines and reducing his powers of jurisdiction, Britain and the Transvaal united to punish him.[65] However, this was not reflective of the two colonial governments' wider relations. A year after the 'Mbhabha affair', they engaged in the second Boer–Anglo War which lasted from October 1899 to May 1902.

As hostilities broke out, white settlers were ordered out of the Swazi kingdom, many fleeing to a nearby Portuguese-occupied territory that forms much of present-day Mozambique. They left Bremersdorp a ghost town, although Boers returned in 1901 to set it on fire, flames swallowing up the town's school, newspaper office, banks and more.[66] It's said that Labotsibeni sent elderly women to loot what they could from the burnt-out colonial carcass, sifting through ash and crawling past embers in search of beads and other treasures to send back to her Zombodze royal kraal.[67] It would take almost a century before this razed ground would officially become the city of Manzini, leaving its Boer name resting in the dust.

Before heading off to take on the British, a Boer general said the

following to Ngwane V, formerly Bhunu, on behalf of his government: 'And now, Ubunu, the Government places Swaziland under
your care, and trusts that you will act accordingly. Where upon
I want to advise you, purely as a friend, to rule Swaziland well
and in peace. This is the advice of a sincere friend of Umswazi, of
Umbandini and also of Ubunu.'[68] After delivering what he perhaps
believed were the bolstering words required from a protector to
their dependants, the Transvaal representative departed.

Cast adrift by both powers during this warring period, the Swazi
ruled themselves once more.

Yes, in a way, the *incwala* is a first fruits ceremony. A heralding
of the first sprouts brave enough to push their way into the world
to announce that summer has come. It's the annual manifestation
of an exhale of relief and an exuberant belly laugh because, again,
the earth has provided, its treasures unlocked via sunbeam. More
importantly, it's a time of renewal, cleansing, shucking off the husks
and emerging anew. Moving from lack to abundance.[69] However,
above all, the event – which would historically span weeks – is a
celebration of the *iNgwenyama*, with the people, the nation-wide
military regiments, the chieftaincies. When there is no male sovereign, there is no *incwala*. But when there is, it sucks the attention
of the entire realm.

The *incwala* is an extensive ritual that feeds the senses. The
thrum of *lusekwane* – a sacred acacia shrub – branches being cut
under moonlight by unmarried young men. The vision of brightly
coloured *emahiya*, each clashing with the next, wrapped around the
bodies of women and girls. The caress of the *sigeja* – a neckpiece
connected to cascading tan, brown and black fur – against the
waists of the *iNgwenyama* and his regiments as they dance in full
war attire. The pageantry inside the cattle byre. The charging bull
that must be caught. The day of abstinence that must be spent
without intimate contact, bathing or wearing anything ostentatious.
The sexual, carnal release that would follow. The crackling fire that
swallows up the thrown objects that must remain in the old year.
The flowing beer. The seemingly never-ending sustenance.[70] As the

Swazi teetered on the edge of the unknown, two months into the 'white men's war' that had erupted around them, was there another way to usher in a better, more abundant year?[71]

Except during the *incwala* of 1899, something was wrong. It was carefully kept from the Swazi people until after the ceremony was complete. That way, their merriment could subside into an unhampered bliss, full bellies could be rubbed without a second thought, eyelids could droop under the weight of alcohol and fatigue. This wouldn't have been possible if they had been made aware of the discovery. One that would've seen their joy swallowed into the bowels of mourning. That December during the *incwala*, mere months after 'full authority' had been ceded to him, Ngwane V died.[72]

Moving forward, it would be the *iNdlovukazi* who ruled her people – alone. Labotsibeni took power with speed and in secret. Elders of the council were called, the Ngwenya clan was summoned for their embalming rites, and members of the Dlamini family council were rallied for the task of selecting their heir.[73]

As she operated with alacrity, the ruler left the other elites on edge. Both her distaste for her eldest son's methods and the favour with which she viewed the younger Malunge had been well emphasised – certainly enough that some believed she had been responsible for Ngwane's death.[74] As strongly as they may have felt about Labotsibeni's manoeuvres, there were those who just as staunchly stood by the side of Mbandzeni's widow. Ultimately, she emerged as victor.

From 1899, Labotsibeni became the Swazi regent, supported by a prince and the council. Rather than her prized Malunge, she stood in the place of her babbling baby grandson Nkhotfotjeni – or Mona. And until he was old enough to take up what his father, the late Ngwane, had left behind, it was up to her to preserve Swazi sovereignty. She would retain their rights, regain their land and keep their kingdom a neutral space while white colonials sought claim to it.

*

An hour and a half late, a breathless Njabu blusters into the Lobamba café. With her hair hidden beneath a woolly hat, the woman with mid-tone brown skin that has never known a pore and dazzling clear gloss apologises, explaining that her car had broken down on the way.

Njabu's warm face belies her terse online manner – something I'm not the first to tease her about. Conversation with the producer, journalist and self-styled queer cultural disruptor flows easily. Twenty minutes dissipate into the air as we spin through a carousel of topics but especially queerness and kinship. The time floats out through the nearby balcony doors, cracked open to take in borderless blue skies and the far-off mountain faces of Mdzimba. I almost reluctantly steer us towards our reason for meeting.

When I ask her about Labotsibeni's nickname, after pausing to think, my Swazi companion responds with an admission: 'I've only heard my mum use that word for, you know, soft porridge.' She explains that when cooked mealie meal – or maize meal – has been left to sit and begins separating, sometimes the product is referred to with the same name that the *iNdlovukazi* would be anointed with. Gwamile.

'It translates as resilient, very headstrong,' Njabu states from across our small round table. For her, it feels fitting. Critique of the historic ruler is indivisible from the acknowledgement of her reality: that she had to engage processions of white men who openly, loudly, thought less of her and her people. They were Black, they were African, and she was a woman. And like porridge left open to the air, colonial officers found her stodgy and stubborn.

'Gwamile translates to everything that people admire about good leaders who are men.'

A telegram, sent from the British colony of Natal in 1900, marked a new, escalated era of the Swazi struggle against colonial paperwork and policy. 'Her Majesty has now annexed the Transvaal to her Dominions and Her Majesty's Government therefore stands in the same position towards the Swazis as the Government of the South African Republic did before the war', read the announcement.[75]

Victory for the British and an end to the war came two years later, once the lands of southern Africa had been scorched and Africans were forcibly removed to concentration camps to stop them aiding the Afrikaner forces.[76] In 1902, the Boers officially surrendered and accepted British terms laid out in the Treaty of Vereeniging: their republics came under the sovereignty of the British Crown with the promise that the Transvaal and the Orange Free State would eventually govern themselves – as British colonies.[77]

The 'right of conquest' which had passed to Edward VII, who inherited the British throne after his mother's passing in 1901, was handed right back to the Transvaal. The king granted all his powers and jurisdiction to the Transvaal's governor. 'All revenues collected in respect of Swaziland were to be paid into the Transvaal Treasury and all expenditure incurred under the provisions of the Order in Council was to be paid out of the revenues of the Transvaal,' writes scholar F. J. Mashasha.[78]

Labotsibeni remonstrated furiously against the 1903 legislation which would be known among the Swazi as *madla ngengwenya* – the power of the crocodile.[79] Her lands and her people were being placed under the direct control of a powerful predator that had laid in wait until it was ready to pounce. In the petition she and her council put forward at the end of 1904, the *iNdlovukazi* described the Order-in-Council as a means to 'destroy our national life and put an end to our separate existence, merging us indiscriminately among the scattered tribes of the Transvaal'.[80]

The events of the years that immediately followed would've only strengthened Labotsibeni's convictions. Although the British would then 'disannex' the Swazi kingdom from the Transvaal in 1906, placing it directly under the British High Commission for South Africa alongside present-day Lesotho and Botswana, the attempts to undo Swazi sovereignty were well under way.[81] The Swazi were discovering that it didn't matter *which* settlers came to occupy their territory. Even to the empire they had prostrated themselves before in hopes of protection, free African people on African soil would always be a threat to be feared and a target to subdue. After the 1906 order, eSwatini was a 'British protected state' with an 'undefined and uncertain' legal status in relationship with the British Crown – but, for all intents and purposes, the British understood themselves as eSwatini's true government.[82]

In swept the policies under Edward VII's banner. Rather than the Transvaal, the Swazi appeal process now went from the *iNgwenyama*'s court to the resident commissioner's court based in the central hub of Mbabane. Any criminal jurisdiction in the Swazi realm was now exclusively handled by the colonial courts, with final decisions taken by the British high commissioner's office in Pretoria.[83]

The embattled Gwamile had made her complaints known to the commissioner in 1905:

> Under our shade, we say the sun is burning us ... We ask
> where do we rule, if our people do not obey the law and
> customs of our nation? [...] How is it that when we try our
> cases – an appeal is allowed to the White Court, and yet
> there is a Court of our own where all cases connected with
> natives should be settled? [...] Where is the power of our
> Sovereignty? This is the first mark of the sun.[84]

Transferring true power to the British and leaving the Swazi with its veneer was the point. And it was only the beginning. By 1909, Labotsibeni's kingdom was partitioned in a move to deal with the concession land claims: two-thirds of the total Swazi land area were shared between the British Crown and individual European concession-holders.[85] The concessions were legally valid, a deputation headed by Malunge, would be told when they arrived in England in 1907 for a sit-down with the king.[86]

The British perhaps even felt they were being generous by instating a five-year grace period, after which, all Swazi people – now a subjugated class – would be required to evacuate privately held concessions. They'd instead move into one of the thirty designated reserves around the kingdom.[87] Even if Swazi inhabitants were able to work out an agreement with the concession-holders of private land, they had no permanent rights and could be evicted at any time. Many were forced to come to terms with their position as labour tenants indebted to newly instated landlords. On top of settler farmers now having many trapped locals to extort labour from, the land partition also drove some of the population out of the kingdom as migrants, with masses of Swazi headed west to work the mines of Witwatersrand and eastern Transvaal.[88]

The Swazi had peacefully submitted to disarmament in 1903 and largely used diplomacy and passivity as modes of defence – some historians even assert that uprisings and military campaigns were 'alien' to the Swazi as they 'had no precedent for such black and white confrontation' compared to the Zulu, the Ndebele and other peoples.[89] It didn't matter. The British still feared the formation of a Zulu–Swazi alliance, particularly after the Zulu uprising of 1906, and so Western weapons – mainly gifts from concessionaires – were seized. Labotsibeni's kingdom was left militarily powerless.[90]

Taxation, imposed since 1903, only squeezed further. The Swazi were consistently more heavily taxed than any other inhabitants in Southern Africa – this would go some way to explaining why eSwatini would become a nation of labour migrants by the First World War.[91] The kingdom's ruling dynasty wasn't exempt. Tax raids were undertaken in the *iNdlovukazi*'s royal village of Zombodze to try to wrangle the royals into submission while reducing the coffers of their hugely diminished military regiments.[92] Alongside trying to demote Gwamile to 'paramount chief' – the British-imposed term that would stick until 1967 – the British also cancelled an order of concessions to the sovereign which substantially reduced her income.[93]

The Swazi kingdom was being slowly and deliberately defanged. This wasn't a pessimistic conclusion Labotsibeni came to, nor was it conjecture. It was a clear goal, a stated interest. Prominent settlers like Allister Miller, who would go on to be recognised as a 'South African aviation pioneer' and receive an Order of the British Empire for his contributions, made their position clear. Security for his people could only come through the 'denationalisation' of the Swazi. For settlers to flourish, eSwatini had to be levelled completely, making room for a nation of serfs ready to serve.[94]

The large, round performance hut offers cool respite from the morning heat. After being dropped off by my driver, Tom, I had purchased a ticket for the Matenga Cultural Village and historical tour before promptly encountering a strolling Nguni cow. A number of Swazi locals had told me to come here – including Tom, and Anele, my lodge's always beaming receptionist with decadent acrylic claws who I spent a few of my evenings with.

'You have to go to the cultural village in order to understand what it means to be Swazi,' Tom told me when we had zoomed away from King Mswati III International Airport. A replica of a mid-nineteenth-century Swazi village built using the same materials and techniques, it is one of eSwatini's most prized tourist attractions.

I find a seat at the back of the chairs arranged for the audience, a half-crown that lines one side of the hut. The amphitheatre-like arrangement means that I have an eagle eye's view over my fellow spectators. From here, I can watch the watchers. The rows are filled with mostly white faces, with smatterings of Black and brown ones. As the room fills up with visitors who have just clambered off tour coaches, the kindly faced Black American man to my right asks if he can move along into the chair between us.

In a room heavy with anticipation, there are ripples of different accents: Dutch flows over French, English meets Swedish. All the voices quieten when one of the village's leaders steps into the hut's centre to introduce himself and the heritage site. Behind him, the space is largely bare except for a handful of traditional drums with goat-skin heads. A bowl is pointedly placed near the front row for tipping and we're instructed on how we'll proceed to the village tour following the 'show'. Shortly after his departure, human-made birdcalls and climbing harmonised notes precede the entrance of the Swazi performers.

Singing while their feet keep rhythm, the first line of performers is made up of women clad in the signature red, black and white *emahiya.* Staffs and shields flash in their hands as they move to the music of their mouths. Bare-chested men stand behind, many sporting *emajobo* – furred loin-skins – around their hips. White fur trim encircles their arms and calves. Some smile, giving themselves to the performance. A few look tired, most are simply unfazed – their work sees them repeat this routine twice a day every day; the Matenga Cultural Group can also be booked for private and additional performances. Plus, their performances aren't limited to just eSwatini: since 2004, they've toured a host of European countries, the Americas and the African continent for festivals and appearances, including a slot during the 2010 World Cup.[95]

The many unblinking eyes of phone cameras are on them, including mine. They capture the siSwati marriage dance, as well as the *Umhlanga* dance of unmarried women and girls. Our purposes for recording may differ but we're all voyeurs, flattening the richness before us and preserving it as a digital file for later viewing.

Our phones in the midst of this traditional homestead aren't the only stubborn reminders of modernity. The white tricot trim of sports shorts flash beneath a pelt as the performers each kick one leg up, then the other, in unison with each other and the drums. Their legs flick up so high and so quickly that their feet flash above their heads and, in an instant, they're back on the ground. LED strip lights hang from cables that run around the thatched, domed roof. I sit under it conflicted and complicit. My guilt is doubly edged: as a child of the diaspora and as one raised in the innards of the largest and most violently successful empire the world has ever seen.*

What does it mean to perform your cultural rituals daily before a room of foreigners, many of them white? To stand before rows

---

* The British Empire colonised roughly a quarter of the world's landmass. In a survey of two hundred of the world's countries, it was discovered that Britain established some kind of military presence – through force, threat of said force, negotiation, payment – in all but twenty-two of them. This stands at roughly 90 per cent. The figure includes British pirates and armed 'explorers' who undertook operations with the approval of their government.[96]

of faces expecting to be entertained as beers disappear down their throats? What is signified when engagement and appreciation can be measured by how many green, purple and orange *lilangeni* notes those foreigners felt moved to drop in a wooden bowl?

Some theorists describe cultural tourism within the Global South as 'the final stages of colonialism and empire' where travellers from former and current colonising nations enjoy remnants of the cultures that have resisted globalisation.[97] Local people face exploitation, with their ecosystems and environment polluted and their cultures bastardised.[98] Others contend, however, that local identities and traditions are preserved, in part, because of a touristic presence. Resources are funnelled into recreating historical events and efforts are made to maintain heritage sites. There's also, of course, the economic benefit which means jobs for indigenous populations and vendors for local markets and industries.[99]

Later, after we tour the village, my guide, a man also adorned in a *lihiya* who sports excellent bone structure, will tell me that the performance element is crucial to get people to engage with the history. 'If there was no performance, some will not have their job. People would not be interested to come if there's no dance. It's a complementary element to the museum.'

It's a blunt acknowledgement of the state of play and one shared by other Swazi working in the tourism industry. 'It is what it is,' Anele would tell me that evening. She's used to the task of capturing foreigners' attention. In response to my question of whether it ever feels conflicting for him to work in this environment, the guide lays it out plainly. 'Sometimes you don't connect with the audience. You can see that they don't understand, or that they just want to relax or are afraid. Sometimes you see school children who enjoy the dance but they don't connect with the Black people who are living here.'

He'll point to some of the advantages of the work like meeting new people and getting to learn new languages – alongside fluency in English, he can hold a conversation in German, French and Portuguese among others. But that doesn't detract from the emotional toll. 'When [people] don't connect with the dancers, the dancers become heavy. There's no reason to dance for them because they dance for the connection. Even on the tour, if I can see in your eyes that you're not connecting, I'll just brush through because I can see you aren't interested.'

Back in my seat, lilting harmonies wash over me and ululations reverberating around the hut anoint me. Complicated feelings are pulled through me, leaving me both nourished and nauseous. It's only a matter of time before I realise that the ululations are coming from Black members of the audience, responding to the call of the performers. At no point is that more clear than with the hymn, one of the final songs of the set.

The drums have stilled. The room is carried on the voices of sopranos, altos, tenors and basses meeting in siSwati. Black audience members are standing, swaying, singing back at the performers, singing at one another. One woman, her eSwatini flag wrapped around her like a shawl, leaves her seat to deposit money at the front. She returns to it with the half-step, half-dance of an older aunty guided by the spiritual to go and pay her tithe, white handkerchief in hand. I wonder how many of my previously assumed fellow tourists are Swazi, how often they attend these performances and whether they are based locally or have come to connect from afar.

Humming and more ululations fill gaps that words cannot. The voices rise, gaining steam, fervour and meaning. The sound floats above us all like a prayer.

Outside of Labotsibeni's borders, former colonies – Cape, Natal, Transvaal and Orange River – were officially unified in 1910 as the 'Union of South Africa'. Although it would be another few decades before it was a sovereign state free of the British, the Union was a self-governing dominion. The Union codified informal racial seg-regation with legislation, like the system of pass laws – an internal passport system for indigenous Africans – and restrictions to land ownership. The ground was being laid for Apartheid. Observing what was taking place around her, the *iNdlovukazi* saw that the political, social and economic conditions had shifted; the fight needed new tools.[100] (That said, her skill for diplomacy endured: during the Second World War, she purchased an aircraft for the British to the tune of £1,000. Labotsibeni ensured that it was named after her.[101])

Gwamile became acquainted with Africans pursuing social justice in the surrounding territories, including two of the founders of the South African Native Congress; it would later be known as the African National Congress.[102] She financed its communications arm, the *Abuntu Batho* newspaper which first published in 1912. Here, she was finally granted the freedom to put Swazi grievances in the public domain and gradually build the case her grandson Mona would one day present before courts.[103]

In order to do this, however, the ageing sovereign saw emphasis needed to be placed on education. The late Mbandzeni had been bewildered by documents, clenched in the fists of concessionaires, that he couldn't read. Labotsibeni's dealings with colonial administrators had brought her before the same kinds of documents, alongside European written laws and procedures that were essentially indecipherable. Both rulers were dependent on white advisors, lawyers and interpreters to tread through the bureaucratic maze. 'We hold the feather but do not understand what we are signing.'[104]

Her hopes for an educated Swazi kingdom – where skills training in various trades was offered alongside academic education to the population, where their chiefs and *indvunas* were also better equipped to cope with an evolving landscape – wouldn't be realised in her lifetime.[105] Aside from establishing the Zombodze National School near her royal residence and setting up a Swazi National Fund in 1911 which taxed the Swazi for the education of the young *iNgwenyama*-in-waiting, chiefs and councillors (it would later be extended to any Swazi child in need), Labotsibeni expected her grandson to fulfil her vision.[106] It was why she risked the wrath of the council to have him sent to a boarding school outside of Swaziland, to improve his chances of successfully taking on their colonial overlords.[107]

Seemingly prioritising her grandson's advancement over all else – including the advancement of her subjects – Labotsibeni laid the groundwork for the future Sobhuza II to build upon. Bolstered by what she had seen take place with the Union of South Africa, perhaps she hoped – willed – that eSwatini would be free under the child in whose name she ruled. Although the old *iNdlovukazi* didn't live to see it, that day would arrive. Mona, later *iNgwenyama* Sobhuza II, would reign over a sovereign kingdom.

But before she died, Labotsibeni stepped down from the position she had held for three decades. 'This is the day I have always longed for,' began her address, read and translated by a secretary. It was addressed to the British resident commissioner, as well as the representatives of the colonial government.[108] Labotsibeni stood before them, before her Swazi people, her stooped shoulders hidden under her large leopard-skin cloak: 'It has now come at last like a dream which has come true. King Mbandzeni died in October 1889 (thirty-two years ago). As from that day my life has been burdened by an awful responsibility and anxiety. It has been a life full of the deepest emotion that a woman has ever had.'[109]

On that day – 21 December 1921 – Labotsibeni was officially ending her regency. There, the people had gathered for Sobhuza's first *incwala*. It was, in fact, the first since 1899.[110] No *iNgwenyama*, no *incwala*. The ceremony was ushering in rebirth and fresh fruits in more ways than one.

> The Swazi nation placed me in charge of all the affairs of the country as Queen in place of the dead King, and I have acted as Regent during the minority of two subsequent kings. Bhunu died after only a very short life, leaving me with the responsibility of bringing up his infant son and heir. I rejoice that I now present him to Your Honour in your capacity as head of the Administration of Swaziland.[111]

White spectators, photographers and film crews had all made the journey, eager to capture the moment Gwamile Mdluli passed full authority of the kingdom to her 22-year-old grandson.[112]

I have brought him up as a Swazi prince should be brought up.
His spirit is in entire accord with the traditions and feelings
and the aspirations of his countrymen and, what is more, I
have given him the opportunity to obtain the very best training which any Native youth can obtain here in South Africa
[...] In him I feel that I have done all as his Grandmother and
Queen I could possibly do.'[113]

She was shedding the duties she had borne for decades, finally
relinquishing the kingdom into trusted hands. The ongoing struggle against colonial occupation now had a new leader.

When eSwatini's independence was realised in 1968, it would
be attached to Sobhuza II and his reign but its roots can be found
in some of Labotsibeni's contributions. Even so, she lingers at the
edges of Swazi public memory. The sister of my interviewee, Njabu,
is only a decade younger than her but didn't know who she was.
Outside of a statue in Mbabane, there is little that marks her life
in eSwatini today.

'I remember even when that statue came out, there were people
asking what the purpose of [it] was,' Njabu had remarked in our
last minutes together. 'What's the point of a statue without the
story?'

As if she had pre-empted the questions of future Swazi and
historians, Labotsibeni made pains to reference her husband's
concessions in her final address as *iNdlovukazi*: 'I have asked your
Highness to come here and bear me witness before him, and the
council of the Nation to the effect that I have never sold even a
single right of the Nation, I have never given away any of their land
or people to others. I stand before them with clean hands. All my
books are open for his inspection.'[114]

Four years after giving the address, in 1925, Labotsibeni passed
away, believed to have been nearing her seventies. While the *iNg-
wenyamas* of eSwatini are buried in the royal burial mountain of
Mbilaneni, Gwamile was laid to rest in Zombodze, the village she
had called home for much of her life.

The survival of the Kingdom of eSwatini has been credited to

Labotsibeni by some scholars. 'It was she who remoulded the wreckage of the shattered monarchy, the result of the disastrous reigns of the Swazi kings who had preceded her, into the working institution that she handed on in 1921 to her grandson, Sobhuza II (whom she had meticulously tutored throughout his youth),' says one.[115] However, for some Swazi like Njabu, to present the ruler's legacy in such a way is to obfuscate a core truth. 'While her husband may have given away land for stupid things like gin, she gave it away under the guise of protection.'

When we spoke via DMs, Njabu had given a frank appraisal of Labotsibeni's legacy. 'On the surface, I think she was a great leader given the highly patriarchal nature of the monarchy,' she had written. 'I think though that pointing out the negative about her humanises her. Our monarchy has bloody hands. We just hold on to her [as an ideal for] Swazi women because our place in society is always reduced to breeding and raising children.'

The journalist elucidates further as we sit across from one another, picking apart one of the café's giant muffins as a team.

'My gripe is that history has taught me nothing about what she did for women at that time.' If anything, Njabu sees Labotsibeni's reign as a missed opportunity to cement the place of Swazi women in politics. 'I don't even know of a woman who is associated with her governance at that time.'

She pauses for a sip of water. 'I'm sure she was great, I really am, but as a woman, I say, what did she do for women during that time?' At this time, answers are not forthcoming.

As we reduce our baked good to crumbs, I tell Njabu about my tour of the cultural village that followed the performance.

How we were told that men and women lived separately within their east-facing huts, with children also separately educated from the age of six. How we were shown the *esangweni* – a semi-enclosed gathering space for the men of the family – where no women should be found as it was here that fathers educated boys on how to be a man. How a small fire had crackled and snapped at the *esangweni*'s centre, ejecting ash and smoke as our guide told us that when women brought food, they knelt at the entrance, placed the food down and sent boys to pick it up to hand to the elders. How we weren't shown the *edladleni* – the women's area. How the group of tourists both tittered and frowned when told that the head and feet of animals could only be eaten by men because if women ate it, they'd become more intelligent than men. How 'if she eats the tongue, she'll talk too much and disrespect men which is not good also' elicited a laugh.

How conflict is resolved by the grandmother. How she holds the respect of the elders and her decision within the kraal is final. How ceremonies take place in her hut – the *kagogo* – which is the nucleus of the traditional homestead. How we all stood inside the hut, men on the right and women on the left, where we were told that a crime is considered moot once the would-be perpetrator runs into the *kagogo*. How a father spends his last night before working away from home in the *kagogo*, asking for protection and blessing from the ancestors. How it mirrored the father's first night back, spent in the same hut as an expression of gratitude. How the men were instructed to leave first in order to check that it was safe for those of us stood on the left. How we had to wait until each man had exited before we could trail out.

I ask my companion how it's possible that men are presented as protectors and yet, for everyone in the homestead, the grandmother is the ultimate shield. Njabu, having nodded along with my description of my visit, responds with her own string of questions.

'Am I only valuable to the family when I'm a grandmother? How do I get to a place of being valuable if I've been invaluable my whole life? If Granny's protecting, why do you need to protect me? What are you protecting me from? If we're all seeking protection from her, aren't we all equally protected?'

She stresses that, too often when we talk about Swazi – and African history at large – analysis is often limited to European colonisation. 'Say we forget about these white people – what are we doing to each other?' she asks.

'Let's not glamorise our histories. There's something wrong with these traditions. The reason why we were so eager to accept [British colonisation] was because, somehow, it fit.'

CHAPTER 11

Ririkumutima

The Cunning Mother

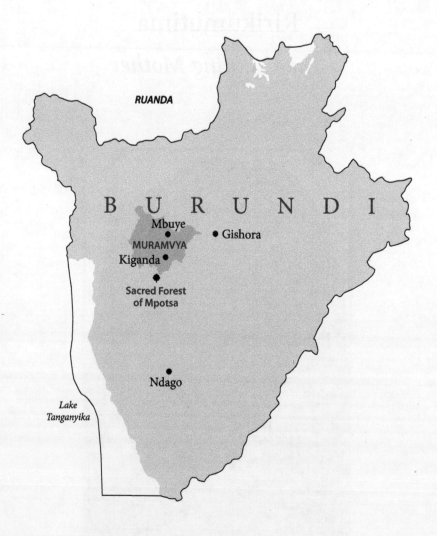

The girl who will become a woman learns at her mother's side. Her siblings, boys who will become men, will too until they reach the age where a mother has no more to teach them; a father takes over.

Her mother will teach her that how she walks, talks, speaks and dresses around an Urundi homestead will be scrutinised. That eyes – of her kin, of the administrators, of the ancestors – are always watching as life unrolls around her.

As a girl who is not yet a woman, she will not be allowed to cover her chest, with just her hips wrapped in an *akabindo* – the Kirundi word for a cloth made of hammered bark.[1] Her partly plaited, partly shaved head symbolises virginity. She'll learn that it is forbidden to become pregnant before marriage and therefore, her nipples must be supervised – they will betray her by changing colour, they say. She'll learn that discoloured nipples would be the least of her problems as she discovers stories of pregnant women weighed down by stones and thrown into ditches, their lovers caught and struck with spears.[2] This is one of many lessons.

Quickly, she'll absorb the ways of her people. The way her people do not smoke tobacco, but rather snuff it; how they sit outside their bristled homes with *inengo* (pincers) holding pinches of tobacco in their noses. That when they're not using snuff, the enduring smell of incense would reliably reach their nostrils. The way that Imana – the omnipotent vital power shared with people of Ruanda – moves through their communities and can be found in animals, trees and any sacred object, including the straw huts built to home the spirits of their ancestors. That the accompanying rites and worship is overseen by a *kiranga*, a highly placed devotee. The manner in which brewed banana beer is a tool of unification, peace and reconciliation; that a court overseeing interpersonal issues can rule that a certain number of beers is to be given as appeasement. That the Batutsi and Bahutu have always lived together in the hills as they reared livestock and farmed their lands, often intermarrying, while the pottery-making Batwa live apart. That if any interpersonal conflict arises in their village, it will be dealt with swiftly by their locally appointed *mushingantahe*, whose lauded reputation for wisdom, integrity and mission of justice precedes them.[3]

The girl who will become a woman is educated through her hands. Hands that will knead and sweep and feed; hands that will direct livestock, tend to fields and weave baskets and mats. The domed thatched building that homes her is considered her domain. She'll find that being able to keep a home and being diligent is closely aligned with her value as a spouse.[4]

As the girl becomes a woman, her prescribed role takes form. The structures and institutions within Rundi society tell her that it's her calling to be the tie that binds two families, perhaps even two clans or ethnic groups. Frankly speaking, in accordance with traditions, she's not considered to actually belong to an ethnic group. When the girl becomes a woman, she will marry and bear children to other ethnic groups.[5] This is why she is the link and this is why compassion, patience and modesty – virtues believed to be intrinsic to womanhood – are expected of her. Like all other girls who are becoming women, she is being shaped into a peacemaker.[6] Discretion will be expected of her. Do not contradict your husband in public but ask his opinion in private. You must allow your husband to beat you should you fall into disobedience and fault.[7]

She'll learn that fertility is prized among her people. When she nurses her newborn, an *urugori* – a motherhood crown made of papyrus strips or sorghum stalks – will rest atop her deep-brown shaven head. She'll get one with each child. Should she have a seventh child, a special, ceremonial *urugori rw'ingara* will be hers to claim. The number of crowns in her possession will dictate how much special treatment she's entitled to.[8] Any spouse of hers would be considered a rich man, thanks to her clutch of offspring. The inverse is also true: if, after consulting a *kiranga*, women still encounter fertility problems, they will be maltreated and ostracised. The girl will become a woman, but, she learns, she *must* become a mother.

The woman who was once a girl will discover that while the domestic sphere is considered her domain and her fellow women under her purview, there is more than one way to cultivate influence. She'll counsel directly when matters involve women; she'll act through her husband when the men of the village are in discord. When it comes to public affairs, the woman who used to be a girl is almost invisible. Almost. There are traditionally no titles for her to hold, no mandate for her to oversee. But she is there, central to administrative machinations. Maybe she'll take on new responsibilities when the husbands and brothers are called to conflict, or make reports to the *mwami* (male sovereign). She might even hold a chieftainship.[9]

Like many girls who became women, her name will be unknown. However, a few – namely those tied to the kingdom's rulers – will survive. One of those names is Nidi Ririkumutima Bizima Bitzazimiza Mwezi.

There are four dynastic names that once rang around the Kingdom of Urundi. They were Ntare, Mwezi, Mutaga and Mwambutsa.

Depending on where they were in the cycle, each freshly ascended *mwami* took possession of one of the well-worn names and made it their own. Much like the Tutsi dynasty in Ruanda, once the latest wearer of 'Mwambatsu' was no more, a successor bearing 'Ntare' would follow, bringing the cycle full circle once more. At least, that was the intention – some historians believe that four cycles were actually completed, others only two.[10]

The four names have moulded early history of today's Burundi, a republic in name that was built on the embers of a Bantu kingdom. Not all of the reigns of the *abami* (plural of *mwami)* have been preserved; we know much about a few and scarcely anything about others. We know about Ntare I Rushatsi, the kingdom's first *mwami* that Burundian sources place in the fourteenth or fifteenth century; as sovereign, he is credited with its unification as well as its strengthening.[11] He's often confused with Ntare III Kivimira (or Semugazashamba) who ruled in the latter half of the seventeenth century and expanded the reach of the kingdom.[12] Between them float Mwezis and Mwambutsas; their names pad out the traditional list of the *abami*, pushed into the shadows created by their better-known counterparts.

Each followed their predecessor into power that they had been selected for by birth. They were *Ganwa*, the name given to the class made up of *baganwa* (princes). They were not labelled 'Hutu', 'Tutsi' or 'Batwa' like the population they ruled over. They were distinct, set apart. Once the ruling *mwami* grew old, his weakened state understood as a reflection of the kingdom, he was required to relinquish power to his son. Hydromel, a honey wine, or milk were offered, always laced with poison. The sovereign was obliged to pass away to allow the dynastic sequence to grind forwards once more.[13]

The cycle eventually ticked over to the reign of Ntare IV Rugamba (or Rubogora) – the sovereign who led the Rundi people into the nineteenth century. Under this Ntare, the area of the kingdom is said to have doubled. He spearheaded invasion and subjugation which saw the territory swell in all directions, increasingly resembling the contours of the Burundi we know today. As its size increased, so, too did its unwieldiness. Relying on his sons to administer the newly occupied regions could only serve Ntare IV so much and by the time he passed away, the expanded kingdom was still not fully under *Ganwa* control.[14]

When one of his younger sons, Mwezi IV Gisonga (or Gisabo), took power around 1852, it wasn't without infighting. It didn't help that Gisabo came to power under the regency of his older brother Ndivyariye, nor that there were buzzing questions about his parentage. His struggle against his siblings was a mere microcosm of the long-standing conflicts between the *baganwa*, their differing descent lines carving through the royal class. Against a backdrop of the Batare (the sons of Ntare) standing in opposition to the Bezi (the sons of Mwezi), Gisabo managed to seize the seat of sovereign.[15]

Although *mwami* in name, Gisabo's reign was characterised by the different administrative systems that emerged. Aside from nominal acknowledgement of the central area of Muramvya controlled by the ruler and his allies, the Batare based in the east and south-west, for example, oversaw their region as though they were autonomous. Meanwhile, in the north-east, revolt spluttered into the open with the baying for the overthrow of Gisabo. After all, the *mwami* had quickly disposed of his principal regent, Ndivyariye. Despite being a strong early supporter of his younger sibling's claim to rule, he wasn't spared: accusations of plotting had driven Ndivyariye from the court and into the path of his assassin. It was his descendants in the north who rose up against the *mwami*.[16]

As the 1900s loomed, the Urundi kingdom's internal fabric was being pulled in disparate directions. The latest to be adorned with a dynastic name, Gisabo and his realm hovered at the edge of the unknown.

There are a few sepia-toned photographs of Ririkumutima. They capture her hooded eyes which pierce the layers of time separating her from her viewer, the patterned fabrics that hide much of her head from view, the way highlights dance across her face and reflect off her smooth, near-obsidian skin.

The third daughter of Chief Sekawonyi of the Watussi (or Batutsi) Munyakarama clan and his spouse Inankinso, *Mwamikazi* Ririkumutima was rumoured to be Gisabo's favourite wife.[17] Out of the thirteen – potentially fourteen – marriages that united various clans through their sovereign, she had jostled her way to the front. Such favour, however, may have come with designs on the Urundi seat of power. Although listed as Gisabo's seventh wife with no reputed firstborns, Ririkumutima saw one of her sons – out of the *mwami*'s believed twenty-five male offspring – as Gisabo's successor.[18]

The Watussi woman didn't just hold favour; she wielded some power in her own right. According to oral accounts, when one of her subjects stood falsely accused by members of the royal court and faced threats of eviction by her husband, Ririkumutima intervened. After she insisted that the case be judged by the *bashingantahe* of the royal council, the persecuted man was acquitted.[19] Contrary to the embedded traditions of her people, the *mwamikazi* did not always require intercession via her husband's ear; rather, she felt free to publicly challenge him and his advisors. She had come a long way from her former home of Ndago, a village in the south of the kingdom, to the royal seat of Muramvya.[20] And she wanted more.

Whatever thoughts of succession lay hidden behind Ririkumu-tima's face, one that would be eventually captured by a nineteenth-century camera, would soon be laid out in the open.

By the 1890s, Ririkumutima would've witnessed firsthand the way her husband and sovereign was being squeezed from all sides. Resistance to the court was a growing public sentiment; disease and ecological crises laid waste to the kingdom and its resources; attacks from other kingdoms came thick and fast; while nearby territories swelled with commercial power. Meanwhile, threats from within continued to bubble.[21]

There was no shortage of potential usurpers swirling around Gisabo in wait. Kilima, a man from Bushi, had emerged in the north-west, claiming *Ganwa* parentage. He would later be remembered as one of the *mwami*'s half-brothers. He obtained weapons from his Swahili commercial contacts near Lake Tanganyika, while successfully riding popular resentment towards the central court. There was also Chief Maconco. His early support of the *mwami* had been sealed with marriage to at least one of Gisabo's daughters. The alliance soon fell apart, however. A 'dispute over a hunting dog' and the death of his spouse loosened any ties of fealty as Maconco readied to stand against his late wife's father.[22]

While the internal clamour around Gisabo's rule refused to quieten, the *mwami* was invisible beyond his kingdom. His domain was so deeply centralised around Muramvya and the royal court that colonial powers doubted his existence until the early 1900s. This was despite the fact that Europeans made first contact with the kingdom dated from 1858 (although in regions that did not recognise Gisabo's authority), maintained a presence there from the 1870s and permanent residence from 1896.[23] Across Ririkumutima's lifetime, European intrusion had been slowly inching closer.

As far as the Europeans – specifically the Germans who'd laid claim to Urundi at the Berlin conference in 1888 – were concerned, it was time to set about making a house a home.

Mr Boniface's car sweeps us into the parking area in front of the building. It's less a parking lot, more an expanse of orange-red sand that cars can park on. There's only one other vehicle, a grey sedan parked as close to the entrance steps as possible. IRATIRO RY'AKARANGA K'UBURUNDI is emblazoned on the front of the building, below much bigger text which reads MUSEE NATIONAL DE GITEGA. I didn't expect Mr Boniface to leave the car – at the Living Museum in Bujumbura, he had settled into his seat for a snooze – but today, my elderly driver seems curious. Together, we step inside.

The Gitega museum is Burundi's national museum and one of the nation's three public museums; the final of the trio is the Geological Museum in Bujumbura, where my accommodation is, which has been closed to the public since 2018. Gitega is the biggest, with its collection housed in one room – albeit a long and packed one. A model replica of a chief's hut sits in one corner, while a life-size statue of a *mushingantahe*, replete with robes and a spear, stands in another. Various receptacles line the surface of an *uburiri*, a bed made of poles and reeds, covered in rushes. There's an *imbungo*, a small woven basket once used to offer hydromel to the king; an *inkongoro* made from a long, hollowed-out pumpkin used to give children milk; both an *indosho* and an *igisuku* are present, the ladle used to make butter from milk and the earthenware jar used to store it.

Among the feeding troughs for cattle, the time-eaten litter for carrying persons of import, the hip-height drums and the real, large preserved head of a hippo, are other relics of a bygone society and the people who formed its tapestry.

Framed photographs line the little corridors that have been created in the room by the display cabinets. A trio of young women stand dressed in clothing made of bark, one of them smiling coyly at the camera. The upturned mouth and squeezed eyes of a grey-bearded elder relay satisfaction as an *inengo* holds their nostrils shut, allowing the snuff to work its magic. A defendant sits on the ground before the *bashingantahe*, a stick which allows its holder to speak is extended from the hand of one of the council members. In other displays, artefacts rest behind glass. Beads and bangles hang in one, talismans and divination rattles dangle in another. A fighter's bow with a rope made of cow tendon sits above adjoining arrows while a number of *icumu* (spears) stand proudly, a symbol of authority, virility and legacy as men handed down their *icumu* to their chosen heir.

Abami, presidents, prime ministers and de facto dictators stare down from the walls, whether from a frame, a poster listing the date of their reign or from realistic-looking busts, including an aged Mwezi Gisabo who sits crouched with his forlorn-looking head propped up in his hands.

Mr Boniface and I walk through the museum alongside Jean-Bosco, the museum's manager. Our tall, weathered guide seems to enjoy the questioning, perhaps given that its already midday and I'm the second person to sign the visitors' log. There isn't another soul on the site during our hours there. When we take breaks to allow me to furiously scribble notes – audio recordings are not allowed, Jean-Bosco had smiled apologetically – the museum worker and my driver chat in Kirundi until my next question or the next artefact we're led to.

He has so much to tell me about Gisabo. How, if the Germans hadn't been attuned to Gisabo's existence before, they were well aware by the turn of the century as they sought to bring the kingdom under German authority. How Kilima and Maconco allied themselves with the colonials as their attempts to seize the *mwami* got under way. The way the sovereign would elude their attempts for almost a year, thanks to his subjects.

'The people of Gishora (an area 7km north of Gitega) saw the king was running from Muramvya,' Jean-Bosco explains. 'They hid him in their big [grain] storage in Gitega and enemies passed by without noticing.' Gisabo hid out there for nine months, he tells us, before finally facing the Germans.

When it comes to Ririkumutima, however, the museum worker's knowledge is thin. There is nothing to be found about the
mwamikazi in the museum. There are no images of her to gaze out
at visitors, no preserved relics that we know passed through her
hands. She's an afterthought, a footnote, to her husband's reign,
despite playing a part in one of the most important periods in
Burundi's history, including the signing of the 1903 Treaty of
Kiganda.

After keeping the Germans at bay for seven years, perhaps Gisabo
was tired of fleeing, of jeopardy, of knowing that bows and arrows
were weak competition for German guns, of watching and waiting
to see who would turn on him next.

Of course, the instability affected much more than him – a
ruler driven from his compound had implications for his realm,
his people, his fellow *Ganwa*, his kin. German military expeditions into the centre of the country sought to cow and punish
the people for their perceived stubbornness, killing and brutalis-
ing Rundi people as they went.[24] When Ririkumutima and the
baganwa advised Gisabo to sign for peace and halt their kingdom
being taken by force, the *mwami* listened.[25] The Urundi ruler had
a high regard for his most favoured wife and her counsel. It was
perhaps why he had placed Mbikije, the son of another wife named
Ntibanyiha, under Ririkumutima's tutelage as he was primed as the
heir apparent.[26] Some accounts have alluded to the *mwamikazi*'s
persistent attempts to change her husband's mind about his heir
but it's possible, in keeping with Rundi traditions, that sorghum
seeds had been placed in Mbikije's hands immediately after he
was born; it would've bestowed upon him an 'inviolable right to
succeed his father.'[27] Ririkumutima's powers of persuasion could've
only extended so far. She had to settle for being entrusted as
Mbikije's mentor and successfully urging Gisabo towards a treaty.

When the *mwami* accepted German authority on 6 June 1903,
it came with additional terms: he would respect the presence of
missionaries slowly proliferating within the kingdom and would
accept the administrative authority of German allies like Kilima

and Maconco. In return, the German empire would support Gisabo in consolidating his power as ruler of Urundi. He'd retain his royal title but relinquish true power.[28]

Maconco, however, learnt a bitter lesson in gambling on colonial support. Despite earning a prominent administrative position, he was eventually accused by the Germans of stealing a gun, arrested and hanged.[29] When it came to preserving German interests, allies – even those who had placed themselves at great risk – were expendable. Maconco's execution at the hands of Europeans highlighted the ever-shifting field of power and right now, it tilted firmly towards the German occupation. They had no one to answer to for the killing of a figure of great stature in the kingdom.

There could be no equivocation: the Kingdom of Urundi was now a colony.

Gisabo passed away not long afterwards in 1908, and it's not clear whether his death came about through hydromel or other means. The late sovereign's demise came during spiralling existing diseases in the region, and the introduction of new ones too. Trypanosomiasis (or 'sleeping sickness'), smallpox, cerebrospinal meningitis and influenza swept through the occupied kingdom, disabling and killing as they went.[30] Disease-bearing tsetse flies and whispered rumours about his beloved Ririkumutima's culpability both flitted about Urundi.

When the fifteen-year-old Mbikije was selected as the next *mwami*, it still came as an apparent surprise to the freshly widowed Ririkumutima. She was said to be 'severely disappointed' when the German occupation and her fellow royal family members intervened on behalf of the son of Ntibanyiha.[31] Despite stubborn belief, again her offspring had been overlooked.

Regardless, Ririkumutima worked the situation to her advantage. After a time, the Watussi royal decided that, actually, Mbikije should ascend at the expense of all other candidates. With the concerned parties in accord, the teenager became *Mwami* Mutaga IV Mbikije and Ririkumutima became *umugabekazi* – the queen mother. She was now the new ruler's most trusted advisor and, crucially, his regnant until he came of age. It was a break from the common practice. In accordance with tradition, that role should've belonged to his mother. Instead, to secure her grip on power and nullify a future challenge, Ririkumutima allegedly had Ntibanyiha murdered.[32] For all intents and purposes, Mutaga was *her* son.

Did Ririkumutima understand her role strictly as being a guiding force? Or did she, as has been loosely hypothesised, attempt to dupe the kingdom into believing that she had always been the *mwami*'s mother? However it initially manifested, the fiction largely prevailed. Her place as regnant was sealed – although, under German occupation, she was little more than a regional administrator.[33]

The successful ascension of Mutaga – and by extension, his new *umugabekazi* – was not without challengers. His uncle and a senior member of the royal class, Ntarugera, vied with Ririkumutima for control over the realm's governance. He believed that the royal seat had been usurped, opening a bitter chasm between those who supported the *mwami* and those who didn't. It swallowed the *Ganwa* class, seeding dissent amid royal family members and leaving the monarchy vulnerable to the Germans. Taking advantage of the internal fissures, the Europeans divided the kingdom into three districts, with the titled pair only ruling the central part of Urundi. In the north, they installed long-time ally Kilima, guaranteeing that a united Rundi administration rising up against them was an unlikely scenario.[34]

Although the Rundi monarchy was deeply fractured, haemorrhaging sovereignty and resources, Ririkumutima was at least padded by her new status. Her position appeared so impenetrable that it even withstood the death of Mutaga in November 1915, just seven years after his father.

Some sources state that the *mwami* died after contracting malaria while others point the accusing finger towards his mentor.[35] The number of children Ririkumutima had with Gisabo is disputed but among her offspring were two sons named Nduwumwe and Bangura. Some traditions suggest that the pair followed their mother's orders to strangle Mutaga. Others point to a romantic tryst as the catalyst. Those oral accounts suggest that Ririkumutima informed the young *mwami* that Bangura was seducing one of his wives. Having flown into a rage, the brothers came to blows which proved fatal for the ruler. It played out as the *umugabekazi* had intended, the accounts relay.[36]

Ultimately, the truth didn't matter as Ririkumutima's fiction was enduring – so enduring, in fact, that she was able to manoeuvre herself as the regnant of Mutaga's infant son and successor, Bangiricenge, after having his mother, Ngenzahago, assassinated. This was just the beginning: her son Nduwumwe led a massacre, seen as the best way to secure her position. Under Ririkumutima's orders, another of Mutaga's wives was killed, alongside many members of her clan.[37]

Her sons, particularly Nduwumwe, rose through the ranks under the *umugabekazi*. Although she maintained her authority from Muramvya's royal capital of Mbuye, the royal uncle who still claimed usurpation, Ntarugera, continued to needle in her side with his accusations. 'To try and prevent an even greater civil war, the German authorities created at Mutaga's death an awkward arrangement of having Ntarugera share power with Ndumumwe and Ririkumutima,' writes historian Jeremy Rich.[38] It was perhaps not an ideal arrangement but it didn't stop the ruler from favouring her offspring and her Munyakarama clan above others.

Although they would never wear the title of sovereign, Ririkumutima had managed to fashion her wish into a workable reality. Together with her sons (and reluctantly, Ntarugera), she was the face of Urundi rule under occupation.

A year before Mutaga died, the assassination of Archduke Franz Ferdinand in the summer of 1914 set in motion a series of escalating hostilities that would culminate in the First World War. The European belligerents drew their colonies around the globe into the deadly conflict that spanned four years.

African lands became the theatre of Western fighting and colonised people their makeshift soldiers. 'German East Africa' was no different as the Germans hunkered in to defend the territory against

British, and later Belgian, forces. Rather than the trench warfare that epitomises the period in Europe, guerilla warfare and effectively '[chasing] each other up and down the region, often at a pace of 30km a day' stretched out across almost half a decade.[39] 'They levelled villages for supplies and enlisted civilians as soldiers to fight and carriers to shift their supplies,' details Tanzanian historian and cultural curator Kathleen Bomani. 'Most soldiers and porters died from malnutrition, fatigue, malaria, tsetse fly and black fever, rather than bullets.'[40]

As their kingdom was ravaged by a war not of their own making, the Rundi royals were split on where their support should lie. When the Belgians made their way towards Urundi from the nearby 'Belgian Congo', Ntarugera gave the new wave of colonisers his backing. Conversely, Ririkumutima continued to affirm German overlordship while remaining a prominent opponent of a Belgium colonial empire now headed by Leopold II's nephew.[41]

Unfortunately for her, the German colonial empire was haemorrhaging under the pressure of Allied forces. Two years into the First World War, it had lost most of its colonies and although it would maintain an armed German presence in the Great Lakes region until the war's official end, by 1916, Belgian troops had seized Urundi. So egregious was Ririkumutima's 'insolence', after she and the *Ganwa* surrendered the kingdom to them, the Belgians still sought to make her pay.[42] 'I am going to launch a *coup d'état* which will count as a major moment in the history of the country,' the governor of 'Belgian Congo' opined in his diary in June 1917. 'Ntarugera will be the only regent [of Urundi].'[43]

However, many of Belgium's problems were solved within a couple of months. The circumstances of her death remain inconclusive, with traditions ranging from illness to strangulation but at her home in Mbuye on 29 July 1917, Ririkumutima took one last breath. She joined the *umugabekazi* who had gone before her, nestled under the soil of the sacred forest of Mpotsa.[44]

Although she escaped whatever specific retribution their new overlords had concocted, Belgium and the eventual legacy it would imprint on the kingdom would punish Ririkumutima and her people in more ways than one.

With Urundi held under military occupation from 1916, Belgium was officially handed Urundi and Ruanda in 1923. With the spoils of a fallen German empire split and gorged upon by European victors through a League of Nations mandate, the Belgians now temporarily governed Ruanda–Urundi, acting as a trustee until the people could be trusted to rule themselves.[45] The two kingdoms would be governed as one despite their marked differences (so marked in fact, that they would later twice refuse offers by the United Nations to be granted independence as a single entity[46]).

In the late *umugabekazi*'s kingdom, the Belgians got to work. They quickly abolished *mwami* authority over life and death and reorganised the districts and administration. In efforts to capitalise on the region's economy, they introduced the cultivation of maize and sweet potatoes and concepts of crop rotation. They established cotton production which would go on to become the second largest export.[47] Coffee, however, was the occupied territory's mainstay, eventually representing 80 per cent of Ruanda–Urundi's exports.[48] The introduction of coffee production and forced labour came hand in hand.[49] Meanwhile, priests, missionaries and educators trundled their way through the region, powered by a Catholic mission to replace the *kiranga* with Jesus Christ.[50]

All the systems established across the colonial territory were built on the basis of flawed Western assumptions around African ethnicity. Colonialists who had previously spent time in Ruanda brought their hypotheses on the Hutu and Tutsi to Urundi.[51]

Within their self-made conceptualisations of race, Europeans believed that 'Hutu' and 'Tutsi' were completely distinct: the former falling into the 'Negroid' racial grouping and the latter assumed to be of the more 'superior' race of 'Hamites'.[52] The appearances of both Bantu-speaking groups only seemed to confirm the racial classification they had devised. Colonial historians replicated and normalised these distinctions, with antiblackness seeping from the lines of their articles and books. 'The tall, aristocratic

Tutsis . . . invaded the country from the east some four centuries ago and easily mastered the indigenous Hutu societies,' writes one.[53] Elsewhere, the Tutsis' 'tall stature, light skin pigmentation and Ethiopid features' is contrasted with the 'ungainly figures betoken hard toil' of the Hutus who 'patiently bow themselves in abject bondage to the later arrived but riling race, the Tutsi'.[54]

Given that Hutus and Tutsis made up both the occupied Ruanda and Urundi dominions, in line with colonial logic, there was no reason why their reductive understanding of the former couldn't be applied to the latter. This was despite the fact that in Ruanda, the chasm between Tutsi and Hutu was much greater, with Tutsis over-represented in the monarchy and in chieftainships. While intermarrying took place in Urundi, it carried greater taboos for their northern counterparts.[55] It also didn't matter to the colonials that the Rundi *Ganwa* weren't considered Hutu or Tutsi, nor that Hutus could hold positions of power and Tutsis could be poor and nomadic. As far as the Belgians were concerned, across Ruanda–Urundi, all chiefs were Tutsi and all subjects were Hutu.[56]

This was but only the beginning of how the colonisers would strain the ethnic lines that ran through Urundi and the wider region. Belgian rule created ripe conditions for tensions that would erupt into devastating violence, ripping Burundi and Rwanda apart long after independence had been declared in 1962.

Nidi Ririkumutima Bizima Bitzazimiza Mwezi wouldn't live to see the 1966 military coups and depositions of Mutaga's son, Mwambutsa IV Bangiricenge, who ruled in his own right from 1929, and his grandson, Ntare V (the latter only reigned from July to November 1966 before being ousted). She was long gone by the time the Tutsi-dominated army committed genocide against Burundi's educated Hutus in 1972, slaughtering hundreds of thousands. Nor would she witness the primarily lower-class Hutus conduct mass killings of Tutsis across the closing months of 1993, after the assassination of the Burundian president, with Tutsi-led massacres carried out in response.

The harmonious living formations that had existed centuries

before Ririkumutima had even learnt to walk had been set ablaze and fanned enthusiastically by a colonial presence, leaving the descendants of Urundi to pick through the smoking remnants.

'Ririkumutima was a brave woman and the Germans hated her because of her influence,' Jean-Bosco had said as he walked Mr Boniface and I to the museum's entrance. 'She was a politician. She influenced the king.'

However, it's the next sentence he said that remains on my mind as Mr Boniface navigates the mountain road, whizzing us away from Gitega. Shrubs, banana trees and grass line the red dusty road, while people and homes flash by. In the distance, deep green valleys swell and dip, no level ground to be seen. Every now and again, the land is divided into green and clay-coloured squares; the straight lines running through them say that this land is fertile and will shortly offer up its fruit.

'She was an anti-imperialist,' our museum guide had said. Yet, the traditions we have access to right now suggest otherwise. There is scant evidence that she sought to rise up against the Germans and their colonial rule, while opposition to the Belgians can be interpreted as the late *umugabekazi* having identified an external threat to an internal hierarchy that favoured her and her family. What does it mean when a figure like Ririkumutima, who appears to have been principally driven by her own interests, can be considered 'anti-imperialist'? Is emphasis placed on the fact that she was able to hold some power rather than what she did with it? In some domains, has 'anti-imperialism' come to mean 'existing and surviving under colonial rule'? Which other African historical figures have been swept up under the term, their actions unexamined? Although, as my mentor and scholar Christienna Fryar noted to me, being 'anti-imperialist' doesn't necessarily mean that the person is against wielding the power themselves, as we've seen with Ranavalona and, at times, Njinga.

These distortions are possible because there is barely any evidence of Ririkumutima's life to speak of. Her omission within the national museum stays with me as Mr Boniface winds our way towards Muramvya, halfway between Gitega and Bujumbura – towards the royal palaces Gisabo had erected there. An examination of Ririkumutima's life is a process of collecting the dribs and drabs filtered through the men around her and the absences around her aren't limited to the museum. In the Kirundi-language newspapers organised by Catholic missionaries, Rundi authors disparaged Ririkumutima. In 1956, the Belgian and Burundian editors of the *Ndongozi* newspaper disappeared her role in Mutaga's assassination in a review of his life. Ruins of her former Ndago home had survived until the early 1980s when they were destroyed during construction work.[57]

Elsewhere, traditional architecture has been preserved, including the royal estate in Muramvya. My feet are just the latest to tread orange dust that has been walked by Rundi rulers, chiefs, *baganwa, bashingantahe*, farmers, warriors, vendors, delegations passing through and more. The palaces – each one thick with straw thatching with a stone path leading to its opening – are off-limits with a metal fence denying access. A sign next to the palace closest to me reads INZU Y'UMWAMI. *Home of the ruler.*

Exorcised and expunged, we're forced to make approximations about Ririkumutima and, as I stand as close as I can to the fence, I make another. The estate is described as the residence of Mwezi Gisabo and Mutaga Mbikije, as well as Ntare Rugamba. It was here that they administered justice with the voices of the *baganwa* and other court officials, it was here that the *Ganwa* mingled and the kingdom's subjects came for places of worship or to seek audiences.[58] We can infer that, given this space housed her husband and her 'son', it would've regularly seen Ririkumutima's presence, if not her occupancy. It's no great marvel by itself but inches us closer to locating her, plotting her life and exhuming her contributions. This is the work we must do for such figures, these are the tiny morsels we must snatch from the margins.

The colonisation of Urundi sharply defined the codes that already ran through a deeply patriarchal society; the political, religious and social discrimination against women that missionaries brought with them found already fertile soil.

Women have been historically rendered invisible, with even Ririkumutima – one of their most privileged, highly positioned number – left struggling to puncture the national narrative of her own land.

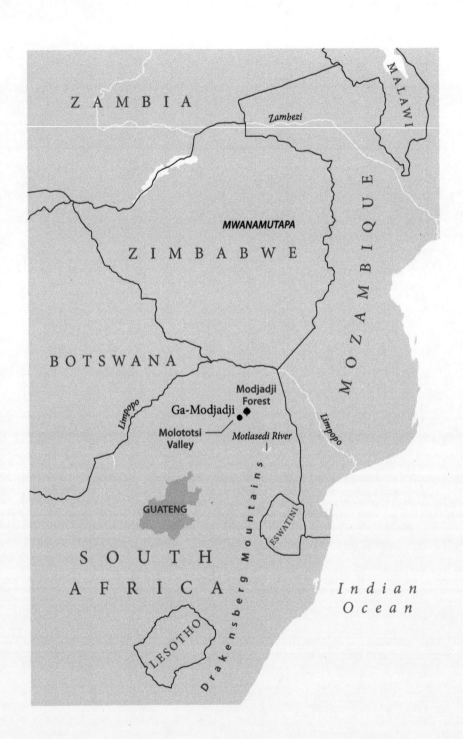

Z A M B I A

Zambezi

MALAWI

MWANAMUTAPA

Z I M B A B W E

M O Z A M B I Q U E

B O T S W A N A

Limpopo

Modjadji
Forest

Ga-Modjadji

Molototsi
Valley

Motlasedi River

Limpopo

GUATENG

ESWATINI

S O U T H

A F R I C A

Drakensberg Mountains

LESOTHO

Indian
Ocean

CHAPTER 12

Makobo Modjadji VI
The Rain Queen

Her eyes rove around, down and then up once more. She doesn't commit to a smile, not like the wide grins or proud pursing of many around her. A slightly upturned corner of her mouth will have to be enough for the hungry cameras before her. She stands to receive a leopard-skin mantle but eventually turns to aid both the VhaVenḓa king and the premier of Limpopo Province who appear to struggle with presenting the skin the right way round. Their slow confusion had not been hastened by the pulsing rhythm of drums, the feverish cacophony of wooden flutes, nor the pounding of feet into red dust.

Now suitably cloaked and seated, she is flanked on all sides by men – some from her twenty-two-strong and exclusively male royal council. Before her dance the aged women of her people, the BaLobedu (or Lobedu). They sing, stamp and swirl around the drummers in their uniform of yellow and green, flashing white feathered reeds and coiled anklets. She looks on. She will not speak today. Her people, made up of fifty-three villages in South Africa's Limpopo, will likely never hear her speak.[1] They'll hear instead from her male advisors as they profess her delight and relish in the responsibilities before her.

The bulk of the ceremonial fanfare concluded, her entourage threads its way through ululating masses, some with MODJADJI CORONATION 2003 emblazoned on the back of their shirts, legible under belts and sashes of beads. Head bowed, 25-year-old Makobo Caroline Modjadji VI leads, preceded only by a press pack angling for photos of the woman wrapped in the embrace of a leopard. Dignitaries stream after her. Mining billionaire businessmen jostle for space with political icons like Winnie Madikizela-Mandela as they wind their way through the throng. Royal representatives have made the journey from their respective kingdoms, such as Ndzundza-Mabhoko and AbaThembu.

Above them, a haze of grey clouds coddles the land, the sharp edges of the leafy landscape smoothed out of focus. Drizzle greets the parched earth, a gratefully snatched good omen. Today, her reign begins.

When I asked TC, a historian and village poet, how his family and the family of the Modjadjis are related, the writer, clad almost entirely in leopard print, adjusted his grip on his polished walking aid and closed his eyes. It was as though gathering himself would quiet the din of the Polokwane fast-food restaurant around us. 'The history of us and Modjadjis was as follows,' he began solemnly.

TC's people, the Kalanga (or Bukalanga) have long been a drifting people. By 1000 CE, they had worked their way down from the north of the continent, before making a home of the western and southern present-day Zimbabwe and surrounding lands that fall within today's Mozambique and South Africa.[2] They brought with them a reputation for dance, drinking, and dancing while drunk. Alongside a predilection for revelry, these early Kalanga people established themselves as miners, traders of gold and architects of the city-states of Maphungubgwe and Khami.[3] As they built and spread, Bukalanga numbers swelled. Family branches, later clans, established their own traditions. The BaLobedu, VhaVenda, BaKalanga (not the same as the wider Bukalanga family), and BaTembe sit among at least twelve tribes that trace their origins back to the Kalanga.[4]

'By 1200, [the Modjadjis] began to have their own tradition of leading,' explained TC. Three hundred years later, the early sixteenth century saw the emergence of Dzugudini, considered one of the earliest Lobedu chiefs. Her life has been painted vividly through Khelobedu – the language of the BaLobedu people – oral traditions over centuries. They detail how the daughter of a *mambo* ('chief' or 'king' in Shona) was forced to flee her father's domain within the kingdom of Mwanamutapa in present-day Zimbabwe. She had fallen pregnant and the father was presumed to be her brother. The refusal of Dzugudini and her mother to reveal his identity to her father incurred a wrath that drove the pair – and some of his followers – away from the royal kraal and across the rushing waters of the Limpopo River.[5]

Dzugudini's son, Makhaphele, followed by his son Mohale, led the BaLobedu tribe further south into the Molototsi valley, the site of today's Ga-Modjadji. Under Mohale, the BaLobedu settled in lands already occupied by the Kheoga people, who they killed and subjugated.[6] There, they established themselves as an agricultural people, working the land and exchanging produce for subsistence.[7] Over the next few centuries, *Mambo* Mohale's rule, and that of his descendants, reached across the entire valley.

By the late 1700s, Chief Mugodo – also referred to as Mokoto – was feeling the pressure. The authoritative and unchallenged status of his ancestor, Mohale, had long dissipated as Mugodo's sons and councillors lay plans to overthrow him. In the face of looming defeat, the chief issued a prophecy: he could only be succeeded by a queen and her veins must run red with the blood of Mwanamutapa.[8] Not only must the successor be a woman, but she had to be his child.

As the oral tradition goes, it was the wish of his ancestors that he sire a child with his daughter, Maselekwane. She would succeed Mugodo, and her child would succeed her. The prophecy dictated that it was only through such an act that the sanctity of their rituals could be preserved – the ability to call upon the skies to lay open, beckoning rain to fall. Mugodo's daughter was given a throne name: Modjadji. It means 'ruler of the day'.[9]

The throne was not intended for Makobo Modjadji whose coronation was marked on 16 April 2003. At least, not yet. Tragedy had padded the path for the 25-year-old's ascent as the sixth Rain Queen. Her mother, Princess Mmakheala Modjadji, had been lined up as the next designated successor. With plenty of time before she was expected to lead, Makobo was the first Rain Queen to receive a formal education.[10] There was perhaps little harm seen in allowing the young child to flirt with modernity beyond the royal cradle.

The passing of Makobo's grandmother, Mokope Modjadji V, while a significant blow to her people, was likely unsurprising to those in the royal kraal. At the age of sixty-four, she succumbed to her failing body with heart, kidney and lung failure claiming her in late June of 2001. What had not been planned for was the death of Mmakheala, two days before her mother, at the age of just thirty-seven. 'A short illness' is all that would be given as a cause.[11]

Newspapers – both South African and international – homed in on a crisis of succession, creating such a furore that a spokesperson shared that the Modjadji family were upset that their internal workings had been shared with the world before succession discussions or funeral arrangements had been made.[12] Yet, the decision always appeared clear: a granddaughter of the fifth Rain Queen still stood among them, the only woman left in the royal family.[13]

At just under the age of twenty-three, Makobo had lost both her grandmother and mother, and gained a kingdom.

'I am baptized by my own god,' Makobo's grandmother once said in an interview. Mokope Modjadji V was not a Christian but would allow African Christian leaders to court her, competing for her attention and approval. Yet she wouldn't commit herself any which way. The head of a traditional monarchy, one recognised by the South African government, sought to channel the rule of her mother, and her mother's mother: the Rain Queen as unknowable.

Since 1800, the Modjadji dynasty and the BaLobedu people had been overseen exclusively by women. Mothers passing secrets of rain onto daughters, aunties relinquishing the leopard-skin mantle to nieces. Alongside those sacraments, the expectations of what made a traditional monarch were relayed from one generation to the next, traits necessary for successful rule over the nearly 150 villages and towns under their authority.

The Modjadji queen was to live a secluded life, only seen by – or giving audience to – royal relatives and nobles. Mokope Modjadji V could often be found sat barefoot in front of her thatched reception hut, sometimes sporting the leopard-skin cloak that had rested on the shoulders of five generations, but rarely dressed more ostentatiously than other BaLobedu women.[14] Traditional homesteads belonging to affiliated families made up the royal compound in Khehlakoni village with rounded huts encircled by low clay walls – this was her domain. It was here that she would entertain *iNdunas* (village headsmen) as they issued reports on the rural communities they oversaw in her name. So tightly bound was the monarch to the land over which she ruled, a Modjadji chief couldn't leave the kingdom or traverse its borders. In fact, observing these codes had made it impossible for Khesethwane Modjadji, the third Rain Queen, to register her vote for the Native Council in the 1930s.[15]

There was a certain infallible air to the monarch. Among the BaLobedu people, it was understood that it was not possible for the queen to fall ill, with Modjadji III believed to never have experienced illness a day in her life. Though a select audience would be entertained in the presence of a Rain Queen, they were not allowed to address her directly.[16] Much like the descendants of Dahomey's Hangbé, remarks to and from the queen could only be made through an intermediary, often a member of her royal council.

Largely eschewing public functions, when the Rain Queen was to be presented before her people, precautions were taken to keep a studied distance between the ruler and her subjects. Like her granddaughter, footage of the coronation of Modjadji V saw the newly enthroned ruler maintain a bowed head, avoiding the possibility of curious eyes locking onto hers. This same queen emerged as notable for having kept the then-president of South Africa and also of the African National Congress (ANC), Nelson Mandela, waiting on her, aligning with her reputation for having little patience with visitors.[17] Having visited her several times, Mandela would tell reporters that his relationship with Modjadji V was close, but would warn them to never quiz her. 'She does not answer questions,' he said.[18]

For scholars like Kabelo O. Motasa, the seclusion demonstrates the way the Royal Council held full control over the women of the royal house, including its rulers. 'If the Modjadji queen had a mind of her own, insisting on marrying a man of her choice or going against tradition by living a more public life, the Royal Council would ban the husband from the royal house and the village, and would not recognise the children as possible successors in the event of the Modjadji's death.'[19]

The famed abilities of the Modjadjis coupled with their seclusion combine to produce a potent cocktail of mystery, intrigue and implicit threat. It's why, TC told me, that for many generations, they have largely been left alone, despite having war-ready neighbours that included Shaka of the Zulus. 'Swazis and Zulus didn't want to fight them because everyone survives through water,' he had said with a smile. 'They knew without rain, they would die.' Even the Christian converts among the BaLobedu, who amounted to 5 per cent of the population in the 1930s, believed in the power of the Modjadji to bring forth rain – albeit through the will of God.[20]

To honour, and sometimes appease, the most famous rainmaker in the region, other chiefs would send her gifts. Trundling caravans of gifts – perhaps baskets and calabash filled with the season's latest offerings – followed by cattle led with rope, passed the fragrant Modjadji Forest, brushing past the fern-like cycads it has become known for. Each gift sent up to the BaLobedu homeland in a high valley in the Drakensberg Mountains held a desperate plea to the monarch: somewhere, there was a drought that only she could end.[21]

Gift and I stand in front of the grey slate column, sweating under a cloudless sky. A two-hour journey from central Polokwane has brought us here, to Ga-Modjadji, in search of anything and everything I can find on the Rain Queens. Before us stands the Modjadji Dynasty Memorial, inscribed with names, dates and the villages of the early kings and queens who passed power onto one another. Behind it sits a large gated building, the sun's beams only highlighting the stubborn rust of its corrugated roof. MODJADJI TRADITIONAL AUTHORITY reads the sign next to it.

With a few quick words in Pedi, Gift – the driver I bonded

with from the moment he picked me up at Polokwane Airport –
grabs the attention of a nearby young man. Before long, an older
gentleman stands with us in front of the structure. Anthony speaks
slowly and cautiously. He asks what we're looking for and why I've
come from London for this information. We explain my work and
the larger project this falls under – I just want to know more about
Makobo Modjadji. That she is not the only historical figure I'm
researching and, judging by Anthony's body language, feel moved
to assure him that we have no insidious agenda.

After further exchange between the two men, Anthony's cagi-
ness gives way ever so slightly as he offers a brief, carefully worded
explanation: 'We're still fighting for Masalanabo to be the Rain
Queen.' He mentions a Supreme Court case and, again, we make
it clear that we're not here to trouble any ongoing disputes. Gift
gestures towards the memorial and asks him to explain more
about each ruler inscribed on the side being kissed by the sun. My
driver-turned-research assistant is just as hungry for information
as I am.

I pepper Anthony with questions. He offers to take a picture of
Gift and I in front of the memorial. It all seems to have softened
him because when I ask him about *dithokola* – the annual October
rainmaking ceremonies – he turns to lead us away and says, 'I can
show you.'

We head towards the kraal, gleaning what I can from him on our
short walk. Anthony has been a tour guide for almost a decade. I
sense his role encompasses more, namely around the dispute, but
his trust is understandably too fragile for further query. Before the
establishment of the nearby tribal office, all the problems used to
be solved within the kraal but now everything has been Westernised, he tells us. He points out tall trees with thick trunks and
outstretched emerald stems; 'Modjadji's palm' is the name of the
sacred cycad. 'You can only find this species here,' Anthony notes
with pride.

A gate made of metal and wood greets us at the opening of the
kraal, part of the fence that guards an expanse of burnt-orange
dust. Openings in the fence lead off to the areas belonging to

the four families that inhabit the kraal today. But before we can cross the threshold, we must remove our shoes. This is hallowed ground and accepting its heat on bare soles is our dues. Chattering children observe us from the shade of trees and between gaps in the wooden fence as we slowly make our way through their home. Later, TC will tell me that, in pre-colonial times, men would sit to one side of the kraal and women the other. If women were on their period, they wouldn't be allowed to enter the traditional kraal, made to sit outside. Today, this rule is no longer enforced.

As we pass the modern homes within the royal compound, I assume we won't be going much further. This is already more than I had dared to hope for. Instead, our guide says, 'I'll take my chances and show you the chalet where we pray for the rain.' Our weak protests against getting Anthony in trouble are wordlessly dismissed – he's already leading the way.

When the ancestor of the BaLobedu, Dzugudini, escaped the reach of her father's power, she took more than a following with her. She crossed the waters of the Limpopo with the tribe's sacred beads, the rain charms and the knowledge of their use.[22] With each generation of the Modjadji dynasty, those secrets floated on a whisper from the reigning monarch to their expectant successor. However, the Modjadjis were never the only rainmakers in the area.

'The Kalanga, [they would] do rituals in a certain way – in a way that they were using it for protection and rain,' explained TC. Unlike the physical fight and sheer numbers of the Zulu, they turned to rituals that involved the mixing of different traditional herbs to induce rain, and when necessary, fire.[23] While the Modjadjis are considered among the most powerful rainmakers found in the lands that make up today's South Africa, their duties have historically involved facilitating the rainmaking of others.[24]

South African social anthropologist Isak Niehaus outlines the rainmaking rites organised by Sethlare chiefs in the region until 1956, as detailed by elderly informants. Just before ploughing season approached, chiefs summoned the rainmakers in their kraal, while sending out village headmen to collect donations.

Crops, livestock and, later, cash were collected from all the village people. The rainmakers would then send delegates to plead with the Modjadji monarch: both for rain, and for the collection of rain medicines from her in a goat's horn. Upon their return, the medicine would be handed to the rainmakers. Locating a secluded spot, they would then mix the medicine in a large earthen pot with other ingredients, while making public invocations to the ancestors of the Sethlare chiefs and the Modjadji Rain Queen.

The next day, 'virgin' boys and girls were assembled at the *mošate* (royal residence) and would be given rain medicines before sleeping overnight on the banks of the Motlasedi River. Early in the morning, the children poured the medicines into the water and then placed medlar leaves, smeared with medicines, along the boundaries of the chiefdom.[25] The rituals of rainmaking were so widespread and commonplace, children would grow up hearing stories of rainmakers killing the sons of neighbouring chiefs in order to strengthen their rain medicines. They were told to be careful to never stray too far from the homestead, lest a stranger decide to trade their life for rainfall.[26]

Dithokola involves three ceremonies carried out by the Rain Queen, Joooo, one at each of three sacred shrines, including the pouring out of locally brewed beer to be lapped up from the ground by important individuals, before dancing to the beat of a sacred drum.[27] Modjadji V refused to share the ceremonial rituals innate to the process, spurning the enduring interest in the BaLobedu practice, and the greatest secrets are held within the walls of the round building before us.

'After our ceremony, we pray here at the chalet.' Anthony gestures to the structure topped with thick thatching, enclosed by a low brick wall. It's an anomaly, nestled among tiled homes with windows and, as far as I can see, the chalet's only opening is a battered wooden door.

We move closer to the chalet but still beyond its walls the squeals of nearby playing children accompany us. Gift asks if I can take pictures.

'Yes, but there's just one thing,' says Anthony before quickly slipping into a Pedi exchange with my companion.

'Oh, um,' Gift stumbles over his words as he glances at me. He looks back to our guide for clarification. 'Okay. So she's not allowed if she's there?' Anthony nods in the affirmative.

'Ah,' my driver turns to me, the words sheepishly creeping out of his mouth, 'you're not allowed to take pictures if you're at your ... if you're at that time of the month.' There's no doubt he's recalling my fairly vocal complaints of period cramps as his van navigated the pothole-ridden incline leading to Ga-Modjadji. I've always been a firm believer in making men uncomfortable with menstrual patter.

Having offered to take pictures for me, Gift steps beyond the wall and onto what looks like a stone reception area in front of the chalet. After further questioning, we learn that the believed connection between menstruation and witchcraft is what prohibits me. Should I have breached the perimeter, there would be repercussions, Anthony tells me. 'Even if you don't tell us and you enter, you'll see what happens to you.'

Access to the hut and its threshold all rests on personal discretion and blood, in all senses. You enter at your own risk, with menstruation being just one facet. TC explained later that the rainmaking secrets of the Kalanga cannot be shared beyond the traditional tribe; you must be of the same blood to learn them – and to enter the chalet. Only the Rain Queen and her designated *sangoma* – a term borrowed from the Zulu people for traditional healers – know what takes place within those rounded walls. And, for that reason, the *sangoma* is only allowed to care for the family of the Modjadjis, for the fear that they'd pass on those innermost confidences.[28]

'If you can't enter in the house where they put the pots or where they put their systems of rituals, you cannot become the king or queen.' He recalled that Mugodo, the father of the first Modjadji, had taken his daughter to the chalet – or pot house, as TC calls it – when she was young. They had believed that if she died upon entry, then she was not a child of the same blood.

'In that house, if you are not part of the blood of the family, unfortunately, you won't come out, the house will eat you.' TC's leopard-print *kofi* cap bobbed enthusiastically as he spoke. His words reached me clearly, cutting through the hubbub of customers communing over chicken and chips.

'If you can't come back, you can't blame anyone,' he adds with a chuckle. 'You can tell your ancestors, wherever you're going, that you didn't follow the rules.'

During the reign of Khesethwane Modjadji (r. 1894–1959), Makobo's great-great-grandmother, the people and their land were subjected to the laws of Apartheid, formally introduced in 1948. Her domain had been folded into the Transvaal Colony, which had been merged with the Cape, Natal and Orange River colonies to form the Union of South Africa in the early twentieth century.

This wasn't the first time that the Modjadji Dynasty had come into contact with white colonists aiming to oversee their lands. At the tail end of the nineteenth century, Khesethwane's aunt, Masalanabo Modjadji II, had come into increasing conflict with the independent, self-governing Zuid-Afrikaanse Republiek – or the Transvaal Republic.[29] When they had arrived at the land of the BaLobedu in the late 1880s, they began imposing taxes, while steadily encroaching on the kingdom. The people of the Modjadjis, who had themselves killed and cowed the pre-existing natives, were on the other end of occupation. By 1892, the Republic had demarcated a reserve for the local people – they named it 'Modjadji Location' – with imposed boundaries. Lobedu land had been reduced to less than 10 per cent of their previous territory.[30]

The next two years of dispossession and required taxes heightened both fury and insult. In 1894, the aggrieved Modjadji II led an armed confrontation against the Republic, only to be subdued by their army of commandos – fully enfranchised white Burgher men who had been called up to service and joined their local commands. From the Modjadjis to the Republic, 10,000 heads of cattle changed hands. Whether they were confiscated from the BaLobedu as retribution, or they were paid to the new settlers in the hopes of peace and protection, the message was clear. This white presence was not here to just set down roots but also a new social order, and this was just the dawn.

'In 1956 or 1957, they built a place called Seshego for Black people, another called Westenberg for coloureds, and Nirvana for Indians,' explains Freddie as he sits across from me in another Polokwane restaurant booth. A friend of Gift, the driver had set up the interview. All I knew was that Freddie had been an MK – a member of the ANC's paramilitary arm – and that I 'need to speak to him'. Freddie's recall of the oppressive constraints under which he was born is delivered matter-of-fact, reeling off dates and locations at impressive speed.

Townships, like Seshego, were termed as such to specify its status as a 'non-white' – usually Black – neighbourhood deliberately located away from white suburbs.[31] It's how Soweto, one of the more widely known examples, got the name it still goes by today: **South Western Townships**. In these townships, access to basic infrastructure – public services, recreation and green spaces, transport – was minimal with the movement of Black Africans restricted through a slew of laws like the 1913 Native Land Act, the 1923 Native (Urban Areas) Act and the 1951 Prevention of Illegal Squatting Act.[32] These all folded into apartheid doctrine instituted under the National Party, an Afrikaner ethnic nationalist party which governed South Africa for almost fifty years. Their ultimate aim was to corral all Black South Africans into territories designated for them – homelands – and leave the rest of South Africa for the white population. Between 1950 and the early 1980s, over 3.5 million people were removed from their homes in line with this ideal.[33]

When Freddie's parents relocated to Seshego in 1965, he – a gabbling one-year-old – stayed with his grandfather until he followed them to the township four years later. There, he was met with an environment roughly split into designated areas, with the colour of your skin denoting where you could and could not go. This only became more pronounced if you were a 'guest worker' – a Black person travelling in and out of white areas to make a living.

'Every day during the week, from about five-thirty p.m., there must be no Black found in the town,' Freddie tells me. 'We grew up knowing that by around four forty-five, five p.m. latest, you must run to the buses or to the outskirts of town, otherwise they would beat or arrest you.'

Though the National Party sought to constrict and contain Black South Africans, they couldn't stifle the airwaves, especially when transmitted from outside of the country. That's how Radio Freedom, via Zambia, reached the townships. Getting it on the radio was never guaranteed but, should the frequency allow, young Black people like Freddie were introduced to the words of anti-apartheid activist Oliver Tambo and concepts of political consciousness.

'We'd stay in some dark corners listening to Radio Freedom,' he remembers. 'We'd switch the stations when guys we didn't trust came around. When they left, we'd look for the frequency again. Maybe it would be lost for a week or two but the day we got it back, we'd run around calling each other to listen. That's how we got the influence.'

That influence eventually led him to Peter Mokaba, a figure in the paramilitary arm of the ANC, uMkhonto we Sizwe (MK). 'Everything he was saying, I could associate with. I saw him as the one and started going to political classes.' By the early 1980s, Freddie was juggling school, and later university, with political activism – the latter saw him arrested in June 1984 and completing his exams from prison the following year.

From there, the details become vague. There's much that Freddie says he still can't talk about and likely never will, adding that there are many events he has never shared with his wife. 'Remember, we were not fighting a war that was in the open. We were fighting an underground war and, with most of the operations, we still don't feel comfortable talking about them.' The enemy, as far as MKs like Freddie were concerned, was any apartheid installation, anything that promoted apartheid. 'White museums, white radio broadcast-ing, a white filling station. We targeted areas that we knew would cripple their electrical platforms.'

When his class schedule allowed, the Seshego man increasingly did more with MK. He started making frequent trips in and out of the country 'carrying things,' he says cryptically. He had three passports. He started meeting 'the big bosses' and in 1987, underwent underground military training before quickly working his way up the ranks into operations. He voted from exile in Zambia, based at an ANC military camp, when the first democratic elections were held in April 1994, returning to South Africa seven months later.

Today, Freddie is a caucus leader and a councillor for the Economic Freedom Fighters, a pan-Africanist group that draws from Marxist-Leninist and Fanonian schools of thought. He became disillusioned with what he observed of the ANC – embroiled in corruption scandals and rampant tribalism – and he wasn't the only one.

During President Mandela's several visits to Mokope Modjadji V following his elevation in 1994, the Rain Queen made it clear that she did not care much for his movement with the ANC. Reports emerged that when its party representatives approached the BaLobedu people with a message of 'a better life for all', they received firm reproaches for not being respectful to traditional ways, to which Mandela would quickly assure Makobo's grandmother that there was no intention on the government's part to erode her authority.[34]

Reaching equilibrium between a desired democratic future and an institution steeped in ancestral custom would be a finely tuned balancing act.

Lashing, unseasonable rains hit Johannesburg on the day of Mokope's death in June 2001 and continued into the next twenty-four hours. Just days prior, an eclipse had left portions of South Africa cloaked in darkness.[35] 'I think the African heaven chose to mourn her demise in this spectacular way,' Ngoako Ramathlhodi, the premier of Limpopo, would tell mourners. The fifth Rain Queen left behind a heavy mantle for her granddaughter to take up.

Though the dawn of the twenty-first century brought uncertainty, the customs of the BaLobedu that Makobo grew up absorbing have remained stalwart, particularly when it comes to women. Women have a high status, both as sisters and wives, and exercise the right to acquire and control property.[36] Under their queen, women can vie for political office and, if successfully elected, undertake a coveted position as the head of a district. Above them, sit the 'mothers' of the district who can be any gender, and are the go-betweens of district heads and the queen.[37] They have full control over the wealth they earn after marriage, and it is the woman's house that inflates with stature upon the receipt of that wealth – although it remains to be inherited by her son.[38] While the BaLobedu people may have been ruled by women for the last 200 years, with the authority usually passing from mother to daughter, the society still follows lines of patrilineal descent. However, another right held by BaLobedu women is that of entering into marriage with another woman.

Woman-marriage has been documented in at least forty pre-colonial African societies and, for some like the BaLobedu, it has remained a fundamental institution to this day.[39] Socially, it strengthens the bonds of kinship that underpin societies that depend on co-operative labour and exchange. But, ironically, the concept of woman-marriage rests on the flux of gender. While a gender position such as 'husband' might normally be occupied by a man, the flexibility of the concept did not exclude other genders, namely women, from being chosen, or even born into the position.[40] Similar to the district 'mothers', a number of roles among the BaLobedu, like officiating at a beer-offering to the gods, can be undertaken by any gender.[41]

Preservation of lineage is central to the institution of woman-marriage. For example, the Kuria people, a Bantu patrilineal community found in present-day Tanzania and Kenya, feared being unable to have children. It was an ill omen that marked a person even after death: to die *omogomba* – leaving no offspring behind – required burial outside in an arid place. As a result, a Kuria woman, whose hope of giving birth to sons had been eroded by time, could take a wife.[42]

Among the BaLobedu, there are different forms of woman-marriage. Alongside infertility, ageing women within the society have the right – enforceable by law – to a daughter-in-law from any house to offer services and care to her, as well as marry her son. Should there not be a son, the ageing woman can marry the woman herself.[43] These practices do not exist solely within the reach of the wealthy and powerful; they're open to any woman with the means to build up a compound and provide for its occupants. However, the women in question are often girls, prized for their potential as wives and mothers, coveted as a means of payment – a girl could be handed over by her family in a transaction in lieu of repayment for a large debt. The early 1900s saw BaLobedu girls used as compensation for unintentional homicide, where they were sent to the family of the deceased to bear them a child.[44]

Back in the restaurant with TC, filled with the noises of boisterous consumption, he specifies – insists – that the ongoing practice is not a lesbian one, that these girls would be married for a woman to have assistance with farmwork and housework. A woman wanting for nearness or desiring another woman are impossible to preclude but those infinite, intimate possibilities are crowded out by duty, continuity and power. Bloodline rules all – and nowhere is that more visible than with the Rain Queen and her *vatanoni* (wives, plural).

I picture a girl picking her way through the village. With each step, her trepidation rises only to be met with mounting pride. She's headed to the royal kraal, sent by her family to court the favour of their ruler; perhaps her mother has newly set her sights on heading up her district or her father hopes to remedy a ritual offence. She's one of many – there are other girls who have been sent from different villages in Ga-Modjadji. The honour is significant, the girl reminds herself, she will be a *matanoni*.

Life as one of the Rain Queen's wives won't be too dissimilar to what she already knows, largely tending to her monarch's fields and other farmwork. If she's of royal blood herself, or closely related to the queen, she'll have the privilege of cooking her food – if she remains a virgin, of course. Virginity is her ticket. Should the girl fall to the seduction of a man after a year or two, she'll be sent home to deliver her child in disgrace. Only when they are weaned will she be brought back to the queen by her father with pardon beer. Another will take her place – maybe the girl's younger sister or even her brother's daughter. In some cases, her promised replacement is yet to be born.[45]

If she stays the course and remains untouched for years, she'll be given a house of her own and be allowed to bear children to the queen, their progenitor a royal relative of the Rain Queen. Those children will not belong to the girl. They will, instead, call the Modjadji ruler 'father'. They will call the children birthed by the queen their siblings. Because she, too, can have children but only with a relative whose identity is never revealed. There's no room for the Western parlance of single motherhood. This queen is mother, father, parent. She is whole. She is complete.[46]

The future of this *matanoni* is bright. It has to be. She has been kept home instead of going to school for this exact purpose, it was her destiny to marry the queen. If she fulfils her duties, proves herself worthy of the title she bears, maybe she'll be given her own village in the royal district. Maybe she'll even be given other *vatanoni* as her wives. And if royalty is encoded in her lineage, another district could be hers to rule.[47]

This might not be her path though, she must remember. Her queen might choose to give her in marriage to one of her relatives or a political client, and her child will take the name of that man. And one day, the girl and her spouse will have to give the queen a daughter to take the place of her mother. A circle has no beginning nor end.

But the honour, the honour is great. The girl will strengthen ties, tethering her own district to the royal house. Her family will be able to call the Rain Queen their *tsetse*, their bridegroom, their son-in-law. And the children that she brings forth – screaming their way into the world through blood and fluid – will wear the Modjadji name.

The girl crosses the threshold.

*

From across the booth, Freddie tells me that he had once studied anthropology, focusing specifically on the BaLobedu people – something I'm not sure even Gift knew when he arranged for us to meet. 'What are the chances?' bounces around my head.

'At some point,' he says coyly, 'I nearly got involved with their chief.'

'Wait,' I pause, brow furrowed, 'one of the Rain Queens?'

'Yah!' is the response, before we both collapse into laughter – my confounded hooting merging with his mischievous chuckles.

They had met at a fast-food place with introductions made by the former premier of Limpopo's older brother. I'm balanced on the uncomfortable edge of my bench, as far forward as the table between us will allow.

'Which Rain Queen was it?' I ask. History work involves dealing with dates but guessing people's ages approximately has never been something I've excelled at.

'The last one, the one who passed on,' Freddie replies, visibly searching for her name.

'The mother of the princess? Makobo?!'

'EH HEH!' he exclaims with acute satisfaction, the itch finally scratched. 'That one, yes. We spoke but, you know what, I realised it wasn't—'

Our server has arrived and stands ready to take our order. Reluctantly, I reach to pause my recording and turn to the menu.

The day before her crowning ceremony, Makobo Modjadji, the imminent ruler of the BaLobedu people, was busy laying out cutlery for the banquet in her honour alongside her wives. In a T-shirt and jeans, she silently nodded and smiled while getting things in order around her palace. Meanwhile, her advisors chattered with journalists from the *Guardian* about the sense of responsibility she felt towards her upcoming duties.[48]

After her official ascension in 2003, Makobo was the first in her dynasty to be able to read and write, thanks to a formal education. She could drive, frequented dance clubs, had control over her own bank account, was tech-savvy, chatted on the phone and enjoyed soap dramas.[49] Within a dynasty that sought out seclusion, Modjadji VI was an outlier. Despite being surrounded by advisors like Mathole Motshekga, the former premier of Gauteng, she pushed up against – and burst through – the customs imbued within her genealogy, including how she conducted her romantic dalliances.

To have a boyfriend was one thing. To have a boyfriend who was a municipal office manager and the father of her two children was another. To the council, it didn't matter that he was of the Mohale house who were 'traditionally entitled to marry the Modjadji queens'. Nor did it seem to matter that other Modjadji rulers may have been fathered by Mohales.[50]

Not only did David Mohale live openly with her in the palace, but Makobo also acknowledged him as the father of her second child and only daughter, Masalanabo, who was born in 2005.[51] It was so great an affront to their traditional ways, it would be reported that the royal council refused to acknowledge Mohale, banning him from the royal village.[52] Questions were being asked with a fervour, within and beyond the kraal.

Tucking into a leafy chicken salad, Freddie recalls his first encounter with the Rain Queen in 1996, almost a decade before the birth of her daughter. It was one of initial blissful ignorance on his part, unaware of who she was.

'She's not the kind of person you can detect comes from the royal family or that she has these powers,' he recalls. 'When I met her, I didn't even notice because there was nothing showing, unlike when you meet the Zulu king, you'd see from afar that something was happening.'

But, over the next three years of talking intermittently on the phone, he'd learn that she was a Modjadji but believes that it was not the life she would have chosen for herself. When describing the pomp and grandeur that royalty tends to entail, he says quite simply: 'She didn't like that.'

The more Freddie learnt, the more he eventually feared. There was the issue of her name regularly appearing in the press. He recalls reading stories in the papers about her with 'the municipal manager of some municipality'. There was also the fact that her movements were closely watched, with stringent protocols to be observed. 'That is the only kingdom that is very secretive in South Africa.' He refers to the Zulu royal family again, describing it as relatively accessible to meet their king. 'You want to meet the Rain Queen?' My companion chuckles. 'You have to write an essay. People come from Uganda, Kenya, as far as Egypt, just to talk to the Rain Queen.'

Above all, however, Freddie feared her might, her gift for making rain and what could come with such ancestral power. Things petered out. 'She went her way and I went mine,' he concludes.

It's her temperament that he returns to, how open and receptive he felt she was – and how wholly unsuited for queenship she might be.

'She wanted to live a life that was not of royalty and now it is not possible.' He pauses. 'Her death to me is controversial because she didn't want to adapt to those traditions.'

When a Rain Queen was deemed to have reached a suitable age, around sixty, she named her successor before ingesting poison. Through this ceremony, she passed on her essence and power, fortifying the next monarch.[53] It's a ritual that some scholars argue was forced upon them by the all-male Royal Council, displaying the control they held over them.[54] Modjadji I died by this form of suicide in 1854 after naming her daughter. Modjadji II followed the example of her mother, naming her niece as the next ruler before taking the poison in 1894. Makoma Modjadji IV, however, refused to take her life and, instead, reigned until she died naturally.[55]

The ceremonial secrets of a Rain Queen's burial remain elusive, Modjadji V having refused to discuss them. This hasn't stopped press and scholars alike from hypothesising, finding the chasm in their knowledge or the wish of internal preservation unsatisfactory. The same can be said for the circumstances of Makobo's death in 2005, which appears equally as murky.

The official cause of her death, two years after she became

queen, would be given as 'chronic meningitis', however, contra-
dictory rumours would abound – from poison to HIV/AIDs.[56]

For local people, Makobo Modjadji's powers followed her
beyond death. Our guide, Anthony, would tell Gift and I, as we
walked back from the royal kraal, that while her body lay in a
chalet – a different building to the rainmaking structure – it burnt
down while she lay inside. They managed to put out the fire before
the flames licked the coffin. Some say arson, others say it was
supernatural. The cause of the fire remains unknown.[57]

Four years before Makobo's grandmother died, Mokope complained that no one asked her to make rain anymore. That young
people had lost touch with religion and, economically, it was
creating problems.[58] And the rise of modern meteorology has
sparked greater questions around their powers, not helped by the
geographical location of the BaLobedu people. Cascading waterfalls, rich biodiversity and tropical climates combine to sow seeds
of doubt.

'Geographically, [Ga-]Modjadji finds itself in a rainy tropical
place, like in Brazil with the Amazon,' Freddie had offered. 'If it
was a desert, or a semi-desert, we can say that these people came
with these powers and made it rain. Unfortunately we can't say
that here.'

I asked if he thinks there's an emerging generational gap. Has the
mystique been tugged away? Has what was once a given become
a subject of query, possibly even suspicion? Freddie believes so.
'The influence that technology has had on [younger people] has
exposed them to information – everyone now can google how rain
is manufactured in the natural [world] and which types of areas
are prone to rain worldwide.'

For TC, the suspicions run deeper. Having yielded most, if not
all, of his insights with infectious chuckles, the serious manner
adopted by the local historian is almost startling.

'The problem came when Modjadji II couldn't make the rain
fall,' TC explains gravely. 'Neither could Modjadji III.' The Kalanga
clansman paints a picture of Modjadji monarchs faltering in their
ability to carry out the rituals – the same rituals that had protected

them from outsiders and watered their lands. He wonders whether these circumstances could have played a part in the death of Modjadji II, circumstances that, he says, are ongoing. 'Even today, they still can't make the rain, even though it's what their traditional house is known for.'

Absorbing my surprise, the man clad in the marks of a leopard shares his theory: that somewhere along the dynasty, one of the queens had a child with a person who was not of the BaLobedu – or the wider Bukalanga – lineage. He's adamant that the first Modjadji was able to make the rain but then the problems began with the second, perhaps with the introduction of *vatanoni*, and have endured to this day.[59]

'If you're not of the same blood, you cannot make the rain,' TC repeats. 'It runs in the bloodline.'

It was Mathole Motshekga, today an MP for the ANC, who raised Princess Masalanabo after her mother's death. The man who had once advised Makobo was granted custody of her daughter. The next potential heir was just a few months old at the time of her mother's burial.

Prince Mpapatla Bakhoma Modjadji stepped into the vacuum left by the death of his sister, Makobo. He was designated regent for Masalanabo with the assurances that she would take her place as the seventh Rain Queen once she turned eighteen. Things would change, however, when the Modjadji Royal Council decided to appoint the princess's older brother, Prince Lekukela Modjadji, as king with the support of the regent in 2021.[60] In spite of the South African government recognising Masalanabo as the future Rain Queen in a 2016 memorandum, the council cited Masalanabo's lack of preparation as the focal reason for turning to Lekukela, as she had been living primarily with the Motshekga family in Gauteng.

'Unfortunately, Masalanabo has missed several divine and sacred processes in our culture and tradition as a potential heir,' Mpapatla told onlookers in a briefing held by the royal council in Limpopo. Appraising the history of their people, he argued that the throne had never been attached to gender and, additionally, according to their customs, the child born to the reigning queen is not supposed to exit the royal household before the age of six.[61] Instead, the regent intends for the princess to assume the position of *khadi-kholo* – great aunt of the kingdom.

The battle has split both the BaLobedu people and the Modjadji advisors, as the siblings and their advisors struggle back and forth over the succession. In 2022 Masalanabo was endorsed as the next Rain Queen by the BaLobedu Royal Council, established in the December of that year to support her claim to the throne, having turned eighteen in January 2023. Pictures from her birthday celebrations show the teenager, dressed in traditional beads paired with Nike trainers, stood under a portrait of her late mother. While South African media reported that she was set to be inaugurated as Rain Queen a few months later in August, Lekukela had already been installed as king-elect in October 2022.[62] His official day of coronation, however, remained pending judicial approval following a court application from the princess's legal team to challenge their decision.[63]

'President Cyril Ramaphosa introduced Her Majesty Queen-elect Masalanabo Modjadji and told the Balobedu nation and South Africa that she will ascend the throne when she turns eighteen,' explained Gabriel Selomela Rasebotsa, secretary of the Balobedu Royal Council. 'Masalanabo Modjadji is the rightful queen.'

This has since been affirmed by the South African president, following the announcement of his legal recognition of 'Her Majesty Queen Masalanabo Modjadji VII' on 13 December 2024.[64] Unsurprisingly, this remains fiercely contested by Lekukela and his supporters, with the Prince stating that 'the government has overlooked our customs and traditions in identifying an heir to my mother's throne.'[65] At the time of writing, preparations are underway for the seventh Rain Queen's inauguration in March 2025, although it feels like this contested process is far from concluded. At least for now, it appears that the uninterrupted rule of women over the BaLobedu people may yet continue.

*

Heralded as a female monarchy, the Rain Queens are part of a
dynasty that has been widely romanticised by literature, journalism, tourists and local people themselves. I've been told tales of
young rambunctious children playing outside their Polokwane
compounds, reluctant to return indoors, until an auntie issues an
all-powerful threat: 'Do you want to play outside tomorrow? I'll tell
Modjadji and you won't be able to play.'[66]

The mystery of a legendary queen who holds deep ancestral
knowledge and normally spurns public clamour is one that has
long evoked the interest of tourists. On our trip back to Polokwane,
driving away from the mountains that loom over Ga-Modjadji, Gift
compares the royal family to that of a growing megachurch, with
the benefits that come with being a visible leader. Government
funding and recognition of their traditional authority and sub-
sidised cars and houses are just a few of the incentives he lists.

The power of the Rain Queen, scholars have argued, lay in her
seclusion, where absence allowed the imagination to fill in the gaps
of this almighty presence.[67] The Modjadji queen, the 'transformer
of clouds', becomes whatever is desired of her. And, by all accounts,
Makobo desired autonomy – an existence beyond her name and
her ancestors.

Unlike the other rulers in this book, Makobo was the latest face
of a long-standing dynasty of women rulers. Unlike many of the
other sovereigns we've encountered, whose legacies are fragmented
and barely celebrated, there was no man who could replace, usurp
or outmanoeuvre a Modjadji queen for 200 years. However, as
Royal Councils of past and present have demonstrated, over time,
true power no longer belongs solely to the sovereign.

The Modjadji dynasty to which the late queen belonged is
one wracked with tragedy. And today, two feuding siblings, children that Makobo Modjadji VI left behind, are writing its latest
chapter.

CONCLUSION

Africa heaves with trauma. This has gone largely unexamined by the countries that have emerged from historic colonial empires, African politicians and holders of power, and some of its own people.

You can trace the lines back with a roving finger. For example, from the United Arab Emirates' direct involvement in the ethnic cleansing and displacement currently taking place in Sudan (which they deny), to Leopold's similarly devastating regime in the Congo, to the missionaries, to the slave ships, to the first 'explorers' who came before them.[1]

You can follow the line forward to present day. The way we've been led to believe that 'colonisation is over' while neo-colonialism abounds under the guise of 'developing' Africa. Foreign corporate behaviour and military interventions, Western donor 'aid', EU–Africa trade ties, ongoing missionary work.[2]

It's hard not to constantly appraise all that we've lost. It's difficult not to ask questions that I know can never be answered and yet, I still ask. I ask even though I know that many traditions have survived in different parts of the continent, carefully sheltered from the desecration of colonisation, the brutality of enslavement and the cruelty of a world ordered by antiblackness. What might 'otherwise' have looked like?

What could kinship formations have looked like? How might we have understood gender and queerness? How would we read one another without the introduction of 'ethnic groups'? How might we have read ourselves? Who could we have been?

Too many have and too much has been stolen. However, what soothes me somewhat is the ingenuity that has always crackled across the continent, some in response to colonisation. Survival and salvaging has gifted us with what we know today. The way our histories have been preserved acts as a salve against a burning gash. Those from periods gone by have provided us a framework with which we can examine and engage their lives, extrapolating from what they've left behind.

These histories have been retold through my lens. So much of me is in this work and it is by design. One of the biggest fallacies peddled in history work is that we can remove ourselves from it. The myth of objectivity is a denial of the way our worldviews, our biases, the language we write in utterly mould the stories we choose to retell.

I chose to embrace my subjectivity but crucially, the fictive. The latter is hugely inspired by Saidiya Hartman's practice of critical fabulation. It's a writing practice that the scholar describes as 'playing with and rearranging the basic elements of the story... [attempting] to jeopardize the status of the event, to displace the received or authorized account, and to imagine what might have happened or might have been said or might have been done.'[3] It's a method that recognises 'the archive' as an embodiment of colonial violence, where omissions, oversights and agenda have ensured which retellings have been pushed to the surface. Working from the intersection of the fictive and the historical, critical fabulation is a search for the counter-fact, the counter-histories. Like Stephanie Smallwood, I understand this practice as one that 'disturbs the archive's naturalization of the violence it narrates'.[4]

That said, there are boundaries. We must 'respect the limits of what cannot be known.'[5] We can never concretely speak to the interiority of these historical figures, we cannot 'give voice' to the subaltern. That is not our task nor our right. Instead, we probe, interrogate and extrapolate from what cannot be verified. While Hartman focuses on the enslaved Africans funnelled through the Atlantic slaving complex, I've attempted to extend the practice. My subjects – elite rulers – could not be more different, but they too have been consigned to colonial retellings. And, in the case of many of these queens and warriors, have been lionised in nation-alist canons. Both are reductive. They disappear what has been threaded throughout this book: that these African rulers could and did also wield violent power against their people. This has been an attempt to attend to African figures whose lives come to us garbled through colonial – and archival – violence. 'It's a narrative of what might have been or could have been; it is a history written with and against the archive.'[6]

Perhaps you picked up this book with the expectation or desire for a 'straightforward' history of these twelve African figures. I hope I've presented a case for why that would never have been possible since such a thing doesn't exist.

The rulers whose lives we've explored together are of the com-munities that raised them up and devoured most whole. Their own subjects have been the keepers of time, the attendants of memory. A monarch is nothing without their people, and history work is worthless without complexity. Njinga, the binary-defying sovereign who bargained with the lives of enslaved people. Məntəwwab and Ririkumutima, the rulers determined to maintain power at all costs. Makobo, a Rain Queen who pushed against a dynastic institution that demanded her invisibility. We must engage all parts of them, not simply what serves us.

History can never and will never be complete. I write with the expectation, with the hope that this book will be disassembled, challenged and reconstructed, just as I have done with the work of others through this book.

We write across one another. We write towards each other. Built on our engagement with the past, we write ahead of liberated African futures that are yet to be penned.

ENDNOTES

Introduction

1 Interview with Mafoya Glélé Kakaï, Cotonou, 6 May 2023
2 Stephanie E. Smallwood, 'The Politics of the Archive and History's Accountability to the Enslaved', *History of the Present*, Vol. 6(2), Fall 2016, pp. 117–32, p. 117
3 Stephanie E. Smallwood, *Saltwater Slavery: A Middle Passage from Africa to American Diaspora*, 2007, 33, in Smallwood (2016), p. 117
4 Katherine Everett, Emily Hardick, Damarius Johnson, 'The Year of Africa', *Origins: Current Events in Historical Perspective*, Dec 2020, https://origins. osu.edu/article/year-of-africa-1960-rumba-pan-africanism-Kariba
5 Margaret Jean Hay, 'Queens, Prostitutes and Peasants: Historical Perspectives on African Women, 1971–1986', *Canadian Journal of African Studies / Revue Canadienne des Études Africaines*, Vol. 22(3), 1988, Special Issue: Current Research on African Women, pp. 431–47, p. 433
6 Susan Otto, 'Chapter Six: Centering African Indigenous Women within the Context of Social, Economic and Political Development', *Counterpoints*, Vol. 443, 2014, pp. 117–27, p. 123
7 Agnes Akosua Aidoo, 'Asante Queen Mothers In Government And Politics In The Nineteenth Century', *Journal of the Historical Society of Nigeria*, Vol. 9(1), 1977, pp. 1–13, p. 13
8 Smallwood (2016), p. 118

Chapter 1: Mọrèmi Àjàṣorò

1 Philip K. Neimark, *The Way of Orisa: Empowering Your Life Through the Ancient African Religion of Ifa* (San Francisco: HarperCollins, 1993), pp. 57–58; Research notes from ayọ̀délé olọ́fintúádé, Feb 2025
2 Ibid.
3 R. C. C. Law, 'The Heritage of Oduduwa: Traditional History and Political Propaganda Among the Yoruba', *The Journal of African History*, Vol. 14(2), 1973, pp. 207–22, p. 210; J. Sina Ojuade, 'The Issue of "Oduduwa" In

Yoruba Genesis: The Myths and Realities', *Transafrican Journal of History*, Vol. 21, 1992, pp. 139–58, p. 139

4 Law (1973), p. 211

5 Research notes from ayọ̀délé, Feb 2025

6 Law, p. 210

7 Baba Ifa Karade, *The Handbook of Yoruba Religious Concepts*, (Massachusetts: Weiser Books, 2020), p. 2

8 Law (1973), pp. 208–10

9 Karade, p. 3

10 Law (1973), p. 208

11 Ibid.; Samuel Johnson, *The History of the Yorubas: From the Earliest Times to the Beginning of the British Protectorate* (London: Cambridge University Press, 1921), p. 3

12 Mathews, p. 5

13 Ibrahim Anoba, 'African Heroes of Freedom: Queen Moremi Ajasoro', Libertarianism.org, 2019, https://www.libertarianism.org/columns/african-heroes-freedom-queen-moremi-ajasoro#_ednref3; Alabidun, Shuaib Abdulrahman, 'The Cognomen of "Ijakadi L'Oro Offa", and Benevolence History of Offa People', Ilorin.info, 27 Dec 2017: https://www.ilorin.info/fullnews.php?id=22217

14 Rowland Abiodun, 'Àṣẹ: Verbalizing and Visualizing Creative Power through Art', *Journal of Religion in Africa*, Vol. 24(4), 1994, pp. 309–22, p. 310

15 Neimark, p. 38

16 Research notes from ayọ̀délé, Feb 2025

17 Akinola Segun Gabriel, 'Ifá Guiding Principles in Pre-Marital Counselling Towards a Happy Family', *Pharos Journal of Theology*, Vol. 103, 2022, p. 4

18 Ibid., p. 5

19 Research notes from ayọ̀délé, Feb 2025

20 Anoba (2019)

21 Laura S. Grillo, 'Ironic Reversals: Gender, Power, and Sacrality in Ilé-Ifẹ̀', *Journal of Africana Religions*, Vol. 2(4), 2014, pp. 465–76, p. 470

22 Muyiwa P. Awodiya, 'Form & Technique in Femi Osofisan's Plays' in Eldred Durosimi Jones & Marjorie Jones (eds.) *New Trends & Generations in African Literature: A Review* (Suffolk: James Currey Publishers, 1996), p. 113; NEBO TV, 'Yoruba Historian Abiodun Narrates the Hstory [*sic*] of a Powerful Woman, Moremi Ajasoro', youtube.com, 23 May 2020 https://www.youtube.com/watch?v=ObgLA1Ipg2Q&ab_channel=NEBOTV

23 G. T. Stride and Caroline Ifeka (1971), *Peoples and Empires of West Africa: West Africa in History, 1000–1800*, Africana Pub. Corp (University of Michigan), pp. 309–10

24 Research notes from ayọ̀délé, Feb 2025

25 Balogun Bisi Omidiora, 'The Place Of Oranmiyan In The History

Of Ile–Ife', vanguardngr.com, 22 Feb 2016: https://www.vanguardngr.
com/2016/02/the-place-of-oranmiyan-in-the-history-of-ile-ife/

26   Ibid.

27   Research notes from ayọ̀délé, Feb 2025; A. O. Y. Raji & T. S. Abejide, 'The
     Guild System and Its Role in the Economy of Precolonial Yorubaland',
     Arabian Journal of Business and Management Review, (OMAN Chapter),
     Vol. 3(3), Oct 2013, pp. 14–22, p. 15

28   M. A. Fabunmi, (1969) *Ife Shrines* (Ibadan), p. 17

29   Suzanne Preston Blier, 'Art in Ancient Ife, Birthplace of the Yoruba',
     African Arts, Vol. 45(4), 'Gender and South African Art', Winter 2012,
     pp. 70–85, p. 73; Dayọ̀ Ológundúdú, *Yoruba Religion*, Center for Spoken
     Words, Institute of Yorùbá Culture, 2014, p. 63

30   Oluwole Coker & Adesina Coker, 'Folklore as Folklaw in Yoruba
     Indigenous Epistemology', *Journal of Afroeuropean Studies*, Vol. 2(1), 2008,
     pp. 1–20, p. 2

31   Abiola Odejide, 'Children's Biographies of Nigerian Figures: A Critical
     and Cultural Assessment', *The Reading Teacher*, Vol. 40(7), March 1987,
     pp. 640–44, p. 640

32   Ibid.

33   Ibid., p. 641

34   Oyèrónkẹ́ Oyěwùmí, *The Invention of Women: Making an African Sense of
     Western Gender Discourses* (Minneapolis: University of Minnesota Press,
     1997), p. 29

35   Ulli Beier, *Yoruba Poetry: An Anthology of Traditional Poems* (London:
     Cambridge University Press, 1970), 11 in ibid., p. 162

36   Ibid., p. xxiii (content in paratheses added by this author)

37   Ibid.

38   Interview with ayọ̀délé, Ìbàdàn, 9 Apr 2023

39   Oyěwùmí, pp. 66–67 & 73; B. W. Hodder, 'Rural Periodic Day Markets
     in Part of Yorubaland', *Transactions and Papers (Institute of British
     Geographers)*, no. 29, 1961, pp. 149–59, p. 154

40   Hodder, p. 158; Oyěwùmí, p. 66

41   Ibid.; G. J. Afolabi Ojo, *Yoruba Culture: A Geographical Analysis* (London:
     University of London Press, 1966) in Oyěwùmí, p. 67

42   Oyěwùmí, p. 67

43   Ibid., p. 68

44   Neimark, p. 127

45   Ibid., pp. 76–80

46   Mathews, p. 1

47   Anoba (2019)

48   Richard Akresh, Sonia Bhalotra, Marinella Leone and Una Osili, 'War
     and Stature: Growing Up During the Nigerian Civil War', *The Centre for
     Market and Public Organisation*, Dec 2011, pp. 1–10, p. 1

49 Ọmọlade Adunbi, 'Mythic Oil: Resources, Belonging and the Politics of Claim Making Among the Ìlàjẹ Yorùbá of Nigeria', *Africa: Journal of the International African Institute*, Vol. 83(2), 2013, pp. 293–313, p. 297

50 Anoba (2019)

51 Ibid.; Ade Obayemi, 'Ancient Ile-Ife: Another Cultural Historical Reinterpretation', *Journal of the Historical Society of Nigeria*, Vol. 9(4), Jun 1979, pp. 151–85, p. 172

52 Grillo, p. 465

53 Neimark, p. 95 & 105; Nadia Milad Issa, 'The Body as Layered Divinity: Regla de Ocha-Ifá Ritual Kinship', *ReVista: Harvard Review of Latin America*, 1 Mar 2021: https://revista.drclas.harvard.edu/the-body-as-layered-divinity/

54 J. Omosade Awolalu, *Yoruba Beliefs and Sacrificial Rites* (London: Longman Group Limited, 1979), p. 114

55 Research notes from ayọ̀délé, Feb 2025

56 Awolalu, p. 114

57 NEBO TV (2020); Anoba (2019)

58 Gbenga Faturoti, 'Osun Remembers Icon of Culture, Duro Ladipo', Independent.ng, 4 Mar 2018: https://independent.ng/osun-remembers-icon-culture-duro-ladipo/

59 Ibid.; Obayemi, p. 166; Grillo; p. 470

60 Adaobi Onyeakagbu, 'Queen Moremi: Did you know about the courageous legend whose statue is the tallest in Nigeria?', pulse.ng, 21 Jun 2022: https://www.pulse.ng/lifestyle/food-travel/queen-moremi-did-you-know-about-the-courageous-legend-whose-statue-is-the-tallest-in/hr4llg4

61 Jacob K. Olúpọ̀nà, *City of 201 Gods: Ilé-Ifè in Time, Space, and the Imagination*, (Berkeley: University of California Press, 2011), p. 206

62 Jacob Olúpọ̀nà, 'Feminine Ritual Power and African Politics', *Journal of Africana Religions*, Vol. 7(2), 'Special Issue: James H. Cone and Black Theology', *Africana Perspective* (2019), pp. 307–10, p. 310

63 Research notes from ayọ̀délé, Feb 2025

64 Olúpọ̀nà (2011), p. 205

65 Grillo, pp. 470–71; ibid., p. 206

66 Odejide, p. 642

67 Interview with ayọ̀délé, Ìbàdàn, 9 Apr 2023

68 Blier (2012), p. 73

69 Research notes from ayọ̀délé, Feb 2025

70 Interview with ayọ̀délé, Ìbàdàn, 9 Apr 2023

71 LaRay Denzer, 'Yoruba Women: A Historiographical Study', *The International Journal of African Historical Studies*, Vol. 27(1), 1994, pp. 1–39, pp. 6–7

72 Johnson, p. 245

73 Denzer, p. 7

74   Ibid., pp. 24–25

75   Ibid., pp. 31–32

76   Cheryl Johnson-Odim and Nina Emma Mba, *For Women and the Nation: Funmilayo Ransom-Kuti of Nigeria* (Urbana: University of Illinois, 1997), p. 78

77   Ibid., p. 81

78   Olúpọ̀nà (2011), p. 205

79   United Nations Centre for Human Settlements [Habitat], 'The Partner System', *Bulletin of the International Year of Shelter for the Homeless*. Tenth Issue, Jul 1987: https://www.gdrc.org/icm/partner-sys.html

80   Olúpọ̀nà (2011), p. 205

81   Maureen Warner-Lewis, *Guinea's Other Suns*, (Dover, MA: The Majority Press, 1991) in Karade, p. 5

82   Karade, p. 6

83   Ibid., pp. 5–6

84   G. O. Ajibade, 'Same-Sex Relationships in Yorùbá Culture and Orature', *Journal of Homosexuality*, 60(7), 2013, pp. 965–83, pp. 970–71

85   Ibid.

86   Bright Alozie, 'Did Europe Bring Homophobia to Africa?', *Black Perspectives*, 21 Oct 2021: https://www.aaihs.org/did-europe-bring-homophobia-to-africa/

87   Ayodele Sogunro, 'Against "The Order of Nature": Towards the Growth of Queer Lawfare in Nigeria' in Adrian Jjuuko et al., (eds), *Queer Lawfare in Africa: Legal Strategies in Contexts of LGBTIQ+ Criminalisation and Politicisation* (Pretoria University Law Press, 2022), pp. 205–36, p. 205

88   Interview with ayọ̀délé, Ìbàdàn, 9 Apr 2023

89   Babatunde Lawal, 'The Living Dead: Art and Immortality among the Yoruba of Nigeria', *Africa: Journal of the International African Institute*, Vol. 47(1), 1977, pp. 50–61, p. 51

90   Ibid., p. 56

Chapter 2: Njinga a Mbande

1   Morarji Peesay, 'Nuchal cord and its implications', *Maternal Health, Neonatology and Perinatology*, Vol. 3(28), 2017

2   Linda M. Heywood, *Njinga of Angola*, (Cambridge, MA: Harvard University Press, 2017), p. 57

3   Ibid., p. 17 & 35

4   Cavazzi, MSS Araldi Giovanni Antonio Cavazzi da Montecuccolo, 'Missione evangelica nel Regno de Congo' (1668), volume A, book 2, p. 20; Giovanni Antonio Cavazzi da Montecuccolo, Istorica Descrizione de' tre' regni Congo, Matamba et Angola (Bologna: Giacomo Monti, 1687), book 5, para. 106; Antonio da Gaeta, La Maravigliosa sione alla Santa Fede di

Cristo della Regina Singa, ed. Francesco Maria Gioia (Naples, 1669), 146 in Heywood (2017), p. 57

5   John K. Thornton, 'The Kingdom of Kongo, ca. 1390–1678. The Development of an African Social Formation (Le Royaume Du Kongo, ca. 1390–1678. Développement d'une Formation Sociale Africaine)', *Cahiers d'Études Africaines*, Vol. 22(87/88), 1982, pp. 325–42, p. 335

6   Heywood (2017), pp. 8–9

7   Ibid., p. 58

8   Kit Heyam, *Before We Were Trans: A New History of Gender* (London: John Murray Publishers, 2022), p. 34; Daniel F. Silva, '(Anti-)Colonial Assemblages: The History and Reformulations of Njinga Mbande', in Janell Hobson (ed.), *The Routledge Companion to Black Women's Cultural Histories* (London: Routledge, 2021), pp. 75–86, p. 77

9   Heywood (2017), p. 58

10 Ibid.

11 Selma Pantoja, 'Njinga a Mbande: Power and War in 17th-Century Angola', *Oxford Research Encyclopedia of African History*, pp. 1–23, p. 3

12 Pantoja, pp. 3–4

13 Heywood, p. 11 and p. 13

14 Pantoja, p. 3; Heywood, (2017), p. 13

15 Pantoja, p. 4

16 Heyam, p. 33; Heywood (2017), p. 21

17 Thornton (1982), p. 331

18 John Thornton, 'Early Kongo-Portuguese Relations: A New Interpretation', *History in Africa*, Vol. 8, 1981, pp. 183–204, p. 186

19 Heywood (2017), pp. 4–6

20 Ibid., p.7; Thornton (1982), p. 334

21 Heywood (2017), pp. 22–23

22 Ibid., pp. 23–24; Pantoja, p. 4

23 Wheeler DL, 'The Conquest of Angola'; *The Portuguese Conquest of Angola*, by David Birmingham, (Oxford University Press; London: Institute of Race Relations, 1965) p. 50, maps, 6s, *The Journal of African History*, Vol. 7(1), 1966, p. 162; Beatrix Heintze, 'Historical Notes on the Kisama of Angola', *The Journal of African History*, Vol. 13(3), 1972, pp. 407–18, p. 411

24 Heyam, p. 33

25 Heywood (2017), pp. 24–25; Manuel Ruela Pombo, *Angola-Menina, 1560–1565* (Lisbon, 1944), p. 29

26 Heywood (2017), pp. 25–26; Pantoja, p. 4

27 Pantoja, p. 4

28 Luís Filipe Campos da Silva Santos, 'Rehabilitation Techniques and Repair of Cambambe Fortress', Masters Thesis: Técnico Lisboa, Sep 2016, p. 2;

E. Morais e A. Matoso, História dos Portugueses em Angola, Luanda: Edições Luanda.

29 Cunha Matos, M. (2010), Colonial Architecture and Amnesia, Mapping the Work of Portuguese Architects in Angola and Mozambique, L'Afrique, c'est chic, Architecture and Planning in Africa 1950–1970, OASE, (82), 25–30. Retrieved from https://www.oasejournal.nl/en/Issues/82/ColonialArchitectureAndAmnesia

30 Rede Angola, 'Museu de Antropologia', http://www.redeangola.info/roteiros/museu-de-antropologia/

31 Cavazzi, *Istorica Descrizione*, book 2, para. 134 [258].

32 Heywood (2017), p. 44

33 Ibid., p. 45

34 Cavazzi, MSS Araldi, book 2, pp. 94–95.

35 Heywood (2017), p. 58; M. L. Rodrigues de Areia, 'Les symboles divinatoires: Analyse socio-culturelle d'une technique de divination des Cokwe de l'Angola (Ngombo Ya Cisuka)', Online access: OAPEN DOAB Directory of Open Access Books, Imprensa da Universidade de Coimbra / Coimbra University Press, 2019, p. 519

36 Silva, p. 76

37 Heywood (2017), p. 45

38 Ibid.

39 Silva, p. 76

40 John Thornton, 'The African Experience of the "20. and Odd Negroes" Arriving in Virginia in 1619', *The William and Mary Quarterly*, Vol. 55(3), Jul 1998, pp. 421–34, p. 429

41 Heywood (2017), pp. 26–27

42 Pantoja, p. 4

43 Jan Vansina, 'The Foundation of the Kingdom of Kasanje', *The Journal of African History*, Vol. 4(3), 1963, pp. 355–74, p. 358

44 Thornton (1998), p. 429

45 Ibid., pp. 429–30

46 Heywood (2017), pp. 31–32; Pantoja, p. 4; Father Baltasar Barreira to the Father General, 3 Jan 1582, *MMA* 15:274.

47 Pantoja, p. 12; Alberto Oliveira Pinto, *História de Angola: Da Pré-História ao Início do Século XXI* (Lisbon: Mercado das Letras, 2015), p. 332.

48 Pantoja, pp. 4–5

49 Heywood (2017), p. 48

50 Ibid., p. 49

51 António de Oliveira de Cadornega, História Geral das Guerras Angolanas, ed. José Delgado, 3 vols. (1940–42; repr. Lisbon: Agência-Geral do Ultramar, 1972), 1:94 in Heywood (2017), p. 60

52 Heywood (2017), p. 60

53 Ibid., pp. 50–51

54 Cavazzi, *Istorica Descrizione*, book 5, para. 106; Ribeiro, Orquídea
    Moreira, Fernando Alberto Torres Moreira, and Susana Pimenta, 'Nzinga
    Mbandi: from Story to Myth', *Journal of Science and Technology of the Arts*
    11, No. 1 (2019), pp. 51–59, p. 52

55 Blogs, Harvard Network, 'The Enigmatic Queen Nzinga of Ndongo', The
    Shelf: Preserving Harvard's Library Collections, 2013, https://archive.
    blogs.harvard.edu/preserving/2013/11/18/the-enigmatic-queen-nzinga-of-
    ndongo/ ; Heywood (2017), p. 62

56 Heywood (2017), p. 62

57 R. Briard, 'Creating the Identity of Queen Njinga', *The Mirror –*
    Undergraduate History Journal, Vol. 42(1), 2022, pp. 83–94, p. 84

58 Ribiero et al., p. 52; Williams, Hettie V. (2010), 'Queen Nzinga (Njinga
    Mbande)'. In Alexander, Leslie M.; Rucker, Walter C. (eds.), *Encyclopedia*
    of African American History, 1. Santa Barbara, California: ABC-CLIO

59 Silva, p. 76; Pantoja, p. 5

60 Cavazzi, MSS Araldi, book 2, p. 24; Feo Cardoso, Memórias, 159 in
    Heywood (2017), p. 51

61 Cavazzi de Montecúccolo, João António (1965 [1687]). Descrição Histórica
    dos Três Reinos do Congo, Matamba e Angola, 2 Vols, Lisboa: Junta de
    Investigações do Ultramar, p. 65

62 Pantoja, p. 4

63 Joseph C. Miller, 'Nzinga of Matamba in a New Perspective', *The Journal of*
    African History, Vol. 16(2), 1975, pp. 201–16, p. 207

64 Heyam, p. 35; Heywood (2017), p. 50 and p. 75

65 Heywood (2017), p. 75; Njinga to Bento Banha Cardoso, 3 March 1626
    [misdated 1625], as quoted in 'Governador a Seus Filhos', FHA 1:261 in
    Heywood (2017), p. 75

66 Miller, p. 207

67 Heywood (2017), p. 55; Pantoja, p. 6; Cavazzi, Descrifdo historica dos tres
    reinos, I, 259, II, 7; António de Oliveira de Cadornega, História Geral
    das Guerras Angolanas, ed. José Delgado, 3 vols. (1940–42; repr. Lisbon:
    Agência-Geral do Ultramar, 1972), 1:161

68 Thornton (1991), p. 38

69 Miller, p. 205

70 Heywood (2017), p. 65

71 Ibid.; Cavazzi, MSS Araldi, book 2, p. 33; Thornton (1991), p. 32; Miller,
    p. 209

72 Cavazzi, p. 26; Heywood (2017), p. 64

73 Kevin Dawson, *Undercurrents of Power: Aquatic Culture in the African*
    Diaspora (Philadelphia: University of Pennsylvania Press, 2018), p. 29

74 Heywood (2017), pp. 65–66; Pantoja, p. 8

75 Heywood (2017), p. 68; Pantoja, p. 8

76 Thornton (1991), p. 32

77 Lingna Nafafé, 'J. Ndongo's Political and Cultural Environment: Alliance, Internal Struggle, Puppeteering and Decline'. In: *Lourenço Da Silva Mendonça and the Black Atlantic Abolitionist Movement in the Seventeenth Century*. Cambridge Studies on the African Diaspora, (Cambridge: Cambridge University Press, 2022), pp. 138–92, p. 161

78 Pantoja, p. 8

79 Heywood (2017), p. 24 and p. 69

80 Heywood (2017), p. 69; Pantoja, p. 8

81 'O Extenso Relatório do Governador a Seus Filhos' (s.d., 1625–30), FHA 1:229–30 in Heywood (2017), p. 70; Pantoja, p. 8

82 Lingna Nafafé, pp. 164–65

83 'Carta de Fernão de Souza a El-Rei', 21 Feb 1626, MMA 7:417–20 in Heywood (2017), p. 71

84 Thornton (1991), p. 26

85 Heywood (2017), p. 85

86 Ibid., p. 86

87 Lingna Nafafé, p. 164

88 Pantoja, p. 9

89 Ibid., pp. 8–9

90 Thornton (1991), p. 32

91 Miller, p. 209; Pantoja, p. 8

92 Miller, p. 209–10

93 Miller, p. 210

94 Ibid.

95 Heywood (2017), p. 126

96 Cadornega, Historia Geral, I, 194–211; Cavazzi, Descricao historica dos tres reinos, I, 21, and II, 79–81; Miller, pp. 210–11

97 Heyam, p. 48

98 Ibid., p. 49; Heywood (2017), p. 83; John Ogilby, *Africa* (London: Printed by Tho. Johnson for author, 1670), sig 3B6 & sig 3C1 in Heyam, p. 49

99 Heywood (2017), p. 101; Thornton, p. 38

100 Awuor Onyango, 'In the Shape of an African', Sep 2023, https://www.curationist.org/editorial-features/article/in-the-shape-of-an-african

101 Silva, p. 78

102 Ibid.

103 Heyam, pp. 48–49

104 Vansina, p. 360

105 Heyam., p. 49

106 James H. Sweet, *Recreating Africa: Culture, Kinship, and Religion in the African-Portuguese World, 1441–1770* (Chapel Hill: University of North Carolina Press, 2003), p. 56

107 Cheryl M. Schmitz, 'Kufala! Translating witchcraft in an Angolan–Chinese

labor dispute', *HAU: Journal of Ethnographic Theory*, Vol. 10(2), 2020, pp. 473–86, p. 476

108 Amara Das Wilhelm, *Tritiya-Prakriti: People of the Third Sex: Understanding Homosexuality, Transgender Identity and Intersex Conditions Through Hinduism* (Bloomington, Indiana: Xlibris Corporation, 2004), p. 227

109 Marc Epprecht, *Heterosexual Africa?: The History of an Idea from the Age of Exploration to the Age of AIDS*, (Athens: Ohio University Press, 2008) p. 37

110 Joana Bahia and Farlen de Jesus Nogueira, 'If You Have Faith, Exu Responds on-line: The Day-to-Day Life of Quimbanda on Social Networks', *Open Theology*, Vol. 9(1), 2023, pp. 1–13, p. 1–4

111 Heyam, p. 61

112 Heyam, pp. 29–30

113 Heywood, 'Njinga', *Dictionary of African Christian Biography*, 2020, https://dacb.org/stories/angola/njinga/; Thornton (1991), p. 7

114 Ronaldo Vainfas, 'The New Christian Cadornega and His Work on the Angolan Wars in the Seventeenth Century', *Tempo Niterói*, Vol. 29(2), Maio/Ago. 2023, pp. 1–23, p. 5; Briard, p. 91; Heywood (2020)

115 Miller, p. 207

116 Beatrix Heintze and Katja Rieck, 'The Extraordinary Journey of the Jaga Through the Centuries: Critical Approaches to Precolonial Angolan Historical Sources', *History in Africa*, Vol. 34, 2007, pp. 67–101, pp. 68–69

117 Ibid., p. 75

118 Pantoja, p. 9

119 Jan Vansina, 'Confinement in Angola's Past', *A History of Prison and Confinement in Africa*, ed. Florence Bernault (Portsmouth, NH: Heinemann, 2003), p. 61

120 Briard, p. 87

121 Arquivo de Identidade Angolano, 'Who We Are', https://www.arquivode identidadeangolano.com/quem-somos-1 [website has expired: 01.12.2024]

122 Graeme Reid, 'Progress and Setbacks on LGBT Rights in Africa – An Overview of the Last Year', Human Rights Watch (2022), https://www.hrw. org/news/2022/06/22/progress-and-setbacks-lgbt-rights-africa-overview-last-year

123 Equaldex, 'LGBT Rights in Angola', https://www.equaldex.com/region/angola

124 Pantoja, p. 10

125 Heywood (2017), p. 134

126 Pantoja, p. 10; Manuel Pedro Pacavira, Nzinga Mbandi (Lisbon: Edições 70, 1978), p. 164.

127 Pantoja, p. 10

128 Heywood (2017), p. 134

129 Pantoja, p. 11
130 Heywood (2017), pp. 137–39
131 Ibid., p. 158; Pantoja, p. 10
132 Heyam, p. 51; Silva, p. 78
133 *Monumenta Missionaria Africana, Vol. 11, West Africa (1651–1655)*, 1971, (Lisbon: Agência Geral do Ultramar), p. 70
134 *Monumenta Missionaria Africana*, p. 524
135 Pantoja, pp. 10–11; Miller, p. 212
136 Miller, p. 212; Thornton (1991), p. 32
137 Miller, p. 212; Thornton (1991), pp. 32–33
138 Thornton (1991), p. 39
139 Antônio da Gaeta and F. M. Gioia, La Meravigliosa Conversione alla Santa fede di Cristo della Regina Singa, e del suo Regno di Matamba nell'Africa Meridionale. Descrita com historico stile dal P.F. Francesco Maria Gioia da Napoli (Naples: Giacinto Passaro, 1669), ch. XVIII, 233.
140 Heywood (2017), p. 1
141 Thornton (1991), p. 25
142 Susan Seligson, 'The Enduring Power of Queen Njinga', 2011, https://www.bu.edu/articles/2011/the-enduring-power-of-queen-njinga/
143 Miller, p. 215
144 Heyam, p. 51; Thornton (1991), p. 32
145 Miller, p. 201
146 Pantoja, p. 11
147 Heyam, p. 53
148 Ibid., p. 51

Chapter 3: Tassi Hangbé

1 Interview with Adaze, Royal Palaces of Abomey, 5 Apr 2023
2 Edna G. Bay, 'On the Trail of the Bush King: A Dahomean Lesson in the Use of Evidence', *History in Africa*, Vol. 6, 1979, pp. 1–15, p. 7
3 Bay (1979), p. 7; Auguste Le Hérissé, *L'ancien royaume du Dahomey: mœurs, religion, histoire* (Paris, 1911), p. 291
4 Interview with Adaze, 5 Apr 2023
5 Le Hérissé, p. 294–95; Stanley B. Alpern, 'On the Origins of the Amazons of Dahomey', *History in Africa*, Vol. 25, 1998, pp. 9–25, p. 11
6 Suzanne Preston Blier, 'The Path of the Leopard: Motherhood and Majesty in Early Danhomè', *The Journal of African History*, Vol. 36(3), 1995, pp. 391–417, pp. 401–03
7 Ibid., p. 395 and p. 403; Robin Law, 'An Alternative Text of King Agaja of Dahomey's Letter to King George I of England, 1726', *History in Africa*, Vol. 29, 2002, pp. 257–71
8 Blier (1995), pp. 403–04

9 Ray A. Kea, *Settlements, Trade and Polities in the Seventeenth-Century Gold Coast* (Baltimore, 1982), 401, n. 168 in Robin Law, 'Dahomey and the Slave Trade: Reflections on the Historiography of the Rise of Dahomey', *The Journal of African History*, 1986, Vol. 27(2), Special Issue in Honour of J. D. Fage, 1986, pp. 237–67, p. 242

10 Law (1986), p. 239

11 Ibid., p. 258

12 Augustus A. Adeyinka, 'King Gezo of Dahomey, 1818–1858: A Reassessment of a West African Monarch in the Nineteenth Century', *African Studies Review*, Vol. 17(3), Dec 1974, pp. 541–48, p. 542

13 Tashjian, V., & Allman, J. (2002), Marrying and marriage on a shifting terrain: Reconfigurations of power in early colonial Asante, In J. Allman, S. Geiger, & N. Musisi (Eds.), Women in African colonial histories (pp. 237–59). Bloomington: Indiana University Press, p. 220 in Amoah-Boampong and Agyeiwaa, p. 6

14 Amoah-Boampong and Agyeiwaa, p. 6

15 Bay (1979), p. 7

16 Alpern, p. 13

17 Robin Law, 'History and Legitimacy: Aspects of the Use of the past in Precolonial Dahomey', *History in Africa*, 1988, Vol. 15, 1988, pp. 431–56, pp. 433–34

18 Edna G. Bay, 'Belief, Legitimacy and the Kpojito: An Institutional History of the "Queen Mother" in Precolonial Dahomey', *The Journal of African History*, Vol. 36(1), 1995, pp. 1–27, p. 10

19 Ibid., p. 9; Law (1988), p. 434

20 Law (1988), p. 434

21 Le Hérissé, p. 295

22 Anatole Coissy, 'Un regne de femme dans l'ancien royaume d'Abomey', *Etudes Dahoméennes*, 2 (1949), pp. 5–8 in Alpern, p. 13

23 Bay (1979), p. 7

24 UNESCO World Heritage Convention, 'Royal Palaces of Abomey' (n.d.) https://whc.unesco.org/en/list/323/

25 On human sacrifice in Dahomey, see Robin Law, 'Human Sacrifice in Pre-Colonial West Africa', *African Affairs*, Vol. 84(334), 1985, pp. 53–87; Patrick Manning, 'The Slave Trade in the Bight of Benin, 1640–1890' In Hogendorn Gemery (ed.). *The Uncommon Market. Essays in the Economic History of Atlantic Slave Trade* (New York: Academic Press, 1979), pp. 107–41; Adeyinka, 'King Gezo of Dahomey, 1818–1858' (1974)

26 Alpern, p. 13

27 Law (1988), p. 442; Coissy, pp. 5–8

28 Public Record Office, London: C.113/276, letter of William Baillie, Whydah, 18 Jan 1718 in Law (1988), p. 442

29 Law (1988), p. 431

30 Stanley B. Alpern, *Amazons of Black Sparta: The Women Warriors of Dahomey* (New York : New York University Press, 1998), p. 165

31 Bay (1995), p. 1 and p. 7

32 Edna G. Bay, 'The Royal Women of Abomey' (Ph.D. thesis, Boston University, 1977); 'Servitude and Worldly Success in the Palace of Dahomey', in Clare C. Robertson and Martin A. Klein (eds.), *Women and Slavery in Africa* (Madison, 1983), pp. 340–67

33 Boniface Obichere, 'Women and Slavery in the Kingdom of Dahomey', *Revue d'Histoire d'Outre-Mer*, Vol. 66, 1978, pp. 5–20, pp. 11–12

34 Robin Law, 'Further light on Bulfinch Lambe and the "Emperor of Pawpaw": King Agaja of Dahomey's Letter to King George I of England', *History in Africa*, Vol. 17, 1990, pp. 211–26, p. 217; de Chenevert and Abbe Bullet, 1776: 'Reflexions sur Juda', ms. in Archives d'Outre-Mer, Aix-en-Provence: Depot des Fortifications des Colonies, Cotes d'Afrique, p. 7 in Robin Law, 'The "Amazons" of Dahomey', *Paideuma: Mitteilungen zur Kulturkunde*, Bd. 39, 1993, pp. 245–60, p. 248

35 Law (1993), p. 248

36 Law (1990), p. 217

37 Ibid.

38 Amoah-Boampong and Agyeiwaa, p. 3; N. Sudarkasa, (1986), 'The status of women in indigenous African societies', *Feminist Studies*, Vol. 12(1), pp. 91–103

39 Z. Zevallos, 'Sociology of Gender', *The Other Sociologist*, 28 Nov 2014, Online resource: https://othersociologist.com/sociology-of-gender/; ibid.

40 Obichere, p. 12 and pp. 15–16

41 Ibid., pp. 14–15

42 Ibid., p. 16

43 Arch. nat. Dahomey, Fonds hist., Aff. pol., E. Trabloux to Alby, 26 Jul 1895, No. 92. Governor Ballot to Résident of Abomey, No. 152. Résident to Governor, 19 Nov 1895, No. 125 in ibid., p. 11

44 Agbenyega Adedze, 'The Amazons of Dahomey', *Oxford Research Encyclopedia African History*, 2020, pp. 1–16, pp. 6–7

45 Elizabeth Abbott, *A History of Celibacy: From Athena to Elizabeth I, Leonardo da Vinci, Florence Nightingale, Gandhi, & Cher*, p. 238; Meilan Solly, 'The Real Warriors Behind "The Woman King"', *Smithsonian Magazine*, 15 Sep 2022, https://www.smithsonianmag.com/history/real-warriors-woman-king-dahomey-agojie-amazons-180980750/

46 Photography by Peter Nissen, Hamburg, 'Kingdoms of Oyo and Dahomey', University of Cambridge, Museum of Archaeology and Anthropology, https://maa.cam.ac.uk/schools/resources/african-collections-schools-resources/kingdoms-oyo-and-dahomey

47 Law (1993), pp. 252–53

48 Ibid., p. 253; Mike Dash, 'Dahomey's Women Warrors', *Smithsonian*

Magazine, 23 Sep 2011, https://www.smithsonianmag.com/history/dahomeys-women-warriors-88286072/

49 John Duncan, 1847: Travels in Western Africa, London, 2 vols, I: p. 233 and pp. 245–46

50 Adedze (2020), p. 7

51 Law (1993), p. 251

52 Auguste Bouet, 1852: *Le Royaume de Dahomey*, L'Illustration, 20, nos. 490–2, p. 42

53 Obichere, p. 12

54 Ibid., p. 16

55 Ibid.; Abbott, p. 239

56 Law (1993), p. 256

57 Abbott, p. 239

58 Richard Burton, 1864: A Mission to Gelele, King of Dahome, London, 2 vols, II: 68 n. in Law (1993), p. 256

59 Ibid, II: 222 in Law (1993), p. 256

60 Edna Bay, 1983, 'Servitude and worldly success in the palace of Dahomey, in Claire C. Robertson & Martin A. Klein (eds): *Women & Slavery in Africa*, (Madison), pp. 340–67, p. 344

61 Kapya K. Kaoma, *Christianity, Globalization, and Protective Homophobia: Democratic Contestation of Sexuality in Sub-Saharan Africa* (Cham: Palgrave Macmillan, 2017), pp. 22–24; Leah Buckle, 'African Sexuality and the Legacy of Imported Homophobia', *Stonewall*, 2020, http://www.stonewall.org.uk/about-us/news/african-sexuality-and-legacy-importedhomophobia; S. O. Murray and W. Roscoe, eds. 1998, *Boy wives and female husbands: Studies of African homosexuality*, (New York, NY: St. Martin's Press); George Olusola Ajibade, 'Same-Sex Relationships in Yorùbá Culture and Orature', *Journal of Homosexuality*, Vol. 60(7), pp. 965–83, p. 972

62 Jesse Brimmer, ' "Un-African" African Sexualities: Post-Colonial Nation Building and the Conditioning of Citizenship in Sub-Saharan Africa with Analysis of Uganda and Kenya', (MA Long Thesis, 2020, Central European University Collection), p. 7

63 Alpern, p. 9

64 Ibid., p. 14

65 Ibid.; Amélie Degbelo, 'Les amazones du Danxomè, 1645–1900' (Master's thesis, Université Nationale du Bénin, 1979), p. 35 and p. 174

66 Victor-Louis Maire, *Dahomey-Abomey: la dynastie dahomeenne. Les palais: leurs bas-reliefs* (Besanqon, 1905), 43 in Alpern, p. 10

67 Alpern, p. 10

68 Manohla Dargis, 'The Woman King' Review: She Slays', *The New York Times*, 15 Sep 2022: https://www.nytimes.com/2022/09/15/movies/the-woman-king-review-viola-davis.html

69 Anton Bitel, 'The Woman King: must history intrude on such heady mythmaking?' *BFI*, 3 Oct 2022: https://www.bfi.org.uk/sight-and-sound/reviews/woman-king-must-history-intrude-such-heady-mythmaking

70 Robin Law, 'Introduction', *Dahomey and the Ending of the Transatlantic Slave Trade: The Journals and Correspondence of Vice-Consul Louis Fraser, 1851–1852*, Edited by Robin Law, Fontes Historiae Africanae, New Series 10, (Oxford: Oxford University Press, 2012) p. 10

71 For more on the apprenticeship system, see S. Boa 'Experiences of women estate workers during the apprenticeship period in St. Vincent, 1834–38: the transition from slavery to freedom', *Women's History Review*, Vol. 10(3), 2001, pp. 381–407; James Latimer, 'The Apprenticeship System in the British West Indies', *The Journal of Negro Education*, Vol. 33(1), 1964, pp. 52–57.

72 Obichere, p. 13 and p. 18

73 Law (1986), p. 256

74 Law (1993), p. 258

75 Forbes (1851), 2: 108 in ibid.

76 Alpern, p. 13; Law (1993), pp. 249–50

77 Alpern, p. 12; Le Hérissé, pp. 363–64

78 Alpern, pp. 11–12

79 Law (1993), p. 250

80 Ibid., p. 250 and p. 255

81 Ana Lucia Araujo, 'Dahomey, Portugal and Bahia: King Adandozan and the Atlantic Slave Trade', *Slavery & Abolition: A Journal of Slave and Post-Slave Studies*, Vol. 33(1), 2012, pp. 1–19, p. 6; I. A. Akinjogbin, *Dahomey and its Neighbours 1708–1818*. (London: Cambridge University Press, 1967), p. 193 and p. 200 in David Ross, 'The Anti-Slave Trade Theme in Dahoman History: An Examination of the Evidence', *History in Africa*, Vol. 9, 1982, pp. 263–71, p. 263

82 Araujo (2012), p. 12; 'History, Memory and Imagination: Na Agontimé, a Dahomean Queen in Brazil', In *Beyond Tradition: African Women and their Cultural Spaces*, edited by Toyin Falola and Sati U. Fwatshak, 2011, (Trenton, NJ: Africa World Press), pp. 45–68, p. 46

83 Alpern, p. 10

84 Ibid., p. 11

85 Interview with the incumbent Queen Tassi Hangbé, Palais Royal Tassi Hangbé, 5 Apr 2023; Interview with Mafoya, Cotonou, 6 Apr 2023

Chapter 4: Abla Pokou

1   Artefacts from descendants of Queen Abla Pokou at Musée des Civilisations de Côte d'Ivoire, Abidjan

2   Timothy C. Weiskel, 'The Precolonial Baule: A Reconstruction (Le Baule

précolonial: reconstruction)', *Cahiers d'Études Africaines*, Vol. 18(72), 1978, pp. 503–60, pp. 507–10

3 Emmanuel Akyeampong and Pashington Obeng, 'Spirituality, Gender, and Power in Asante History', *The International Journal of African Historical Studies*, Vol. 28(3), 1995, pp. 481–508, pp. 492–93

4 Ibid., p. 492; A. A. Boahen, 'The State and Cultures of the Lower Guinean Coast', in B. A. Ogot, ed., *General History of Africa*, V (Berkeley, 1992), p. 412

5 Akyeampong and Obeng, p. 493

6 A. Norman Klein, 'Slavery and Akan Origins?' *Ethnohistory*, Vol. 41(4), 1994, pp. 627–56. JSTOR, https://doi.org/10.2307/482768, p. 628

7 K. Y. Daaku, Osei Tutu of Asante (London, 1976), pp. 14–17; Akyeampong and Obeng, p. 494

8 T. C. McCaskie, 'Denkyira in the Making of Asante c. 1660–1720', *The Journal of African History*, Vol. 48, 2007, pp. 1–25, p. 1

9 Ibid.

10 Akyeampong and Obeng, p. 495

11 Gareth Austin, 'Developmental Divergences and Continuities between Colonial and Pre-Colonial Regimes: The Case of Asante, Ghana 1701–1957', the working papers of the second GEHN Conference, Irvine, California (15–17 Jan 2004), p. 3 https://www.lse.ac.uk/Economic-History/Assets/Documents/Research/GEHN/GEHNConferences/conf2/Conf2-GAustin.pdf

12 'Divine Kingship in Asante', James B. Duke Memorial Library / Johnson C. Smith University https://library.jcsu.edu/divine-kingship-of-asante/; Austin, p. 3; Ivor Wilks, *Asante in the Nineteenth Century: the Structure and Evolution of a Political Order* (London: Cambridge University Press, 1975).

13 A. Adu Boahen, 'When Did Osei Tutu Die?' *Transactions of the Historical Society of Ghana*, Vol. 16(1), 1975, pp. 87–92. JSTOR, http://www.jstor.org/stable/41406582, p. 87; Timothy C. Weiskel, 'L'histoire Socio-Économique Des Peuples Baule: Problèmes et Perspectives de Recherche (The Socio-Economic History of the Baule Peoples: Research Problems and Perspectives)', *Cahiers d'Études Africaines*, Vol. 16(61/62), 1976, pp. 357–95, JSTOR, http://www.jstor.org/stable/4391456, p. 379

14 Emancipation Support Committee Trinidad and Tobago, 'Profile of Otumfuo Osei Tutu II Asantehene (King of Ashanti)' https://www.emancipationtt.com/wp-content/uploads/Profile-of-Otumfuo-Osei-Tutu-II.pdf

15 Weiskel (1978), p. 507

16 Ibid., p. 510; Wilks, pp. 327–28

17 Zeinab Badawi, *An African History of Africa: From the Dawn of Humanity to Independence* (London: WH Allen, 2024), p. 302

18 Weiskel (1978), p. 508; M. Delafosse, 1900, *Essai de manuel de la langue agni (Paris)*, pp. 159–65

19 McCaskie, T. C. 'People and Animals: Constru(Ct)Ing the Asante Experience', *Africa: Journal of the International African Institute*, Vol. 62(2), 1992, pp. 221–47. JSTOR, https://doi.org/10.2307/1160456, p. 223

20 Iba Ndiaye Diadji, ' "Life-Water" to "Death-Water" or on the Foundations of African Artistic Creation from Yesterday to Tomorrow', Leonardo, Vol. 36(4), 2003, pp. 273–77, p. 273

21 Véronique Tadjo, 'Lifting the Cloak of (In)Visibility: A Writer's Perspective, Research in African Literatures', Vol. 44(2), (In)Visibility in African Cultures / Zoe Norridge, Charlotte Baker, and Elleke Boehmer, Guest Editors, Summer 2013, pp. 1–7, p. 2

22 Badawi, p. 24–5

23 Ibid; Diadji, p. 274

24 Tadjo (2013), p. 2

25 Agbenyega Adedze, 'Commemorating the Chief: The Politics of Postage Stamps in West Africa', *African Arts*, Vol. 37(2), Summer 2004, pp. 68–73 (& p. 96), p. 72

26 Delafosse, p. 163

27 Tadjo (2013), p. 5

28 Bernard Dadié and Melvin Dixon, 'The Baoulé Legend', *Callaloo*, No. 7, Oct 1979, pp. 6–7, p. 7; Tadjo (2013), p. 5

29 McCaskie, p. 223

30 Dadié and Dixon, p. 7

31 J. W. Tufuo and E.E. Donkor, *Ashantis of Ghana: People with a Soul*, (Accra, Ghana: Anowuo Educational Publications, 1969) p. 54

32 Talkeu Tounouga, Camille and Odile Brock, 'The Symbolic Function of Water in Sub-Saharan Africa: A Cultural Approach', *Leonardo*, Vol. 36(4), 2003, p. 283, *Project MUSE* muse.jhu.edu/article/45618; 'Pharmacognostical Profile of Selected Medicinal Plants', in *Handbook of African Medicinal Plants* au. Maurice M. Iwu (Boca Raton: CRC Press, 4 Feb 2014), Routledge Handbooks Online.

33 Misty L. Bastian, 'Married in the Water: Spirit Kin and Other Afflictions of Modernity in Southeastern Nigeria', *Journal of Religion in Africa*, Vol. 27(2), 1997, pp. 116–34. JSTOR, https://doi.org/10.2307/1581682, p. 123

34 Douglas J. Falen, 'Vodún, Spiritual Insecurity, and Religious Importation in Benin', *Journal of Religion in Africa*, Vol. 46(4), 2016, pp. 453–83. JSTOR, http://www.jstor.org/stable/26358824, p. 463

35 Henry John Drewal, 'Performing the Other: Mami Wata Worship in Africa,' *TDR (1988–)*, Vol. 32(2), 1988, pp. 160–85. JSTOR, https://doi.org/10.2307/1145857, p.161; Bastian, p. 124

36 Diadji, p. 274

37 Ibid.

38 Weiskel (1978), p. 508; Reseau Ivoire, 'The history of Bouake' https://rezoivoire.net/ivoire/villes-villages/760/lhistoire-de-bouake.html

39 Interview with *Tante* Lucie, Abidjan, 29 Mar 2023

40 ANRCI X.38.9, 'port du Lieutenant d'infanterie coloniale hors cadres Carpentier, chef de poste – Sakasso, sur le régime politique du district de Sakasso, circonscription de Bouaké', n.d. (Oct 1905), Archives nationales de la République de Côte d'Ivoire (ANRCI)

41 Weiskel (1978), p. 542

42 Ibid.

43 Delafosse (1900), p. 207

44 Kahiu, Wanuri, director. Pumzi. Focus Features, 2009 quoted in Jane Bryce, 'African Futurism: Speculative Fictions and "Rewriting the Great Book"', *Research in African Literatures*, Vol. 50(1), Spring 2019, pp. 1–19, p. 3; Peggy Kolm, 'Pumzi: African Science Fiction,' *Biology in Science Fiction*, 24 Jan 2010, https://blog.sciencefictionbiology.com/2010/01/pumzi-afican-science-fiction.html

45 Nick Wood, 'Our Ancestors Are Not Ghosts,' SF in SA #11, Dec 2010, https://nickwood.frogwrite.co.nz/?p=607

46 M. Ghasemi, (2014). Revisiting History in Hayden White's Philosophy. Sage Open, 4(3). https://doi.org/10.1177/2158244014542585

47 Véronique Tadjo, *Queen Pokou: Concerto for a Sacrifice*, 2009, p. 7

48 Ibid.

49 Bryce, p. 43

50 Ute Fendler, 'Superheroes for Africa?' *Africa Today*, Vol. 65(1), 2018, pp. 87–105, p. 96

51 Ibid.

52 Jean-Paul Azam, 'The Redistributive State and Conflicts in Africa', *Journal of Peace Research*, Vol. 38(4), 2001, pp. 429–44, p. 436

53 Interviews with *Tante* Lucie and scholars at Université Félix Houphouët-Boigny, Abidjan, 29 Mar 2023

Chapter 5: Məntəwwab

1 Habtamu Mengistie Tegegne, 'Land Tenure and Agrarian Social Structure in Ethiopia, 1636–1900', Doctoral dissertation, University of Illinois, 2011, p. 128

2 James Bruce, *Travels to Discover the Source of the Nile: In the Years 1768, 1769, 1770, 1771, 1772 and 1773*, Volume 2 (Edinburgh: Printed by J. Ruthven, for G. G. J. and J. Robinson, Paternoster-Row, London, 1790), pp. 598–99

3 Ibid.

4   Bahru Zewde, 'Review: History of Ethiopia', *The Journal of African History*, Vol. 36(3), 1995, pp. 501–03, pp. 502–03

5   Bruce, p. 599

6   Tegegne (2011), p. 119

7   Donald Crummey, *Land and Society in the Christian Kingdom of Ethiopia: From the Thirteenth to the Twentieth Century* (Illinois: University of Illinois, 2000), p. 95

8   Tegegne (2011), p. 113

9   Ibid.

10 Ibid., p. 115

11 Ibid., p. 116

12 Ignazio Guidi, Annales Regum Iyasu II et Iyo'as, Corpus Scriptorium Christianorum Orinetalium, Scriptores Aethiopici, versio, *Series Altera*, Vol. 6 (Rome 1912), pp. 283–84, 307–09 in ibid., p. 116

13 Merid Wolde Aregay, 'Society and Technology in Ethiopia 1500–1800', *Journal of Ethiopian Studies*, Vol. 17, Nov 1984, pp. 127–47, p. 127

14 Donald Crummey, 'Society and Ethnicity in the Politics of Christian Ethiopia during the Zamana Masafent', *The International Journal of African Historical Studies*, Vol. 8(2), 1975, pp. 266–78, p. 268

15 Richard Pankhurst, 'Tedla Hailé, and the Problem of Multi-Ethnicity in Ethiopia', *Northeast African Studies*, 1998, New Series, Vol. 5(3), 1998, pp. 81–96, pp. 81–82

16 Mulugeta Gebrehiwot Berhe and Feseha Habtetsion Gebresilassie, 'Nationalism and self-determination in contemporary Ethiopia', *Nations and Nationalism*, Vol. 27, 2021, pp. 96–111, p. 98

17 Ibid., pp. 98–9

18 Jon Abbink, 'Ethnicity and Constitutionalism in Contemporary Ethiopia', *Journal of African Law*, Vol. 41(2), 1997, pp. 159–74, p. 159

19 Ibid., p. 160

20 Atlas of Humanity, 'Nyangatom Tribe, Ethiopia' (n.d.): https://www.atlasofhumanity.com/nyangatom

21 John Young, 'Ethnicity and Power in Ethiopia', *Review of African Political Economy*, Vol. 23(70), Dec 1996, pp. 531–42, p. 532; John Ishiyama, 'Ethnic Identity and Conflict: The Case of Ethiopia', *Georgetown Journal of International Affairs*, Vol. 24(1), Spring 2023, pp. 12–18, p. 13

22 Young, p. 532

23 Ishiyama, p. 13

24 Tegegne (2011), p. 119

25 Steyn, p. 3

26 Tegegne (2011), p. 119

27 Crummey (2000), p. 95

28 Tegegne (2011), pp. 119–20

29 Habtamu Mengistie Tegegne, 'Rethinking Property and Society in

Gondärine Ethiopia', *African Studies Review*, Vol. 52(3), Dec 2009, pp. 89–106, p. 94

30 Ibid., p. 95

31 Ibid.; Tegegne (2011), p. 16

32 Tegegne (2011), p. 191

33 Tegegne (2009), p. 95 and p. 103; Antoine D'Abbadie, *Dictionnaire de la langue amarinna*, Actes de la Societe philologique 10; (Paris: F. Vieweg, 1881) p. 722

34 Tegegne (2009), p. 97

35 Tegegne (2011), p. 42 and p. 84

36 Tegegne (2009), p. 97

37 Tegegne (2011), p. 116 and p. 128

38 Ibid., p. 128

39 Joe Tenn, 'More on Gasha' (n.d.): http://abyssiniagateway.net/info/gasha.html#:~:text=The%20unit%20employed%20in%20this,about%2080%20to%20100%20acres

40 Tegegne (2011), p. 130

41 Ibid., p. 137

42 Salome Gebre Egziabher, 'The Changing Position of Women in Ethiopia', *Zeitschrift für Kulturaustausch* (Sonderausgabe 1973), p. 113 in Donald Crummey, 'Women and Landed Property in Gondarine Ethiopia', *The International Journal of African Historical Studies*, Vol. 14(3), 1981, pp. 444–65, p. 445

43 Crummey (1981), p. 464

44 Ibid., p. 465

45 Bruce, p. 612

46 Tegegne (2011), p. 120

47 Ibid.; Steyn, p. 4

48 Tegegne (2011), p. 120

49 Guidi, *Annales Regum Iyasu II et Iyo'as*, pp. 54–58 in Crummey (2000), p. 95

50 Crummey (2000), p. 95

51 Tegegne (2011), p. 120

52 Crummey (1975), p. 272

53 Yohannes Woldemariam, 'The romantic rewriting of Haile Selassie's legacy must stop', *London School of Economics Blogs*, 4 Feb 2019: https://blogs.lse.ac.uk/africaatlse/2019/02/04/the-romantic-rewriting-of-haile-selassies-legacy-must-stop/

54 Ishiyama, p. 13

55 Ibid.; World Without Genocide, 'Ethiopia, 2020–Present' (updated 2021): https://worldwithoutgenocide.org/genocides-and-conflicts/ethiopia-tigray

56 World Without Genocide (2021)

57 Mattha Busby and Martin Belam, 'Nobel Peace Prize: Ethiopian prime

minister Abiy Ahmed wins 2019 award – as it happened', *The Guardian*, 11 Oct 2019: https://www.theguardian.com/world/live/2019/oct/11/nobel-peace-prize-greta-thunberg-abiy-ahmed-jacinda-ardern-among-those-tipped-win-live-news

58   World Without Genocide (2021)

59   Ibid.

60   Magdalene Abraha, 'There's a brutal conflict in Ethiopia. My family there ask: why does no one hear us?', *The Guardian*, 17 Nov 2021: https://www.theguardian.com/commentisfree/2021/nov/17/conflict-ethiopia-tigray-war-starving

61   Ibid.

62   Al Jazeera, 'Strong evidence that Ethiopia committed genocide in Tigray war: Report', *Al Jazeera*, 4 Jun 2024: https://www.aljazeera.com/news/2024/6/4/strong-evidence-that-ethiopia-committed-genocide-in-tigray-war-report

63   Magdalene Abraha, 'Think the war in Ukraine is the world's deadliest conflict? Think again', *The Guardian*, 28 Dec 2022: https://www.theguardian.com/commentisfree/2022/dec/28/war-ukraine-deadliest-conflict-tigray-ethiopia

64   Tegegne (2011), pp. 120–21

65   Ibid., p. 57 and p. 83

66   Ibid., p. 239; Richard Pankhurst, 'Ethiopian Dynastic Marriage and the Béta Esra'él (or Falashas)', *Africa: Rivista trimestrale di studi e documentazione dell'Istituto italiano per l'Africa e l'Oriente*, Settembre 1997, Anno 52, No. 3 (Settembre 1997), pp. 445–54, p. 445

67   Tegegne (2011), p. 239

68   Andrew Lawler, 'Church Unearthed in Ethiopia Rewrites the History of Christianity in Africa', *Smithsonian Magazine*, 10 Dec 2019: https://www.smithsonianmag.com/history/church-unearthed-ethiopia-rewrites-history-christianity-africa-180973740/

69   Tegegne (2011), p. 96; Raita Steyn, 'An Ethiopian "Renaissance" Queen? Mentewab as Protector of Arts and Patron of Iconography', *Pharos Journal of Theology*, Vol. 105(2), 2024, pp. 1–11, p. 2; Elias Kiptoo Ngetich, 'Catholic counter-reformation: A history of the Jesuits' mission to Ethiopia 1557–1635', *Studia Historiae Ecclesiasticae*, Vol. 42(2), pp. 104–15, pp. 111–12

70   Tegegne (2011), p. 85

71   Ibid.

72   Ibid., pp. 114–15

73   Ibid., p. 121

74   Makda Teklemichael, 'Contemporary Women Artists in Ethiopia', *African Arts*, Vol. 42(1), Spring 2009, pp. 38–45, p. 38

75   Stanislaw Chojnacki, 'New Aspects of India's Influence on the Art and

Culture of Ethiopia', *Rassegna di Studi Etiopici*, Nuova Serie, Vol. 2(45), 2003, pp. 5–21, p. 10–11

76 Elisabeth Biasio, 1994, 'Art Culture and Society: Consideration on Ethiopian Church Painting Focusing on the 19th Century', In Proceedings of the 11th International Conference of Ethiopian Studies (Addis Ababa 1991), eds. Bahru Zewde, Richard Pankhurst, Taddesse Beyene, pp. 541–62, p. 552, Addis Ababa: Institute of Ethiopian Studies, Addis Ababa University in Teklemichael, p. 38

77 Teklemichael, pp. 38–39

78 Claire Bosc-Tiessé, 2004, 'The Use of Occidental Engravings in Ethiopian Painting in the Seventeenth and Eighteenth Centuries: From the Success of the Book Evangelicae Historiae Imagines by Nadal at King Susniyos' Court (c. 1610–11) to the Murals in the Narga Sillase Church (c. 1738–50)', In The Indigenous and the Foreign in Christian Ethiopian Art: On Portuguese-Ethiopian Contacts in the Sixteenth-Seventeenth Centuries, ed. Manuel Joao Ramos and Isabel Boavida, pp. 83–102. London: Ashgate. p. 314 in Estelle Sohier, 'Hybrid Images: From Photography to Church Painting: Iconographic Narratives at the Court of the Ethiopian King of Kings, Menelik II (1880s–1913)', *African Arts*, Vol. 49(1), Spring 2016, pp. 26–39, p. 33; Steyn, p. 7.

79 Tegegne (2011), p. 122

80 Richard Pankhurst, 'An Eighteenth Century Ethiopian Dynastic Marriage Contract between Empress Mentewwab of Gondar and Ras Mika'el Sehul of Tegre', *Bulletin of the School of Oriental and African Studies*, (University of London, 1979) Vol. 42(3), 1979, pp. 457–66, pp. 457–58

81 Ibid., p. 458

82 Terry Stewart, 'James Bruce', *Historic UK* (n.d.): https://www.historic-uk.com/HistoryUK/HistoryofScotland/James-Bruce/

83 National Galleries of Scotland, 'Pompeo Batoni: James Bruce of Kinnaird, 1730–1794. African explorer' (n.d.): https://www.nationalgalleries.org/art-and-artists/1915

84 Devon & Exeter Institution, 'James Bruce of Kinnaird (1730–1794)' (n.d.): https://devonandexeterinstitution.org/james-bruce-of-kinnaird-1730-1794/

85 Terry Stewart (n.d.)

86 Ibid.

87 Pankhurst (1979), p. 461

88 Crummey (1975), p. 273

89 Paul B. Henze, *Layers of Time: A History of Ethiopia* (New York: Palgrave, 2000), p. 121

90 Bruce, p. 655–56 in Pankhurst (1979), p. 457

91 Tegegne (2011), p. 121; Pankhurst (1979), p. 458

92 Pankhurst (1979), p. 462

93 Ibid., p. 458; Henze, p. 121

94 Tegegne (2011), p. 217

95 Pankhurst (1979), p. 461

96 Tegegne (2011), p. 141

97 Crummey (1975), p. 273; Donald Crummey, 'Čäčäho and the politics of the northern Wällo-Bägémder border', *Journal of Ethiopian Studies*, Vol. 13(1), Jan 1975, pp. 1–9, p. 5

98 Crummey (1975), p. 272; Tegegne (2011), p. 141

99 Joseph Tubiana, 'Turning Points in Ethiopian History', *Rassegna di Studi Etiopici*, Vol. 21, 1965, pp. 162–66, p. 166

100 Crummey (1975), p. 272; Crummey (1975), p. 5

101 Tegegne (2011), p. 140

102 Ibid., p. 141

103 Ibid.

104 Ibid.

105 Royal Ark, 'Ethiopia: Tigray Genealogy' (n.d): https://www.royalark.net/Ethiopia/tigray.htm

106 Tegegne (2011), pp. 141–42; Tubiana, p. 166

107 Henze, p. 104

108 Interview with Mags at Addis Restaurant, London, 14 Jun 2024; Bruce, p. 599

109 Interview with Mags, 14 Jun 2024

110 Fred Harter, ' "If you had money, you had slaves": how Ethiopia is in denial about injustices of the past', *The Guardian*, 18 Jan 2023: https://www.theguardian.com/global-development/2023/jan/18/ethiopia-slaves-in-denial-about-injustices-of-the-past

111 Ibid.

112 Tegegne (2011), p. 141

113 Steyn, p. 1

Chapter 6: Nandi kaBhebhe

1 'Welcome to the Wonderful World of the KwaZulu-Natal Battlefields Route' (n.d.), https://www.battlefieldsroute.co.za/

2 Babanango Game Reserve website: https://babanango.com/

3 E. Eldredge, (2014), 'Shaka's Early Life: Oral Traditions, Tales, and History'. In *The Creation of the Zulu Kingdom, 1815–1828: War, Shaka, and the Consolidation of Power* (pp. 42–58) (Cambridge: Cambridge University Press), doi:10.1017/CBO9781139871686.005, p. 42; E. A. Ritter, *Shaka Zulu: The Rise of the Zulu Empire*, (London: Book Club Associates, 1971), p. 12

4 Ritter, p. 12; Thabisile Buthelezi, 'The One Who Has Eaten It, Has Only Eaten a Part: Exploring Traditional Zulu Premarital Sexual Practices', *Sexuality in Africa Magazine*, Vol. 3(2), pp. 3–5, pp. 4–5

5 Ritter, p. 5

6 Ritter, p. 11; Johan H. Koeslag, 'Population homeostasis during the Demographic transition', *South African Journal of Science*, Vol. 81(2), 1985, pp. 66–72, p. 66

7 C. W. Kies, 'Family Planning in Rural Kwazulu: Transition from Traditional to Contemporary Practices', *Southern African Journal of Demography*, Vol. 1(1), 1987, pp. 16–19. JSTOR, http://www.jstor.org/ stable/20853751 p.16; Mark Hunter, 'Courting Desire?: Love and Intimacy in Late 19th and early 20th Century Kwazulu-Natal', *Passages: A Chronicle of the African Humanities*, no. ns 2, Jun 2005, http://hdl.handle.net/2027/ spo.4761530.0010.016; Ritter, p. 11

8 Kies, p. 16

9 Hunter, 2005

10 Nompumelelo Zondi, 'Critiquing the Male Writing of Female Izibongo: A Feminist Approach', p. 31; Msimang C T (1975) Kusadliwa ngoludola (Pietermaritzburg: Shuter and Shooter)

11 Ritter, p. 11

12 Goqozile Masango, 'Understanding how inhlawulo works' https:// www.702.co.za/articles/404304/understanding-how-inhlawulo-works

13 James W. Fernandez, *The Shaka Complex* (1967), p. 11

14 Ibid., p. 9

15 Ibid., p. 11

16 Harriet Ngubane, 'Some notions of "purity" and "impurity" among the Zulu', *Africa*, Vol. 46(3), Jul 1976, pp. 274–84

17 Ritter, p. 12; https://beingafrican.com/zuli-test/ [webpage has expired]

18 Maxwell Z. Shamase, 'The royal women of the Zulu monarchy through the keyhole of oral history: Queens Nandi (*c.*1764–*c.*1827) and Monase (*c.*1797–1880)', p. 2

19 Ritter, p. 12

20 Ritter, p. 13; Stephen Taylor, *Shaka's Children: A History of the Zulu People*, (London: HarperCollins, 1994), p. 43

21 Anna Ridehalgh, 'Some Recent Francophone Versions of the Shaka Story', *Research in African Literatures*, Vol. 22(2), 1991, pp. 135–52, p. 135

22 J. Malherbe, M. Kleijwegt and E. Koen (2000) *Women, society and constraints, Unisa: A collection of contemporory South African gender studies*, Institute of Gender Studies (Pretoria: University of South Africa) p. 195

23 Fernandez, p. 11

24 Ibid.

25 Duncan Brown, 'Poetry, History, Nation: The Praises of Shaka kaSenzan-gakhona', *English in Africa*, Vol. 24(1), 1997, pp. 7–36, p. 13

26 Fernandez, p.12

27 Fernandez, p. 11; Ritter, p. 13; Taylor, p. 39 & p. 44

28 Ridehalgh, p. 135

29 Fernandez, p. 12

30 Daphna Golan, 'The Life Story of King Shaka and Gender Tensions in the Zulu State,' *History in Africa*, Vol. 17, 1990, pp. 95–111, p. 96

31 Rebecca Ray, 'Epic Hero Definitions and Activities' (n.d.): https://www.storyboardthat.com/articles/e/epic-hero

32 Mark R. Lipschutz and R. Kent Rasmussen (1986), 'Senzangakhona', *Dictionary of African Historical Biography* (2nd ed.), (Berkeley: University of California Press), p. 213

33 Ridehalgh, p. 135

34 Tinyeko Captain Ndhlovu, 'Shaka Zulu's Famous Impondo Zenkomo / The Bull Horns Tactical Battle Formation', *Ditsong: National Museum of Military History* (2023): https://ditsong.org.za/en/shaka-zulus-famous-impondo-zenkomo-the-bull-horns-tactical-battle-formation/ 5

35 Nompumelelo Zondi, 'Critiquing the Male Writing of Female Izibongo: A Feminist Approach,' *Agenda: Empowering Women for Gender Equity*, no. 68, 2006, pp. 30–38. JSTOR, http://www.jstor.org/stable/4066760, p. 31

36 Fernandez, p. 12

37 Golan, p. 96; Ridehalgh, p. 135

38 Cyril malibongwe Mbeje, 'the Zulu Identity (South African Ingenious tribes)' https://www.researchgate.net/publication/312189041_the_Zulu_Identity_South_African_Ingenious_tribes

39 Brown, p. 13

40 Golan, p. 107

41 L. D. Ngcongco, General history of Africa, VI: Africa in the nineteenth century until the 1880s, 6, pp. 90–123, p. 90 https://unesdoc.unesco.org/ark:/48223/pf0000084956

42 C. A. Hamilton, 'Traditions of Origin and the Ideological appropriation of the Past in the Zulu Kingdom Under Shaka', 1987, p. 4 https://core.ac.uk/download/pdf/39666789.pdf

43 Elizabeth A. Eldredge, 'Sources of Conflict in Southern Africa, C. 1800–30: The "Mfecane" Reconsidered', *The Journal of African History*, Vol. 33(1), 1992, pp. 1–35, p. 1

44 Fernandez, p. 12

45 Golan, pp. 99–100

46 Dan Wylie, ' "Proprietor of Natal": Henry Francis Fynn and the Mythography of Shaka', *History in Africa*, Vol. 22, 1995, pp. 409–37, p. 409

47 Isaacs to Fynn, 10 Dec 1832, cited in P. R. Kirby, 'Unpublished Documents Relating to the Career of Nathaniel Isaacs, the Natal Pioneer', Africana Notes and News 18/2(1968), 67.

48 Wylie, p. 409

49 No author, 'The Diary of Henry Francis Fynn', *Emandulo* (n.d.): http://emandulo.apc.uct.ac.za/metadata/FHYA%20Depot/1188/1237/index.

html#:~:text=It%20was%20then%20subjected%20to,1950%20by%20
Shuter%20and%20Shooter

50 Wylie, p. 409

51 Mathieu Deflem, 'Warfare, Political Leadership, and State Formation:
    The Case of the Zulu Kingdom, 1808–1879', *Ethnology*, Vol. 38(4), 1999,
    pp. 371–91, p. 388

52 Karen Elizabeth Flint, *Healing Traditions: African Medicine, Cultural
    Exchange, and Competition in South Africa, 1820–1948*, p. 76; Diane
    Canwell, *Zulu Kings and their Armies*, p. 34

53 David Chichester, *Religions of South Africa* (Routledge Revivals), p. 27

54 Ritter, pp. 159–60

55 Alfred T. Bryant, 'Olden Times in Zululand and Natal: Containing Earlier
    Political History of the Eastern-Nguni Clans', Volume 13 of *Africana
    collectanea*, 1965, p. 608

56 Fernandez, p. 12

57 Ritter, pp. 159–60

58 Jordan K. Ngubane, 'Shaka's Social, Political and Military Ideas', *Shaka,
    King of the Zulus in African Literature*, Ed. Donald Burness (Washington,
    DC: Three Continents, 1976), pp. 127–64, p. 132

59 Henry Francis Fynn, *The Diary of Henry Francis Fynn*, 1950

60 Interview with the museologist, Durban, 17 Apr 2023

61 Somadoda Fikeni, (2006), 'The Nature and Function of Izibong-Panegyric
    Legends: The Case of the Xhosa People of South Africa', In Kunnie,
    Julian; Goduka, Nomalungelo Ivy (eds.). Indigenous Peoples' Wisdom
    and Power: Affirming Our Knowledge Through Narratives, Ashgate,
    pp. 225–45, p. 230

62 Zondi, p. 31

63 N. N. Canonici (1994) Zulu orol poetry, Durban: University of Natal,
    pp. 21–22

64 Nondi, p. 31

65 Taylor, *Shaka's Children;* Laband, 1995 (pp. 10–18) cited in Maxwell Z.
    Shamase, p. 4

66 Ritter, p. 199

67 Ibid., p. 286

68 Laband, 1995 (pp. 22–26) cited in Maxwell Z. Shamase, p. 5

69 Ibid.

70 Stuart, J.1926. *uBaxoxele (Incwadi Yezindaba za Bantu ba KwaZulu, na ba
    seNatal)*. London: Longmans, pp. 24–28.

71 Ritter, p. 311

72 Ibid., p. 312; Fernandez, p. 12

73 Ritter, p. 312; Gardiol J. van Niekerk, 'Death and sacred spaces in South
    Africa and America: a legal-anthropological perspective of conflicting

values', *The Comparative and International Law Journal of Southern Africa*, Vol. 40(1), March 2007, pp. 30–56, p. 32 (a footnote in the article)

74 Taylor, p. 94; Ritter, p. 313
75 Ridehalgh, p. 138
76 Ibid., p. 136
77 Babacar M'Baye. 14 May 2020, Literary Pan-Africanism in African epics from: *Routledge Handbook of Pan-Africanism*, Routledge, p. 401 https://www.routledgehandbooks.com/doi/10.4324/9780429020193-27
78 Interview with the museologist, Durban, 17 Apr 2023

Chapter 7: Ranavalona I

1   Gwyn Campbell, *David Griffiths and the Missionary 'History of Madagascar'*, Volume 41 of Studies in Christian Mission, (Leiden–Boston: Brill Academic, 2012), p. 285
2   Campbell (2012), p. 285; Stephen Ellis, 'Witch-Hunting in Central Madagascar 1828–1861', *Past & Present*, No. 175, May 2002, pp. 90–123, p. 97
3   Ibid.
4   Campbell (2012), pp. 285–86
5   Ibid., p. 286
6   Jean-Pierre Raison, 'For a geography of *hasina* (Imerina, Madagascar)', *Higher School of Theology and Religious Studies*, (1974), pp. 709–16, p. 709
7   Ibid., pp. 709–10
8   Ibid., p. 710
9   Alan D. Rogers, 'Human Prudence and Implied Divine Sanctions in Malagasy Proverbial Wisdom', *Journal of Religion in Africa*, Vol. 15(3), 1985, pp. 216–26, p. 218
10 Raison, p. 710
11 Campbell (2012), p. 500
12 François Callet, *Tantara ny Andriana eto Madagasikara (Histoire des rois)* (Antananarivo: Imprimerie catholique, 1908)
13 J. F. Ade Ajayi, 'Madagascar 1800-80' in *General History of Africa VI: Africa in the Nineteenth Century until the 1880s*, ed. J. F. Ade Ajayi (Paris: UNESCO, 1998), pp. 164–75, p. 164
14 Gerald M. Berg, 'Writing Ideology: Ranavalona, the Ancestral Bureaucrat', *History in Africa*, Vol. 22, 1995, pp. 73–92, p. 75
15 Ibid.
16 Edward A. Alpers, *Ivory and Slaves: Changing Pattern of International Trade in East Central Africa to the Later Nineteenth Century* (Berkeley: University of California Press, 1975), pp. 94–95
17 Sandra Evers, *Constructing History, Culture and Inequality: The Betsileo in*

the Extreme Southern Highlands of Madagascar, (Leiden: Brill Academic, 2002), pp. 167–72

18 Ibid., 175

19 C. Keller, *Madagascar, Mauritius and The Other East-African Islands* (London: Swan Sonnenschein & Co, 1901), p. 90

20 Campbell (2012), p. 634

21 Gwyn Campbell, 'Eating the dead in Madagascar', *South African Medical Journal* [Online], 103.12 (2013): pp. 1032–34

22 Interview with Mihaja and our guide, Antananarivo, 22 Apr 2023

23 Sandra Razafimahazo, 'Vazimba, Myth or Reality?' *Indian Ocean Review* (n.d.): https://www.madatana.com/article-vazimba-mythe-ou-realite.php

24 Ibid.

25 Françoise Raison-Jourde, *Les Souverains de Madagascar: l'histoire royale et ses résurgences contemporaines,* (Paris, Éditions Karthala: 1983)

26 Masika Sipa, 'Tribes of Madagascar', *Mada Magazine* (n.d.) : https://www.madamagazine.com/en/volksgruppen-madagaskars/

27 Alexander Ives Bortolot (2003), 'Kingdoms of Madagascar: Maroserana and Merina', In *Heilbrunn Timeline of Art History.* New York: The Metropolitan Museum of Art, 2000–. http://www.metmuseum.org/toah/hd/madg_1/hd_madg_1.htm

28 Campbell (2012), p. 51 and p. 87

29 Ibid, p. 51

30 Philip M. Allen and Maureen Covell, *Historical Dictionary of Madagascar: Second Edition* (Maryland: The Scarecrow Press, Inc., 2005), p. 225

31 Campbell (2012), p. 51

32 Gwyn Campbell, 'The Adoption of Autarky in Imperial Madagascar, 1820–1835', *The Journal of African History*, Vol. 28(3), 1987, pp. 395–411, p. 405

33 Ibid.

34 Ibid., p. 398

35 Ibid., pp. 398–99

36 Ibid., p. 406

37 Ibid., pp. 406–08

38 Campbell (2012), pp. 49–50

39 Berg, p. 85; William Ellis, *History of Madagascar: Comprising also the progress of the Christian mission established in 1818, and an authentic account of the persecution and recent martyrdom of the native Christians* (London: Fisher, Son & Co., 1838), p. 421

40 W. Ellis, pp. 423–25

41 Ibid., p. 428

42 Ibid., p. 426

43 Stefan Amirell, 'Female Rule in the Indian Ocean World (1300–1900)', *Journal of World History*, Vol. 26(3), Sep 2015, pp. 443–89, pp. 446–47

44 Ibid., 447
45 S. Ellis, p. 98; Berg, p. 79
46 S. Ellis, p. 113
47 W. Ellis, p. 360; Gwyn Campbell, *The Travels of Robert Lyall, 1789–1831: Scottish Surgeon, Naturalist and British Agent to the Court of Madagascar* (Berlin: Springer Nature, 2021), p. 165
48 S. Ellis, p. 113; Niel Gunson, 'Sacred Women Chiefs and Female "Headmen" in Polynesian History', *The Journal of Pacific History*, Vol. 22(3) 1987, pp. 139–72, pp. 139–40
49 Campbell (1987), p. 395; Berg, p. 85
50 Kelly Brignac, 2021. 'Free and Bound: Abolition and Forced Labor in the French Empire,' Doctoral dissertation, Harvard University Graduate School of Arts and Sciences, pp. 1–258, p. 100
51 Quoted in Lt Larevanchère, 'Souvenirs de l'expédition de Madagascar en 1829 et 1830', *Journal de l'Armée* [Paris] (1834), 45–46 in Berg, p. 86
52 Brignac, p. 100; Berg, p. 81
53 Berg, p. 79
54 Ibid.
55 Ibid., p. 74
56 Campbell (1987), p. 406
57 Berg, p. 81
58 Ibid., p. 82
59 Ibid., p. 82–83
60 Campbell (1987), p. 407
61 SOAS The Library, University of London, 'Guide to the London Missionary Society Archive (1764–1977), p. 128: https://digital.soas.ac.uk/content/AA/oo/oo/o8/85/oo001/LMS.pdf; C. Silvester Horne, *The Story of the L.M.S.* (Oswestry: Quinta Press, 2009), p. 175
62 H. Deschamps, *Histoire de Madagascar* (Paris, 1972), p. 151; W. Ellis, p. 403; Horne, p. 175
63 Deschamps, p. 163
64 Berg, p. 79
65 S. Ellis, p. 113; Allen and Covell, p. 225
66 Allen and Covell, p. 225; Gunson, p. 139
67 Pat Morton, 'A Study in Hybridity: Madagascar and Morocco at the 1931 Colonial Exposition', *Journal of Architectural Education (1984–)*, Vol. 52(2), 1998, pp. 76–86, p. 81; 'Manjakamiadana Rova', MadaCamp.com, text from Passport for Madagascar, 44th edition, Jan/Feb 2008: https://www.madacamp.com/Manjakamiadana_Rova
68 Gwyn Campbell, 'Architecture and Labour' *The Journal of African History*, Vol. 47(1), 2006, pp. 153–54, p. 153
69 *MadaCamp.com* (2008)
70 Interview with Mihaja and our guide, 22 Apr 2023

71 Ibid.

72 Stephen Ellis, 'Review: [Untitled]', *Africa: Journal of the International African Institute*, Vol. 76(4), 2006, pp. 601–02, p. 601

73 Donald G. McNeil Jr., 'Antananarivo Journal; A Palace Inferno Sears Madagascar's Very Soul', *The New York Times*, 22 Jun 1996: https://www.nytimes.com/1996/06/22/world/antananarivo-journal-a-palace-inferno-sears-madagascar-s-very-soul.html

74 Isabelle Ratsira, 'Twelve Sacred Hills', MadaCamp.com: https://www.madacamp.com/Twelve_Sacred_Hills

75 Yildiz Aumeeruddy-Thomas, Verohanitra Miarivelomalala Rafidison, Finn Kjellberg and Martine Hossaert-Mckey. 'Sacred hills of Imerina and the voyage of Ficus lutea Vahl (Amontana) in Madagascar', *Acta Oecologica*, Vol. 90, 2018, pp. 18–27

76 Interview with Mihaja and our guide, 22 Apr 2023

77 Patricia Ramavonirina, 'National Heritage – The Ambatondrafandrana Court gets a makeover', *La Vérité*, 9 Oct 2020: https://laverite.mg/societe/item/11695-patrimoine-national-le-tribunal-d-ambatondrafandrana-fait-peau-neuve.html

78 S. K. Croucher (2007). 'Clove plantations on nineteenth-century Zanzibar: Possibilities for gender archaeology in Africa', *Journal of Social Archaeology*, Vol. 7(3), pp. 302–24, pp. 302–03; Valerie J. Hoffman (2005). 'Ibadi Muslim Scholars and the Confrontation with Sunni Islam in Nineteenth- and Early Twentieth-Century Zanzibar', *Bulletin of the Royal Institute of Inter-Faith Studies*, Vol. 7(1), pp. 91–118, p. 91

79 Raombana, 'AnnaTes', 1853, p. 330, *Archives de l'Acad6mie malgache*, Tsimbazaza, Antananarivo in Gwyn Campbell, 'Crisis of Faith and Colonial Conquest: The Impact of Famine and Disease in Late-Nineteenth-Century Madagascar (Crise de la foi et conquête coloniale: les conséquences de la famine et de la maladie à Madagascar à la fin du XIXe siècle)', *Cahiers d'Études Africaines*, Vol. 32(127), 1992, pp. 409–53, p. 414

80 Campbell (1992), p. 414

81 Ibid., p. 411; Rogers, p. 218

82 Rogers, p. 218

83 Vivy Madagascar, 'Sampy' (n.d.): https://www.vivytravel.com/sampy/

84 Berg, p. 80

85 Francois Callet, ed. *Tantara ny Andriana eto Madagascar* [4 vols.: Antananarivo, 1873–1902], reference edition (2 vols.: Antananarivo, 1908), p. 1159 in Berg, p. 80

86 Johns and Freeman to Ellis (10 March 1835), LMS-LI, V/2/A in ibid.

87 Quoted in Bloch, *From Blessing to Violence*, p. 19 in S. Ellis, p. 121; Horne, p. 181

88 Horne, p. 181

89 Edward Baker, 'Brief Account of the Suppression of Christianity in Madagascar, 1835', SOAS/LMS MIL Bx5 F2 JC in Campbell (1992), p. 416

90 Horne, pp. 184–86

91 Ibid., p. 185

92 S. Ellis, pp. 112–13

93 Campbell (1992), p. 415; Gwyn Campbell, 'The State and Pre-Colonial Demographic History: The Case of Nineteenth-Century Madagascar', *The Journal of African History*, Vol. 32, 1991, pp. 415–45

94 Campbell (1991), p. 421

95 Campbell (1992), p. 417; Horne, pp. 188–89

96 M. K. R, 'Rova Manjakamiadana: 15 ans après', *La Gazette de la Grande Ile* (2010): https://web.archive.org/web/20110713183217/http://www.lagazette-dgi.com/index.php?view=article&catid=64%3Anewsflash&id=7716%3Arova-manjakamiadana--15-ans-apres&format=pdf&option=com_content&Itemid=67

97 Arianne Chernock, 'Queen Victoria and the "Bloody Mary of Madagascar"', *Victorian Studies*, Vol. 55(3), Spring 2013, pp. 425–49, p. 429

98 Ibid., p. 425

99 Ibid., pp. 425–26; W. Ellis, pp. 524–25

100 W. Ellis, title page in Chernock, p. 426

101 Ibid., p. 425 and pp. 428–29

102 *Madagascar Envoys Foreign and Domestic Various 1836–38.* FO 48/1. National Archives, Kew in Chernock, p. 429

103 Chernock, pp. 428–29

104 *Madagascar Envoys 1837* in Chernock, p. 430

105 Chernock, p. 430

106 *Madagascar Envoys 21 Feb 1837* in ibid., p. 431

107 *Madagascar Envoys 16 Jun 1837* in ibid.

108 Phares M. Mutibwa, *The Malagasy and the Europeans, Madagascar's Foreign Relations 1861–1895* (London: Longman Group, 1974), p. 25

109 Martin Willis, 'Battle of Madagascar 1845', The National Archives, Nov 2015: https://blog.nationalarchives.gov.uk/battle-madagascar-1845/#note-25005-1

110 Ibid.

111 Chernock, p. 435; William Ellis, *Three Visits to Madagascar During the Years 1853-1854-1856.* (New York: Harper, 1859), p. 20

112 Chernock, p. 435

113 'Foreign Miscellany', *The Manchester Guardian*, 18 Apr 1846: 3

114 Chernock, p. 437

115 J. A. Lloyd, 'Memoir on Madagascar', *Journal of the Royal Geographical Society of London*, Vol. 20, 1850, pp. 53–75, p. 67

116 Chernock, p. 442

117 Ibid, pp. 431–32

118 Ibid, p. 433
119 Chernock, p. 444; S. Ellis, p. 99
120 Deschamps, p. 151 and p. 163
121 R. O. The Great Island – Histoire de Madagascar. By Hubert Deschamps. Paris: Berger-Levrault, 1960. pp. 348, 31 plates. NF 19.50. *The Journal of African History*, Vol. 1(2), 1960, pp. 319–21; Robert F. Gray, *Africa: Journal of the International African Institute*, Vol. 31(3), 1961, pp. 283–85
122 Samuel Pasfield Oliver, *Madagascar: An Historical and Descriptive Account of the Island and Its Former Dependencies, Volume 1* (London: Macmillan and Co., 1886), p. 87
123 Ibid., pp. 87–8
124 Campbell (2012), p. 569; Ajayi, p. 170; Campbell (1992), p. 417
125 'Madagascar and its Christianity', *The British Quarterly Review*, Vol. 74, Apr 1863, pp. 300–13 in Chernock, p. 441
126 Horne, p. 189; Campbell (1992), p. 416
127 Chernock, p. 441
128 Oliver, p. 118 and pp. 240–42

Chapter 8: Nana Yaa Asantewaa

1 K. A. Busia, *The Position of the Chief in the Modern Political System of Ashanti* (London, 1951), p. 90
2 C. C. Reindorf, *The History of the Gold Coast and Asante*, (Basel, 1895), p. 90
3 Ivor Wilks, *Asante in the Nineteenth Century: The Structure and Evolution of a Political Order*, (African Studies, Series Number 13), Cambridge University Press, 1989, p. 38; Robin Law, 'Wheeled Transport in Pre-Colonial West Africa', *Africa: Journal of the International African Institute*, Vol. 50(3), 1980, pp. 249–62, p. 254
4 A. Adu Boahen, *Yaa Asantewaa and the Asante-British War of 1900–1*, 2003, edited with an editor's note by E. Akyeampong. Accra and Oxford: Sub-Saharan Publishers and James Currey, p. 116
5 Peter Herndon, Section 5: The Ashanti Way of Life, Family Life Among the Ashanti of West Africa, Curricular Resources, Unit 4 (91.02.04), Yale-New Haven Teachers Institute https://teachersinstitute.yale.edu/curriculum/units/1991/2/91.02.04/5
6 Boahen (2003), p. 117
7 R. S. Rattray, *Religion and Art in Ashanti* (Oxford: Clarendon Press, 1979), pp. 84–85
8 T. C. McCaskie, 'The Life and Afterlife of Yaa Asantewaa', *Africa: Journal of the International African Institute*, Vol. 77(2), 2007, pp. 151–79, pp. 155–56
9 Agnes Akosua Aidoo, 'From the Archives: Women In The History And

Culture Of Ghana', *Contemporary Journal of African Studies*, Vol. 9(2), 2022, pp. 187–213, p. 191

10 Ibid.

11 McCaskie (2007), p. 155

12 Ibid., pp. 151–52

13 Ibid., p. 152

14 Agnes Akosua Aidoo, 'Asante Queen Mothers in Government and Politics in the Nineteenth Century', *Journal of the Historical Society of Nigeria*, Vol. 9(1), 1977, pp. 1–13, p. 1

15 C. A. Diop, *The cultural unity of Black Africa: The domains of matriarchy & of patriarchy in classical antiquity* (London, England: Karnak House, 1989), p. 32

16 F. Boateng, 'African traditional education: A tool for intergenerational communication' in M. K. Asante & K. W. Asante (Eds), *African culture: The rhythms of unity* (pp. 109–122). (Trenton, NJ: Africa World Press), p. 114

17 Simphiwe Sesanti, 'African Philosophy in Pursuit of an African Renaissance for the True Liberation of African Women', *Journal of Black Studies*, Vol. 47(6), Sep 2016, pp. 479–96, p. 489; C. A. Diop, *Precolonial Black Africa* (New York, NY: Lawrence Hill Books, 1987), p. 48

18 Malcolm D. McLeod, The Asante (London, 1981) pp. 25–26 in Emmanuel Akyeampong and Pashington Obeng, 'Spirituality, Gender, and Power in Asante History', *The International Journal of African Historical Studies*, Vol. 28(3), 1995, pp. 481–508, p. 489

19 R. S. Rattray, Ashanti (London, 1923), p. 79

20 Akyeampong and Obeng, p. 489

21 Ibid., p. 498; Joseph Dupuis, *Journal of a Residence in Ashantee* (London, 1824), pp. 114–16; Aidoo (2022), p. 205

22 P. A. Owiredu, 'The Akan System of Inheritance Today and Tomorrow', *African Affairs*, Vol. 58(231), 1959, pp. 161–65, p. 161

23 'The "Abusua" or Family System', modernghana.com, https://www.modernghana.com/ghanahome/ashanti/ashanti.asp?menu_id=6&sub_menu_id=496&menu_id2=67&s=c

24 Kofi Awusabo-Asare, 'Matriliny and the New Intestate Succession Law of Ghana', *Canadian Journal of African Studies / Revue Canadienne Des Études Africaines*, Vol. 24(1), 1990, pp. 1–16, p. 5

25 Interview with Kobi, Kumasi, 31 Mar 2023

26 Manhyia Palace Museum, 'The Museum', https://web.archive.org/web/20110511063233/http://manhyiapalacemuseum.org/about-us.html

27 Interview with the Manhyia Palace guide, Kumasi, 1 Apr 2023

28 M. Leslie, 'Beyond hearsay and academic journalism: The black woman and Ali Mazrui', *Research in African Literatures*, 24(1), 1993, pp. 105–12, p. 109

29 Aidoo (1977), p. 2
30 Ibid., p. 4
31 McCaskie (2007), pp. 154–55
32 Ibid., p. 154; T. C. McCaskie (1984) 'Ahyiamu – "a place for meeting": an essay on process and event in the history of the Asante state', *The Journal of African History*, Vol. 25(2), pp. 169–88.
33 McCaskie (2007), p. 155
34 Aidoo (1977), p. 2
35 Akyeampong and Obeng, p. 488
36 Ibid., p. 490; Michelle Gilbert, 'The Cimmerian Darkness of Intrigue, Queen Mothers, Christianity and Truth in Akuapem History', *Journal of Religion in Africa*, Vol. 23(1), 1993, p. 9
37 Akyeampong and Obeng, p. 491; Aidoo (1977), p. 9
38 B. Stoeltje, 'Asante Queen Mothers in Ghana', *Oxford Research Encyclopedia of African History*, 25 Mar 2021, p. 5
39 Aidoo (1977), p. 2
40 Ibid.
41 McCaskie (2007), p. 156
42 Sharon F. Patton, 'The Stool and Asante Chieftaincy', *African Arts*, Vol. 13(1), 1979, pp. 74–77 and pp. 98–99, p. 74
43 Ibid.; K. Edusei. (2004) 'Art Forms in Ghana: The Stool as a Socio-Politico-Religious Symbol', *Journal of Science and Technology*, 24(1), pp. 59–67, pp. 59–61
44 Edusei, p. 66
45 Patton, p. 74
46 Alexander Y. A. Kyerematen, *Panoply of Ghana* (London: Longman Green & Co, 1964), p. 11
47 Edusei, p. 61
48 E. A. Degan (1988) *Asante Stools*, Galerie Amrad African Arts: Montreal, Canada.
49 Edusei, p. 62; Art Institute Chicago, 'Ceremonial Stool' [wood and brass], 1950–1999. 1995.148. Art Institute Chicago, Arts of Africa, Chicago, Illinois, https://www.artic.edu/artworks/137130/ceremonial-stool
50 Ibid.
51 Ibid.; Patton, p. 76
52 Osei Kwadwo (2000), *An Outline of Ashanti History* (O. Kwadwo Enterprise: Agona, Ashanti), p. 18; Patton, p. 74
53 Akyeampong and Obeng, pp. 483–86
54 Ibid.
55 McLeod, p. 57 in Akyeampong and Obeng, pp. 483-4
56 Degan (1988) in Edusei, p. 63
57 A. Kyerematen, 'The Royal Stools of Ashanti', *Africa: Journal of the*

International African Institute, Vol. 39(1), 1969, pp. 1–10, pp. 2–3; Ibid., p. 64

58 Kyerematen (1969), pp. 3–5; Akyeampong and Obeng, p. 498; Otto, p. 120

59 Edusei, p. 65

60 William Tordoff, 'The Ashanti Confederacy', *The Journal of African History*, Vol. 3(3), 1962, pp. 399–417, p. 401; Margaret Priestley and Ivor Wilks. 'The Ashanti Kings in the Eighteenth Century: A Revised Chronology', *The Journal of African History*, Vol. 1(1), 1960, pp. 83–96, p. 84

61 Priestley and Wilks, p. 86

62 Amanda L. Logan, 'Tasting Privilege and Privation during Asante Rule and the Atlantic Slave Trade', *The Scarcity Slot: Excavating Histories of Food Security in Ghana*, 1st ed., Vol. 75 (Berkeley: University of California Press, 2020), pp. 61–94, p. 70

63 Kwasi Konadu, 'Euro-African Commerce and Social Chaos: Akan Societies in the Nineteenth and Twentieth Centuries', *History in Africa*, Vol. 36, 2009, pp. 265–92, p. 266

64 Perbi, Akosua Adoma (2004). *A history of indigenous slavery in Ghana: from the 15th to the 19th century.* (Legon, Accra, Ghana: Sub-Saharan Publishers), p. 23

65 Konadu, p. 266; National Museums Liverpool, 'Abolition of the transatlantic slave trade' (n.d.): https://www.liverpoolmuseums.org.uk/history-of-slavery/abolition; UK Parliament, '1807 Abolition of the Slave Trade' (n.d.): https://www.parliament.uk/about/living-heritage/evolutionofparliament/2015-parliament-in-the-making/get-involved1/2015-banners-exhibition/maria-amidu/1807-abolition-of-the-slave-trade/

66 Ibid., p. 267

67 S. R. B. Attoh Ahuma (1972), 'One-Man Policy – A Curse to West Africa', *The Gold Coast Nation and National Consciousness*, Routledge, pp. 54–59, doi:10.4324/9781315033044-11; 'Thorburn, James Jamieson, (1864–14 Sep 1929), Governor and Commander-in-Chief, Gold Coast Colony, 1910–12; *Who's Who* (Oxford University Press, 1 Dec 2007) doi:10.1093/ww/9780199540884.013.u218141

68 Patterson R., The Third Anglo-Asante War, 1873–1874. In: Miller SM, ed. *Queen Victoria's Wars: British Military Campaigns, 1857–1902,* (Cambridge: Cambridge University Press, 2021), pp. 106–25. doi:10.1017/9781108785020.006

69 Aidoo (1977), pp. 6–8

70 W. E. F. Ward, 'Britain and Ashanti, 1874–1896', *Transactions of the Historical Society of Ghana*, Vol. 15(2), 1974, pp. 131–64, p. 131

71 'Asante Gold', The Victoria and Albert Museum, http://www.vam.ac.uk/content/articles/a/asante-gold/

72 A. Adu Boahen, 'Prempeh I in Exile', Paper presented at the national Cultural Centre, Kumasi, 19 Aug 1972, p. 4; Aidoo (1977), pp. 9–11

73 McCaskie (2007), p. 155

74 W. J. Donkoh, 'Yaa Asantewaa: a role model for womanhood in the new millennium', *JENdA: A Journal of Culture and African Women Studies*, 2001: http://www.jendajournal.com

75 McCaskie (2007), p. 155

76 Aidoo (1977), p. 12

77 Boahen (1972), p. 5

78 King of Asante to Governor, 7 May 1891 quoted by Tordoff, *Ashanti Under the Prempehs: 1888–1935*, 1965 (Oxford: Oxford University Press), pp. 43–44.

79 Boahen (2003), p. 13

80 Boahen (1972), pp. 5–6; Akyeampong and Obeng, p. 504; Harcourt Fuller, 'Commemorating an African Queen: Ghanaian Nationalism, the African Diaspora, and the Public Memory of Nana Yaa Asantewaa 1952–2009', *African Arts*, Vol. 47(4), Winter 2014, pp. 58–71, p. 60

81 Interview with Kobi, Kumasi, 31 Mar 2023

82 Akyeampong and Obeng, p. 504

83 Fuller, p. 60

84 UK Parliament Hansard archives, 'The Ashanti Expedition, Volume 91: debated on Tuesday 19 March 1901' https://hansard.parliament.uk/Commons/1901-03-19/debates/19ea3bcc-b7f4-4dab-9afc-0b9abe700ab4/TheAshantiExpedition?highlight=savage

85 Gaurav Desai, 2001, *Subject to Colonialism: African Self-Fashioning and the Colonial Library* (Durham: Duke University Press), p. 82

86 UK Parliament Hansard archives (1901)

87 B. Wasserman, 'The Ashanti War of 1900: A Study in Cultural Conflict', *Africa: Journal of the International African Institute*, Vol. 31(2), 1961, pp. 167–79, p. 170

88 Parliamentary Papers 1901: 'Correspondence relating to the Ashanti War 1900', p. 17 in Wasserman, p. 170; Asirifi-Danquah (2007), *The Struggle Between Two Great Queens, 1900–1901: Yaa Asantewaa of Edweso, Asante and Victoria of Great Britain* (Kumasi: Asirifi-Danquah Books Ltd), p. 60

89 Rattray, *Ashanti*, p. 292 in Wasserman, p. 169

90 McCaskie (2007), p. 157

91 Aidoo (1977), p. 12

92 Kofi Agyekum, 'The Ethnopragmatics of the Akan Palace Language of Ghana', *Journal of Anthropological Research*, Vol. 67(4), 2011, pp. 573–93, p. 583

93 Aidoo (1977), p. 12

94 Akyeampong and Obeng, p. 504

95 Aidoo (1977), p. 12

96   Boahen (2003), p. 168
97   Emmanuel Akyeampong, 'Christianity, Modernity and the Weight of
     Tradition in the Life of "Asantehene" Agyeman Prempeh I, c.1888–1931',
     Africa: Journal of the International African Institute, Vol. 69(2), 1999,
     pp. 279–311, p. 301
98   Fuller, pp. 60–61
99   Akyeampong and Obeng, p. 492
100 Akyeampong fieldnotes: Interview with Mawere Poku, Accra, 6 Aug 6 in
     Akyeampong and Obeng, p. 492
101 Ibid, p. 491
102 Fuller, p. 61; Otto, p. 121
103 Obrecht to Basel, 30 Jul 1900 (No. 1900.II.169); Paul Jenkins, 'Abstracts
     Concerning Gold Coast History from the Basel Mission Archives' (n.p.,
     n.d.)
104 Andrew Apter, 'History in the Dungeon: Atlantic Slavery and the Spirit of
     Capitalism in Cape Coast Castle', Ghana, The American Historical Review,
     Vol. 122(1), 1 Feb 2017, pp. 23–54, p. 49
105 Fuller, p. 61
106 Interview with Kumasi Armed Forces Museum guide, Kumasi, 1 Apr 2023
107 Nana Pokua Wiafe Mensah, 'Nana Yaa Asantewaa, The Queen Mother
     of Ejisu: The Unsung Heroine of Feminism In Ghana', MA thesis
     submitted to University of Toronto https://tspace.library.utoronto.ca/
     bitstream/1807/25684/3/WiafeMensah_Nana_P_201011_MAThesis.pdf p. 62
108 Akyeampong and Obeng, p. 505
109 Interview with Kumasi Armed Forces Museum guide, 1 Apr 2023
110 Lynda R. Day, 'What's Tourism Got to Do with It?: The Yaa Asantewa
     Legacy and Development in Asanteman', Africa Today, Vol. 51(1), Autumn
     2004, pp. 99–113, p. 109; Obrecht to Basel, 1900; Jenkins (n.d)
111 Aidoo (1977), p. 13
112 Day, p. 109
113 Akyeampong fieldnotes: Interview with Mawere Poku, Accra, 30 Aug, 19
     in Akyeampong and Obeng, p. 506
114 Interview with Kumasi Armed Forces Museum guide, 1 Apr 2023
115 Mensah, p. 65
116 Tom C. McCaskie, 'Local Knowledge: an Akuapem Twi History of Asante',
     History in Africa, Vol. 38, 2011, pp. 169–92, p. 188
117 McCaskie (2007), p. 159–60; Fuller, p. 61
118 Day, pp. 106–07
119 Ibid., p. 99 and p. 103
120 Ibid., pp. 59–60
121 Fuller, p. 64

Chapter 9: Muhumusa

1   National Museums of Rwanda (archived in 2008): http://www.museum.
gov.rw/2_museums/kigali/kandt_house/pages_html/intro/page_intro.htm

2   Ibid.

3   Visit Rwanda, 'Kandt House Museum': https://visitrwanda.com/interests/
kandt-house-museum/

4   Rwanda Cultural Heritage Academy, 'Traditional Hairstyles of Rwanda',
Google Arts and Culture (n.d): https://artsandculture.google.com/story/
traditional-hairstyles-of-rwanda-rwanda-cultural-heritage-academy/
xwWRUcIyLjxKcg?hl=en

5   Dominique Uwizeyimana, 'Social Exclusion in Rwanda Under Different
Leadership Regimes', *International Journal of Applied Business and
Economic Research*, Vol. 15, 2017, pp. 1–39, p. 10

6   K. Firestone, 2014. 'The Pygmy Peoples Living in the Rwenzori Mountain
Forest in Uganda', http://www.zoharafricansafaris.com/the-pygmy-peoples-
living-in-the-rwenzori-mountain-forest-in-uganda/ in Uwizeyimana, p. 10

7   E. Galloway (2010), Created for Vinny Ferraro's World Politics class,
Mount Holyoke College, https://www.mtholyoke.edu/~gallo22e/classweb/
Website-World%20Politics/History.html in Uwizeyimana, p. 10; African
Studies Center, 'Rwanda – History', University of Pennsylvania (n.d.):
https://www.africa.upenn.edu/NEH/rwhistory.htm; African Studies
Center, 'Rwanda – Ethnic Groups', University of Pennsylvania (n.d.):
https://www.africa.upenn.edu/NEH/rwethnic.htm

8   Jan Vansina, *Paths in the Rainforests: Toward a History of Political
Tradition in Equatorial Africa*, (Wisconsin: University of Wisconsin Press,
1990), p. 1

9   J. D. Gasanabo (2004), 'Mémoires et Histoire Scolaire: Le Cas du Rwanda
de 1962 à 1994'. PhD thesis submitted to the University of Geneva: http://
archive-ouverte.unige. ch/unige:282, p. 115 in Uwizeyimana, p. 10; Aimable
Twagilimana, *Historical Dictionary of Rwanda* (USA: Scarecrow Press Inc,
2007), p. 80; African Studies Center, 'Rwanda – History'

10   Gasanabo, p. 115

11   Uwizeyimana, p. 11

12   Billy Batare, 'Rwandan Ethnic Conflicts: A Historical Look at Root
Causes' (Austria: European Peace University, 2012), p. 3

13   Galloway, p. 1

14   Batare, p. 3

15   Newbury, p. 306

16   Ibid., p. 307

17   Ibid.

18   Ibid., p. 307 and p. 309

19   René Lemarchand, 'Power and Stratification in Rwanda: A

Reconsideration', *Cahiers d'Études Africaines*, Vol. 6(24), 1966, pp. 592–610, p. 599

20 Ibid.; Uwizeyimana, p. 12

21 Uwizeyimana, p. 12

22 E. Rurangwa, (2013), 'Land Tenure Reform. The Case Study of Rwanda: International Gorilla Conservation Program, Rwanda.' Paper presented at the Conference on Land Divided: Land and South African Society in 2013, in Comparative Perspective. University of Cape Town, 24–27 March 2013 in ibid., p. 13

23 African Studies Center (n.d.)

24 Uwizeyimana, p. 13

25 Batare, p. 1 in ibid., p. 13; M. I. Midlarsky, *The Killing Trap* (New York: Cambridge University Press, 2005), p. 162

26 F. Keane, Second-class Citizens, p. 1 in Uwizeyimana, p. 13

27 Human Rights Watch, 'Rwanda: History' (1999): https://www.hrw.org/reports/1999/rwanda/Geno1-3-09.htm

28 Newbury, pp. 306–07

29 Patrick Gathara, 'Berlin 1884: Remembering the conference that divided Africa', *Aljazeera.com*, 15 Nov 2019: https://www.aljazeera.com/opinions/2019/11/15/berlin-1884-remembering-the-conference-that-divided-africa

30 Ibid.; Matthew Craven, 'Between law and history: the Berlin Conference of 1884–1885 and the logic of free trade', *London Review of International Law*, Vol. 3(1), 2015, pp. 31–59, pp. 31–32

31 Elizabeth Heath, 'Berlin Conference of 1884–1885', *Oxford Reference*: https://www.oxfordreference.com/display/10.1093/acref/9780195337709.001.0001/acref-9780195337709-e-0467

32 Gathara (2019)

33 Ibid.

34 Aaron O'Neill, 'Number of African countries under European control 1914 (based on current borders)', *Statista.com*, 19 Jun 2024: https://www.statista.com/statistics/1039152/number-african-countries-under-european-control-1914/

35 George Shepperson, 'The Centennial of the West African Conference of Berlin, 1884–1885', *Phylon (1960-)*, Vol. 46(1), 1985, pp. 37–48, p. 43

36 Gathara (2019)

37 Eleanor Masters, 'The Berlin Conference and the New Imperialism in Africa', AMdigital.co.uk, 7 March 2023, https://www.amdigital.co.uk/insights/blog/the-berlin-conference-and-the-new-imperialism-in-africa

38 Gathara (2019)

39 Terence Ranger, 'The Invention of Tradition in Colonial Africa', In: Hobsbawm E, Ranger T, eds. *The Invention of Tradition*, Canto Classics, (Cambridge University Press, 2012) pp. 211–62, p. 221

40 Aaron O'Neill (2024)
41 Atrocities Watch Africa, 'King Leopold of Belgium in Congo' (n.d.): https://atrocitieswatch.org/publications/king-leopold-of-belgium-in-congo/
42 Newbury, p. 310
43 Paul Rutayisire, 'Rwanda Under German and Belgian Colonization' in *History of Rwanda* (Kigali: National Unity and Reconciliation Commission), pp. 165–410, p. 211
44 Newbury, p. 310
45 Mwambari, Walsh & Olonisakin, p. 482
46 Rutayisire, pp. 211–12
47 Alison Des Forges, *Defeat is the Only Bad News: Rwanda under Musinga, 1896–1931* (Wisconsin: University of Wisconsin Press, 2011), p. 103
48 Interviews with Christian and Jean at the Roots of Nyabinghi Heritage Center, Burera, 3 May 2023
49 Des Forges, p. 103
50 David L. Schoenbrun, 'A Past Whose Time Has Come: Historical Context and History in Eastern Africa's Great Lakes', *History and Theory*, Vol. 32(4), Beiheft 32: History Making in Africa, Dec 1993, pp. 32–56, p. 34
51 Rutayisire, p. 168
52 Ibid., p. 202 and p. 217
53 Interview with Jean, 3 May 2023
54 Rutayisire, p. 216
55 Human Rights Watch (1999)
56 Des Forges, p. 79
57 Rutayisire, p. 214
58 Des Forges, p. 104
59 Ibid., p. 189
60 Uwizeyimana, p. 16
61 Gudrun Honke, *Au plus profound de l'Afrique* (Wuppertal: Hammer Verlag, 1990), p. 100
62 Rutayisire, p. 173
63 Ibid., p. 179
64 Bernard Lugan, 'Sources écrites pouvant servir à l'histoire du Rwanda (1863–1918)' in *Etudes Rwandaises*, XIV, numéro spécial (1980), p. 46 in ibid, p. 180
65 Rutayisire, pp. 186–87
66 Interview with a tour guide at the Kandt House Museum, 3 May 2023
67 Jaques J. Maquet, 'The Kingdom of Ruanda', in *African Worlds*, ed. Daryll Forde (Oxford: Oxford University Press, 1954), pp. 164–89, pp. 172–73
68 Eric Lane, 'Kigeri II Meets That Peculiar Lady, Nyirabiyoro: A Study in Prophecies', *History of Religions*, Vol. 13(2), Nov 1973, pp. 129–48, p. 134, emphasis added by author

69 Ibid.; J. Nyirahabimana & J. C. Nkejabahizi, 'Ndorwá Famous Women', *Rwanda Journal, Series A: Arts and Humanities*, Vol. 1(1), 2016, pp. 17–31, p. 18

70 King Ndahura II Imara Kashagama of Busongora, 'Queen Kitami and the Rise and Fall of Mpororo', Busongora Kingdom, 8 Jan 2016, https://www.busongora-chwezi.org/history/queen-kitami-and-the-rise-and-fall-of-mpororo

71 E. M. Jack, 'The Mufumbiro Mountains', *The Geographical Journal*, Vol. 41(6), Jun 1913, pp. 532–47, p. 544

72 Interviews with Christian and Jean at the Roots of Nyabinghi Heritage Center, Burera, 3 May 2023

73 Jack, p. 544–5

74 Elizabeth Hopkins, 'The Nyabingi Cult of Southwestern Uganda' in *Protest and Power in Black Africa*, ed. Robert Rotberg and Ali Mazrui, (New York: Oxford, 1970)

75 Max Dashu, 'Shamanic priestesses of East Africa' (2007), Suppressed Histories, https://www.suppressedhistories.net/articles/nyabingi/bagirwa.html

76 Lane, p. 139

77 Ibid., p. 140; Hopkins, p. 99

78 M. J. Bessell, 'Nyabingi', *Uganda Journal*, Vol. VI(2), 1938, pp. 73–86, p. 77

79 Des Forges, pp. 103–04

80 Bessell, p. 78

81 Jack, p. 538

82 Ine Van Caekenberghe, 'Was traditional Rwandan high-jumping really Olympic class? What we found', *The Conversation*, 17 May 2021, https://theconversation.com/was-traditional-rwandan-high-jumping-really-olympic-class-what-we-found-159160

83 Interviews with Christian and Jean, 3 May 2023

84 Interview with Jean, 3 May 2023

85 Ibid.

86 Lane, p. 140

87 Hopkins, p. 61

88 Schoenbrun, p. 41

89 Bessell, pp. 78–79

90 Des Forges, pp. 117–18

91 Ibid., p. 120

92 Ibid.; Bessell, p. 80

93 Bessell, p. 80

94 Ibid., p. 81

95 Terisa E. Turner, 'Women, Rastafari and the New Society: Caribbean and East African roots of a popular movement against structural adjustment',

Labour, Capital and Society / Travail, capital et société, April / avril, Vol. 24(1), Apr 1991, pp. 66–89, p. 71

96 Ibid.
97 Interview with Christian on Lake Burera, Burera, 3 May 2023
98 Turner (1991), p. 73
99 Safiya Sinclair, *How to Say Babylon: A Jamaican Memoir* (London: 4th Estate, 2023), p. 9
100 Addison E. Southard, *National Geographic*, Jun 1931 in Derek Bishton, 'The Coronation of His Imperial Majesty Haile Selassie' (n.d): https://derekbishton.com/the-coronation-of-his-imperial-majesty-haile-selassie/
101 Ibid.
102 Horace Campbell, *Rasta and Resistance: From Marcus Garvey to Walter Rodney* (New Jersey: Africa World Press, Inc., 1987), p. 73
103 C. L. R. James, 'New society: new people', pp. 73–84, 1984 (1964), p. 164 in Turner, p. 68
104 Lisa-Anne Julien, 'Great Black Warrior Queens: An Examination of the Gender Currents within Rastafari Thought and the Adoption of a Feminist Agenda in the Rasta Women's Movement', *Agenda: Empowering Women for Gender Equity*, No. 57, Urban Culture, 2003, pp. 76–83, p. 77
105 Sinclair, p. 30
106 H. Campbell, p. 72
107 Ibid.; Sinclair, p. 30
108 H. Campbell, p. 72
109 Ras Zuke, *The Rastaman Vibration* (Florida: Far-Eye Productions, 2002), pp. 39–40
110 Joan French and Honor Ford-Smith, 'Women's work and organisation in Jamaica, 1990–1944', unpublished research study for the Institute of Social Studies, The Hague, Netherlands, 1987, p. 5 in Turner, p. 74
111 Turner, p. 74
112 Julien, p. 78
113 Turner, p. 73 and p. 75
114 Ibid., p. 72
115 Julien, p. 79
116 Sinclair, pp. 9–10
117 Interview with Christian, 3 May 2023
118 Turner, p. 71
119 Ibid., pp. 71–72; Dashu (2007)
120 Ras Zuke, pp. 38–42
121 Flyer for 1987 St Paul's Carnival on loan from Bristol Archives, included in the Beyond the Bassline exhibition at British Library, London, Jun 2024
122 Human Rights Watch (1999)
123 Information from the Kigali Genocide Memorial, visited on 5 May 2024
124 D. S. Wilson, 'Navigating the Dark Waters of Evil: The Roles of Colonial

Interference, Propaganda, and Obedience in the 1994 Rwandan Genocide', *The Alexandrian*, Vol. 1(1), 2012, pp. 1–7, p. 1

125 Uwizeyimana, p. 17

126 The Kigali Genocide Memorial

127 Deborah Mayersen, 'A political monopoly held by one race: The politicisation of ethnicity in Colonial Rwanda', University of Wollongong, 2011, pp. 167–80, pp. 171–72

128 Latham-Koenig, p. 292

129 Ibid.

130 Ibid.

131 Ibid., pp. 292–94

132 The Kigali Genocide Memorial

133 Interview with Paul, Kigali, 5 May 2023

134 The Kigali Genocide Memorial

135 Tharcisse Seminega, 'The Hutu Ten Commandments', No Greater Love, https://www.rwanda-nogreaterlove.com/hutu-10-commandments

136 The Kigali Genocide Memorial

137 Human Rights Watch, 'Genocide in Rwanda: Numbers' (1999): https://www.hrw.org/reports/1999/rwanda/Geno1-3-04.htm

138 Al Jazeera, 'France 'enabled' 1994 Rwanda genocide, report says', Apr 2021: https://www.aljazeera.com/news/2021/4/19/france-enabled-1994-rwanda-genocide-report-says

139 Uri Misgav, 'The Israeli Guns That Took Part in the Rwanda Genocide', Jan 2015, Haaretz: https://www.haaretz.com/2015-01-03/ty-article/.premium/the-israeli-guns-in-the-rwanda-genocide/0000017f-db06-df9c-a17f-ff1ef7130000; i24NEWS, 'Israel was aware of violence against Hutus before Rwandan genocide, new documents show', May 2019, i24NEWS: https://www.i24news.tv/en/news/international/africa/1556826403-israel-was-aware-of-violence-against-hutus-before-rwandan-genocide-new-documents-show

140 Dick Wittenberg, ' "He killed my sister. Now I see his remorse": the extraordinary stories of survivors of the Rwandan genocide who forgave their attackers', *The Guardian*, 6 Apr 2024: https://www.theguardian.com/world/2024/apr/06/he-killed-my-sister-now-i-see-his-remorse-survivors-of-rwandan-genocide

141 The Kigali Genocide Memorial

142 Wittenberg (2024)

143 Michael Ferragamo, 'Thirty Years After Rwanda's Genocide: Where the Country Stands Today', Council on Foreign Relations, Apr 2024: https://www.cfr.org/in-brief/thirty-years-after-rwandas-genocide-where-country-stands-today

144 Ibid.

145 Shola Lawal, 'As Rwanda votes, tensions with neighbouring DR

Congo deepen over M23', 15 Jul 2024: https://www.aljazeera.com/features/2024/7/15/as-rwanda-votes-tensions-with-neighbouring-dr-congo-deepen-over-m23

146 Shola Lawal, 'Rwanda-DRC tension: Have rebels taken control of Congolese city? What next?', *Al Jazeera*, 27 Jan 2025: https://www.aljazeera.com/news/2025/1/27/rwanda-drc-tension-have-rebels-taken-control-of-congolese-city-what-next; Carlos Mureithi, 'Rwandan-backed rebels M23 claim capture of eastern DRC city Goma', *The Guardian*, 27 Jan 2025: https://www.theguardian.com/world/2025/jan/27/m23-rebel-group-goma-drc-democratic-republic-congo-rwanda; Wedaeli Chibelushi & Marina Daras, 'Rebels kill DR Congo governor as fighting intensifies', BBC News, 24 Jan 2025: https://www.bbc.co.uk/news/articles/ckgy6qlv5kro

Chapter 10: Labotsibeni Mdluli

1   Leroy Vail, editor, *The Creation of Tribalism in Southern Africa*, (London: Currey; Berkeley: University of California Press, 1989) p. 290

2   Sabelo Gumedze, 'Swaziland', *Human Rights Law in Africa Online*, 2004, pp. 1580–81

3   Vail, p. 290

4   Balam Nyeko, 'Pre-Nationalist Resistance to Colonial Rule: Swaziland on the Eve of the Imposition of British Administration, 1890–1902', *Transafrican Journal of History*, Vol. 5(2), 1976, pp. 66–83, p. 71

5   Ibid.

6   Thoko Ginindza (1997), Labotsibeni/Gwamile Mdluli. Annals of the New York Academy of Sciences, 810: pp. 135–58, p. 139

7   Hilda Kuper, *Sobhuza II: Ngwenyama and King of Swaziland* (New York: Holmes and Meier, Africana Publishing Co., 1978), p. 18

8   Ibid.

9   Ibid.

10 Ginindza, p. 139

11 Kuper (1978), pp. 18–19

12 Sarah Mkhonza, 'Queen Labotsibeni and Abantu-Batho', *The People's Paper: A Centenary History and Anthology of Abantu-Batho*, edited by Peter Limb, (Wits University Press, 2012), pp. 128–50, p. 131

13 Nyeko, p. 72

14 Five Hundred Year Archive (FHYA) and Historical Papers, University of the Witwatersrand, Johannesburg (WITS), 'Nkambule, edited typescript', WITS A2760 Inventory 2015: Transcript: 24/04/70, (?) Nkambule, area Buseleni, 1 page: https://fhya.uct.ac.za/nkambule-edited-typescript?query=Madsolomafisha%20Nkambule.

    It is important to note that there is confusion as to whether Mbandezi's mother was Tibati or her sister Nandzi Nkambule who is said to have died young.

15 Nyeko, p. 72
16 Hugh MacMillan, 'Decolonisation and the Triumph of "Tradition"', *The Journal of Modern African Studies*, Vol. 23(4), Dec 1985, pp. 643–66, p. 645
17 Hamilton Sipho Simelane, 'Swazi Resistance to Boer Penetration and Domination, 1881–1898', *Transafrican Journal of History*, Vol. 18, 1989, pp. 117–46, p. 119
18 Ibid.
19 Ibid., pp. 119–20
20 Nyeko, p. 72
21 Ibid.; Simelane (1989), p. 120
22 Simelane (1989), p. 120
23 Ibid.
24 Hilda Kuper, *An African Aristocracy: Rank Among the Swazi* (New York: Holmes and Meier, Africana Publishing Co., 1947), p. 25
25 Ginindza, pp. 141–42
26 Kuper (1947), p. 24
27 Ginindza, p. 155
28 Ibid.
29 Ibid.
30 Ibid., p. 136
31 Nyeko, p. 68
32 Ibid., pp. 68–69
33 Alan R. Booth, ' "European Courts Protect Women and Witches": Colonial Law Courts As Redistributors of Power in Swaziland 1920–1950', *Journal of Southern African Studies*, Vol. 18(2), Jun 1992, pp. 253–75, p. 256
34 Nyeko, p. 69
35 Ibid.
36 Ibid., p. 75
37 Kuper (1978), p. 26
38 Simelane (1989), p. 121
39 Ibid.
40 Ryan Moore, 'The Rise and Fall of the Orange Free State and Transvaal in South Africa', Library of Congress Blogs, 28 Jun 2018: https://blogs.loc.gov/maps/2018/06/the-rise-and-fall-of-the-orange-free-state-and-transvaal-in-southern-africa/
41 Ibid.
42 J. E. Yarett, 'The British annexation of the Transvaal: an American view', *Historia*, Vol. 19(1), Jan 1974, pp. 46–59; John Laband, The First Anglo-Boer War, 1880–1881. In: Miller SM, ed. *Queen Victoria's Wars: British Military Campaigns, 1857–1902* (Cambridge: Cambridge University Press, 2021), pp. 167–86.

43 Simelane (1989), p. 121

44 Ibid., p. 122

45 Ibid., p. 123

46 Nyeko, pp. 72–73 and p. 76

47 Simelane (1989), p. 126

48 C. 6201 Vol. L11, Enclosure in No. 3, Report on Swaziland by F. De Winton, p. 95 in ibid.

49 Quoted in Ronald Hyam, *The Failure of South African Expansion, 1908–1948* (London: The Macmillan Press, 1972), p. 6

50 Nyeko, p. 75–76

51 Ibid., p. 77

52 Ibid.; Kuper (1978), p. 26

53 Ginindza, pp. 143–44

54 Ibid., p. 140

55 Ibid., p. 144

56 Simelane (1989), pp. 130–32

57 Ibid., p. 133

58 Ibid., p. 134

59 Ibid., p. 137

60 Kuper (1978), p. 29

61 C. 9206, Vol. LXIII, p. 831, Enclosure 2 in No. 11, From Her Majesty's Consul, Swaziland, to High Commissioner, 20 May 1898 in Simelane (1989), p. 137

62 Simelane (1989), pp. 136–37

63 Ibid., pp. 137–38

64 Ibid., pp. 140–41

65 Ibid., p. 141

66 Manzini City Council, 'History of Manzini' (n.d.): https://mzcitycouncil.sz/history-of-manzini/

67 Ginindza, p. 144

68 Quoted in J. S. M. Matsebula, *A History of Swaziland* (Johannesburg: Longman, 1976), p. 139.

69 Bruce Lincoln, 'Ritual, Rebellion, Resistance: Once More the Swazi Ncwala', Man, New Series, Vol. 22(1), March 1987, pp. 132–56, p. 133; The Kingdom of Eswatini, 'Incwala Festival' (n.d.): https://www.thekingdomofeswatini.com/eswatini-experiences/events/incwala-festival/

70 Ibid., p. 135; 'Incwala Festival'; The Kingdom of eSwatini, 'A look back on Incwala, a blend of colour and culture', Dec 2021: https://www.thekingdomofeswatini.com/news-blogs/a-look-back-on-incwala-a-blend-of-colour-and-culture/

71 Simelane (1989), p. 141

72 Ginindza, p. 144

73 Kuper (1978), p. 30

74 Ginindza, p. 145
75 PRO. DO. 119/472/C4, Administration of Swaziland: Telegram No. 235 from High Commissioner to Governor of Natal, 21 Sep 1900 in Hamilton Sipho Simelane, 'Landlessness and Imperial Response in Swaziland 1938–1950', *Journal of Southern African Studies*, Vol. 17(4), Dec 1991, pp. 717–41, pp. 718–19
76 South African History Online, 'Black Concentration Camps during the Anglo-Boer War 2, 1900–1902' (2011): https://www.sahistory.org.za/article/black-concentration-camps-during-anglo-boer-war-2-1900-1902
77 South African History Online, 'Peace Treaty of Vereeniging – transcript' (2012): https://www.sahistory.org.za/archive/peace-treaty-vereeniging-transcript
78 F. J. Mashasha, (1974) *The Swazi and Land Partition (1902–1910)*. Collected Seminar Papers. Institute of Commonwealth Studies, 17, pp. 87–107, p. 87
79 Ginindza, p. 142
80 Kuper (1978), p. 38
81 Mashasha, p. 87
82 Ibid., p. 88
83 Booth, pp. 256–57
84 Swaziland National Archives, RCS 186/2, Queen Regent Labotsibeni to High Commissioner (1905)
85 David E. Torrance, 'Britain, South Africa, and the High Commission Territories: An Old Controversy Revisited', *The Historical Journal*, Vol. 41(3), Sep 1998, pp. 751–72, p. 754; Simelane (1991), p. 719
86 Ginindza, p. 142
87 Simelane (1991), p. 719
88 Macmillan (1985), p. 645
89 Mashasha, p. 101; Macmillan (1985), p. 645
90 Ginindza, p. 143; Hugh Macmillan, 'Administrators, Anthropologists and "Traditionalists" in Colonial Swaziland: The Case of the "Amabhaca" Fines', *Africa: Journal of the International African Institute*, Vol. 65(4), 1995, pp. 545–64, pp. 551–52
91 Macmillan (1985), p. 645
92 Macmillan (1995), p. 552
93 Ibid.; Booth, p. 259
94 Kuper (1978), pp. 71–74 in Macmillan (1985), pp. 645–46
95 eSwatini National Trust Commission, 'Matenga Nature Reserve and Cultural Village': https://entc.org.sz/mantenga/ [website error: 01.12.2024]
96 For more, see Stuart Laycock, *All the Countries We've Ever Invaded: And the Few We Never Got Round To* (Gloucestershire: The History Press, 2012), Caroline M. Elkins, *Legacy of Violence: A History of the British Empire* (New York, NY: Alfred A. Knopf, 2022) and Sathnam Sanghera,

Empireworld: How British Imperialism Has Shaped the Globe (London: Penguin, 2024).

97   Dean MacCannell, *The Tourist: A New Theory of the Leisure Class* (New York: Schocken Books, 1976) in Lynda R. Day, 'What's Tourism Got to Do with It?: The Yaa Asantewa Legacy and Development in Asanteman', *Africa Today*, Vol. 51(1), Autumn 2004, pp. 99–113, p. 101; Day, p. 101

98   Dr. Koson Srisang quoted in David Nicholson-Lord (1997) 'The Politics of Travel: Is Tourism Just Colonialism in another Guise?' *The Nation*, 265, pp. 11–18, p. 14

99   Day, p. 101; Victor T. C. Middleton, with Rebecca Hawkins, *Sustainable Tourism: A Marketing Perspective*, (Oxford: Butterworth-Heinemann, 1998), p. 76

100 Ginindza, p. 143

101 Ayanda Dlamini, 'Celebrating the woman of steel: Gwamile!', *eSwatini Observer*, 9 Aug 2020: http://new.observer.org.sz/details.php?id=13373

102 Ibid.

103 Kuper (1978), p. 47

104 Ginindza, p. 146

105 Ibid., pp. 147–48

106 Ibid., p. 148

107 Kuper (1978), pp. 48–49

108 Ginindza, pp. 155–57

109 Labotsibeni's address from the Swaziland Archives, quoted in ibid., p. 157

110 Macmillan (1985), pp. 646–47

111 Labotsibeni's address in Ginindza, p. 157

112 Macmillan (1985), p. 646

113 Labotsibeni's address in Ginindza, p. 157

114 Ibid.

115 Alan R. Booth, 'Review: The Kingdom of Swaziland by D. Hugh Gillis', *The International Journal of African Historical Studies*, Vol. 32(2/3), 1999, pp. 476–77

Chapter 11: Ririkumutima

1   Interview with Jean-Bosco at the Museum of Gitega, Gitega, 7 May 2023

2   Ibid.

3   Josephine Ntahobari & Basilissa Ndayiziga, 'The role of Burundian women in the peaceful settlement of conflicts' in Women and peace in Africa: Case studies on traditional conflict resolution practices (Paris: UNESCO, 2003), pp. 11–26, p. 19

4   Ibid., p. 19

5   Interview with Jean-Bosco, Gitega, 7 May 2023

6   Ntahobari & Ndayiziga, pp. 19–20

7   Jean Berchmans Ndihokubwayo & Apollinaire Ndayisenga, 'Reflection on the place of women in Burundian society', Conference paper (2019), p. 3, https://www.researchgate.net/publication/331284817_Reflection_on_the_place_of_women_in_Burundian_society

8   Interview with Jean-Bosco, Gitega, 7 May 2023

9   Ntahobari & Ndayiziga, pp. 19–20

10 David Newbury, 'Precolonial Burundi and Rwanda: Local Loyalties, Regional Royalties', *The International Journal of African Historical Studies*, Vol. 34(2), 2001, pp. 255–314, p. 284

11 Présidence de la République du Burundi, 'Barundi, Barundikazi, Bakunzi b'Uburundi', INTAHE 2019: https://www.presidence.gov.bi/wp-content/uploads/2019/06/INTAHE-2019.doc; Jean de Dieu, 'The State House Ntare Rushatsi Has Been Inaugurated', Agence Burundaise De Presse, 2 Oct 2019, https://abpinfos.com/the-state-house-ntare-rushatsi-has-been-inaugurated

12 Newbury, p. 282

13 Interview with Jean-Bosco, 7 May 2023

14 Newbury, p. 284

15 Ibid.

16 Ibid., p. 285

17 Christopher Buyers, 'Burundi Genealogy – Modern' (n.d.), https://www.royalark.net/Burundi/burundi6.htm; Jeremy Rich, 'Ririkumutima', *The Dictionary of African Biography, Book 5* ed. by Henry Louis Gates, Emmanuel Akyeampong, and Steven J. Niven (Oxford: Oxford University Press, 2012), pp. 204–05, p. 204

18 Buyers (n.d.)

19 Rich, p. 204; Ntahobari & Ndayiziga, p. 21

20 Rich, p. 204

21 Newbury, pp. 285–86

22 Ibid., p. 287

23 Ibid., p. 286

24 Roger Botte, 'Rwanda and Burundi, 1889–1930: Chronology of a Slow Assassination, Part 1', *The International Journal of African Historical Studies*, Vol. 18(1), 1985, pp. 53–91, pp. 82–83

25 Interview with Jean-Bosco, 7 May 2023

26 Rich, p. 204

27 Ndihokubwayo & Ndayisenga, p. 3

28 Newbury, p. 287

29 Ibid.

30 Botte, p. 59

31 Rich, p. 204

32 Ibid.

33 Ntahobari & Ndayiziga, p. 21

34   Rich, pp. 204–05
35   Buyers (n.d.)
36   Rich, p. 205
37   Buyers (n.d.); ibid.
38   Rich, p. 205
39   Laura Cole, 'Untold history: The WWI battles that levelled East Africa', Al Jazeera, 6 Nov 2018, https://www.aljazeera.com/features/2018/11/6/untold-history-the-wwi-battles-that-levelled-east-africa
40   Ibid.
41   Rich, p. 204
42   Ibid., p. 205
43   Jacques Vanderlinden, *Pierre Ryckmans, 1891–1959: Coloniser dans l'honneur* (Brussels: DeBoeck, 1994), p. 70
44   Rich, p. 205
45   A. L. Latham-Koenig, 'Ruanda-Urundi on the Threshold of Independence', *The World Today*, Vol. 18(7), Jul 1962, pp. 288–95, p. 288
46   Augustin Nsanze, 'Contributions to the Understanding of Recent History', *African Studies Review*, Vol. 45(1), 2002, pp. 150–54, p. 154
47   Latham-Koenig, p. 289
48   Ibid.
49   Arthur Blouin, 'Culture and Contracts: The Historical Legacy of Forced Labour', *The Economic Journal*, Vol. 132(641), Jan 2022, pp. 89–105, p. 90
50   Latham-Koenig, p. 290; Interview with Jean-Bosco, 7 May 2023
51   Latham-Koenig, p. 289
52   Timothy Longman, *Christianity and Genocide in Rwanda*, African Studies (Cambridge: Cambridge University Press, 2009), p. 44
53   Latham-Koenig, p. 288
54   René Lemarchand, 'Political instability in Africa: the case of Rwanda and Burundi', *Civilisations*, Vol. 16(3), 1966, pp. 307–37, p. 311; Frederick Duke of Mecklemburg, *In the Heart of Africa* (London: Cassei and Co., Ltd., 1910), p. 47
55   Latham-Koenig, p. 288 and p. 291
56   Lemarchand (1966a), p. 312; Longman, p. 44
57   Rich., p. 205
58   UNESCO World Heritage Convention, 'The sacred natural landscapes of Muramvya, Mpotsa and Nkiko-Mugamba', 9 May 2007, https://whc.unesco.org/en/tentativelists/5143/

Chapter 12: Makobo Modjadji VI

1   Interview with Anthony, Ga-Modjadji, 27 Apr 2023
2   Thembani Dube, 'The Kalanga in Historical Perspective', *Oxford Research Encyclopedia of African History*, 2020, pp. 1–2

3   Ndzimu-unami Emmanuel, *The Rebirth of Bukalanga* (Maphungubgwe: Maphungubgwe News Corporation, 2012), p. 10

4   Ibid., p.7

5   Moyahabo Rosinah Mohale, *Khelobedu Cultural Evolution Through Oral Tradition* (Pretoria: University of South Africa, 2014), p. 2

6   M.W. Prinsloo, 'Queenship of the Lobedu of Modjadji: aantekeninge', *Journal of South African Law / Tydskrif vir die Suid-Afrikaanse Reg*, Vol. 4, 2005, https://journals.co.za/doi/10.10520/EJC54994

7   Beth Greene, 'The Institution of Woman-Marriage in Africa: A Cross-Cultural Analysis', *Ethnology*, Vol. 37(4), 1998, pp. 395–412, p. 397

8   Mohale, p. 4

9   Interview with TC Kgopa, Polokwane, 27 Apr 2023

10 Gosiame Amy Goitsemodimo, 'Modjadji – the Rain Queen', *National Museum Publications*, 6 Sep 2019, https://nationalmuseumpublications.co.za/modjadji-the-rain-queen/

11 Donald G. McNeil Jr., 'Modjadji V, Rain Queen, Dies in South Africa at 64', *The New York Times*, 30 Jun 2001, https://www.nytimes.com/2001/06/30/world/modjadji-v-rain-queen-dies-in-south-africa-at-64.html

12 Ibid.

13 Ngwako Modjadji, 'Rain queen's heir yet to be named', *Mail & Guardian*, 6 Jul 2001, https://mg.co.za/article/2001-07-06-rain-queens-heir-yet-to-be-named/

14 Patricia Davison and George Mahashe, 'Visualizing the Realm of a Rain-Queen: The Production and Circulation of Eileen and Jack Krige's Lobedu Fieldwork Photographs from the 1930s', Kronos, No. 38, Special Issue Documentary, Nov 2012, pp. 47–81, p. 65; McNeil Jr (2001)

15 Eileen Jensen Krige, 'The Place of the North-Eastern Transvaal Sotho in the South Bantu Complex', *Africa: Journal of the International African Institute*, Vol. 11(3), Jul 1938, pp. 265–293, p. 271

16 Cheryl Fish, 'Review: Traveling Hopefully', *The Women's Review of Books*, Vol. 19(1), Oct 2001, pp. 21–22, p. 22

17 McNeil Jr (2001)

18 AP, 'Queen Modjadji', *The Economist*, 5 Jul 2001, https://www.economist.com/obituary/2001/07/05/queen-modjadji

19 Kabelo O. Motasa, 'Patriarchal Usurpation of the Modjadji Dynasty: A Gender-critical Reading of the History and Reign of the Modjadji Rain Queens', *Pharos Journal of Theology*, Vol. 102, 2021, pp. 1–19, pp. 8–9

20 Davison and Mahashe, p. 51

21 Interview with TC Kgopa, 27 Apr 2023

22 M. W. Prinsloo, 'Queenship of the Lobedu of Modjadji: aantekeninge'; Eileen Krige and Jacob Daniel Krige, *The Realm of a Rain Queen: A Study*

of the Pattern of Lovedu Society (London: Oxford University Press, 1943), pp. 24–25

23 Interview with TC Kgopa, 27 Apr 2023

24 Krige (1938), p. 271

25 Isak Niehaus, 'Coins for Blood and Blood for Coins: From Sacrifice to Ritual Murder in the South African Lowveld, 1930–2000', *Etnofoor*, Vol. 13(2), 2000, pp. 31–54, p. 38

26 Ibid., p. 39

27 Interview with Anthony, 27 Apr 2023

28 Interview with TC Kgopa, 27 Apr 2023

29 Davison and Mahashe, p. 71

30 Ibid.

31 Ulrich Jürgens et al., 'Townships in South African cities – Literature review and research perspectives', *Habitat International*, Vol. 39, 2013, pp. 256–60, p. 256

32 Ulrich, p. 257

33 Ibid.

34 McNeil Jr (2001)

35 CNN, 'S. Africa buries queen with power over the skies', 1 Jul 2001, http://edition.cnn.com/2001/WORLD/africa/07/01/safrica.queen.reut/index.html [website inaccessible]

36 Davison and Mahashe, p. 50

37 Krige and Krige, p. 180

38 Eileen Jensen Krige, 'Woman-Marriage, with Special Reference to the Lovedu. Its Significance for the Definition of Marriage', *Africa: Journal of the International African Institute*, Vol. 44(1), Jan 1974, pp. 11–37, p. 16

39 Greene, p. 395; Bright Alozie, 'Woman-to-Woman Marriage in West Africa', *Oxford Research Encyclopedia of African History*, 30 Jan 2024 (Oxford University Press)

40 Greene, p. 399

41 Krige (1974), pp. 31–32

42 L. A. Binagi, 'Marriage among the Abakuria', *MILA; A Biannual Newsletter of Cultural Research*, Vol. 5(I), 1976, p. 22 in Kirsten Alsaker Kjerland, 'When African Women Take Wives: A Historiographical Overview', paper for 'Poverty and Prosperity in Africa: Local and Global Perspectives' research programme, Nordiska Afrikainstituet, 1997, pp. 1–21, p. 1

43 Krige (1974), p. 18.

44 Ibid., p. 16

45 Ibid., p. 21

46 Ann Jones, 'Looking for Lovedu', *The Women's Review of Books*, Vol. 15(5), Feb 1998, pp. 11–12, p. 12

47 Ibid., p. 22

48 Rory Carroll, 'She who must be surveyed', *The Guardian*, 2003: https://
    www.theguardian.com/world/2003/apr/14/worlddispatch.southafrica

49 Susan Njanji, 'SA queen with 'mystical' powers', *Gulf Times*, 2017 https://
    www.gulf-times.com/story/552970/sa-queen-with-mystical-powers;
    Nwando Achebe, *Female Monarchs and Merchant Queens in Africa* (Ohio:
    Ohio University Press, 2000), p. 52; Liz McGregor, 'Rain queen's heir is
    pawn in a battle royal', *The Guardian*, 2007 https://www.theguardian.com/
    world/2007/oct/14/southafrica.theobserver

50 Ndivhuwo Khangale, 'Rain queen dreamt of me, says bereft lover', *IOL*, 18
    Jun 2005: https://www.iol.co.za/news/south-africa/rain-queen-dreamt-of-
    me-says-bereft-lover-244116

51 McGregor, 'Rain queen's heir is pawn in a battle royal'

52 Christopher Munnion, 'Rain Queen's mysterious death could signal end
    of dynasty', *The Telegraph*, 2005 https://www.telegraph.co.uk/news/world
    news/africaandindianocean/southafrica/1492519/Rain-Queens-mysterious-
    death-could-signal-end-of-dynasty.html

53 Krige (1938), p. 270

54 Motasa, p. 9

55 Ibid., p. 12

56 Munnion, 'Rain Queen's mysterious death could signal end of dynasty';
    The Sydney Morning Herald, 'A descendant of original 'she who must be
    obeyed', 22 Jun 2005: https://www.smh.com.au/national/a-descendant-of-
    original-she-who-must-be-obeyed-20050622-gdljyx.html

57 Michael Wines, 'Rain Queen Is Dead, but Debate Over Her Power
    Lives On', *The New York Times*, 21 Jun 2005: https://www.nytimes.
    com/2005/06/21/world/africa/rain-queen-is-dead-but-debate-over-her-
    power-lives-on.html

58 McNeil Jr (2001)

59 Interview with TC Kgopa, 27 Apr 2023

60 Getrude Makhafola, 'Prince Lekukela Modjadji ascends to Balobedu
    royal family throne – instead of his sister Masalanabo', news24, 9 May
    2021: https://www.news24.com/news24/southafrica/news/prince-lekukela-
    modjadji-ascends-to-balobedu-royal-family-throne-instead-of-his-sister-
    masalanabo-20210509

61 Capricorn FM, 'Modjadji royal house united on decision for Prince
    Lekukela to ascend the throne', 17 May 2021: https://www.capricornfm.
    co.za/modjadji-royal-house-united-on-decision-for-prince-lekukela-to-
    ascend-the-throne/; Shonisani Tshikalange, 'Modjadji Royal Council on
    ascension to the throne that caused a rift', *Times Live*, 17 May 2021: https://
    www.timeslive.co.za/news/south-africa/2021-05-17-modjadji-royal-council-
    on-ascension-to-the-throne-that-caused-a-rift/

62 Zingiswa Mndayi, 'Prince Lekukela Modjadji installed as King of the

Balobedu', SABC News, 1 Oct 2022, https://www.sabcnews.com/sabcnews/
prince-lekukela-modjadji-installed-as-king-of-the-balobedu/

63 Shonisani Tshikalange, 'Modjadji Royal Council on ascension to the
throne that caused a rift'

64 The Presidency of the Republic of South Africa, 'President Ramaphosa
legally recognises Her Majesty Queen Masalanabo Modjadji VII of the
Balobedu Queenship', 13 Dec 2024: https://www.thepresidency.gov.za/
president-ramaphosa-legally-recognises-her-majesty-queen-masalanabo-
modjadji-vii-balobedu-queenship

65 Modiegi Mashamaite, 'Queen Masalanabo Modjadji VII makes history
with matric success amid royal dispute', *Sunday Times Live*, 15 Jan
2025: https://www.timeslive.co.za/news/south-africa/2025-01-15-queen-
masalanabo-modjadji-vii-makes-history-with-matric-success-amid-royal-
dispute/

66 Interview with Betty Mayeya, London, 25 Jun 2023

67 Davison and Mahashe, p. 50

Conclusion

1 Husam Mahjoub, 'It's an open secret: the UAE is fuelling Sudan's
war – and there'll be no peace until we call it out', *The Guardian*, 24 May
2024, https://www.theguardian.com/commentisfree/article/2024/may/24/
uae-sudan-war-peace-emirates-uk-us-officials; Talal Mohammad, 'How
Sudan Became a Saudi-UAE Proxy War', *Foreign Policy*, 12 Jul 2023,
https://foreignpolicy.com/2023/07/12/sudan-conflict-saudi-arabia-uae-gulf-
burhan-hemeti-rsf/; Alma Selvaggia Rinaldi, 'How Sudan's RSF became a
key ally for the UAE's logistical and corporate interests', *Middle East Eye*,
1 Sep 2024, https://www.middleeasteye.net/news/sudan-rsf-key-ally-uae-
logistical-and-corporate-interests

2 Mark Langan, 'Let's talk about neo-colonialism in Africa', London
School of Economics Blogs, 15 Nov 2017, https://blogs.lse.ac.uk/afri-
caatlse/2017/11/15/lets-talk-about-neo-colonialism-in-africa/

3 Saidiya Hartman, 'Venus in Two Acts', *Small Axe*, Vol. 12(2), Jun 2008,
pp. 1–14, p. 11

4 Smallwood (2016), p. 129

5 Hartman, p. 4

6 Ibid., p. 12

ACKNOWLEDGEMENTS

Many hands have shaped this work.

To Zaahirah Adam, thank you for being a beautiful menace I can't shake after twenty years and, more importantly, funding a chunk of my research trip. Thank you to The Society of Authors and the Authors' Foundation for a grant that also made the trip possible.

To every person I spoke to – like Njabu, ayòdélé, Shema, Shakia and more – it has been an honour to commit your knowledge and insights to paper.

To my agent, Abi Fellows, my sweet Cap, what a ride. Thank you for your fierce advocacy, soothing words and top-tier cheerleading.

To my editor, Katie Packer, thank you for believing in me. Thank you for fighting for this book in all ways. To the wider Trapeze team, thank you for your enthusiasm and excitement when all I wanted to do was delete the Word doc. In particular, huge thanks to Yadira Da Trindade, Georgia Goodall, Pablo Pizarro Janczur, Aoife Datta and Paul Stark for your care and attention.

To Jodi Hunt, Jessica Hart and the wider design team, thank you for your work on a cover that continues to stun me. To my illustrator, Tosin Akinkunmi, thank you for saying yes and for producing art that rendered me speechless.

To my mentor, my teacher, Christienna Fryar, I'm honoured to count you as kin. Thank you to the other brilliant scholars I met while studying, including Hannah Elias and Justin Bengry.

To my Black queer history babes, Havana McElvaine, Kate Bernstock, Yancé-Myah Antonio Harrison and Don Crossfield, that first year of our masters was like a dream because of you and our beautiful cohort.

To Ray Okiya, my football bestie, thank you for letting me drag you up and down SE London for games. To The Arsenal, and football at large, thank you for holding down my sanity. Except for VAR, that can fuck off.

To my cheerleaders and early readers: Auntie Esi Bentil, Samantha-Louise Hayden, Merryn Thomas, Sarah Zadie Baiden, Dani Adekoya, Sophie Nye, Jordan Daley, Taylor Garron, Tianna Viviean Johnson, Aleema Gray, Holly Cooper, Lemara Lindsay-Prince, Candice Carty-Williams, Char, Nick Jeffreys and the French girls (Marion, Amandine, Fredo, Franciane, Moriba, Assa *et le go!*) Jeffreys and Nick Jeffreys. Writing this was a deeply lonely process so to know that you were thinking of me and excited about the book brought me more comfort than I can say.

To my other gay Gooners, Lauren 'Loz' Corelli and Susana Ferreira, your friendship is one of my warmest treasures. To Betty Mayeya, Nicole Thomas and little baby River, thank you for bringing me into your family. Big up the Black Footy Babes massive!

To my top bird Ellie Crocker, thank you for loving me with gusto. To Alex Provan, thank you for your unwavering moral clarity which anchors me. To Dani Scott-Haughton, your laughter, affirmations and friendship are precious and priceless. To Leyla Reynolds, my world would be duller without you.

To my brothers, Josh Akpan and Sam Akpan, thank you for championing me always. It's been my greatest pleasure to watch you grow from annoying boys to kind, funny and annoying men.

To Leila Davis and Fleur Finch, your flat became my refuge when I had to escape my laptop but, as it turns out, wherever you both are, I'm always held. Thank you.

To Rianna Walcott, my chargie, I'd be a much lesser friend, thinker and person without you. To Jade Bentil, my favourite historian, your love and encouragement kept me together; deep in the trenches, you were always there.

To my love, Maëva Vitéla, thank you for everything. There's no book without you; you can find yourself on every page.

Many hands have shaped this work. More – particularly Black women and trans scholars – have shaped my approach to history work. To name a few, thank you Christienna Fryar, Jade Bentil, Havana McElvaine, Kate Bernstock, Yancé-Myah Antonio Harrison, Holly Cooper, ayòdélé olófintúádé, Aleema Gray, Varaidzo, Saidiya Hartman, Christina Sharpe, Stephanie E. Smallwood, Tiffany Lebatho King, Marisa J. Fuentes, Audre Lorde, Octavia E. Butler, Barbara Smith and Oluwatoyin Salau.

Many imprints have been left on me by the indigenous communities across Africa and throughout the globe today fighting for their land, their dignity, their sovereignty, their lives. Our struggles for liberation have always been interconnected.

Free Congo. Free Sudan. Free Haiti. Free the Uyghurs. Free Palestine. Free the people, free the land.

CREDITS

Trapeze would like to thank everyone at Orion who worked on the publication of *When We Ruled*.

Agent
Abi Fellows

Editor
Katie Packer

Inventory
Jo Jacobs
Dan Stevens

Copy-editor
Deborah Balogun

Editorial Management
Georgia Goodall
Pablo Pizarro Janczur
Jane Hughes
Charlie Panayiotou
Lucy Bilton
Patrice Nelson

Audio
Paul Stark
Louise Richardson
Georgina Cutler-Ross

Proofreader
Clare Hubbard

Contracts
Dan Herron
Ellie Bowker
Oliver Chacón

Design
Jessica Hart
Nick Shah
Deborah Francois
Helen Ewing

Photo Shoots & Image Research
Natalie Dawkins

Finance
Nick Gibson
Jasdip Nandra
Sue Baker
Tom Costello

Marketing
Yadira Da Trindade

Production
Hannah Cox
Katie Horrocks
Amy Knight

Sales
Dave Murphy
Victoria Laws
Esther Waters
Group Sales teams across
Digital, Field, International and
Non-Trade

Publicity
Aoife Datta

Operations
Group Sales Operations team

Rights
Rebecca Folland
Tara Hiatt
Ben Fowler
Maddie Stephens
Ruth Blakemore
Marie Henckel

ABOUT THE AUTHOR

Paula Akpan is a historian, journalist and public speaker. Her work mainly focuses on Blackness, queerness, social politics and our relationship with technology. She regularly writes for a variety of publications including *Vogue*, *Teen Vogue*, the *Independent*, *Stylist*, *VICE*, *i-D*, *Bustle*, *Time Out London* and more. Paula has also interviewed the likes of Oprah, Lupita Nyong'o, Reese Witherspoon, Jada Pinkett Smith, Syd and Ray BLK. *When We Ruled* is her first book.